GREENE & GREENE

Edward R. Bosley

2

Charles Sumner Greene and Henry Mather Greene are rightly known as architects who gave high-art form to the American Arts and Crafts movement in the early years of the twentieth century. A handful of highly refined and exquisitely crafted dwellings are the legacy for which the brothers are best known, but before these could exist, the Greenes had made a long, quiet journey from the traditional aesthetics of the day toward a profound sensitivity to their adopted home of Southern California. For a fortunate few, they brought to bear their formal training and fraternal symbiosis at the height of their careers together to envision and create a fresh and artistic range of possibilities for living in harmony with the land.

The Greenes believed that to succeed as classically trained architects in this remote and newly developing region of the country meant rejecting classicism. The warm climate, more relaxed lifestyles, and rugged topography demanded it, as did their own creative impulse. They also believed that the mix of academic and progressive architecture that they had seen as students at the Massachusetts Institute of Technology, and as apprentices in Boston, had posed meaningful questions but did not necessarily offer appropriate answers for building in their new environment. They realized, too, from their teenage days at the Manual Training School of Washington University in St. Louis, that their work, if it were to be done at all, must be done with care and precision. Adhering to these simple tenets—looking beyond the dictates of history, profiting from good examples of contemporary architecture, and executing work to the highest standards—succesfully sustained the Greene and Greene firm for more than twenty years. In the final anaylsis, however, it was the automatic, fraternal bond between two talented men that would incite a rare collective genius and make possible the creation of exceptional works of art and craft.

Charles and Henry Greene were perfectly matched, yet utterly different. Their strengths were at once poles apart and flawlessly sympathetic. Charles tended toward a critical, artistic, and random intellect, while Henry's approach to life was more methodical, precise, and dependable. Over time, these tendencies became traits. During their professional years together, Henry ran the office with consummate skill while Charles exercised his design creativity on the jobs at hand. He processed daily stimuli into a

particular artistic vision: rocks in a stream bed, trees on the landscape, images in books of faraway temples and cliff-side castles all contributed to the firm's unique aesthetic. Henry organized and transformed his brother's visions into practical, buildable form, thereby allowing Charles's muse to flourish undistracted. In the early days of the practice, the Greenes cultivated clients who provided the opportunities they needed to prove themselves as sound architects. Influential periodicals began to recognize the firm for home designs that reflected their region's conditions in creative and artistic ways. Soon, they were free to choose clients who were willing to take risks to create houses of artistic beauty and careful craft. With few exceptions they shunned classicist imagery, but their designs were born of classical proportions, appropriate materials, traditional methods of construction, and relentless attention to detail.

Artistic expression of structure was the basis of the Greenes' design philosophy, and wood was their favored medium. Wood could be sculpted, carved, left rough, or polished. It could be useful and decorative at the same time, and it was plentiful and inexpensive. The Greenes, using many different species and methods of working woods, boldly drew attention to structure by articulating it prominently throughout their houses. They did not abandon applied ornament, nor did they allow it to overtake the expression of rationality and structure. It became instead a graceful evocation of natural surroundings. Gradually, the brothers attracted increasingly wealthy clients who allowed them to set their artistic sights higher and higher. They began to use exotic materials—mahogany from Honduras, teak from Burma, vermillion from Indonesia—to mill and sculpt into the temple-like pavilions on which their reputations rest. Contractors and craftsmen who worked with the Greenes, notably Peter and John Hall and William Isaac Ott, were held to the same high standards to which the architects held themselves. Nothing was spared in the quest to make whole their vision of beauty.

External economic forces are sometimes blamed for the decline of the Greene and Greene firm after 1911. The real reasons are more complex, and lie among the same bonds that made the brothers' work a success. Charles had never wanted to be a professional architect but an artist, and he viewed

1 Frontispiece:
   David B. Gamble house, Pasadena, 1907–09.
   View of rear (west) terrace from entry hall.

2 **Robert R. Blacker house, Pasadena, 1907–09.**
   Detail of living room with original chairs and
   mahogany drop-front desk.

3 **Henry M. Greene, Walter D. Valentine cottage,
   Wild Wood Park, Altadena, 1922–24.**
   Detail of portico on a work previously unknown to
   be by Henry Greene.

3

architecture as only one of several vehicles through which he could express his creativity. The others—painting, writing, and wood carving—he feared would remain neglected as long as he continued in professional practice. Moving with his family to Carmel in 1916, Charles began a radically different phase of his life that ultimately served spectacularly to solidify his identity as an artist/architect in the cliff-top dwelling for D. L. James. His later retreat into self-observation and a personal language of symbolism is demonstrated in the design and decoration of his own Carmel studio.

After the split, Henry Greene was also more able to explore the scope of his own talents. He ably upheld the legacy of Greene and Greene and its reputation for building in harmony with nature, but developed a prodigious talent for garden and landscape design as well, evidence of which, unfortunately, is all but obliterated today. His iconic adobe ranch house, designed for Walter L. Richardson in Porterville, remains the great outward expression of his essentially self-effacing character and of his personal, anti-modernist interpretation of "less is more." Two heretofore unpublished cottages that Henry designed for Walter D. Valentine in Altadena also evince a remarkable sensitivity to their surroundings in a way that suggests the profound value of Henry's previously overlooked contributions to the firm.

The early and late works of the Greenes, however, will inevitably be seen as bookends to the great wooden conflations of their classic period, from 1907 to 1910. Charles, who once remarked bitterly that he was "prostituting his art" in Pasadena, would later take great pride in this period of his career. The simple fact is that the brothers were at their best as progressive architects when they worked together. It was then that they stretched each other's creativity and productivity, and called each other to account to bring their clients exceptional value.

While other, more commercially successful architects adjusted their methods of working to the increasing standardization of homebuilding in the 1920s and 1930s, the Greenes independently remained of the opinion that the architect had an obligation to create an artistic dwelling of unique and lasting value. Henry had a greater affinity than his brother for designing economical housing, but both believed that an inexpensive house need not be a cookie-cutter reiteration of its neighbor. This was a view held, but one that

had little bearing on their work. As Henry Greene put it, "Our clients were rich. No one had to borrow money to complete their homes once started."[1] As anti-modernists in a modernist age, though, fewer and fewer clients were willing to approach house design in the Greenes' way. Nor should it be ignored that by 1911 they had gained a justified reputation for being slow and expensive. Recognition of the significance of their earlier work came late in life, by which time they had long since put aside their drafting tools.

In the twilight of their lives Charles and Henry Greene may have glimpsed in the future the remarkable surge of appreciation that attaches to their work and careers today. The Gamble House, owned by the City of Pasadena and administered by the University of Southern California School of Architecture in a joint agreement with Gamble-family heirs, is the only house designed by the Greenes that contains nearly all of its original, architect-designed furnishings, offering the public a unique opportunity to experience their architectural genius. The Huntington Library's Virginia Steele Scott Gallery in San Marino, California, exhibits the largest assembly of the Greenes' decorative arts outside the Gamble House. It should not be surprising that both venues are more visited than ever. In an era of mass marketing, machine-driven production, and instantaneous global communication, it is sometimes comforting to be immersed, however briefly, in an environment that soothes the senses with its rootedness in nature and the echo of a slower-paced society. It was, after all, for similar reasons—to escape the dehumanization of the factory economy of the nineteenth century—that the Greenes, their craft-workers, and their clients collaborated to create such exceptional works of art.

1

Yankee Forebears, Midwest Boys

1   Page 6:
    Massachusetts Institute of Technology Department
    of Architecture. Detail of student and faculty
    photograph taken on the steps of the Walker building,
    corner of Bolyston and Clarendon streets, Boston,
    March 1891. Left to right: Ernest M. Machado '90,
    Charles Sumner Greene '92, Smith (?), Henry Mather
    Greene '92 (top), William H. Punchard '91.

2   Brighton Station rail crossing, Cincinnati, Ohio,
    c. 1890.

3   The steamer *Bostona* on the Ohio River at
    Huntington, West Virginia, c. 1880.

Charles Sumner Greene and Henry Mather Greene came into the world during the physical and psychological reconstruction of the United States in the years following the Civil War. "Charlie" arrived on October 12, 1868, and "Hallie" was born fifteen months later, on January 23, 1870. When Charles was born, his parents, Lelia Ariana Greene (*nee* Mather) and Thomas Sumner Greene, had been married less than a year. She was twenty-four, he, twenty-six. Born in Cincinnati, Ohio, their sons enjoyed a happy childhood in the city's 24th Ward, near Brighton Station on Walker Miller Road (now State Street) overlooking Mill Creek.[1] The Greenes' solidly working-class neighborhood was distinguished by a largely German-immigrant population and successful industry, including several of the city's famous breweries, the Procter and Gamble candle and soap plant, and the Singer Sewing Machine factory. The boys' paternal grandparents, Elihu and Mathilda Greene, lived nearby.[2] Their mother's parents, Oscar and Augusta Mather, lived a short train or riverboat journey to the east on a farm along the banks of the Guyandotte River, just south of Barboursville, West Virginia.[3] While Elihu and Mathilda Greene were the grandparents closest to the boys on a daily basis, it was with their mother's parents that Charles and Henry spent their childhood summers. Thomas Sumner Greene planned his sons' upbringing seriously. He believed that they would fare better in the nation's competitive post-war industrial economy if they joined forces to develop the same skill sets and pursue a profession together. Their mother, Lelia, was less inclined to insist on sameness, and saw to it that her boys developed the inherent traits and talents that naturally distinguished them. The parents' two approaches, while seemingly at odds, proved to be complementary, producing an automatic bond between the brothers and a genuine affection for their parents.[4]

Thomas Greene was steering his sons toward the building arts as early as Christmas 1876, when Charles, then eight, received from his father a copy of *The Boy's Book of Trades and the Tools Used in Them*. Detailed descriptions of more than twenty building-trade occupations filled its pages, including those of brick maker, mason, plasterer, carpenter, painter, plumber, and cabinetmaker.[5] House design and construction was not only promoted as a growing profession with a bright future in America, but it was a natural

2

3

4 Thomas Waldron Sumner (del.), Unitarian Church, Peterborough, New Hampshire, steeple elevation dated 8 February 1825. Ink and color wash on heavy paper.

5 Thomas Sumner Greene (1842–1931) in Civil War uniform, c. 1861.

5

choice for the Greene boys, since architecture was represented by several leaves on the family tree.[6] Most notably, their father's maternal grandfather, Thomas Waldron Sumner (1768–49), had been an accomplished Boston architect, who worked in the style of Charles Bulfinch. He was a founding member of the Society of Associated Housewrights in 1804 and was its president from 1808 to 1817. Sumner's father, James, had also been a housewright, as were his cousins, Samuel and John Gabriel Sumner.[7]

New England roots ran deep in the family. The Greenes' earliest American ancestor, John Greene, arrived in Boston from Salisbury, England, in 1635 and was awarded landholdings in Rhode Island in consideration for his service to Governor William Roger. Among his descendents was Major General Nathaneal Greene (1742–1786), who had served with distinction in the Revolutionary War under George Washington. Nathaneal Greene's brother, Christopher, was Thomas Sumner Greene's grandfather.[8] Lelia Ariana Mather Greene was also of New England stock, descending from the Massachusetts Mathers, among whom figured the prominent Congregationalist ministers Richard Mather, Increase Mather, and Cotton Mather, the latter known especially for his role in the Salem "witch trials" of the 1690s.

The variety and depth of Thomas and Lelia Greene's life experiences, as well as their pedigrees, gave uncommon richness and texture to their sons' development. Thomas Sumner Greene had volunteered for service in the Union Army (5th Ohio Light Artillery) at the age of eighteen and served the entire span of the Civil War, the bloodiest conflict ever to take place on American soil.[9] As a private, he served under the commands of John Charles Fremont, General Ulysses S. Grant, and General William Tecumseh Sherman. His service was marked by long periods of personal hardship, including troop movement under appalling conditions punctuated by dramatic and violent episodes of engagement with the enemy. In his memoirs, Greene described a personal meeting with Abraham Lincoln ("his hand was the softest I ever touched") and gave vivid detail to the intense fighting at Shiloh and hand-to-hand combat at the siege of Vicksburg.[10] Greene's particular talent for legible penmanship gained him promotions to the level of captain. He was luckier than his older brother,

4

6 Guyandotte River at the former Mather family farm
   near Salt Rock, West Virginia.

7 Lelia Ariana Mather (1844–1931), c. 1861.

GREENE & GREENE

6   7

Charles, who had also fought at Vicksburg but died in 1866 from lingering wounds. Despite having been personally grieved by the death of his brother and by seeing his fellow soldiers die on a huge scale, Thomas exhibited few outward signs of trauma in the aftermath of the war.

Following the cessation of hostilities, as he was completing his army commission in Baton Rogue, Louisiana, Thomas met Lelia Ariana Mather, a plucky young woman who was visiting relatives she had not seen since before the war. Her youthful energy and her New England roots must have appealed to the young soldier and they were married the next year, on her twenty-third birthday, in Huntington, West Virginia, near Lelia's hometown of Barboursville. The couple settled near Thomas's parents in Cincinnati and he soon took employment as an "honest, industrious, and capable" bookkeeper for the Greenwood Pipe Company.[11] Lelia kept house and prepared to raise a family.

Lelia Mather was born in 1844, in the state of Virginia, to Oscar and Augusta Mather. By 1863, her native Cabell County had joined with twenty-five other anti-rebel counties to gain separate statehood as West Virginia. It was a political division that recognized the people's philosophical alignment with the Union north, but proximity to the enemy nonetheless had its consequences. A federal revenue officer and paymaster during the war, Lelia's father was sometimes trapped behind Confederate picket lines holding the Union Army payroll for the region. Hidden until Union soldiers could regain control of the area, his daughter, Lelia, still a teenager, was chosen to go to her father's aid. Armed with a pistol tucked under her skirt, she rode courageously through the Confederate pickets, carrying food and other supplies to her father under cover of darkness.[12]

Settling into post-war life as a married woman, Lelia Greene pursued china painting to supplement the family income and because it was something she enjoyed and could do well. She earned a reputation for an artistic sensibility by posting charmingly illustrated letters to family and friends depicting animals and flowers drawn from direct observation in her garden. Of her two sons, Charles inherited the greater tendency toward his mother's creative talent and spontaneity, though Henry was also artistically inclined. Both boys doodled in their schoolbooks, sketching caricatures and

everyday objects. Henry's attempts, though sometimes more whimsical, were also more controlled and methodical, showing a conservative tendency toward compact compositions. His watercolors were well planned and executed. Charles's drawings and watercolors were more freewheeling, spontaneous, and impressionistic.[13]

During the summer months of their pre-adolescence, the boys enjoyed breaks from school on the Mathers' West Virginia farm. The hilly, remote region provided the boys with a clear impression of the quickly disappearing pre-industrial life in America. It was a working farm where the family produced what they needed and rarely resorted to cash outlay for manufactured goods. From the farm, Henry wrote enthusiastically to his father about the simple pleasure of riding a horse: "Sumner and I slipped out through the corn field and caught Bird and Sam and then went down through the meadow and to the river and forded and rode around....I can stand up on the horse and I went to town by myself."[14] Because of the distance of a generation between Lelia and her younger siblings, her sons played with uncles who were roughly their own age. Sumner, the playmate of Henry's letter, was born to Charles and Henry's maternal grandparents in February 1868, just eight months before Charles was born to Lelia.[15]

The Thomas Greene family moved from Cincinnati to St. Louis in 1874. Shortly before the move, a photographic portrait was made of "Hallie," a happy four-year-old in a fancy ruffled suit that had been passed down from previous generations.[16] In St. Louis, the boys attended Eads Elementary School, and the family continued to visit the Mather farm. Thomas Greene held a job for nearly five years as bookkeeper and cashier for Edward Martin & Co., a clothing manufacturer based in downtown St. Louis. He wanted to improve his professional prospects, however, and returned to Cincinnati in 1879 to enroll in the Pulte Medical College. During much of the next three years, while Thomas completed his studies, the family lived full time on the Mather farm.[17] Pulte Medical College featured a homeopathic curriculum specializing in Samuel Hahnemann's famous botanical treatments, but the three-year combination of course work and apprenticeship also required examinations based on more traditional medical texts.[18]

Greene graduated in 1882 at the age of forty. His academic mentor, or "preceptor," had been Lelia's younger brother, Dr. Valcon W. Mather of Kansas City, a man five years Greene's junior. Dr. Greene opened a private practice in St. Louis and announced his specialization in the treatment of "Catarrh," a term commonly used to describe ailments of the mucous membrane or respiratory tract.[19] The practice did well, partly due to a specialized cure, which allowed him to advertise a proprietary edge.[20] Professional success, and possibly a family inheritance, gave Greene sufficient funds to make investments and provide comfortably for his family. He also improved his social and business contacts, and by 1884 Dr. Thomas Sumner Greene appeared among the "names of prominent householders" in the second edition of Gould's St. Louis Blue Book.

That year, Dr. Greene enrolled Charles, then fifteen, in the three-year Manual Training School of Washington University, established in 1879 by Calvin Milton Woodward (1837–1914). Henry, aged fourteen, followed his brother the next year, and the two young men began receiving the specific training that would help make it possible for them to build successful careers. Woodward's unique vision for his secondary school—the first such institution in the country—was to educate the hand, heart, and mind of each student. For over a decade, Woodward had loudly criticized the lack of adequate technical training in America and believed that the post–Civil War nation was ill-prepared to embrace industrialization, the dominant force in the urban-American economy. A Harvard graduate of the class of 1860 (students dubbed it the "war class"), Woodward believed that secondary and higher education needed to expand beyond classical course offerings, which had characterized university curricula until then.

In 1869 he established the new Polytechnic Institute of Washington University, with a curriculum that led to professional degrees in chemistry, civil engineering, and mechanical engineering.[21] When Woodward asked his new college-age students to construct models for their course work, however, he discovered that they knew little or nothing about the proper use of tools. Recalling how he had learned to use tools as a boy—by demonstration and practical application—he realized that class instruction on the use of tools was essential if students were to graduate with fuller competence. Woodward then brought the same rationality to secondary education, establishing the Manual Training School of Washington University in 1879. Starting with a younger age group, Woodward reasoned that tool instruction in a dedicated shop environment would eventually show benefits in higher education and in industry.

Woodward had been especially impressed by Russia's highly systematic method of tool instruction, which had been developed by Victor Della-Vos in 1868 and exhibited at the Centennial Exposition in Philadelphia in 1876.[22] Woodward drew from it in planning for the new preparatory school (though he claimed that Della-Vos had merely put into practice much of what he, Woodward, had earlier proposed but not had the chance to implement).[23] After tool instruction, the balance of the curriculum was a combination of academic instruction and mechanical drawing. "The Cultured Mind, The Skillful Hand," was the promise of the school's motto.[24]

As stated in the prospectus the year Charles entered, the purpose of the new high school was "1. To furnish a broader and more appropriate foundation for higher technical education, 2. To serve as a developing school where pupils could discover their inborn capacities and aptitudes ... while securing a liberal elementary training, [and] 3. To furnish those who looked forward to industrial life [the] opportunity to become familiar with tools, materials, drafting, and the methods of construction, as well as with ordinary English branches."[25] The ordinance officially establishing the school also stated the following: "Its object shall be instruction in mathematics, drawing, and the English branches of a high-school course, and instruction and practice in the use of tools. The tool instruction, as at present contemplated, shall include carpentry, wood-turning, pattern-making, iron chipping and filing, forge-work, brazing and soldering, the use

8 Dr. Thomas Sumner Greene in front of the Greene family residence on Washington Avenue, St. Louis, c. 1887.

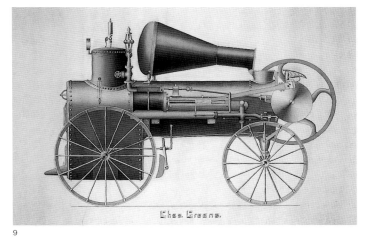

9 Charles Sumner Greene, student drawing of steam locomotive for Manual Training School of Washington University, St. Louis, Missouri, c. 1885. Ink and charcoal on heavy paper.

8

9

10

11

of machine shop tools, and such other instruction of a similar character as may be deemed advisable to add to the foregoing from time to time. The students will divide their working hours, as nearly as possible, equally between mental and manual labor. They shall be admitted, on examination, at not less than fourteen years of age, and the course shall continue three years."[26]

Initially, the MTS was meant to supply a better-prepared body of students to Woodward's Polytechnic Institute, but its influence soon broadened. The curriculum was geared toward shaping students who would be fit to pursue careers in mechanical, industrial, or technical fields, and Woodward even believed that future bankers, lawyers, and other professionals would benefit from his training. In a passage worthy of John Ruskin or William Morris, the prospectus claimed, "One great objective of the school is to foster a higher appreciation of the value and dignity of intelligent labor, and the worth and respectability of laboring men. A boy who sees nothing in manual labor but mere brute force despises both the labor and the laborer." The first year of training included two hours of wood work daily, the balance of the day being used to teach drawing, English, mathematics, and other academic courses. A similar pattern would characterize the second year, which featured the forge shop, and the third year, which was devoted to machine shop. Physics, algebra, Latin, history, geometry, and modern languages were taught within the academic section. As Woodward explained in a four-page circular distributed in 1880, shortly before the new school was officially opened that September, "The Manual Training School is not a mere workshop; the head is to be trained even more than the hand."[27]

At the Manual Training School, as at the Polytechnic Institute, there was also an undercurrent of artistic development and a premium put on attractive presentation within Woodward's classes. Exercises in descriptive geometry included the delineation of intricately shaded forms, beautifully identified by students' precise calligraphy.[28] Woodward believed that technical endeavors merited an artistic approach, though he left it to others to teach. Since the mid-1870s, his Polytechnic Institute had offered special woodcarving courses taught by instructors brought from Washington

University's Art and Design department. One of these, Calista Halsey, taught during the 1877–78 academic year and wrote a vivid description of a carving class in her well-reviewed first novel, *Two of Us*, published in 1879.[29] Her account seems clearly to have been drawn from personal experience, though her female protagonist speaks from the point of view of one of her students:

"Faithfulness in design was one thing insisted upon, and therefore, however crude in execution, as all first work must be, it had a certain artistic value. It meant something. That was the beauty of this handwork. If any article demanded any special decoration, it could be given....Segments of circles, fragments of squares and triangles, sprays of flower and leaf, cut straight across by carved bands—a butterfly, perhaps, with expression of a culprit fay—a bird, poised for flight. 'They are carved with a Japanese *motif*, if you see,' said the young lady....'I try to keep the sketchiness, and the delicacy, and the quaintness. I leave out the grotesqueness, and I Americanize it by using our own leaves and flowers. It is a very free translation of Japanese art.' She began to talk a great deal about the dignity of handwork, especially handwork that called into exercise taste, imagination and artistic feeling, as this did....It was not so much merely technical instruction in wood-carving, as it was an outlook at what was doing in the whole round world of art."[30]

Calista Halsey left Washington University five years before Charles Greene entered classes at the Manual Training School, but her spirit lingered within the institution if credit can be given to Woodward's training of the Greenes relative to their later outlook on the value of art in craftsmanship. Halsey's mention of Japanese art tantalizingly suggests another possible legacy of her woodworking classes at Woodward's Institute, which later shared faculty with the Manual Training School. But whatever influences the Manual Training School had on the Greenes' later work, it can at least be said that Woodward consistently produced students who enjoyed preferential admittance to the best technical and academic institutions in the country. The record of Charles Greene's performance under Woodward reveals his affinity for skills that became artistic passions, but foreshadows ambivalence toward others that he would require as a

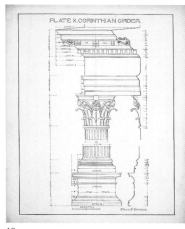

12

professional architect. A perfect score of 100 in freehand drawing, for example, was accompanied by a zero in penmanship (ironically the skill that had helped his father win promotion in the Union Army). Similarly, in wood turning he received a respectable 92, but only a passing grade of 68 in mechanical drawing.[31] Both boys benefited from the program, and on the occasion of Woodward's retirement in 1910, Henry Greene submitted this accolade: "My first impressive lessons in thoroughness and logical analysis were first learned in the 'Old MTS,' and to this early training I feel I owe my success in my profession."[32]

While Henry was completing his course at the Manual Training School, Dr. Greene arranged for Charles to be taken on without pay in a year's apprenticeship with the St. Louis architect Alfred F. Rosenheim (1859–1943). Charles later recalled the feeling he had when his father suggested he enter Rosenheim's office: "I had a feeling of keen disappointment. I wanted to be an artist [but] father dismissed my objections....The year I was with him was for the first few months spent in tracing full size details—this meant stretching one's body over a table four feet by eight feet....Now there came a business depression and the last job was finished. From memory, I began to make water color drawings of steamboats on the Ohio River."[33] Alfred Rosenheim had also graduated from the Manual Training School (class of 1884) and continued his studies in Germany. He attended the Massachusetts Institute of Technology as a "Special Student" in architecture, returning to St. Louis as a designer in the office of Theodore C. Link (1850–1923), best known as the architect of the St. Louis Union Station (1892–94). Rosenheim began his independent practice in 1886, but continued to design for Link. It is therefore possible that Charles Greene was assigned to assist on some of Link's projects during his tenure with Rosenheim from the fall of 1887 until the summer of 1888.[34]

In the fall of 1888, Dr. Greene sent his sons to study architecture in earnest at MIT. Located near the heart of Boston's Back Bay, the Massachusetts Institute of Technology had been the birthplace of formal architectural education in America. In 1865, William R. Ware (1832–1915), of the respected Boston firm of Ware and Van Brunt, was asked by MIT's president and founder, William Barton Rogers (1804–82), to organize the first architecture course. Ware's philosophy of teaching was developed through a direct study of European architectural instruction during his travels abroad in the mid-1860s and through inspiration gained from working in the New York studio of Richard Morris Hunt (1828–95). Hunt had been the first American to graduate from the Ecole des Beaux-Arts and had modeled his office closely along the lines of a Parisian atelier. Ware based the MIT curriculum largely on the French model. Classes began in 1867, and by 1872, to further authenticate the Beaux-Arts experience, Ware hired Eugene Letang, another Ecole graduate, to help develop and expand the department.[35]

By the time the Greenes arrived at MIT—sometimes known as Boston Tech, or simply "Tech"—another Ecole graduate, Francis Ward Chandler (1844–1926), had been named head of the architecture department to succeed Theodore M. Clark, who had been in the post since Ware's resignation in 1881. In 1888, of the seventy-five architecture students at MIT, only eight were candidates for the full degree. The remaining sixty-seven students, including Charles and Henry Greene, had been attracted to the "Partial Course in Architecture," so called because it required just two years of course work rather than four. Partial Course students, also known as "Special Students," were awarded a certificate rather than a full degree. The two-year course emphasized drawing, sketching, and design skills, primarily to develop a student's "wrist" and general artistic and spatial sensibilities. History and French or German were also required during the two-year course, as were geometry and math, though in lesser depth. Classical orders were taught and lectures were given on the fine arts. Included in the full, four-year program, but notably missing from the Partial Course curriculum, were Physics, Calculus, Strength of Materials, and Stability of Structures. For the four-year student, these courses, which dealt with building materials and their actual performance in practical situations, added a valuable and pragmatic component to MIT's offerings that was absent from the Ecole des Beaux-Arts. In this respect, then, the shorter Partial Course was more similar to the Beaux-Arts paradigm in content, if not in length (it lacked two additional years of sketching, history, foreign language, and design instruction, with its final-semester thesis requirement).[36]

13 Charles Sumner Greene, student rendering for
Massachusetts Institute of Technology, Boston,
c. 1890. Ink and watercolor on heavy paper.

14 Charles Sumner Greene, watercolor on heavy paper,
c. 1890.

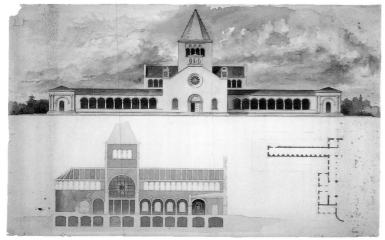

13

14

Admission to the Partial Course was by examination, though Professor Chandler had a great deal of latitude in accepting students based on other criteria. Students who had had a substantial academic history of technical course work at a respected secondary school, or significant experience working with an architect, stood a good chance of gaining admission with special consent from Professor Chandler.[37] Charles and Henry Greene's applications for admission were probably approved with little debate in light of their years at the Manual Training School and Charles's St. Louis apprenticeship with Rosenheim, an MIT alumnus. Even though the Special Students were missing some training as compared with their graduated colleagues, the shortened curriculum represented the norm, not the exception, and therefore more accurately reflects the profession's readiness to practice of that generation.

The Greenes entered the MIT program on September 25, 1888, having found rooms a short walk from Copley Square at Miss Rachel's boarding house at 12 St. James Avenue. They were officially associated with the class of 1892, though as Special Students they were expected to complete their course work by the spring of 1890. It was an exciting time in Boston. From many perspectives, the city was the center of intellectual life in America. The publishing industry was based there and the city's well-established academic community, combined with its philanthropic and religious families, had produced an increasingly rich climate of cultural, scientific and artistic pursuit and patronage. Tangible results of this surrounded the Greenes in their new environment. On Copley Square (known as Art Square prior to 1883), within view of the Greenes' rooms, H. H. Richardson's Trinity Church (1872–77) was already a widely acknowledged triumph of American architecture. The Museum of Fine Arts, Boston, a block-long, Ruskinian gothic structure, designed by John Russell Sturgis in the mid-1870s, also faced the square from St. James Street a few hundred yards from the Greenes' rooms. Perhaps more significantly for young architecture students, one of the city's most anticipated construction projects—McKim, Mead and White's two-million-dollar Boston Public Library—was under way on the west side of the square.

The residential development of Back Bay was also worthy of notice since it was an immense urbanization project (begun 1860) that followed the largest landfill engineering achievement in the world.[38] The building of Back Bay houses involved scores of architects, interior designers, and lavish budgets. Charles and Henry were ideally situated to witness and reflect on the combined activity, and to take part in the debate over the ascendancy of Beaux-Arts academic design theory.[39] The partly built library, as well as MIT's own curriculum, represented the emerging classicist trend. Back Bay houses, as well as Trinity Church, represented the recently progressive, Anglo-American face of the city. Trinity was the paradigm of a design movement that had gathered momentum under Henry Hobson Richardson (1838–86), and therefore the new dichotomy being staged in Copley Square was ironic.

Richardson had been trained at the Ecole des Beaux-Arts, and Charles Follen McKim (1847–1909) and Stanford White (1853–1906) had both worked for Richardson. McKim in particular is credited with significant involvement in Trinity's preliminary designs and White was also involved later.[40] More compelling than any academic discussions that the new students may have had, though, was the very fact of the classicist Boston Public Library rising stone by stone opposite Trinity Church while Charles and Henry attended classes. An aesthetic and philosophical sea change was taking place before their eyes. In a photograph he would keep all his life, Henry Greene captured Richardson's church in a soft, atmospheric pose. Trinity's broad tower rises majestically over the nearby stone townhouses in a misty, tonalist composition.

For his part, Charles had scant interest in MIT's Beaux-Arts approach to instruction and design, let alone in buildings that represented the transformation of Beaux-Arts theory into a new American classicism. Charles complained about the curriculum, complained about completing the two-year Partial Course, and even complained about the French-academic style of the Rogers Building (1865) where many of his classes were held.[41] Both he and his brother were "black-balled" from the student Architectural Club because of an opinion that Charles had expressed to a fellow student regarding the Rogers Building. His chief regret was that his brother, though innocent, was also punished.[42]

Charles's "honor" mark that first year was in Charcoal Drawing. The sketching talent he had developed as a youth in St. Louis, encouraged by his mother, had served him well.[43] During the second year, he excelled in Architectural Specifications, earning a score of 90 as well as another "honor" designation. In that course, Charles successfully combined his Manual Training School background in materials and tools with an innate talent for explaining to others how things should be done.[44] He earned better-than-average grades in Design, Iron Construction, Working Drawings, Materials, and in a drawing course entitled Shades, Shadows and Perspectives. In Materials, he learned the various methods of cutting trees, including the aesthetic and structural merits of quartersawing versus more cost-effective cuts. He learned the details of wood-shrinkage rates by species, and the various ways to treat wood with creosote and other chemicals.[45]

Charles barely passed Pen and Ink in his last semester, possibly because he was by then losing interest in the academic experience. It may also have been because the course required mere imitation, which would have appeared pointless to Charles's increasingly creative nature.[46] In his last semester he received a lukewarm "passing grade with credit" in Water Color, a course taught by visiting lecturer Ross Turner. Despite complaints about school at the time, Charles later recalled his MIT days with genuine fondness in autobiographical notes he jotted in 1943 at the age of 75. He wrote, "I have a kindly feeling for Tech and all of the freedom I knew there…. Professor Chandler … sent me to Cowles Art School and won my everlasting affection…. These were great times." The Cowles School of Art offered Charles a less formal environment than MIT, and stressed "doing" over "thinking." Teachers at Cowles in the 1890s included architect and typographical designer Bertram Goodhue and metalsmith Laurin Hovey Martin.[47] Though Charles never embraced Beaux-Arts design tenets, he later softened on the subject of the MIT-taught classicism. He wrote, "I began to see that meticulous care in reproducing the [classical] architectural order was necessary to make the grade and at last I was thrilled by the dignity and beauty of the antique…."[48]

The individual who held Greene's particular esteem as a teacher was his watercolor instructor. Charles wrote, "I smile yet when I think of Ross Turner situated on a low stool on the bare wooden floor dipping his ebony… brush in his big white bowl of water to whisk a circle of divine colors…."[49] Ross Sterling Turner (1847–1915) was an active *plein-air* watercolor artist in the port town of Salem, north of Boston. He commuted regularly to the city, where he taught painting and maintained a studio. Turner had studied in Munich and Venice before coming to Boston in 1882, and he settled in Salem two years later. He soon became one of the most popular teachers of watercolor in New England, instructing thousands of students at his Boston studio, in his classes at MIT, and at the Massachusetts Normal Art School. Turner's most important published work is the now-scarce manual *On the Use of Water Colors for Beginners* (1886).[50]

Charles Greene admired Turner, though it is unclear how closely, or for how long, they were associated as teacher and student. Charles may have continued taking lessons with Turner after leaving MIT.[51] Had Greene witnessed even the periphery of Turner's social and artistic sphere, as he likely did, he would have had a glimpse into the artistic culture of Boston and Salem, a particularly rich one in the early 1890s. Of interest to an understanding of the Greenes' future work would have been Turner's

15 Henry Mather Greene, painting of coastal Massachusetts, c. 1890. Watercolor on heavy paper.

16 Henry Hobson Richardson, Trinity Church, Boston, 1872–77. View from the west, c. 1900. The Massachusetts Institute of Technology can be seen on the extreme left. St. James Avenue, where the Greenes lived, is to the right of the church.

17 McKim, Mead and White, Boston Public Library, 1887–98.

15

16

17

18 Ross Sterling Turner, center, seated among MIT
    students in an 1887 Department of Architecture
    photograph.

19 Thomas Waldron Sumner, East India Marine Hall,
    Salem, Massachusetts, 1824. Front elevation.
    Ink on paper.

18

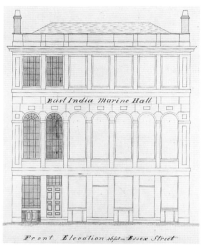
19

contacts in the area of Japan scholarship and collecting. Charles Greene mentioned having difficulty with his "anomalous water colors," which was probably while studying with Turner. Charles lamented, "My disappointment was such that I often took my color box and bicycled to Manchester-by-the-Sea where I produced lugubrious masses of purple rocks and brown sea weed."[52] Manchester, a charming and picturesque seaside town beyond Salem, would have been a forty-mile round trip from Copley Square, but Charles may have stayed over in Salem, where Turner lived and taught some of his students, and where Charles's school friend Ernest Machado lived. Charles shared a number of interests with Machado, including photography and bicycling, and Henry worked alongside Ernest as a fellow apprentice in 1893.[53] On his bicycle rides to Manchester, Charles could see some of the region's most outstanding Shingle Style resort homes along the ocean front, including the G. N. Black house designed by Peabody and Stearns and equally woodsy and rocky dwellings by William Ralph Emerson, whose work Charles Greene included in his personal scrapbook. Perhaps the most compelling reason for Charles and Henry to visit Salem, however, would have been one building in particular. In 1824, their great-grandfather, Thomas Waldron Sumner, had designed one of Salem's best-known landmarks, the East India Marine Hall. This imposing granite structure was designed to contain the East India Marine Society's Museum, of which Edward Sylvester Morse (1838–1925), another Salem resident, was curator. Since the early 1880s, objects of Japanese material culture gleaned by Morse during his extensive travels had significantly augmented the ethnographic collection. It offered (as it does today) a profound understanding of Japanese culture through the eyes of one of the Western world's most respected Japan scholars. Japonism had become an important and popular area of appreciation in America since Philadelphia's Centennial Exposition of 1876, and by the early 1890s, the Boston area was the undisputed center of Japan scholarship.

Charles and Henry Greene had particularly good opportunities to learn about Japan, its art, and its culture, through readily accessible examples of its distinctive painting traditions and decorative arts. In 1890, the Museum of Fine Arts, Boston, established its own Japanese collection with a major gift from Morse. Ernest Fenollosa (1853–1908) was appointed as its curator.

Another Salemite, Fenollosa had traveled with Morse to Japan and amassed his own impressive collection of art. The museum's Japan collection consisted of some five thousand pieces, and was located just yards from the Greenes' boarding-house rooms.[54] The Greenes would have visited the Museum of Fine Arts not only out of personal interest, but because their MIT class in freehand drawing had its sessions in the MFA galleries.[55] Another glimpse of Japan's artistic culture could have reached Charles Greene through Ross Turner's friend Bunkio Matsuki, a Japanese national who had come to Salem as a teenager a few weeks before the Greenes' arrival in the fall of 1888. Matsuki, who had studied in Japan to become a monk, quickly emerged as one of the most colorful and visible promoters of Japanese culture in the Boston area. While enrolled at Salem High School, Matsuki assisted Edward S. Morse with his research, and, in 1890, after a buying trip to Japan, Matsuki opened a Japanese retail department at Almy, Bigelow & Washburn, a fashionable Salem store. Matsuki's popular and well-publicized department sold a mixture of valuable antique pottery and modern manufactured goods.[56] While Charles Greene may have met Matsuki through Ross Turner, he might also have become acquainted with the Salem-Japan connection through the Rantoul brothers, Augustus and William, with whom Charles worked at Andrews, Jaques and Rantoul during his first apprenticeship in Boston. William Gibbons Rantoul (1867–1949) designed a Japanese-style house for Matsuki in 1893, just as the Greenes were leaving Boston for California.[57]

Henry Greene was less restless at MIT, and on the whole had a more even experience in Boston. For one thing, his academic marks were on average ten grade points higher than Charles's were during their first school year. Charles later wrote, "My brother Hal seemed very comfortable and happy and had better marks than I received, which made me very unhappy and discouraged."[58] Henry earned "honor" scores in Freehand Drawing, Charcoal Drawing, and in a course entitled Schools, Churches, and Theatres. His lowest grades were in History of Ornament, and Heating and Ventilation, the latter's exam being the one he and Charles were compelled to make up before receiving their final certificates (a year late) in 1891. Once the late work was completed, however, Henry had still earned only a barely

20

21

20 Andrews, Jaques and Rantoul, William E. Cox house,
"Roughwood" (now Pine Manor College), Brookline,
Massachusetts, 1890–92.
Detail of portico.

21 William E. Cox house, "Roughwood."
Front facade.

passing score. Ironically, he would later emerge as the more proficient of the two brothers in the design of historical ornament and the practicalities of heating and ventilation. Henry's school career passed uneventfully, except for an illness that kept him from classes for a brief period of time in the winter of 1889. Henry managed to write to his parents weekly, often being obliged to pass on news of his brother, who did not write home regularly.[59]

The pressing business of school work and social imperatives for young men in their early twenties kept the Greenes' calendars full, and the weekly correspondence from their parents in St. Louis reflected the schedule of activities in which the two sons were involved, much of it with family. On weekends during the school year they would often travel by train to New Bedford, where they would visit their "Aunt Emily" and "Grandma Greene," daughter of the architect Thomas Waldron Sumner. They would also go to Braintree to visit "Cousin Nannie," and were sometimes asked to bring their musical instruments; Charles played the violin, Henry the flute. When Henry became ill during the Christmas holiday of 1889, he remained in New Bedford with his grandmother, who cared for him until he was well enough to return to school. The Boston-area relations also undertook a certain amount of the boys' social training, encouraging them to associate with good families and to attend proper social events. In a letter written during the winter of 1891, the boys' father, who was also vigilant about his sons' professional and social prospects, wrote, "When do you intend to call on the Phillips and the Thayers and the lady Aunt Emily sent [the] letter of introduction to? I want you to cultivate all [these] acquaintances."[60] The more artistically inclined Lelia had a practical streak that emerged in her letters, too. Charles, it seemed to her, daydreamed too much, to the detriment of his work. She wrote, "Ideal and Art are very fascinating. I can appreciate all that but it is very necessary to someone to work for the means and substance to keep the pot boiling and get the where-with-all to indulge such Luxuries."[61]

Henry managed a better balance between work and society, and even had a serious romance with the daughter of one of his father's investment partners. Annie Callendar and her family had a summer cottage on Nantucket, and Charles and Henry spent brief parts of at least three summers on the island. Henry may have been too preoccupied with Annie to notice that Charles roamed the island to discover the wealth of seventeenth- and eighteenth-century vernacular structures unspoiled by modernization or new development. Charles used his camera to photograph the sights, and wrote to a friend of "threading ... through narrow lanes" and "dwellings ... built by rich ship owners."[62]

In the spring of 1890, with classes finished, it came time for both young men to find employment. Not surprisingly, personal connections came to bear on the Greenes' securing jobs. With a letter of introduction from Mrs. Mary L. Jones, a family acquaintance, Charles found a position with the architectural firm of Andrews, Jaques and Rantoul.[63] Robert Day Andrews (1857–1928) and Herbert Jaques (1857–1916) had both been Special Students in MIT's Partial Course in Architecture, class of 1877. Jaques had worked in the office of H. H. Richardson for three and a half years, and had accompanied Richardson on his famous 1882 trip to Europe.[64] Andrews had worked with Peabody and Stearns for seven years, but had also been with Richardson as a senior draftsman in the early 1880s.[65] Augustus Neal Rantoul (1865–1934) was admitted to the firm as a partner in 1889, and his brother, William Gibbons Rantoul, joined the firm a year or two later.

One commission, which would have come to Charles's attention while in the employ of the firm, was the Cox residence, "Roughwood" (now Pine Manor College), in the Boston suburb of Brookline.[66] A sketch of the house was published in *American Architect and Building News* just one month after Charles joined the firm, and it remained an active project in the office during his entire employment there.[67] The Cox commission was developed as a three-story residence with the volumes typical of the Queen Anne idiom, including a central mass bracketed on either end by substantial turrets with domed roofs. Shingle Style detailing characterizes the exterior skin where multiple layers of shingles form a series of strong horizontal bands across the second story. The third story is concealed under a steep slate roof, with prominent dormers both on the central mass and on the turrets. The two upper levels sit on a first level and foundation of undressed Roxbury puddingstone heavily trimmed in red sandstone bearing chisel marks clearly visible on all surfaces. This may have been Charles

22

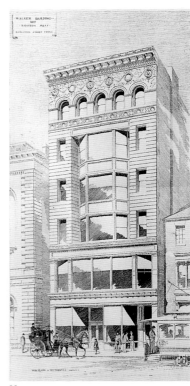

23

22 Charles Greene (fourth from right, in front) in the Boston office of one of his employers, probably Winslow and Wetherell, c. 1892.

23 Winslow and Wetherell, Walker Building, Boston, 1891.

24 H. Langford Warren, Troy Orphan Asylum, Troy, New York, 1893.

25 Edward R. Benton, Albert H. Overman house, Springfield, Massachusetts, 1891–93.

Greene's first professional exposure to the artistic use of masonry to which he would return many times throughout his career. On the nearby Cox carriage house, clinker bricks were combined with standard bricks on a base of granite cobbles, another treatment Charles would turn to again in later years.

The firm employed these elements as a direct result of Andrews and Jaques having worked with H. H. Richardson. Perhaps most significantly for the Greenes, Andrews and Jaques had been with Richardson's firm during the design and construction of the Robert Treat Paine house (1884–87). The bold treatment of rustic exterior materials, and the open planning of the vast stairhall and public spaces, were deftly carried out with colonial and Japanese features and devices, all convincingly echoed in the later Cox residence. While it is tempting to imagine that the Greenes may actually have seen the Paine house, it is more likely that they came by an aesthetic appreciation for those forms and materials through Charles's direct exposure to "Roughwood," the Cox project in Brookline.[68]

Despite this instructive apprenticeship, Charles was unhappy during the four and a half months he was with Andrews, Jaques and Rantoul. "I am sorry dear Charlie your situation is not pleasant, but now that College is open again perhaps you can find some place [that] will suit you better," wrote his father in late September 1890. By the beginning of October, Charles was actively looking for a different job. In particular, he was hoping to find a situation with Charles Howard Walker, one of his instructors at MIT.[69] Charles did not make a move there, though, possibly because Walker's office was not large and may not have had enough work to support him. By early November, Charles had moved to the office of R. Clipston Sturgis, probably at the suggestion of Walker.[70] Sturgis and Walker were both successors to the office of English-trained John Hubbard Sturgis (1834–88), whose firm, Sturgis and Brigham, had designed the Museum of Fine Arts in the mid-1870s. Richard Clipston Sturgis, like Walker, was a founding member of the Boston Architectural Club in 1889, and would have been able to provide Charles with sound training and excellent contacts for future work. Work during the winter months was always slow in Boston, however, so it is not surprising that Charles changed jobs again in February,

to an unidentified firm, and moved yet again the following month, this time to more steady circumstances.[71]

On March 10, 1891, Charles received a brief letter from architect H. Langford Warren: "If you are still disengaged I should like to see you at your early convenience with regard to taking a position in my office." The effect this summons had on Charles's spirits can be imagined after months of unhappiness and uncertainty in his work.[72] Things began to fall into place for Charles. On Sunday, March 28, 1891, the Greenes celebrated the Baccalaureate Sermon at Trinity Church, solemnizing their certificates of completion of the Partial Course in Architecture at MIT.[73] It was another opportunity to appreciate the magnificent polychrome interior of Richardson's famous church, with its bold display of gold leaf, rich reds and blues, earthy greens and browns, and the remarkable mural paintings and stained glass of John La Farge. The Greenes may even have noticed the elegant window, "David Instructing Solomon in the Building of the Temple," designed by Edward Burne-Jones in collaboration with William Morris, one of the firm's most significant works in America.[74] A letter from the Greenes' father, dated April 29, 1891, is ebullient and hopeful: "I shall rejoice when you boys can begin work on your own account. I want to see you swing your own shingle."[75]

Charles enjoyed his employment with Herbert Langford Warren (1857–1917) and would have found him to be a good teacher. Warren had also been a Special Student in architecture at MIT, and had worked in the office of H. H. Richardson from 1879 until 1885. After traveling extensively in Europe, he returned to Boston, primarily to design houses. Eleven years senior to Charles, Warren was an established professional with ambitions. He was soon to be appointed the first professor of architecture at Harvard University. While employed by Richardson, Warren had absorbed the design principles of the Shingle Style, which he used in his own work, but he also migrated freely among the Queen Anne, gothic, and especially Colonial Revival idioms. Warren was English-born and had studied in England (and Germany) before attending MIT. He had the opportunity to develop a first-hand understanding of the English Arts and Crafts movement, which he ably demonstrated in several of his later works. Immediately after Warren

24

25

hired Charles Greene, however, the firm was focused on a large institutional project with few Arts and Crafts pretensions. A preliminary sketch of the firm's Troy, New York, Orphan Asylum was published in *American Architect and Building News* the following month. The commission, which included building and grounds, featured a vast Dutch Colonial structure with crow-stepped gables and dormers, and arcades flanking the wings. The structure was designed for 250 inmates, and was described as one of the most completely appointed buildings of its kind in the country.[76]

This large project was underway during Charles's tenure at the firm, and he may well have been hired specifically to help with the increased workload the project brought. Warren's personal philosophy was that contemporary architects should employ the best of historical forms, especially medieval and classical (and its contemporary moral equivalent, Colonial Revival), and he would have counted on Charles Greene's competency in drafting in these styles.[77] Charles was up to the task, and he declared himself to be happy in Warren's employ for the next eight months. Also among the jobs in the office at that time was the construction of the Town Hall (now Bemis Hall) in Lincoln, Massachusetts. A compact and charming structure, it is nominally a Georgian brick block, but with an astonishing array of details and features that may have provided Charles Greene with valuable insights into the interpretation of classical and colonial forms. In particular, an exquisitely detailed double staircase demonstrates Warren's facility with a variety of colonial baluster designs. On the second level, the meeting hall features an elaborate and exposed wooden truss system, stained dark and secured with iron strapping. Expressed structural elements were important and distinctive aspects of Warren's work that may have made an impression on twenty-three-year-old Charles Greene.

By November 1891, Charles had joined the firm of Winslow and Wetherell and remained there until his departure for California. Heading a large and successful office, Walter T. Winslow (1843–1909) and George H. Wetherell (1854–1930) had distinguished backgrounds. Winslow had studied architecture in Paris before returning to Boston to incorporate with Nathanial Bradlee and George Wetherell as Bradlee, Winslow and Wetherell. George Wetherell had studied at MIT in the class of 1874 before going on to the Ecole des Beaux-Arts. The firm offered Charles Greene yet another high-quality learning opportunity. Notable among the commissions in the office during Greene's employment were several office blocks. Structural iron and steel had become standard materials for new office construction, even in Boston, where the Richardsonian legacy of elegant statements in load-bearing masonry had been among the strongest. The new building method provided Charles Greene with direct experience

that would enable him, with his brother, to submit credible bids for later commercial work in Pasadena. *American Architect and Building News* published two commercial structures by Winslow and Wetherell from this period. The first, published November 19, 1892, was identified simply as a building on Lincoln, Beach, and Utica Streets, the second as a commercial block at the corner of Kingston and Essex Streets. Both structures, while not trend-setting, show a simplicity and lightness compatible with contemporary developments in the design profession. In July 1893, the S. S. Pierce Company announced that Winslow and Wetherell had developed plans for a store in Brookline. The half-timbered Queen Anne shopfronts and offices were not built until 1899, but Charles was in the office when the preliminary schemes were done.[78]

Winslow and Wetherell's 1892 house for Joseph Walker, a lawyer, at 108 Upland Road, Brookline, also used elements that would emerge soon after in Charles's work: the shingle exterior, an octagonal bay with a domed roof, and an octagonal pavilion on the ground level.[79] Charles had witnessed similar design elements used elsewhere, but the instructive effect of focused exposure to consistent principles of design and the use of materials, all within the same firm for nearly two years, would have been especially memorable. Though its design predated Charles's arrival at the firm, the house designed for William Whitman in Brookline in about 1889 may also be considered typical of their domestic designs during this period. The Whitman house plan is the product of Richardson's theory of openness and light, and exhibits careful detailing, honestly exposed materials, and richly textured surfaces. Intricately carved, unpainted wainscoting was of high-grade wood selected for its beauty and expressive grain. During this period, Charles experienced some setbacks, and at one point, after losing a competition he and his brother had entered, he complained bitterly about the profession, saying, "I am about sick of it all and disgusted with architecture generally. I thought I could learn to like it but it is hard work, at least so far."[80] Nonetheless, Charles did well at Winslow and Wetherell and was given at least one promotion while there. He expressed regret when it came time to depart for California in 1893, since he was finally settling comfortably into the architectural profession.[81]

Henry Greene also had the good fortune to apprentice with well-trained and experienced architects in and around Boston. In 1906, for the Los Angeles Public Library's Western History project, Henry Greene described his early work experience as follows: "After leaving the Boston Tech I entered Chamberlin & Austin's office as draughtsman [in] 1890; afterwards worked with Stickney and Austin, Mr. Benton, and Shepley, Routan [*sic*] & Coolidge." Henry began his first job with Chamberlin and Austin at the same time Charles joined Andrews, Jaques and Rantoul, in the spring of

26 Winslow and Wetherell, William Whitman house,
   Brookline, Massachusetts, 1889.

27 Stickney and Austin, Kennebunk River Club,
   Kennebunkport, Maine, 1889.

28 Shepley, Rutan and Coolidge, Joseph H. White house,
   Brookline, Massachusetts, 1893–94.
   Detail of Chinese tile on rear terrace wall.

29 Joseph H. White house.
   Rear of house with terrace retaining wall.

26

GREENE & GREENE

1890. In June 1890, Dr. Greene wrote to his sons, "I hope you like the situations you have and that they will prove instructive." Both young men, though they trained at the prestigious MIT, worked for no pay. This status they would accept for the first eight months, and it was by no means atypical of hopeful young architects.[82] Chamberlin and Austin's office was led by William E. Chamberlin (1856–1911) and William D. Austin (1856–1944), both graduates of MIT as regular students in architecture. Austin was in the class of 1876, Chamberlin in the class of 1877. In his letters Henry apparently made several references to "Mr. Austin," but the only mention of his other employer was made when Lelia Greene commented how odd it was that Henry had not been invited to Mr. Chamberlin's wedding. In any case, Henry seemed more aligned with Austin.[83]

In 1892, William Austin entered into a new partnership with Frederick W. Stickney (1853–1918) of Lowell, Massachusetts, and Henry Greene was sent to work in that office. Stickney had also been a special student in architecture at MIT, and evidence indicates he worked for H. H. Richardson and Henry Van Brunt after receiving his certificate.[84] When Henry arrived at the Lowell office, the firm had a major project under way. Lowell Memorial Hall had been in construction since 1890 and was finished during the summer of 1893. The design is a competent Richardsonian Romanesque essay, though turned subtly toward Classicism with a symmetrical organization of exterior elements and monochromatic use of granite, the light-gray stone that would be the material of choice for American Beaux-Arts architecture. Nonetheless, this may have been the first opportunity for Henry to develop a working understanding of Richardsonian design.[85] Stickney was also remarkably adept at Shingle Style designs considering he did so few. Henry's exposure to that aspect of Stickney's work would have mirrored his brother's exposure during the same period. In particular, it is likely that Henry was aware of Stickney's Kennebunk River Club (1889) in Kennebunkport, Maine, a large and dramatic shingled boat house on the riverbank. Its broad, gable roof shelters the entire three-story structure, its deep porch seeming to float above the beach level, and its wide, arch-covered loggia tucked deep into the upper story. This building represents a romantic yet rational use of a shingle skin in a design that is clearly descriptive of its

function yet welcoming and home-like in its sheltering forms. The Greenes' later work would be described in similar terms.

During the periods of reduced workload in the offices, Henry would take on outside work with other architects.[86] One of these was Edward Raymond Benton, an 1875 Harvard graduate and vice-president of the Boston Architectural Club in the 1890s under Charles's one-time employer R. Clipston Sturgis. Benton seems not to have had a full-time practice, since his office records indicate only two jobs in progress between 1891 and 1893.[87] One of these was an alteration and addition to his father's house near Boston. The other was a mansion, and was probably the reason Henry was hired. Benton was to design a residence for Albert H. Overman, a bicycle and wheel manufacturer in Springfield, capital of the Commonwealth of Massachusetts. The house would cost more than $100,000 to build. Originally located at 34 Federal Street, the Overman house (now demolished) was a Federal-style house with pretensions. Among its eccentricities were prominent sleeping porches on the second level and a compact, lantern-like third level, both of which may have left an impression on Henry. They resemble, in function if not in appearance, concepts the Greenes later proposed for several of their larger houses, including the David B. Gamble house.

Following his tenure with Fredrick Stickney, and his occasional work for Edward Benton, Henry briefly joined the firm of Shepley, Rutan and Coolidge, official successors to the practice of H. H. Richardson. George F. Shepley (1860–1903) was a regular student in architecture in MIT's class of 1882. Charles H. Rutan (1851–1914) did not have academic training in architecture, but was hired in 1869 at the age of eighteen to be Richardson's first office boy. He later became a partner, then a principal in the successor firm. Charles A. Coolidge (1858–1936) graduated with the MIT class of 1883 as a four-year student. Thus, during Henry's last few months in Boston, he would be training with exceptionally qualified and experienced architects.

Henry worked on at least two commissions during the summer of 1893 for which his involvement is clearly documented.[88] The Brookline residence of Joseph H. White at 80 Seaver Street, a "Jacobethan"-style house, was envisioned as one of the more prominent homes on fashionable Fisher Hill.

Because of a drop in elevation on the site, the house was positioned with its entrance close to the street on the uphill side. On the garden elevation, a broad and deep terrace was designed to give easy access to the exterior and to provide scenic views to the north. Henry was required to produce, among other things, detailed drawings of terra-cotta frames set into a brick terrace wall. These terra-cotta elements were designed to hold decorative tiles, identical to the Chinese tiles that would appear more than ten years later in the Greenes' Pasadena work. Chinese decorative tiles had been imported for architectural use for some time, however. As early as 1881, the landscape painter Frederick Church bought several crates of the tiles, both in green and white, for use in the tower and parapets of his Hudson Valley home, Olana.[89] For the Joseph White house, Henry was also responsible for drawing classical details for the entry, including pilasters, arches, columns, and coping. He produced detail drawings for at least one other job for the firm—a remodelling of the Boston and Maine Terminal Station, known as Union Station, or North Station. These drawings included interior iron gates between the lobby and the train shed, elevations of the train shed, and a skylight for the waiting room. This experience was perhaps influential, since skylights would later emerge as a regular theme in Henry's finest independent designs. While anecdotal accounts have often stated that Henry Greene had also worked on the Stanford University Quadrangle project while in the Sheply, Rutan and Coolidge office, extant office records do not confirm his involvement. Indeed, records show that in 1888 the Stanford University project left the Boston office to be completed in California by Charles Coolidge.

27

28

While the Greenes' professional careers in Boston made steady progress, their parents had significant difficulties at home, both with health and financial issues. Thomas Greene had made several disastrous investments totaling some $20,000, and his practice had been declining since 1890.[90] The Greenes moved from their large house on Washington Avenue in St. Louis to a boarding hotel in March 1892, but even with reduced expenses their financial situation continued to deteriorate. Dr. Greene wrote to his sons: "Of course our present way of living has cut our expenses down very materially, and if necessary we can live here in the [office] flat and cut them still further. But I hate to do this, which would publish to everyone how my business has failed...." Added to the financial strain was the fact that Lelia had been suffering from an asthmatic condition. Dr. Greene had recurring "malaria trouble," too. He wrote to his sons that their mother would be cured by the "pure climate of California," and announced that they would depart for California on July 1, 1892.

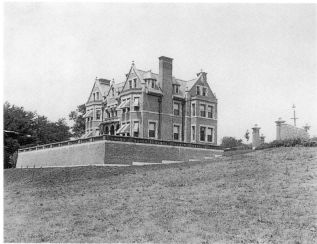

29

Knowing they would probably never return, but not wanting to give the appearance of leaving definitively, Dr. and Mrs. Greene exacerbated their financial straits by purchasing round-trip tickets from St. Louis to Los Angeles.[91] After spending a short time with Dr. Greene's sister, Alice Longley, in South Pasadena, they rented a cottage in the larger town of Pasadena. The change of scenery from St. Louis seemed to do them both good, at least initially, but within a few months their correspondence began to take a gloomy tone once again. The situation went from bad to worse with Dr. Greene's investments, and he described his mood as "blue." His mood swings and many references to poor health indicate a possible clinically depressed state, perhaps the result of long-term effects of his war experiences. He discouraged his sons from coming west at first. Several reasons, most having to do with money, were given: "it breaks my heart not to say come at once, but ... when you get here I would have to support you, as in this small place you would find absolutely nothing to do....There are three architects here and there is probably half a dozen small cottages being built in the whole town."[92]

By January 1893 Charles and Henry decided they would go to California anyway. Their parents' financial difficulties and reports of bad health had probably alarmed them. The next month, however, they changed their

minds, saying they would stay in Boston. That spring, Charles and Henry were given a chance to design a house near Boston for a family friend named Avery, another of their father's investment partners. The commission progressed to drawings, though no evidence has emerged indicating that the house was ever built. This would have been the brothers' first architectural commission together, working as a team.[93] On June 14, 1893, Henry wrote of their intention to come to Pasadena immediately. Dr. Greene wrote back, this time relieved, and suggested that they come by way of Chicago. He would send them enough money to make the detour possible.[94]

By the time the Greenes left Boston during the third week of August, 1893, they had been separated from their parents for nearly five years. Charles would soon turn twenty-five and Henry was twenty-three. Both had matured physically and mentally and had worked with classically trained architects—many of whom were also MIT alumni. It was invaluable experience that had made them bona fide members of a professional elite. It had also given them the confidence to move into the architectural profession on their own.

2

"To Make Pleasurable Those Things"

2

3

T he World's Columbian Exposition attracted nearly everyone who could get to Chicago in 1893. Dr. Thomas Sumner Greene urged Charles and Henry to attend, probably because he thought they would benefit from seeing the architecture and exhibitions. For reasons of health and money, he and Mrs. Greene could not go, but the boys could at least give them a first-hand account.[1] A visit to the fair would give Charles and Henry an opportunity to broaden their impressions of the monumental and unifying effect of Beaux-Arts design and planning. A visit to the "White City" would represent an extension of the Greenes' training at MIT, a kind of graduate-level field trip for further study of the modern application of classical orders and ornament in civic edifices.

The exposition was urban planning writ large—a bold experiment calculated to inspire American cities to remake themselves in a glorious new image. Indeed, in the decades to follow, many communities obliged under the rubric of the City Beautiful movement. For fairgoers who believed that there was more to beauty than monochromatic uniformity and order, some notable exceptions to the Beaux-Arts paradigm could be found. Seeking them out, however, required exploration beyond the main esplanades. On the secluded Wooded Isle, for example, was the Japanese *Ho-o-den*, a series of three half-scale temple buildings modeled after the *Ho-o-do*, or "Phoenix Hall," of eleventh-century Byodin Japan. While often cited as an influence on the Greenes' later work, the *Ho-o-den* would not have been their first exposure to Japanese design, though it may well have been the first authentic Japanese timber construction they had seen. A cause-and-effect relationship between this particular pavilion and their later work, however, is a problematic and tenuous link considering the scarcity of Japanese design references in the Greenes' work during the first ten years of their independent architectural practice. In addition, other building designs and types at the Chicago exposition may have interested the Greenes at least as much, including the Johore Bungalow Village, a collection of deceptively simple thatch huts from the Malay Peninsula featuring intricately carved verge boards and open-air sleeping loggias on the upper levels.

The most prominent structure at the exposition that did not conform to the Beaux-Arts idiom, however, was Louis Sullivan's large, centrally located

4

5

6

Transportation Building, whose colorful exterior provided a vivid contrast to the monochromatic Classicism of its neighbors. Sullivan had inventively combined ceremony with surprise, by massing stairs, terraces, and entries into exotic forms and sheathing them in richly decorated surfaces that made visitors stop, as one souvenir book described it, "in bewildered admiration."[2] Sadly, the true impact of the Greenes' layover in Chicago is impossible to know. The brothers left behind no documentation of their visit.

Leaving Chicago, Charles and Henry continued their journey west by transcontinental railroad to Los Angeles. They rode the last nine miles of their trip by local train and coach to the town of Pasadena, a dusty and hot community of six thousand souls (though it grew to as many as ten thousand during the winter tourist season). Lelia Greene wrote to her sons, "You can look out for Papa's sign and keep on East Colorado Street, for we shall be somewhere here....[Pasadena] is [a] country town, you know, not Boston..."[3] But it was a country town with aspirations, and its mild winter climate and physical beauty had attracted an increasing flow of cultured and socially prominent families since its initial settlement in 1874. One Los Angeles weekly newspaper of the day described Pasadena as "the only place in Southern California where 'society' as it is known in the East exists and flourishes."[4] In another periodical prone to rhapsodize over the area's quality of life, Dr. Francis Fenelon Rowland, a prominent citizen (and future Greene and Greene client), described a local meeting of the Valley Hunt Club preparing to ride to the hounds: "Members and invited guests have arrived, and spend the moments drinking in the health-giving air, laden as it is with the fragrance of the orange and lemon which is wafted from the contiguous groves; or, as if nature is not content with what art has done, thousands of acres on every side as far as the eye can reach are covered with the poppy, all aglow, lupines and the sweet scented wild heliotrope over which the hunters will soon be speeding, thrilled with joy caused by the novelty of a mid-winter's gallop over such a carpet of flowers."[5] In twenty years, Pasadena had developed into a resort land of genteel bohemianism, where pedigree carried at least as much cachet as money, and a robust love of the outdoors bonded a community that was simultaneously refined and progressive.

Charles and Henry arrived with no immediate plans to practice architecture—they and their parents had a vague notion that they would pursue their profession in a metropolis such as Kansas City, or Chicago— but they soon found good reason to consider hanging their shingle in Pasadena. The building boom of the mid-1880s, when more than one thousand new houses were built in two years, had gone bust by 1888, but the local economy had begun to revitalize in the summer of 1892, about the time Dr. and Mrs. Greene arrived from St. Louis. A national financial panic in the spring of 1893 was precipitated by the sudden devaluation of silver and a corresponding surge in the price of gold. In the chaos that followed, western cities fared somewhat less badly than their eastern counterparts, and it proved to be a good time for the Greenes to have left Boston for California. Their former employers would soon be dismissing draftsmen.[6]

Pasadena had enjoyed a busy tourist season during the winter of 1893–94, and many new residences were under construction. While the bank panic caused havoc elsewhere, the fundamental indicators of local business were still robust, and the local outlook was optimistic. Two bank closures in Los Angeles that season had given Pasadena cause for concern, but in a remarkable show of civic solidarity and optimism a pledge was taken by 175 individuals and firms to maintain their deposits at local banks through the crisis. The pledge worked, holding Pasadena's economy relatively sound.[7] Ironically, the city's reputation for having been mildly affected by the panic had unforeseen side effects. Hundreds of unemployed and homeless arrived, setting up campsites in the nearby Arroyo Seco in hopes of finding work (or at least a warmer climate in which to be out of work). Pasadena's civic spirit surfaced once again, and on January 13, 1894, the city trustees announced a plan to house and locate work for unemployed transients, deftly side-stepping the more serious manifestations of the economic crisis. On the same day, during the height of the tourist season, the *Pasadena Star* reported that "Messrs. Henry M. Greene and Charles S. Greene, who arrived from Boston a short time ago, have opened an architects office in the Eldrige block. They are late graduates of the Boston School of Technology and come fully prepared to prove their qualifications as architects."[8]

When the Greenes opened their office, they could lay claim to being the only architects in town whose education had been in the Beaux-Arts tradition. Of the other architects practicing in Pasadena at the time—Harry Ridgeway, T. William Parkes, Frederick L. Roehrig, and J. J. Blick—only Roehrig's education rivaled the Greenes', though it came from an opposing tradition. Ridgeway, the long-established practitioner in town, was a self-taught builder and designer who called himself an architect in the days before certification was required. Of Ridgeway it was said (probably with a straight face), "His idea was not to make two buildings exactly alike, but to utilize all the styles known to architectural science."[9]

T. William Parkes had apprenticed in England for twelve years, and was admitted as an Associate of the Royal Institute of British Architects in 1886. He settled in Pasadena the following year and began a distinguished career.[10] Joseph J. Blick, a draftsman for Parkes, completed his apprenticeship before opening his own practice in Pasadena at about the same time the Greenes opened their office.[11] Frederick Louis Roehrig (1857–1948), on the other hand, was the one the Greenes had to watch. Like the Greenes, he had followed a formal academic curriculum. He attended Cornell University under Professor Charles Babcock, a devoted follower of John Ruskin and an ardent supporter of Gothic Revivalism. Babcock ran his architecture program based on Ruskin's belief that "before an architect can become a true artist, he must be a master of the art of building and a man of science."[12] The Greenes' Beaux-Arts training was very different. Less rigorous in its emphasis on science and building, it stressed instead the mastering of classical orders and historical styles. Because of their education's exotic Beaux-Arts pedigree and its emphasis on an artistic approach to architecture, the brothers presented an attractive alternative for the social and intellectual elite of Pasadena. In addition, they had had a solid grounding in science at the Manual Training School.

During their first two and a half years of independent practice, the Greenes competed for contracts to design nearly twenty moderate-sized residences, receiving commissions to complete about half of these. None was estimated to cost more than $2,900 to build, but for the young and virtually unknown architects this represented a solid start. Their first actual

commission came in September 1894, nine months after their office opened. The contract to design a house for Mrs. Martha Flynn was valued at $2,460.[13] The overall design of the house was simple: clapboard siding covered an essentially rectangular, two-story box. Diamond-pane casement windows on the second level and other features recall images of the late-seventeenth- and eighteenth-century merchant-class houses that the Greenes had seen in Massachusetts. Leaded windows were placed in an angled bay supported by scrolled brackets and positioned off center on the front elevation. Both the bay and brackets were common devices for the period. A porch sheltered under the projecting second level provided shade and outdoor living space near the entry, adjacent to the main living areas. A modest attempt at decorative shingle patterning, similar to that which Charles had seen on the Cox residence in Brookline, was used on the surface between the second-story windows to the left of the central bay.

The Greenes' second commission, which came into the office almost simultaneously, was a house for John Breiner, the local butcher. The meager $1,307 contract afforded less opportunity for artistic exploration, however, and the resulting house provides little evidence of further stylistic development. This changed, ironically, with the Greenes' first encounter with speculative housing. Executed for the Pacific Security Investment Company, the firm's two designs for dwellings were a success, and sold shortly after completion. The first house had a larger budget, and allowed the Greenes sufficient latitude to begin to establish what would soon emerge as distinct design preferences. These included a domed roof over an octagonal bay, a secondary, tripartite bay projecting on a side elevation at a shallow angle, and shingle or clapboard siding over a cobble foundation. They also attempted the Richardsonian device of a stair-hall entry illuminated by windows over the staircase. Flanking this was an octagonal alcove with a built-in window seat, another Richardsonian element used by the Greenes' Boston mentors. While the speculative houses were dramatically scaled-down versions of the grand spatial statements that the Greenes had worked with during their apprenticeships, they demonstrated that the brothers had learned enough of the practical application of architecture to make a promising, if halting, start. An unsuccessful bid to

7   **Martha Flynn house, Pasadena, 1894 (demolished).**
    The first house designed by the Greene and
    Greene firm.

8   **Willis M. Eason house, Pasadena, 1895.**

9   **"Job No. 11" for unidentified client, Altadena,
    1896 (project).**
    Front and side elevations. Ink-on-linen presentation
    drawing.

10 **"Job No. 11."**
    First floor plan. Ink-on-linen presentation drawing.

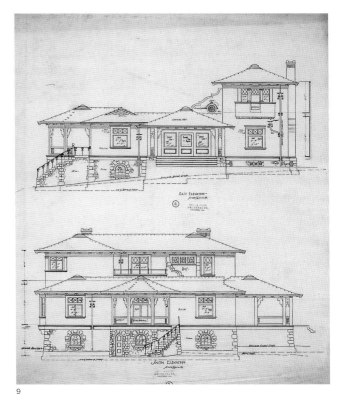

9

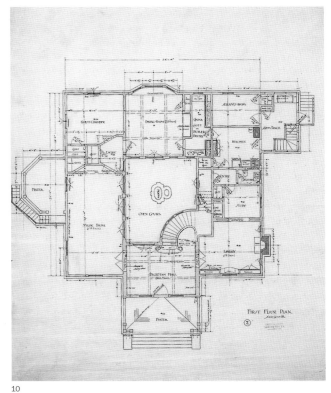

10

design an eight-room residence followed the speculative houses, and, except for the design of a small house for Conrad Covell in January 1895, there was little work in the office for nearly six months.

A side-by-side pair of houses for Robert and Willis Eason was begun that spring. Robert Eason was president, and his son, Willis, bookkeeper, of the Union Savings Bank. Both of the modest cottages had a small porch with a column portico. Like the Covell house, each portico supported a pediment decorated in "stereo relief"—an application of a three-dimensional plaster ornament such as a wreath, garland, or medallion. This form of decoration would emerge as a habitual feature in the Greenes' work during the next four years. The first full year of their active architectural practice concluded with the designs of cottages for T. J. Riggs and Edward S. Crump, and new Sunday school rooms for the Pasadena Presbyterian Church at the corner of Colorado Street and Worcester (now Garfield) Avenue. The church membership planned to install a tracker pipe organ the following year, and the Greenes were contracted to design alterations to the sanctuary to accommodate the changes. Unfortunately, little physical record of this work survives.[14]

Of greater interest from the same period was a design the Greenes produced for a house that was never built. "Job No. 11" was the deceptively sober identification for what was in actuality an elaborate and romantic design for a two-story residence. New commissions had been slow coming into the office following the church work, and it appears that "Job No. 11" may have been a speculative scheme prepared in hopes of attracting a new and wealthy client. The drawings are significant because of their preview of major themes in the Greenes' later work. First, the essentially square plan of the house circulated around a central courtyard open to the sky. The court was open to rooms on all four sides on the first level, and was fitted with a fountain in the center, a feature they would use to dramatic effect more than ten years later for Theodore Irwin. The drawings show a careful concern for how the masonry is expressed, a theme that would soon emerge as an obsession with Charles Greene. Also evident is an artistic love of carved wood, shown in the profiled porch brackets carved to resemble dragons or sea horses. A half-octagon-shaped covered piazza was to project

11

12

from the south elevation to provide indoor-outdoor circulation adjacent to a fifteen-by-thirty-foot music hall, a fantasy that perhaps reflected both brothers' own desires. A basement gymnasium also reflects their shared interest in physical fitness, which was often mentioned in letters from Boston during their days at MIT. A dramatic curved staircase was to rise from the reception area over the open court to the bedroom hallway on the north side of the house. Unfortunately, the music lover's house was never commissioned, but elegant drawings remain as evidence of an imaginative and romantic moment in the early days of Greene and Greene.

During the spring and summer of 1896 the Greenes built an office block for local land investors Joseph N. Kinney and Bela O. Kendall. They designed modern technological advances into the structure, including a skeleton of iron H-beams and cylinder-beams similar to that first used by William LeBaron Jenny in the Home Insurance Building in Chicago of 1884–85. The massing of the Kinney-Kendall building, as well as its decorative scheme, however, apparently derive from the commercial buildings of Winslow and Wetherell during, or just prior to, Charles's apprenticeship there.[15] On the exterior, classical pilasters on all three levels flank three-part window bays. A wreath-and-garland frieze decorates the margin between the second and third levels. The decorative flourishes on the highest frieze are Charles Greene's own invention.[16] A classically detailed cornice (the only original surface that remains visible today) completes the decorative scheme. When Charles joined Winslow and Wetherell, it had recently completed the Walker Building, an office block published in *American Architect and Building News* in October 1891 and illustrated with a picture of the facade (see page 18, fig. 23). Shown is a cornice frieze nearly identical to that of the second-level frieze on the later Kinney-Kendall building. Another Winslow and Wetherell design, for an office block at the corner of Kingston and Essex Streets in Boston, was also published in *American Architect and Building News* (March 1893) and shows the same organization of windows and a corner entry at the street level similar to the Kinney-Kendall block. It is not surprising that the Greenes borrowed heavily from their recent experience to execute their first commercial building, but it is revealing that the Kinney-Kendall design

would be their only significant commercial commission for many years. Their interests and talents would soon lead them almost exclusively to domestic architecture.

Late in 1896 the Greenes competed for the chance to design a large house and stable for Jacob Helmke and his family. The bid was unsuccessful, and the loss of the commission a blow, since it promised working with a much more substantial budget than that to which they were accustomed. The commission was awarded instead to Frederick Roehrig, whose winning design employed a heavily decorated, stereo-relief frieze, a second-level balcony with Georgian balustrade, and a prominent angled bay on the side elevation. The design that prevailed over theirs could not have helped but catch the Greenes' attention. In the ensuing two years they would design several houses with similar features. One of these was a residence for Theodore P. Gordon, commissioned in April 1897, following several unsuccessful bids the firm had made to design houses for other clients.[17] With a contract price of just under four thousand dollars, the Gordon commission came with a more generous budget than any previous job the Greenes had undertaken. An octagonal corner tower—reception room below and bedroom above—distinguished the massing of the exterior. Otherwise, specific exterior features were borrowed from Roehrig's design for the Helmke house: a deep decorative frieze, gables decorated in stereo relief, and a Georgian balustrade guarding the second-story balcony. The Greenes lavished attention on the details of the interior, providing for a built-in dining room sideboard flanked by built-in window benches, and two intricately carved mantels for the library and dining room, subjects of detailed watercolor sketches.

The Hosmer project of the same year gives another view of the Greenes' design tendencies, and establishes their growing attention to specific materials. The Hosmer design relates simultaneously to Dutch Colonial and Mission Revival styles, though classical details were inserted, including fluted columns (wood casings around four-inch iron shafts), scrolled brackets, and a wreath-and-garland relief. The tile roof's galvanized iron gutters channeled rain to gooseneck pipes. The pipes terminated in cement gargoyles' mouths to spit the rain, waterfall-like, into wide collectors and

13 Frederick L. Roehrig, Jacob Helmke house,
     Pasadena, 1896.

14 Theodore P. Gordon house, Pasadena, 1897
     (demolished).
     Watercolor sketch of mantel details for dining-room
     fireplace (left) and library fireplace (right).

13

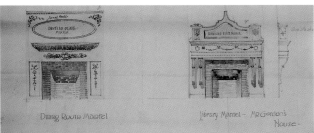

14

downspouts anchored by elaborately scrolled iron straps. The interior rooms were identified by the predominant wood used: the main hall and dining rooms in oak-paneled wainscoting, the living room in curly redwood, and the parlor in Shasta pine. The leaded-glass stair-landing window and stair-hall skylight designs were detailed on a separate sheet of linen.

In the fall of 1895 Dr. Greene and his sons joined the Twilight Club, a new social club founded by Frank S. Abbott. The club was devised as a gathering of men, as Abbott put it, "who might find surcease from their daily business and professional lives and invade the higher realms of science, philosophy, literature or even the more prosaic problems of everyday existence."[18] It was an excellent business opportunity for Charles and Henry, as it afforded a casual and congenial forum in which to make acquaintances among men of means. Eventually, more than a dozen of the Greenes' clients would be counted among the Twilight Club's membership. George S. Hull, a physician, was the first of these, becoming a member in 1896 and a client of the Greene and Greene firm by 1897. In May of that year, Hull had probably heard Dr. Greene's lecture to the club entitled "The Duties and Responsibilities of American Citizenship," followed by a musical presentation—a violin and flute duet—by Dr. Greene's sons.[19] In turn, the Greenes had been able to get the measure of Dr. Hull by hearing his lecture entitled "A Talk on Venice." Dr. Greene's insistence that the boys mingle with society and business associates paid off. A few months later Hull commissioned Greene and Greene to design and supervise for him the building of a two-story residence and separate office building.

As originally designed, the house was a simple block that presented a classically detailed facade with the Greenes' familiar detail on the portico in wreath-and-garland stereo relief. The maximum two-room width of the house faced the street, but the plan narrowed to half its width as it reached deeper into the narrow lot. Owing to the lack of a hallway, and with only a one-room width for most of the length of the house, the in-line arrangement of parlor, living room, dining room, kitchen, and screened porch made each space accessible only from its adjoining rooms. This arrangement allowed for maximum room width within a limited total square footage, but efficiency made for inconvenience, too. The liability was most dramatically

15 **Edward B. Hosmer house, Pasadena, 1897 (project).**
First floor plan. Ink-on-linen presentation drawing.

16 **Edward B. Hosmer house.**
Front elevation. Ink-on-linen presentation drawing.

17 **Dr. George S. Hull house, Pasadena, 1897**
(demolished).
First floor plan. Ink-on-linen presentation drawing.

18 **Dr. George S. Hull house and office.**

19 **Edward B. Hosmer house.**
Interior sections and details, including plan of
skylight. Ink-on-linen presentation drawing.

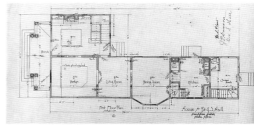

17

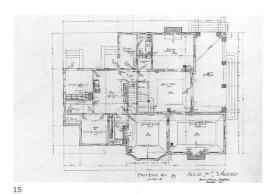

15

16

18

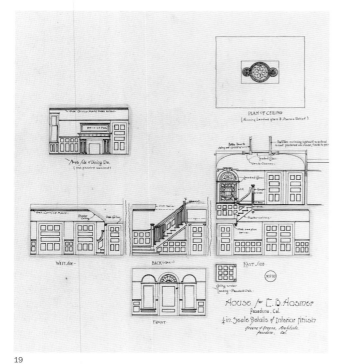

19

shown upstairs, where it was necessary for one bedroom's occupant to invade a neighbor's chamber to gain access to the bathroom facilities. The Greenes did not repeat the Hull residence floor plan in any of their later works, and the client asked them the following year to return to design a sun room and porte cochere addition that alleviated some of the potential distress caused by the confining second-level plan.

Dr. Hull's office, by contrast, was a small outbuilding with three functional interior spaces in a more rational floor plan. A combined hall and reception room, an operating room, and a laboratory made up the plan. This time, three points of entry to each space were allowed for, except in the laboratory, which had two. The exterior hints vaguely at Asian design in the slightly upturned ends of the dormer roof on the elevation over the operating room and in the broad proportions of the portico as it relates to the relatively narrow entry door.

During this same period, the Greenes designed a house for Howard Longley, the brother-in-law of Dr. Greene's sister, Alice, in South Pasadena. This commission provided a much larger budget, but the design process was difficult and went through several significant changes while on the boards. The first scheme, possibly designed by Henry, combined a Mission Revival parapet with a Georgian balustrade and colonial portico, essentially a recapitulation of the Greenes' earlier Hosmer house with a nod to the Georgian detail in Roehrig's Helmke house. This approach did not satisfy the client, however, and a new scheme was called for. It went through at least two conceptual stages, apparently under Charles's guidance.[20] In the final, accepted design, the most dominant feature is the portico, resembling a pagoda-like pavilion. The deep, sheltered space conceals a modified Federal-style doorway flanked by narrow, vertical sidelights and a richly colored fanlight transom in leaded art glass. Decorative flourishes reappear from the earlier "Job No. 11," including animal-head brackets and scrolled downspout hardware. Despite a somewhat inexpert proportioning of exterior elements, the organization of windows communicates interior functions, such as the upper-level stairway clearly indicated by a pair of stepped windows flanked by a downspout and the sweeping skirt of the portico roof.

Early in 1898, the Greenes experimented with an English design for a

20

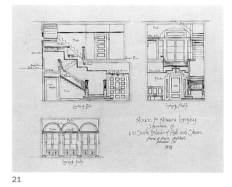

21

20 **Howard Longley house, South Pasadena, 1897.**
Front elevation. Ink-on-linen presentation drawing.

21 **Howard Longley house.**
Detail of hall and stairs. Ink-on-linen
presentation drawing.

22 **Dr. W. H. Roberts office, Pasadena, 1898**
(demolished).

23 **Winthrop B. Fay house, Pasadena, 1898**
(demolished).
A prominent covered piazza foreshadows the
Greenes' outdoor terraces and sleeping porches
of a decade later.

24 **Winthrop B. Fay house.**
First floor plan. Ink-on-linen presentation drawing.

22

23

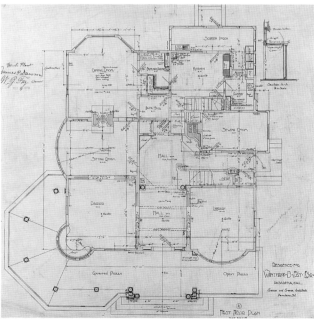

24

small office building for Dr. W. H. Roberts. The traditional vocabulary of
half-timbering on the exterior, leaded-glass windows, and a shingled roof
and gable, showed that the Greenes had a working familiarity with English
country architecture, but the roof pitch is steeper than needed in a climate
such as Southern California's. The Greenes included a semi-heraldic shield
hanging from a decorative wrought-iron rod to announce the doctor's name
and profession.

From this point, the Greenes attracted more and wealthier clients. A few
months after the Roberts office job, they won a contract for a large house
that would exceed by more than double the value of their previous most
expensive domestic commission. The design for a residence for Winthrop B.
Fay reflected Pasadena's fascination with eclecticism and decorative
surfaces. Like the Greenes' earlier house for Theodore Gordon, the Fay
house owed a debt to Frederick Roehrig's design for the Jacob Helmke
house, which also had friezes of swirling bands of stereo relief. A
particularly charming art-glass transom light above the entry doors was
designed with leaded sections of pale lavender, rose, yellow, and green glass
in conventional floral designs surrounding the leaded-in house number.
Much of the decorative exuberance of the Fay house, though, was focused on
the second level. An octagonal tower with a finial marked the southeast
corner of the building while a Palladian window was centered above the
entry, to its right. In the center of this window, french doors opened onto an
elaborately decorated balcony that looked as though it must lead to a grand
space, but was, in fact, accessible only from the unfinished attic space. Like
the Gordon house, however, the Fay house had proportions that gave it a
balanced dignity, an elusive quality in some of the Greenes' other houses of
the same period. The interior public spaces were carried out almost entirely
in oak, with coved ceilings and walls heavily appointed with moldings and
decorative relief. In November of that year the Greenes were also asked to
design the grounds. The drawings show a predominance of grass but include
a plan for two garden seats facing each other on a decomposed granite
walkway leading to a garden plot at the rear of the property. It is the first
known instance of the Greenes extending their designs to formally
incorporate house and garden.

25 **William B. Tomkins house, Pasadena, 1898** (demolished).
Piazza, view from the west.

26 **William B. Tomkins house.**
View from the southwest.

27 **William B. Tomkins house.**
First floor plan. Ink-on-linen presentation drawing.

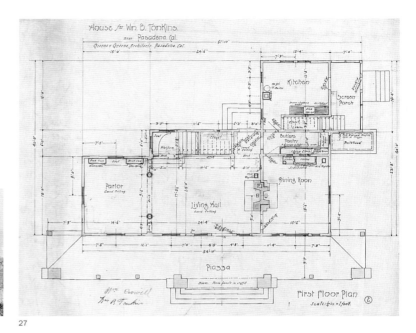

25   26   27

In March 1898 Charles Greene attended a lecture presented by Dr. Norman Bridge entitled "Misfortune of Taste." The evening provoked a passionate response from Charles, who penned his reflections on the discussion a few days later. He wrote that he had gone to the lecture "at the kind invitation of Dr. Hull, who mildly insisted upon my attendance." Summarizing the speaker's argument, Greene wrote, "[let] the proper uses of all things be considered; let ornament follow to make pleasurable those things which are necessary. All ornament for its own sake leads to a hyper-sensitiveness. How shall we know what to do? What is proper today is not tomorrow, ergo, there can be no standard of taste." While this partly paraphrased Louis Sullivan's theory that form should follow function, the idea that there could be "no standard of taste" drove the ensuing discussion that night. Charles was called upon for his own thoughts, which he described somewhat self-consciously in his journal in the present tense: "I verily believe that my tongue will cleve [sic] to the roof of my mouth, but to my astonishment my voice is clear, though a little weak. 'It seems to me that all this may be summed up in two expressions, i.e., the greatest possible amount of Truth with the greatest amount of Pleasure.'" Apparently feeling this to be somewhat enigmatic, he elaborated for the benefit of his journal and no doubt to write what he wished he had said. "Let me examine these two expressions. First, truth—what is true today is true tomorrow. Then what is a day, a year, a century? For truth is eternal. Pleasure may be likened to a line, i.e., direction; but it extends in more than one way, aye further than a square, even as a cube; therefore it is unbounded....Behold the glow of Eternal Truth and Pleasure Unbounded!"[21]

This idealistic and elliptical pronouncement represents the earliest evidence of Charles Greene's life-long struggle to examine his personal philosophy of objective beauty and art. It also signals, at the age of twenty-nine, his increasingly independent and intellectual approach to architecture and a curiosity about philosophical arguments in general. Of more immediate importance, though, it suggests an emerging sympathy for Arts and Crafts ideals that Charles himself may not have recognized, a sympathy that had its beginnings with "Job No. 11" and grew gradually over the next several years.

While the Greenes were ultimately considered to be quintessential architects of the American Arts and Crafts movement, their earliest work was ambivalent toward formal Arts and Crafts expression, even the Shingle Style, one of the movement's legitimate American precursors. This is surprising since the Greenes were near the center of the American Arts and Crafts movement's prenascent stirrings, in early-1890s Boston. Among the founders and leaders of the Society of Arts and Crafts, Boston, were Francis Ward Chandler, H. Langford Warren, Robert Day Andrews, Herbert Jaques, R. Clipston Sturgis, and C. Howard Walker, all of whom were either teachers, mentors, or employers of the Greenes. Established in 1897, the SACB marked the institutionalized beginnings of the movement in America.[22] As has been noted, some of these individuals had been disciples of Henry Hobson Richardson, whose philosophy toward building and design was in accord with that of key figures of the English Arts and Crafts movement. Others circulated within the influential sphere of Charles Eliot Norton (1827–1908), Professor of Fine Arts at Harvard University. Norton posited an intellectual foundation for an American Arts and Crafts movement by promoting the cultural elite's obligation to shape public taste and encourage artistic craft.[23] Norton's personal friendship with John Ruskin (1819–1900) provided additional moral authority for him to promulgate a native movement informed by English precedent. Boston's Tavern Club met to promote this agenda, and the clubrooms served as an important locus for debating and shaping the city's cultural ideals. Norton served as the club's president from 1890 to 1898, and membership included Charles Greene's employers Robert Day Andrews and Herbert Jaques, as well as C. Howard Walker, the Greenes' instructor in History of Ornament.

Through these men, the Greenes would have been at least peripherally aware of the Arts and Crafts movement; but the brothers were not yet ready to accept its message. After all, the movement's original ideals were decidedly anti-machine, a sentiment the Greenes' high-school training had opposed. At the Manual Training School, Calvin Woodward's academic approach was machine-based. His curriculum was specifically designed to prepare students to exploit the opportunities of the industrial age, not to shrink from them. Indeed, Woodward's personal background, including his

28 **Charles W. Hollister house, Pasadena, 1898** (altered).
Front elevation. Ink-on-linen presentation drawing.

29 **Charles W. Hollister house.**
Sections and details of interior finishes. Ink-on-linen
presentation drawing.

28

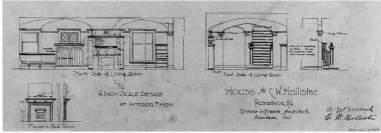

29

youth in the heavily industrial city of Fitchburg, Massachusetts, had prepared him to teach the benefits of machine-age technology to young people. He taught as he had learned. By contrast, the English Art and Crafts movement generally lamented the loss of handcraft caused by the rising influence of the machine as a design and manufacturing expedient. Late-nineteenth-century visionaries, including John Ruskin, William Morris, Charles Robert Ashbee, Ernest Gimson, and Ernest and Sidney Barnsley, battled the negative effects of the Industrial Revolution by promoting the reinstatement of medieval traditions of handcraft in the production of artistic objects of usefulness and beauty. Having benefited significantly from the positive aspects of the Industrial Revolution, America was understandably slower to accept that there was a darker side to the machine age. In 1898, Charles Greene took the first step toward adopting an Arts and Crafts consciousness that was sympathetic with William Morris, expressing the need to combine the "greatest possible amount of Truth with the greatest amount of Pleasure." Architecturally, Charles Greene's "Truth" can be equated with honesty in the expression of natural materials—using materials in a manner sympathetic to their natural state. "Pleasure," to Charles, would have meant beauty, as well as the implied pleasure of the designer in creating that beauty for his client. Charles's designs of the late 1890s reflect this thinking.

While "Job No. 11" was an initial step toward an Arts and Crafts aesthetic, the William B. Tomkins house of 1898 was the Greenes' first executed building to manifest their budding interest in the Arts and Crafts movement. The Tomkins house had a horizontal, site-hugging aspect unlike any of the brothers' earlier work. This was emphasized at each end of a long, open piazza by robust load-bearing pillars edged with stone quoins and filled in with a coat of pebble-dash. A naturalistic treatment of materials distinguished the house, in contrast to the painted surfaces of the Greenes' earlier, more traditionally detailed houses. The house was neither without ornamental flourishes, nor did its design discard the firm's previous vocabulary of architectural elements. The familiar octagonal tower and roof was used again, though more subtly employed to relieve the mass of the long, hipped roof of the central block. The interior was a Moorish fantasy of

pointed arches and interior columns with broad, shallow capitals reminiscent of some of the Greenes' academic sketches of exotic architectural orders. The eaves were deeper than any of those previously designed by the Greenes, and the rafters protruded slightly beyond the eaves, prefiguring a highly recognizable design feature of their later work. Consciously or not, a shift toward Craftsman design ideals began to emerge, too, in the horizontal nature of the piazza, the expressed structure of the posts and brackets supporting the shingled upper level, and the decision to leave the materials unpainted.

The contrast between the progressive Tomkins house design and the more derivative Fay house design is striking, especially since they were executed within just five months of each other. By 1903, Charles emerged as the firm's primary designer. No evidence suggests that in the earlier years Henry did not design equally (and even separately) alongside his brother, and there is some to suggest that he did. While it would be difficult to determine which houses, or which parts of houses, were designed by one brother or the other, it is interesting to reflect on which brother brought which design skills to the firm.

Professionally, Charles had been more exposed to Shingle Style work than had his brother, and he had also had more contact with the future founders of the Boston Arts and Crafts movement. Henry's experience as a draftsman for Chamberlin and Austin, Stickney and Austin, and Edward R. Benton would have led more naturally to traditional Classical and colonial design fluency. His tenure with Shepley, Rutan and Coolidge was brief, but the projects he was assigned to involved designs fully within the range of his education at MIT. Henry's less critical, more deferential personality also may have made it easier for him to observe and adopt ideas from the designs of successful competitors (such as Roehrig). Charles's more opinionated and experimental outlook on work and life made for more idiosyncratic, less traditional ways of working, including the capacity to design fantasy houses for nonexistent clients ("Job No. 11"). Given his experimental streak Charles was also more likely to have produced drawings for the progressive Tomkins house, especially since it followed so closely the more traditional Fay house.

30

30 **James Swan house, "Torrington Place," Pasadena, 1898–99** (altered).
South (front) facade.

31 **James Swan house, "Torrington Place."**
Living room.

32 **James Swan house, "Torrington Place."**
South piazza.

GREENE & GREENE

Not all of the firm's work of this period held as many clues to the future direction of their architecture. The house designed in the fall of 1898 for Charles W. Hollister (the first of two for this client) was not progressive, however notable it was for its generous front porch, which wrapped around to give access to a side door. A rustic stone chimney was discarded early in the design process, the client opting instead for simple brick clad in cement. The pointed-arch doorways, gentle arc of the ceiling in the living room, and twisted-bell-shaped newel posts recall the Moorish decorative touches of the Tomkins interiors. At the far end of the living room, the angled bay was fitted with a semicircular window seat supported by four elaborately turned legs. Two of the second-level bedrooms let onto a balcony above the front porch. This was a refinement of an idea used by the Greenes since their earliest houses: the creation of outdoor living opportunities on both levels by way of an appendage structure serving simultaneously as shelter below and balcony above.

Some commissions were simply too large and demanding for either of the brothers to handle alone. One such was the commission came in May 1899 to design a large residence for the socially prominent James Swan and his wife, who likely kept both brothers busy through the design and construction phases. An earlier design, presented to the clients in December 1898, had been rejected. The final, approved state seems to suggest the brothers' earnest efforts to work out their personal design proclivities in a single structure. Called "Torrington Place," the Swan house, like the Fay and Gordon houses, combined colonial, Georgian, and Classical design elements, albeit in shingle sheathing. The result was a composition compromised by conflicting and unbalanced elements. The budget of $18,500, a considerable sum for the era, allowed for a generous plan of elaborate built-in features and a rich decorative scheme. And, like the Fay house, local precedent may have inspired parts of the Swan design. The Pasadena residence designed by Frederick L. Roehrig in 1897 for Tom S. Wotkyns at 1071 South Orange Grove Avenue (later known as the A. Kingsley Macomber house) shows similarities to the Swan design, especially in the shingle cladding of a two-story gable that sheltered a significant proportion of the house.[24] McKim, Mead and White had used a monumental gable to striking effect in the

31

32

33 Frederick L. Roehrig, Tom S. Wotkyns house,
Pasadena, 1897 (demolished).
View from Orange Grove Avenue, c. 1905.

34 Dinner celebrating the marriage of Henry Mather
Greene to Emeline Augusta Dart in Rock Island,
Illinois, August 22, 1899. Left to right on far side of
table: Louise Dart, Henry Mather Greene, Emeline
Dart Greene, Sidney Mather, and Bess Hulbert.

33

34

design of the W. G. Low house, the Shingle Style icon in Bristol, Rhode Island, built in 1887 (now demolished), but it is unlikely that the Greenes or any other Southern California architects were aware of the Low house, which was not published until 1939.[25] The Greenes may have been introduced to the concept of a large gable, however, by the Mills house (Peabody and Stearns, 1882) in Brookline, Massachusetts.[26] As used by McKim, Mead and White, or Peabody and Stearns, the large gable generally consolidated and unified subordinate details: a shape under which architectural features could be gathered into a coherent composition.[27]

In their design for the Swan house, the Greenes seem to mimic Frederick Roehrig's use of the large gable in the Wotkyns house, though Roehrig is more successful at unification. Unlike the relatively serene and balanced design of the Wotkyns house, the Swan design was weighted with conflicting elements: a bulky portico, a disproportionately large second-level Georgian window molding, and a lone, centrally positioned, hipped dormer with a gabled peak. These combined to draw attention away from the sheltering form of the east gable, effectively fighting any balance and unity it might have provided. On the interior, the profusion of decorative detailing better resembled traditional, high-Victorian fussiness than the restrained richness of the Shingle Style, or even the eclectic elegance of the Aesthetic movement. In short, the Greenes had yet to realize in their work what was later to become one of the firm's greatest strengths: the ability to synthesize, from the best of contemporary design movements and their own natural abilities, schemes that were notable for pleasing proportions and restrained decorative beauty. For its shortcomings, however, the Swan house still allowed the Greenes a chance to further explore accommodations for outdoor living. Its deep piazzas, for example, provide abundant opportunity for enjoying the salubrious Southern California climate.

In June 1899, Leon C. Brockway, a draftsman in the Greenes' office, designed a house for a relative of his with the Greenes acting as consulting architects. The details emanated from the firm's established vocabulary of the period; its spare and subtly asymmetrical elevations gave the house dignity and interest.[28] Following this commission, no new work got under way in the office for several months, in part because Henry Greene had

fallen ill in April with "inflammatory rheumatism" that would keep him in bed for three months. He was still feeling listless when he left in July for Rock Island, Illinois, where he was to be married.

Henry's bride-to-be was Emeline Augusta Dart, one of two children born to William Henry Dart and Charlotte Augusta Sammis Dart in Rock Island. Emeline was six years younger than Henry, but had suffered hardships that had psychologically matured her beyond her age. Her father had died of tuberculosis when she was a child, and it later became apparent that her own health was fragile, too, tending toward respiratory ailments. Emeline was also nearly deaf. In the face of these difficulties, and her strong-willed mother, Emeline took life as it came and allowed herself no time for self-pity. Her mother married a second time, to railroad employee Henry Whitridge, but was soon widowed again. After several visits to California in the early 1890s—during which Emeline's health always improved—the family elected to move to Pasadena permanently. Henry met Emeline at the home of Alice Longley, probably in the summer of 1897. Her sweet personality and determination attracted the sensitive and practical young architect. At about the same time, Henry's brother became friendly with the beautiful and quick-witted young friend of Emeline from St. Louis named Bess Hulbert, and the four shared happy days bicycling and picnicking in the Arroyo Seco. After Henry's illness during the spring of 1899 had finally lifted, he traveled to Rock Island and married Emeline on August 22. Neither Charles nor any of the other Greene family members attended the wedding, but the guests who did included Hal's uncle, Sidney Mather, and Emeline's best friend, Bess Hulbert. The couple honeymooned in Kansas City and soon settled in a rented cottage adjacent to Dr. and Mrs. Greene in Pasadena.[29]

The plans that were prepared in the office that fall led to no new commissions. Drawings for George H. Coffin, for a house to be built across the street from Charles Hollister on Bellefontaine, did not proceed to construction. Similarly, the firm's design submission for an addition to the Pasadena Public Library was unsuccessful. This dry spell—only one built commission in nearly a year—ended in March 1900 when the firm won a contract to design a house for Mr. and Mrs. John M. Smith at the corner of West Colorado Street and Terrace Drive. The Smith house (now demolished)

35 **Mary M. Smith house, Pasadena, 1900**
(demolished).
Living room.

36 **Mary M. Smith house.**
View from the northeast.

35

36

was a straightforward two-story block, but the Greenes' increasingly refined sense of proportion resulted in a design that was significantly more balanced and complementary than that of the Swan house. A stone terrace and second-level balcony dominated the east end of the house, providing outdoor living spaces and views of the town's increasingly busy crossroads at Fair Oaks and Colorado Streets. While the Greenes had designed piazzas for other clients, these had usually been spaces sheltered by porticos, upper levels, or overhangs, such as in the Swan and Tomkins designs. The Smith's terrace projected well beyond the house and its eaves, indicating not only a new interest in the potential of outdoor living, but in integrating the house with its surrounding landscape. The rough stone blocks of the terrace wall also expressly connect to the stone edging of the arches on the east and north elevations of the house.

Within a month following the Smith house contract, in April 1900, the Greenes commenced work on a residence for the physician William T. Bolton, on the east side of North Los Robles Avenue. The design included a barn-like gambrel roof over both major and minor axes of the house, and rustic features including sawed brackets to support the porch posts, saw-tooth edged shingles on the bottom course of the second level, and a cobblestone chimney and foundation. The front porch and second-level balcony faced north, giving a view of the mountains, while living room and dining room faced the street. A seven-foot-long porch bench, like those designed for the Longley house, was conceived to fit adjacent to the entry to take advantage of the view. Overall, the house is notable for its lack of ornament. With the nearly concurrent Smith house, it created an effect far simpler than the Greenes' work of the late 1890s. These two residences signaled another shift in the firm toward Arts and Crafts tendencies, a shift that more fully related decorative detail to underlying structural imperatives. The firm designed two simple houses during the balance of 1900—for Mary R. Milnor and Mrs. Carrie C. Sickler. Other potential projects in late 1900 and early 1901 for which the Greenes had prepared plans—a brick warehouse, an addition to a concrete house, and two beach bungalows—did not proceed to construction. This time it was Charles who had been distracted from his work by a serious romance.

Late in 1899, with Bess Hulbert having returned to St. Louis, Charles became engaged to Alice Gordon White, the daughter of a wealthy English engineer and industrialist who had had business interests in Lancaster, England, and land holdings in Fairfax and Albemarle Counties in the state of Virginia. The White family had come to Pasadena about a year before Dr. and Mrs. Greene; a listing in the 1894 Pasadena directory stated simply: "George S. White, Capitalist." Alice, with her three sisters, Martha, Violet, and Jane, lived with their father and grandmother a few houses east of where Dr. and Mrs. Greene settled.[30] George White suffered from rheumatism and spells of "euremic poisoning," and sometimes called upon Dr. Greene to treat him. The two families became acquainted and the Greenes began to visit the Whites for occasional musical sessions with the charming and worldly White sisters.[31] Charles and Henry were popular at musical evenings since Charles was a good violinist and Henry played the flute and sang well. Alice White eventually became attracted to the quiet and handsome Charles. He no doubt appreciated her gentle demeanor, beauty, and probably her exotic pedigree. Alice had been born in England in 1870, the second daughter of Jane Storey White of Ulverston and George Storey White of Newby Bridge—distant cousins who lived a few miles from each other in what was then the northwest corner of Lancashire (now Cumbria) in the southern Lake District. Five daughters and a son were born to them, though only four girls survived childhood.[32] The children's mother did not live past Alice's fifth birthday, leaving their father and his mother to raise them. By Alice's fifteenth birthday, in August 1885, her father had arranged for the remaining family to sail to America on the *S. S. Celtic* to take up residence at Aspden Grove, a farm west of Charlottesville in the parish of Greenwood, Virginia.[33] Alice had lived in England long enough to become irrevocably English, however, and throughout her life maintained ties to her homeland. She made a total of eleven crossings of the Atlantic.[34]

George White died in 1896, at the age of fifty-two, and in his will named Alice and her older sister, Martha, executrixes of his estate. The four sisters each stood to inherit a comfortable sum from their father, a detail that was probably of less interest to Charles—notorious for his casual attitude toward money—than his father, Dr. Greene, for whom it was a consuming interest.[35]

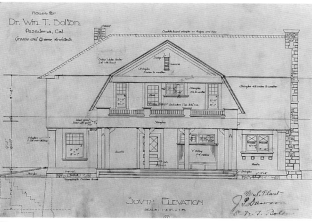

37

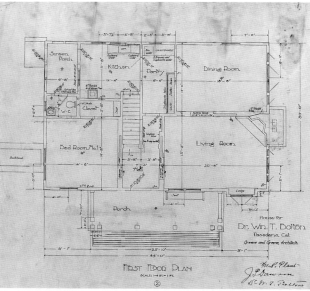

38

39

37 **Dr. William T. Bolton house #1, Pasadena, 1900**
(demolished).
South elevation. Ink-on-linen presentation drawing.

38 **Dr. William T. Bolton house #1.**
First floor plan. Ink-on-linen presentation drawing.

39 Left to right: Jane, Alice, and Violet White, c. 1898.

Charles and Alice had a happy, if protracted, courtship that included picnics and family outings in the natural setting of the nearby Arroyo Seco. During their engagement, Charles designed and constructed his first piece of household furniture: a simple, square-topped pedestal table made from scraps of wood. The piece served as the couple's dining table for some time, at least until a growing family required a larger one.[36] Charles and Alice were wed on February 11, 1901. The printed announcement showed a date two weeks later, but Charles had suddenly fallen ill, and it was felt that Alice should care for him in his apartment, and this could happen with propriety only if they were married.

Thanks to Alice's inheritance the newlyweds were able to enjoy a comfortable four-month honeymoon in Britain and on the Continent.[37] Queen Victoria had just died, signaling a new era for the world, but it was no less so for Charles, whose alliance with Alice would suddenly open to him a vast range of new experiences that would have a profound and lasting impact on his life and work. In particular, the couple came into contact with significant examples of the architecture and decorative arts of the English Arts and Crafts movement, an exposure that would have an immediate effect on his work back home. Charles and Alice began their honeymoon voyage in late March 1901. They traveled by train from Pasadena to New York, by steamship to Southampton, and on to Rome, where sightseeing began in earnest.[38] They visited the Catacombs, the Pantheon, and the Sistine Chapel, and a trip to the coastal city of Naples was followed by a visit to Pompeii. They returned north to Florence, where they saw the Uffizi galleries, Pitti Palace, and the Duomo, and bought postcards of the baptistery doors and the Giotto tower. In Venice, they toured the Doge's Palace, and in Milan they visited the cathedral and art gallery. In Paris, using the Hotel de l'Arcade as their base, they visited the Louvre, the Eglise de la Madeleine, and Père Lachaise cemetery. In short, they were typical tourists. They returned to the Louvre the next day, then visited Notre Dame and Cluny. The indefatigable couple also visited the churches of St. Germain des Près and St. Sulpice. Then, on May 15, they visited the Ecole des Beaux-Arts, where several of Greene's colleagues and instructors had studied under the atelier system. Julia Morgan, then a young protégée of Bernard Maybeck, was studying at

40

the Ecole when the Greenes visited. She had been the first female student
ever to be admitted, and because of this had caused a stir in architectural
circles in Europe and in America, something of which the Greenes would
certainly have been aware.[39]

Traveling to London, the Greenes took rooms in Pembroke Square near
Earl's Court Road. Situated in a reasonably fashionable part of West
Kensington, they were within easy reach of shops and museums. Charles's
travel diary entry for May 28 reads simply: "shopped." On May 30, the entry
"So. Kensington" referred to the South Kensington Museum, whose name
had in fact been changed in 1899 to the Victoria and Albert Museum.
Alice had last visited London in 1898, and she presumably had not broken
the habit of calling it simply "the South Kensington" as many others still
did. The Greenes may well have taken tea in the museum's Green Dining
Room. Designed in 1866 by William Morris's firm, it featured architectural
fittings by Philip Webb and paintings by Edward Burne-Jones and others in
an early collaboration of some of the English Arts and Crafts movement's
greatest visionaries and practitioners.[40] Throughout their travels, the
Greenes purchased postcards in abundance, which today give us an idea of
what interested them. In London, they bought a view of the Law Courts
designed in 1866 by George Edmund Street in the Victorian Gothic style
that had been popularized by A. W. N. Pugin. Street had followed Pugin in
the revived appreciation for Gothic architecture, a style and philosophy that
appealed especially to next-generation figures of the English Arts and Crafts
movement. Indeed, Street's office had been a training ground for Arts and
Crafts figures Philip Webb, John Dando Sedding, Richard Norman Shaw,
and, briefly, William Morris.

Leaving London, the Greenes headed west to Wiltshire, Somerset, and
Devon. They visited Stourhead, the estate of banker Henry Hoare, popular
for its magnificent gardens enhanced by classical pavilions, bridges, and
grottoes. They traveled by rail to Barnstaple, famous for the pottery that
produced Barum ware, and by coach to the North Devon coastal towns of
Lynton and Lynmouth (which Baedeker called "one of the loveliest villages
in England"). Charles and Alice stayed two nights at the venerable Ship Inn
in nearby Porlock, another irresistibly charming seaside town. Near here,

Charles was inspired to paint a small watercolor of the coastline, just as the
Scottish architect Charles Rennie Mackintosh had painted a watercolor at
Porlock Weir three years earlier. Moving north through Manchester, then
northwest to Chester, the couple approached Alice's childhood home.
They stopped in Lancaster, where her family had lived before coming to
America, then in Carnforth, and spent two nights in her father's hometown of
Newby Bridge. They enjoyed vistas of Windermere and the surrounding fells,
and no doubt experienced some of the region's notoriously wet weather.

Nearby, the gifted Arts and Crafts architect and designer Charles Francis
Annesely Voysey had recently completed two important country-house
commissions overlooking the banks of Lake Windermere: Broadleys (1898),
and Moorcrag (1898–99). Both were holiday "cottages" for wealthy
industrialists, the sort of clients the Greenes were beginning to attract in
Pasadena. Voysey's houses, and these in particular, were notable for their
sober, reductive forms and straightforward expression of materials.
At Broadleys and Moorcrag, the soft grayish-green of the local Westmoreland
slate was used for roofs and windows to firmly anchor the houses to their
surrounding terrain, while the stark and uncompromising whiteness of their
roughcast wall surfaces highlighted the progressive and deliberately
unsentimental forms. Voysey's willingness to work with boldly modern forms,
while perpetuating traditional materials and color palettes, probably would
have appealed to the seeker of "truth and pleasure" in Charles Greene,
though it is not documented that he actually saw Voysey's work.[41] Less than
a mile from Voysey's recent constructions was M. H. Baillie-Scott's then-
largest commission, Blackwell, also completed in 1899. Blackwell was a fine
example of a contemporary interpretation of English design, making liberal
use of modern decorative forms within a recognizable and traditional
framework. It was also a house that the Greenes could have seen from the
road or from a boat on Lake Windermere. While it is a matter of speculation
whether Charles Greene noticed these buildings, he and Alice would have
had to pass directly by, either by road or boat, while traveling from Newby
Bridge to Windermere.

They headed across the Scottish border to Edinburgh, where they
checked in for five nights at the Maitland Temperance Hotel near the west

41

end of Princes Street. On their first morning in Edinburgh, however, the Greenes boarded a train for the one-hour-and-five-minute journey west to visit the Glasgow International Exhibition, an event that had been extensively covered in all leading periodicals and art journals.[42] The exhibition was a spectacular public display. Officially billed as a celebration to inaugurate Glasgow's Art Gallery and Museum (today's Kelvingrove Gallery), it was unofficially calculated to put the British Empire's second city on the world stage as a major center in which to celebrate achievements in industry, science, and art. Crowds came from all over Europe and beyond. The temporary Industrial Hall, Machine Hall, and Concert Hall, along with the permanent Art Gallery, were the principle buildings to visit. Smaller outbuildings included pavilions dedicated to foreign countries and commercial enterprises such as photographers T. & R. Annan and Sons, and Miss Cranston's Tea Room, which burned just five days after the Greenes' visit.

Charles Rennie Mackintosh had a modest presence at the exhibition, having been denied the honor of designing the exhibition's principle buildings. In the end, he designed only four display booths, but these provided sufficient opportunity for Charles Greene to witness the influential Scottish designer's work. Mackintosh's effort for the 1901 exhibition, scant as it was, nonetheless convincingly represented a good range of his architectural expression. In the exhibition's Fine Arts building, the Glasgow School of Art booth was a severely geometrical, latticed stall that reflected some of the austerity within the school itself and even presaged the cubist treatment of Mackintosh's Chinese Room for Miss Cranston's Ingram Street Tea Rooms of a decade later. The booth was dedicated to bookbinding displays but appeared more like an exotic animal's cage, with strict quadrants of closed and open panels. In contrast was the voluptuous and curvilinear stall for Pettigrew and Stephens, which catered to middle-class ladies with its displays of Belgian lace. The most refined and characteristic of the Mackintosh designs at the exhibition, however, was his booth for the Rae Brothers Company. Fittings for the stall hint of Mackintosh's own Glasgow flat at 120 Mains Street, especially its cabinetwork, which relates to case pieces Mackintosh had designed for himself and other Glasgow clients, as

well as pieces he designed for the Turin exhibition the following year.[43] Owing to his interest and training in wood and carving, Charles Greene would likely have been enamored of the Russian Village erected under the direction of Russian Arts and Crafts architect Fyodor Osipovich Shekhtel. Native craftsmen painstakingly created a series of fantastic folk-art structures, dense with carved wood, polychrome appliqués, and stenciling, a display that observers called "bizarre."[44]

Soon after visiting Scotland, the Greenes embarked at Liverpool for their return trip to America after nearly four months abroad. On their train trip home from Philadelphia, they also stopped in Buffalo to visit the Pan-American International Exposition. The Buffalo fair was meant to celebrate the progress of the century just concluded, and hoped to inspire international cooperation and peace in the next.[45] Among the commercial exhibits was a display of Joseph P. McHugh & Company's "mission" oak furniture, inspired by a single chair made by Alexander Forbes (designer unknown) sent to McHugh from the San Francisco Swedenborgian Church in 1895. Close to the McHugh exhibit was a four-room display of furniture produced by the little-known Gustav Stickley, whose first issue of *The Craftsman* magazine appeared within three months. Stickley's United Crafts pieces had initially been rebuffed within American furniture-making circles, so the Buffalo exhibition offered him an alternate way to introduce his goods to the public. In a bold and ingenious move, Stickley proposed to bypass the trade and exhibit his products directly to the consumer. He did so in cooperation with one of America's most successful art potteries, the Grueby Faience Company of Boston. Furniture and pottery showed well together, and Stickley's products were soon carried in forty-one cities across the country, including Los Angeles.[46] In October 1901, shortly following the Greenes' return to California, the first issue of *The Craftsman* magazine appeared, dedicated to William Morris. The second issue offered an homage to John Ruskin, and the third gave an account of the guilds of the Middle Ages. In January 1902, an article appeared entitled "A Revival of English Handicrafts." At what point Charles Greene began to clip illustrations from *The Craftsman* is unknown, but his work soon began to reflect an intimate awareness of its aesthetic message, as well as the cumulative influence of his honeymoon travels.

3

A California House

2

While Charles and Alice Greene enjoyed their honeymoon, Henry Greene set about establishing a stronger base of clients for the Greene and Greene firm. The summer of 1901 was especially fruitful in this regard, and several new building projects were under way by the time Charles reappeared in late August. In particular, Henry had concluded an agreement with the Pasadena Ice Company to design an office, ice house, and stable on the west side of Broadway (now Arroyo Parkway) along the Santa Fe railroad tracks on the south end of town. It was not glamorous work, and required more engineering skill than artistic ability, but it helped to pay the bills at a time when expenses were rising, especially for Henry at home. Henry and Emeline's first child, Henry Dart Greene, had been born the previous fall, and the family was preparing to relocate from Pasadena to a larger house on West 24th Street in Los Angeles. Emeline's mother, Charlotte Whitridge, planned to rent the house next door to theirs.[1] The work for the Pasadena Ice Company helped to make this financially possible. Indeed, the company remained a loyal bread-and-butter client to Greene and Greene over the next fourteen years, and significantly more artistic work came about later as a result of the mundane, including residences for the company's president, S. Hazard Halsted, and vice-president, Freeman Ford.

Also in the summer of 1901, Henry designed a retail business block for John Bentz, a local dealer in fine Japanese and Chinese art goods. The Bentz building was to be a two-story brick structure on South Raymond Avenue, near the Greenes' office. The design gave no particular clue as to the nature of the goods to be sold inside, except that the facade was nearly devoid of ornament, which was compatible with the traditional simplicity of Japanese objets d'art. This was in marked contrast to the more ornate Kinney-Kendall business block that the firm had designed five years earlier, but like the Kinney-Kendall, the Bentz building was constructed of brick sheathed in cement, with iron columns for interior structural support. Like the work for the Pasadena Ice Company, the Bentz block itself turned out to be less important than the relationships that would develop between the Bentz family and Charles and Henry Greene. Over the years the Greenes would be frequent visitors to the Bentz shop and another nearby importer, the F. Suie

One Company, which bought its goods exclusively from China.[2] Merchants of exotica such as these not only provided the Greenes with access to design ideas through direct observation of the objects themselves but gave them the opportunity to discuss the goods with the proprietors, who appreciated their sophistication of knowledge. In a few years John Bentz, and later his brother, Nathan, would become residential clients of the Greenes. That same summer, though he shouldered the workload alone until his brother's return from Britain, Henry found time to donate his services for the relocation of a large memorial window for Pasadena's All Saints Episcopal Church.[3]

Returning from Britain in August, Charles and Alice (who was pregnant with their first child) began searching for land on which to build a home of their own. The site chosen was in the sparsely developed Park Place neighborhood, on a sweeping curve of unpaved road at the edge of the Arroyo Seco. The topography was utterly different from any of the flatland, gridiron street sites that the Greenes had designed houses for up to that time. They were on the threshold of wilderness, where views of the mountains above and the rugged flood plain below defined the neighborhood. It was as close as Charles could come—for the time being—to the charming hillside towns he had enjoyed visiting and painting in England. New possibilities to design for the semi-wild California landscape suddenly loomed larger.

Charles and Alice, with the help of Alice's three sisters (and their inheritances), purchased a lot on the uphill side of Arroyo View Drive in the fall of 1901. A few small farms and orchards occupied the picturesque wash of the Arroyo Seco, though much of it was undeveloped. Sycamores and oaks dotted the floodplain, and wild animals descended from the San Gabriel Mountains to forage for food. For the Greenes and the Whites, the Arroyo Seco had been the scene of happy family outings for several years. In a place such as this, they could allow themselves to imagine Alice raising a family in harmony with the natural surroundings while Charles absorbed artistic inspiration. Since early 1900, the Greenes had been searching for a more reductive mode of architectural expression based on the relationship that houses have with their sites, the climate, and their clients. For Charles Greene, the bluffs overlooking the Arroyo Seco promised fertile ground to further explore this relationship.

3 **Pasadena Ice Company.**
Workers in the freezer room.

4 **Anna J. Hansen house, Pasadena, 1901** (demolished).

5 **Metilde Phillips house, Pasadena, 1902** (demolished).
South elevation. Ink-on-linen presentation drawing.

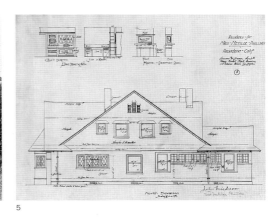

3   4   5

Before Charles's own house would be built, however, more new work came into the office in the fall of 1901 and spring of 1902. Residences for Lorenz P. Hansen and Frank Dowling, and a combined house and dressmaking shop for Mrs. Metilde Phillips, would provide the Greenes with further opportunities to test their simplified aesthetic. The Hansen design was a two-story, shingled house that used an extended and heightened octagonal bay to define one end of the plan. The faceted shape gave intimacy to the interior spaces and enlivened what could have been an otherwise uninspiring rectangular exterior. Similarly, the shingled, two-story design of the Metilde Phillips house included an octagonal, one-story pavilion that extended toward the street on the front elevation. Identified as a "den" on the plans, the room was immediately adjacent to the reception area on the dressmaking side of the structure. From it, through diamond-pane casement windows, Mrs. Phillips could discreetly observe the arrival of her customers. Behind the reception area lay the fitting and work rooms. The family's living room, dining room, and kitchen were aligned on the opposite side of a bisecting hallway, and four bedrooms were arranged around a central upstairs hall. While the plan is hardly adventurous, the simplicity of the surface materials and massing of forms, both of the Phillips house and the Hansen house, is striking when compared with the firm's earlier work. Utterly gone are the decorative flourishes that were still evident even in the relatively clean lines of the Smith and Bolton houses of just two years prior.

Since their return from England, Charles and Alice had been living in Charles's apartment on South Hudson Street, though they knew that they would soon outgrow it. The construction of their new home began none too soon. Their first son, Nathaniel Patrickson, was born in February 1902, one month before ground was broken for the new house on Arroyo View Drive. Construction began on the Phillips house on South Fair Oaks Avenue almost simultaneously, and Henry had gotten the firm additional work from the Pasadena Ice Company. Given Charles's personal supervision of the building of his Arroyo View Drive home (officially designed for Mrs. Charles S. Greene), the Ice Company projects and possibly the Phillips house as well fell to Henry.

Charles's family's house began as a one-story, two-bedroom structure set at an angle to the street and elevated on its wooded hillside behind a cobblestone retaining wall. The wall's top course was brick, with individual "clinkers" (bricks that had melted into irregular shapes from too-close exposure to the kiln's fire) interspersed among the boulders in the body of the wall. Though the stones would ultimately be selected from among the many to be delivered by mule cart from the adjacent arroyo, Charles had detailed the wall's elevation drawings in such a way that they showed that the sizes, shapes, and location of stones had been envisioned in advance. This kind of careful masonry planning would eventually define the entire streetscape: stones from the arroyo, leavened with clinker bricks, established a particular character for the neighborhood and visually connected each house to the next, and to the land on which it stood.

In the case of Charles and Alice's own house, its placement in the shade of a venerable oak tree magnified its connection to nature, and suggested the name "Oakholm." A hallway bisected the plan, with both bedrooms, a bathroom, and a living room placed on one side, and Charles's studio, a store room, the kitchen, and pantry on the other. The dining room was situated at the very back of the house at the end of the long hall, and projected into the garden with its own bay window. The massing of exterior elements showed Charles's continuing interest in octagonal, or partially octagonal, rooms. It is most noticeably expressed here in the projecting living-room pavilion, which is reminiscent of the Phillips den. The west-facing room was positioned to frame views of nature through windows in four facets of the partial octagon: the picturesque sights of the upper and lower arroyo, the then-undeveloped hills beyond the dry wash to the west, and the frequently spectacular sunsets. The initial phase of the house confined all rooms to one level, except for Charles's double-height studio. The compact studio tower consisted of a simple cube with an angled fireplace on the lower level and above it an octagonal space lined with bookcases that were accessible only by way of a steeply pitched ladder. Its design was ingenious—an intimately scaled, useful, and dramatic vertical extension of an essentially square room. An interesting effect was also created on the exterior skin of the studio tower. By alternating the placement of shingles according to their two different

6 **Charles S. Greene house, "Oakholm," Pasadena,**
   1902–15.
   View from the west, 1903.

7 **Charles S. Greene house.**
   Detail of stairway to third level.

8 **Charles S. Greene house.**
   Detail of east wall of living room, showing fireplace
   accented with Pewabic tiles left over from another
   commission.

9 **Charles S. Greene house.**
   Second-floor hallway detail showing pegged
   construction of staircase and railing.

6

7

surface finishes, a checkerboard pattern results, and is clearly visible in a
view of the earliest state of the house. Behind the house was a small, low
stone structure that Charles used as his workshop. Here he could construct
pieces of furniture or other objects and retreat from the bustle of the
household, something even his studio tower could not offer.

Over the years, the house grew as Charles and Alice increased their
family (and household staff). A major addition in 1906 was needed to better
accommodate arriving babies: Bettie Storey, who was born in the fall of
1903; Alice Sumner, born in March 1906; and Thomas Gordon, whose arrival
was anticipated in early 1907. A full upper level was added—two baths, two
bedrooms, and two porches—that subsumed the distinctive octagonal studio
tower into the new mass. A subsequent addition included two children's
bedrooms above the second level, both accessible by a steep and narrow
winding staircase. The new ceiling height of the downstairs bathroom was
the floor level of the first of these, and the height of the upper-story ceiling
became the floor level of the second added bedroom. A tiny bedroom on the
top of the house was a dramatic crow's-nest set among the spreading
branches of the old oak tree. These changes necessitated the removal of
Charles's workshop structure to accommodate the relocated kitchen, utility
room, storage, and servant's room. A brick garage was added in the summer
of 1914 to house the family's new Hudson automobile, and above its roof
Charles designed a pergola structure that would finally be built in 1998,
when recent owners resurrected the original scheme in the course of a
comprehensive restoration.

Ultimately, the Charles Greene house is more significant as an indicator
of what was important to Charles than as a bellwether of the firm's design
direction. Charles was undoubtedly attracted to the hillside site with its
stunning views of undeveloped parkland. There were also sympathetic
neighbors and perhaps even the promise of orchestrating a community
aesthetic as more homeowners arrived. The winding streetscape lent itself
to organic growth, similar to that which Charles's own architectural ideas
were undergoing. It is also possible that Greene's presence in the Park Place
neighborhood encouraged neighbors to consider more carefully the
aesthetically sensitive development of their immediate community.

8

9

A California House

10 **Charles S. Greene house, "Oakholm," Pasadena, 1902–15.**
Master-bedroom fireplace with raised hearth.
Door at left opens to a covered balcony with views of the Arroyo Seco.

11 **George H. Barker house, "Light Hall," Pasadena, 1902** (altered).
View from the southeast. The pergola was added in 1904.

12 **George H. Barker house, "Light Hall."**
View from the east.

13 **George H. Barker house, "Light Hall."**
Two-story entry hall.

11

12

13

Residents lobbied for brick sidewalks, and for culture they participated in the Ludovici family's artistic salon at the nearby Rose Tree Inn. Over a six-year period Greene and Greene designed ten Park Place houses that formed an aesthetic network while establishing a comparative village-like record of their work. The now-famous cluster of homes, still largely intact today, chronicles the phase of the Greenes' work from the period following Charles's exposure to the English Arts and Crafts movement to the establishment of the firm's distinctive architectural language. In time, it would also inspire the identity of the bungalow movement around the country and beyond. With the quiet but intense Charles Greene living and working in the midst of his neighbors, a microcosm of the Greene and Greene vision was created.

Shortly following the construction of Charles and Alice's house, two large and important commissions, and several minor projects, were to occupy the firm's design activities in 1902. In April, the Greenes secured a large commission from George H. Barker, owner of the West Side Light Co., for a mansion on South Grand Avenue in Pasadena. According to the newspapers, the Greenes had prepared plans for a twelve-room house for Barker in 1896 (this may have been the mysterious and unidentified Job. No. 11), but the earlier house was never built. The 1902 design clearly points to a Jeffersonian Colonial inspiration. Both of the Greenes had had practical training in the American Colonial idiom in Boston.[4] The large, symmetrical front elevation of the Barker house, with its two-level, pillared portico, was a preview of the conspicuously grand interior. Aptly named "Light Hall," the mansion's broad, double-storied stair-hall entry, painted white, gave the main public space a generous sense of illuminated openness, also appropriate to Barker's professional affiliation. Despite its undeniable strengths as architecture, the design would come to represent what the Greenes, and especially Charles, would later avoid: the literal translation of a historical style. Though beautifully executed and with strict attention to detail, it was mindless of its context or the environmental imperatives that might have suggested a different, more regionally appropriate design. It seemed to matter little, for example, that Pasadena architecture by 1902 tended toward picturesque wooden cottages, often unpainted; and it

mattered less that twentieth-century Southern California was not Colonial America. Nevertheless, the Arts and Crafts movement was in the rustic treatment of the breakfast room with its unpainted wainscoting, beamed ceiling, and medieval-inspired furniture. The den, too, is an anomaly in the house, showing picture-rail banding similar to the Greenes' Japanese-inspired work.

In July 1902, the Greene and Greene firm was occupied with designing a boarding house for Mrs. Rose J. Rasey and a new rectory for All Saints Episcopal Church. The Rasey building was a voluminous clapboard structure, which may have been partly inspired by boarding houses Charles and Henry had patronized a decade before on Nantucket. However, the Episcopal rectory is more clearly linked to the Greenes' budding idiom, including an overall simplicity of form, unpainted shingle sheathing, and artistic combinations of stone and brick. It is still a transitional design, if the relatively centralized floor plan and overall verticality (accentuated by a steep roof pitch) are contrasted with the rambling plan and lower profile of Charles's own house in its original state. The rectory's details nonetheless show the Greenes' new affinity for the Arts and Crafts aesthetic: a wooden terrace lantern with the house number leaded into an art-glass panel, a newel-post lantern in the entry hall, and the simple, robust gridiron pattern of the entry door. These elements represented close readings of Gustav Stickley's published thoughts on ways to achieve an American Arts and Crafts aesthetic. It is worth noting that Stickley's inspiration had similarly come from England during a visit he had made two years prior to Charles and Alice's honeymoon.

Soon after his return from England, Charles began keeping another scrapbook of design ideas. Among the first of his entries in the new volume was a pasted-in magazine article entitled "A Country House of Moderate Cost," written and illustrated by the Boston architect Ralph Adams Cram for the *Ladies Home Journal*.[5] Cram was aware of English Arts and Crafts design even before Charles and Henry were students at MIT. The article's accompanying illustration showed a house designed by Cram in his characteristically Anglophilic mode. It apparently struck a significant chord with Charles Greene. Prominent on the main elevation is a pair of front-

14 George H. Barker house, "Light Hall," Pasadena, 1902 (altered).
Breakfast room.

15 George H. Barker house, "Light Hall."
Den.

16 Rose J. Rasey boarding house, "Hotel El Morera," Pasadena, 1902 (demolished).

14

15

facing, half-timbered gables with shingled in-fill, Tudor arches over doorways, and diamond-pane casement windows. This published house design bears a striking, and certainly more than coincidental, resemblance to the Greenes' finest early career expression of English Arts and Crafts architecture adapted to Southern California.

While the Greens were still engaged with the Barker house project, lumberman James Alexander Culbertson (1854–1915) provided the opportunity, and probably the impetus, to design a California version of a nominally English house. A native of Girard, Pennsylvania, Culbertson was the eldest son of a wealthy and energetic lumberman, who chose James, age twenty-eight, to become secretary and treasurer of the Girard Lumber Company headquartered in Menominee, Michigan. The company's holdings included 62,000 acres of timberland, mostly white pine, as well as other large tracts.[6] To be closer to his company's operations, James Culbertson moved to Chicago in 1892. Culbertson had heard from a land developer that Joseph Sears's planned suburb of Kenilworth was to be an exclusive, artistically planned community—just what the sensitive and aesthetic-minded Culbertson was seeking. The lot that Culbertson purchased at 220 Melrose Avenue for himself, his wife, Nora, and their four-year-old son, Lloyd, was thick with trees and abutted the natural feature of the Skokie stream. Culbertson selected the architect Frederick Burnham to design his house, which included half-timbered construction, leaded diamond-pane windows, and other features of English country architecture. However, the spatial organization and numerous outdoor-living features, like other Kenilworth houses, were decidedly suburban and purely American. In 1896 the Culbertson's son, Lloyd, died tragically of spinal meningitis at the age of eight.[7] Nora remained in mourning within the confines of their home for years afterward. By the summer of 1902, however, following an extended trip through Europe, the Culbertsons were ready to build again, this time a winter residence. They chose Pasadena and the still relatively sparsely populated Park Place tract. Not surprisingly, Pasadena offered much of what Mr. Culbertson had appreciated about Kenilworth, including a naturalistic suburban setting with houses sensitively designed in concert with their environment.

HOTEL EL MORERA (C. O. RASEY, PROPRIETOR), NORTH EUCLID AVENUE.
16

17 James Alexander Culbertson, c. 1910.

18 **James Culbertson house, Pasadena, 1902–10.**
(altered).

19 **James Culbertson house.**
Detail sketch of leaded-glass lantern for stair-hall
newel-post. Slender stems designed for the end view
recall the work of Scottish designer Charles Rennie
Mackintosh.

17   18

The Greenes' original design for the James Culbertson house was a two-
story, four-bedroom residence with terraces front and rear, generous gardens
surrounding the house, and an abundance of steep gable ends on the four
elevations. The structure was sited near the northwest corner of the lot,
affording views of the Arroyo Seco below and the San Gabriel Mountains in
the distance to the north. The preliminary front elevation design was nearly
identical to Cram's illustration that ended up in Charles's scrapbook, with
two primary gables and a pair of subsidiary gabled dormers to illuminate
the second-level hallway. This plan was ultimately discarded, however, in
favor of a smaller design, which was accomplished by shrinking the
bedrooms and the upper hallway, and by deleting the library. The final plan
had one front-facing dormer instead of two, but the influence of Cram's
published design persisted. Amid the interiors, pithy aphorisms were carved
into wood paneling and mantels throughout the first level. "The Blessing of
the House is Contentment" stretched across the Tudor-arch doorway over
the heads of arriving visitors. Passing through the massive oak entry door,
brightened by a scenic design in leaded art glass, visitors were greeted with
"The Glory of the House is Hospitality," carved in flowing script into the
paneled back of a built-in bench adjacent to the foot of the hall stairs.
A wood-framed newel-post lantern was fitted with opalescent glass to a
design that resembled Charles Rennie Mackintosh's work, with slender,
stylized stemmed plants depicted in the leading.

The Culbertsons' interior would ultimately be appointed with Gustav
Stickley's Craftsman furniture, Tiffany lamps, Native American rugs and
baskets, and imported screens and decorative objects from Japan. Indeed,
the Culbertson's decorative arts blended with the Greenes' architectural
features to present an environment that captured the spirit of the American
Arts and Crafts movement as it began to emerge from behind the shadow of
its English counterpart. There is something peculiarly American about the
motto in the dining room, "The Beauty of the House is Order," which was
carved conspicuously and with particular whimsy across large sections of
the virgin redwood wainscoting to become a major design element in the
room. The stiff-sounding words themselves were embellished and softened
in their meaning by Charles Greene's charming depictions of homey

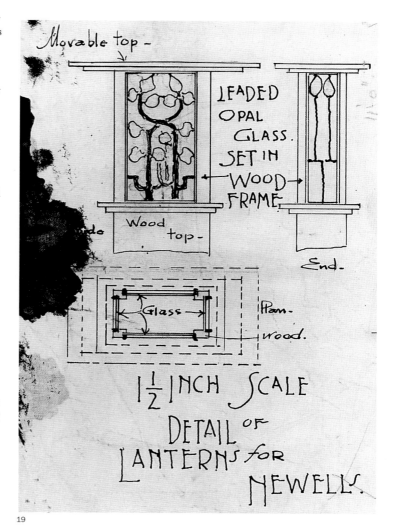

19

20 **James Culbertson garage, Pasadena, 1906.**

21 Charles S. Greene, rare pencil sketch of illustrated
   motto for James Culbertson dining room, 1902.

20

objects—a table, a water jug, a potted tree—fashioned into the letters of the alphabet that make up the words. "The Crown of the House is Godliness," carved into the living room's mantel, was uppermost in the hierarchy of pious sayings, and no doubt served to put visitors on notice about their conduct under the Culbertson roof. Such sayings were stock-in-trade for the other Arts and Crafts promoter in America, Stickley's rival, Elbert Hubbard, whose publication *The Philistine* made a point of nudging its readers frequently with such bits of text in the margins.

James Culbertson had become aware of the Arts and Crafts movement through his involvement with the Kenilworth community as well as through his own interest in art and design. He had found in Pasadena an aesthetic sensitivity among its citizens, not to mention a congenial community of Midwest families with money. He also saw the benefit of working with two young architects who shared his affinity for Arts and Crafts ideals. James Culbertson deserves significant credit for fostering a climate in which the Greenes could exercise new design ideas that they, and especially Charles, in this case, had been developing for his architecture. Culbertson probably encouraged the Greenes' budding interest in Asian design and decorative arts, too. The Greenes' design for the living room's dark-stained, cedar interior (in its original 1902 phase) shows their earliest use of an Asian-inspired bracket detail over the window seat. To be sure, this reflected Culbertson's own collecting tastes, which ran strongly to Asian decorative objects.[8]

With help from Culbertson, the Greenes' work had evolved within the space of only a few months. From designing a competent, though uninspired Colonial Revival house for George Barker they progressed to producing a regionally astute adaptation of English Arts and Crafts architecture for a client who instinctively appreciated the promise of its successful adaptation to America. One explanation for the seemingly aberrant design of the Barker house, and the Greenes' radical shift to the design of the Culbertson house, is that the clients insisted that it be so. But it is worth noting that the Greenes proudly submitted photographs of both houses to the Louisiana Purchase Exposition in St. Louis in 1904. They were the firm's only official design entries for the architectural competition.[9]

21

22 **James Culbertson house, Pasadena, 1902–10 (altered).** Dining-room addition, 1907. As part of a major expansion designed by the Greenes that year, the dining room occupied the space of the former kitchen.

22

Clearly, the Greenes were happy with their work on both projects. Together the designs demonstrated competence and adaptability: the Barker house through its traditional Classical proportions and historical detail, and the Culbertson house through its sensitivity toward a popular design movement of which Charles, at least, had first-hand knowledge from his travels. There may also have been a trace of politics involved in the submission of a colonial and an Americanized English Arts and Crafts design at St. Louis. Among the judges sitting on the Exposition's Advisory Committee on Architecture were two former employers of Charles Greene: Robert Day Andrews, who provided Charles his practical training in the Shingle Style, and his equally influential mentor in the colonial idiom, H. Langford Warren.[10]

After 1902, the Culbertson house took on an extended design life of its own, with James Culbertson acting as enlightened client and the Greenes as professional accomplices. The ultimate result was a different house from the relatively simple Cram-based design the Greenes had first created. In late 1903, the foundation and terrace wall were constructed using Simons blue brick, cobblestones, and clinkers, and in 1906 the Greenes were hired again to undertake minor alterations to the original interior design, and to design the first of Culbertson's two garages.[11] The siting of a utilitarian outbuilding in so conspicuous a place as the front garden was unusual, but then garages themselves were unusual, too. Less than one percent of Pasadena's new houses were built with garages in 1906.[12] The Greenes treated it as if it were a garden pavilion, however, appointing it with a bench, platforms for potted plants, and a sheathing of lattice over the dash-coat walls to encourage vines to climb on it. The structure was topped by a massive trellis made of three layers of wooden beams and rails, built up to provide shade and give the climbing vines additional room to roam. The position of the bench was adjusted to accommodate the siting of the garage next to three existing trees that were so close to the structure that the attached trellis was constructed around the trunks and branches of two of the trees.[13] In 1906, a *Good Housekeeping* article by Pasadena resident Una Nixson Hopkins praised the house as "radiating hospitality," and illustrated the house profusely. This generated for the Greenes a commission that same

year to design an identical house for banker Louis K. Hyde in Plainfield, New Jersey. The plans were drawn up, but the house was never constructed.[14]

In 1907, the year Arroyo View Drive—by then called Arroyo Terrace—was paved, Culbertson commissioned a major expansion of the house to the southwest to accommodate a larger kitchen and service area. A simultaneous reworking of the first level included re-appointing the former dining room as a den and creating a new dining room in the space formerly occupied by the kitchen. The interiors were richly appointed with brushed and carved redwood panels that were stained and gilded to bring added color and highlights to the interiors. The panels depicted scenes from nature, including cloud-topped mountains sitting majestically over the mantel in the new dining room. These reflected the Greenes' fascination with Japanese decorative arts, which had begun when this house was first constructed, but had developed more rapidly beginning in late 1903, at about the time Charles Greene purchased a copy of Edward S. Morse's influential book, *Japanese Homes and Their Surroundings*.

Indeed, the carved panels closely resemble a similar design illustrated in Morse's book.[15] Under these panels in the new dining room, a Japanese-inspired cloud motif, also the kind illustrated in Morse, was used again in the design of the hand-tooled, metal fireplace hood. In the new den, a lakeside mountain scene replaced the original mirror over the mantel, and at the frieze level yet another mountain range surrounded the room, edged by a continuous stand of conifers (celebrating the source of Culbertson's fortune) in low-relief, glazed gesso. The Greenes also designed three panels to be carved and set into the facing panels of the upright piano in the living room. Los Angeles–based architectural sculptor Ernest H. Grassby was contracted by Peter Hall to carve the panels.[16] The style of carving—from the depth of the relief to the sympathetic exploitation of the grain's natural pattern—closely resembles the character of the other Culbertson panels of 1907. It is also similar to panels carved for the Robert R. Blacker house (1907), and the David B. Gamble house (1908).

In 1910, the north end of the house was extended and a second garage added to the south end of the lot. These additions were, like the 1907

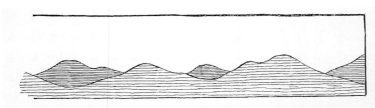

FIG. 150. — RAMMA, COMPOSED OF TWO THIN BOARDS, IN NAGOYA, OWARI.

23

24

23 Illustration from *Japanese Homes and Their Surroundings*, by Edward S. Morse (1895). Superimposed mountain ranges on a carved frieze panel, or *ramma*.

24 **James Culbertson house, Pasadena, 1902–10 (altered).**
Detail of panel over den fireplace, 1907. Formerly the dining room, the den was appointed with carved and stained redwood panels over the fireplace and at the frieze level.

alterations and additions, in the highly refined and articulated wooden style of the Greenes' most celebrated work, and show the skill of Peter Hall's craftsmen. In July 1910, Charles Greene also designed additional light fixtures for the house, including a hexagonal mahogany entry-hall lantern with hardware finished in "dark Florentine gold" and instructions to the craftsman that all wood joints be "housed, mortised and pinned as usual."[17] Charles Greene also designed leaded art-glass wall fixtures for the living room and den at this time.[18] The house was becoming a multifaceted hybrid of the Greenes' evolving language, from the early Arts and Crafts years to well beyond their classic period. In 1914, a pair of two-story window bays of leaded diamond-pane glass and Oregon pine frames was added to the front of the house. On the interior, the addition included a delicately carved flight of birds applied to the cedar ceiling panels of the new dining-room bay.[19] A pergola was erected that same year over the brick wall along the sidewalk, and the gardens were expanded. For the Culbertsons and the Greenes, the house was a constant work in progress that did not end until the death of James Culbertson in 1915.

Following the initial construction of the Culbertson house in October 1902, former client Dr. William T. Bolton awarded the Greenes a contract to design another house for him. The design that emerged was a sober and simple board-and-batten bungalow that further clarified the new direction the firm's designs were taking. It was a simple, linear plan, except for a wing at one end for the kitchen and service areas. At a contract price of $3,600, it was not inexpensive for a small structure. An average of only fifteen to twenty percent of houses built in Pasadena in the first decade of the century cost more than $3,000.[20] For Dr. Bolton, however, who appreciated the Greenes' work, therein lay the ironic attractiveness of their houses. It looked modest, but in reality it was a refined dwelling that appealed to sophisticated if rustic tastes, precisely because it was simultaneously so convincing and deceptive in its simplicity. High-quality materials and careful detailing have never been cheap, even in a cottage. In one sense, Dr. Bolton's plain but expensive bungalow was the logical extension of the simplification of form and careful supervision of work that had interested the Greenes since early 1900. Simply put, the stripping of ornament allowed for reinvestment in craftsmanship.

In February 1903, Greene and Greene announced the move of their Los Angeles office to the Grant Building at 355 South Main Street and the closing of their Pasadena office in the Kinney-Kendall building. It was further announced that Charles Greene would be at his studio on Arroyo View Drive three afternoons a week.[21] Charles no doubt sensed his own potential to make a greater contribution to the firm if he were able to more easily oversee the execution of their designs, and the details of construction had become increasingly important to them. It also may have been tacit recognition on the part of both brothers that Charles was less of an office worker than Henry. And finally, Charles may have realized that in working at home he could better monitor the aesthetic progress of the Park Place neighborhood. His drawings began to contain the admonition to seek the architects' approval on specific details, or that work was to be "supervised by architect," showing his concern about contractors translating his hard-won design solutions from paper to reality.

The exciting promise of the new working arrangement, in which Henry presided over the Los Angeles office and Charles often worked at home, would soon be put to a test in the design of a house for Charles's sisters-in-law, Martha, Violet, and Jane White. The White sisters' house, to be built next to his own family's house on Arroyo View Drive, would serve as a locus for attempting new ideas that the Greenes would refine and use in their highly sophisticated designs in later years. The situation was promising. Alice's sisters had contributed to the purchase of a double lot the previous year, and it had always been the plan that they would live next door to Alice and Charles as neighbors and family in happy proximity. The site, at a bend in the road, occupied one of the finest positions along the arroyo's edge, offering northerly views similar to those from Charles and Alice's house. The plan for the sisters' house reflected the topography of its site. Like the house he had designed for his own family, Charles sited this one on a rise slightly back from the street, allowing for a margin of terraced area between the house and street, and to the west, between the two families' houses. Like "Oakholm" next door, the White sisters' terrace was designed to surround an existing tree that would be retained for its beauty and shade, and to integrate the house with its natural environment.

25

26

27

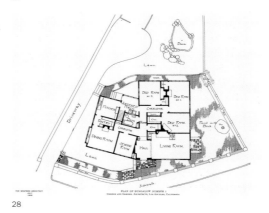

28

The house is distinguished by an extensive use of stone and brick, especially on the exterior—a spirited continuation of the hardscape Charles had designed for his own house. Each functional part of the White sisters' masonry design had a distinctive identity. In the exterior entry stairs, the seemingly random mingling of rocks and brick is deceptive. Boulders were placed among the bricks and smaller stones, looking as though the materials might have been placed as they had naturally been found at the time of construction. In the driveway piers and foundation buttresses, layers of stone alternate with courses of clinker brick in a more deliberate, stratified pattern. Handled differently still is the street-side retaining-wall masonry, which is mostly of smaller cobbles with a top course of brick, stepped to mimic the rise of the main walkway to the front terrace. The varied appearance of the masonry gives the charming (if deceptive) appearance of organic growth over time, rather than the conscious shifting of methods during a single phase of construction. This was part of the Greenes' wizardry, to make new buildings look worn and comfortable, like a favorite tweed jacket. In the rear of the house, to the delight of Charles and Alice's children next door, a boulder-lined basin in the garden held goldfish, lilies, and lotuses.

Above the foundation level, the White sisters' house was originally clad in split redwood shakes, a new addition to the Greenes' material vocabulary in 1903. Shakes, unlike the shingles they had used previously, are cleaved individually from the trunk of a tree. Less-expensive shingles are sawed in large batches from milled lumber. In making shakes, the forced splits occur along the path of least resistance, following the natural contours of the wood's grain. This results in a surface that catches light unevenly and imparts a subtle depth of texture when repeated across the exterior of a house. The front elevation of the White sisters' house, to the left of the entry, projects away from the foundation on cantilevered beams, creating a shadowed recess that increases the sense of detachment of the house from the street. The entry portico is supported by robust wooden brackets that echo the purlins and rafters projecting beyond the edges of the eaves. Inside (now altered), three bedrooms, a living room, and a hallway comprised the rectangular west side of the plan, with a dining room, kitchen, pantry,

A California House

53

29 **Martha, Violet, and Jane White house, Pasadena, 1903.**
Living-room detail with built-in inglenook. A simple
tea table, among the Greenes' earliest furniture
designs for paying clients, can be seen at the far left
of the photograph.

30 Martha White playing with Charles and Alice Greenes'
son, Nathaniel Patrickson Greene, by the fish pond
behind the White sisters' house.

29

30

bath, and porch on the east side. The two sides were angled slightly near the middle, reflecting the shape of the lot and the corresponding contour of the land and street. This was the Greenes' first use of the obliquely angled plan, a device they would later rely on many times to maximize the natural benefits of topography, climate, views, and angles of the sun. The entry hall was directly en suite with the living room, with an overhead beam marking the transition from one space to the other. A broad brick fireplace, with inglenook seats on both sides, dominated the space and faced the views of the arroyo through the large central window on the north. At the east end of the dining room, a bay with four casement windows projected from the main space, creating a window-seat niche for reading in the morning light.

In a 1908 article entitled "Bungalows," written for *The Western Architect,* Charles Greene reflected at length on his designs for the Park Place neighborhood and made a point of mentioning that for the White sisters, "the furniture was designed to fit the room."[22] Furniture design was new for Greene and Greene and seems logically linked to Charles's new home-based role as studio designer for the firm. Among Charles Greene's personal papers was a leaflet entitled "The Simple Structural Style of Household Furniture," authored by Gustav Stickley, "Director of the United Crafts." The single-fold leaflet, which dates from the spring of 1903, contained illustrations of plain oak furniture: dining-room pieces, a living-room library table with chairs, a drop-front desk, and an oak tea table.[23] The text was direct: "The productions of [the United Crafts] workshops embody the principles of the new art which is now developing among us and which promise a long and vigorous existence." Stickley went on to discuss the three principles of the new art as: "the prominence of the constructive idea, the absence of applied ornament, [and] the development of all possibilities of color, texture and substance; the choice being dependent on beauty without regard to the intrinsic value of the material employed." This important and prophetic pamphlet apparently struck a chord of truth with Charles Greene, as his work immediately reflected.

The tea-service table that survives from the White sisters' house shows that the Greenes' initial concepts for furniture designs were indeed aligned with Stickley's, though the table lacks the heaviness of Stickley's designs.

The White sisters' table is a simple design in oak and cedar without any of the sophistication of the Greenes' later work but more elegantly proportioned and executed than the "engagement table" Charles had built from scraps for Alice two years earlier. Pegs, proud of the surface, show where the stretchers are joined. The top surface is cedar, framed by broad oak boards, flush to the center panel, with simple notches along the outside edges as a modest decorative touch. A second cedar panel fills the area between the lower stretchers, serving as an additional surface to hold teacups. Charles also designed dining room furniture for the White sisters in birch, and from this commission forward he would actively seek to continue designing interior furnishings for his architectural clients. Clients who elected to have furniture designed for them would ever remain in the minority, but Charles had a solution to this as well: if he could not design furniture for his interiors, he would at least seek to select it. One such client was Mary Reeve Darling, who commissioned the Greenes to design a small house for her in the town of Claremont, about thirty miles east of Pasadena. It was the Greenes' first commission outside of Pasadena.

The design of the Mary Darling house employed a broad gable reminiscent of the Swan house, but this time with more satisfactory results. Three factors made the mass of the house under a big gable work successfully in concert with the plan. First, the roof ridge is oriented across the center of the narrow part of the plan. Second, the bedrooms on the upper level accommodate a smaller floor area than the lower level. Third, the deep eaves extend down to the top plate of the lower level. In this way the Greenes successfully achieved for Mrs. Darling the unifying effect of the big gable. The gambrel shape of the roof accentuated the effect, making the house seem to fit snugly to the ground. An open loggia on the upper level (now enclosed) acted as a counterpoint to two elevated bays of windows on the lower level. Each of the two bays is perched on a pair of boulders, one at each projecting corner, visually lightening the otherwise ponderous sense of the house being rooted to its site.

The design for the Darling house was published that winter in the British journal *Academy Architecture,* suggesting the firm's heightened confidence and ambition to get work beyond Pasadena. It was the first

31

32 **Mary Reeve Darling house, Claremont, 1903.**
Den fireplace.

33 Illustration from a rare 1903 pamphlet published
by Gustav Stickley's firm United Crafts.

32

33

publication of the firm's work outside of America.[24] Of four sketches that Charles Greene prepared of the house for publication, two of them depict sturdy, Stickley-like pieces of furniture for the living room and study. It is not known if he intended to design furniture for the house, but the illustrations nonetheless show fully furnished and appointed rooms. For the living room, he sketched a long, simple library table at a slight angle in the center of the room. A plain, paneled upright piano is shown on the north wall, with a long, horizontally framed picture or carving, equally plain, centered above it. Next to a built-in bookcase, a desk and chair are shown, drawn in the simple vein of Stickley's United Crafts pieces. Light fixtures in the drawings are sketchily indicated as hanging lanterns with broad brims, but despite the existence of detailed drawings for these fixtures they were never fabricated. In the sketch of the study a desk is set diagonally, and behind it a library table is on a raised dais at the far end of the room. Rugs, embroidered pillows, lamps, and even books are all shown to emphasize Charles's new *gesamptkunstwerk* approach to orchestrating a total living environment. The library table shown in the sketch of the study alcove is nearly identical to the table illustrated in Gustav Stickley's 1903 United Crafts pamphlet. The bookcase surrounds a window, giving it depth similar to the other window bays, and the expressed joinery of the bookcase corners, with tenons protruding slightly from the surface, relates directly to the expressed joinery of the piano stool and the alcove table.

Whereas movable and built-in furnishings were sketched by Charles, it seems that the plan of the house may have been conceived by Henry. The symmetrical organization of space is unlike Charles's plans, for example, either for his own house or for his sisters-in-law. The Darling house plan is linear, relying on subtle manipulation of space to give it character. To be sure, the walls are all at right angles, the staircase is in a predictable location opposite the front door in the middle of the house, and the bedrooms neatly surround a central hall on the upper level. A rich living experience is created through subtle compositional tension on the exterior and equally subtle compression and expansion of space on the interior. The projecting planes of the window bays are in contrast to the deep recesses of the loggia on the front elevation. On the side elevations, the

axially symmetrical recesses of the bedroom balconies similarly balance and contrast with the sunroom bay on one end and the service porch on the other. On the interior, the step up to the study alcove, for example, gives intimacy to its space, and the dark, screened stairway manipulates darkness to make the upstairs hall and bedrooms seem bigger and sunnier by contrast. Materials and surface texture are also subtle enrichments. The Greenes' drawings specify one-by-fourteen-inch redwood boards with battens at the joints on the lower level, with all the wood to be "smoothed by hand," though the marks of the circular saw blade were to be left visible. The modest dignity and genuine comfort of the house come from a combination of simple materials carefully chosen, thoughtful spatial planning, and artistic composition.

Concurrent with the Darling house, a large four-bedroom house was designed for P. L. Auten that was reminiscent of the Tomkins house of 1898: robust granite-block pillars supported a covered porch on the front elevation, and a side terrace with a delicate overhead trellis showed the firm's new design language. On the interior, the familiar octagon bay was used for the redwood-paneled dining room, and coved ceilings in the living room also refer to the earlier Tomkins and Hollister houses.

Josephine van Rossem was the next Park Place landowner to engage Greene and Greene. Recently widowed, and with two young sons, Mrs. van Rossem defied feminine convention by engaging in real estate speculation (her first house designed by the Greenes was a rental property) while keeping her job with a photography laboratory. She was also an artist. The first of three houses to be designed for her by the Greenes would be directly across the street from her family's residence on Arroyo View Drive. Many of her rental properties were nearby so she could keep a close eye on her tenants and investments. Greene and Greene designed for her a simple clapboard cottage with a balloon frame that sat unprepossessingly on the rise of the hill to the east of the White sisters' house. The cobblestone foundation was relatively plain compared with the neighboring work Charles had done for his sisters-in-law and himself, although the oversized boulders he had placed at each outside corner of the foundation created a comforting visual sense of permanence and stability. Two large bays with

34 Illustration from *Academy Architecture* (1903) showing Charles Greene's sketches of the proposed Mary Darling interiors.

35 Illustration from *Academy Architecture* (1903) showing floor plans for the Mary Darling house.

36 **Mary Darling house.** Living-room wall sconce.

37 **Mary Darling house.** Living-room window casing with built-in bookshelves.

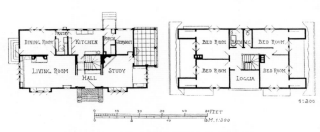

34

35

36

37

shed roofs enlivened the exterior of the otherwise sober box. One contained a trio of casement windows for the living room on the front elevation; the other provided three sash windows to the dining room on the east. Unlike the Darling house, the floor plan was asymmetrical, and the staircase set off to the west side, giving all rooms (including baths) at least one exterior window. Because of a simple but inventive manipulation of the plan, visitors arrived by walking along the front porch, past living-room windows to enter the hall, which, in most of the Greenes' modest houses since the late 1890s, doubled as a reception area. The visitor would then make a full U-turn to the left to enter the living room, creating a dramatic sense of ceremony and surprise. Like the Darling house, Mrs. van Rossem's first Greene and Greene house was fitted with hand-smoothed board-and-batten walls and wood light-fixture brackets. The Greenes did not experiment much with this design, but they did perpetuate in the van Rossem house some of the ideas that had taken shape in the White sisters' house. The distinctive architectural character of Park Place continued to emerge.

Shortly following the van Rossem house, the first scheme for a cottage for Emma Black was rejected, a stable was designed for Samuel Sanborn (for whom the Greenes had prepared plans for an unbuilt two-story house in 1899), and alterations to the chancel for All Saints church were completed. In May 1903, Mrs. Lucretia R. Garfield, the widow of the assassinated president of the United States, was in correspondence with Charles Greene regarding the design for a winter residence in South Pasadena. The Greenes and Mrs. Garfield were related through General Nathaneal Greene, and so their letters sometimes mention genealogy as well as architecture. The design of her house progressed, with Mrs. Garfield and her architect-son's close involvement in the details, though there was often considerable discussion of how to bring costs down. She was delighted with the prospect of her new house, but mentioned that it was difficult to "raise funds" at that time. The project hung constantly under a threatening financial cloud until a letter from Mrs. Garfield to Charles Greene in December 1903 halted the project.[25] Just prior to the cancellation, the Greenes were engaged to design a house that quite literally would reshape their thinking on what it meant to build in, and for, California.

38 **Emma Black house, Pasadena, 1903.**
Structural details of walls and chimney. Ink and watercolor on oil paper.

39 **Josephine van Rossem house #1, Pasadena, 1903.**
East elevation. Ink and watercolor on oil paper.

40 **Josephine van Rossem house #1.**
The clapboard siding and sash windows shown in this 1903 construction-era photograph were replaced in 1906 with shingles and casement windows that were more characteristic of the Greenes' distinctive architectural language.

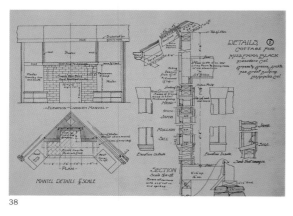

38

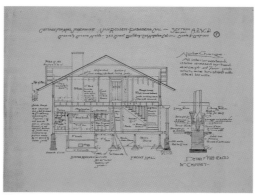

39

The new opportunity came from Arturo Bandini, the son of Don Juan Bandini, an important figure in California's political and economic history. Forging a symbolic link between the state's history and its present political and social structure, Arturo Bandini married Helen Elliott, daughter of Dr. T. B. Elliott, former president of the Indiana Colony that had founded Pasadena in 1874. Arturo Bandini was a dashing socialite who played a leading role in the hunting and field sports of the area. His sister was Arcadia Bandini Stearns, wife of Don Abel Stearns, who had owned the vast Rancho Los Alamitos until his death in 1871. It was Helen Elliott Bandini, however, who was actively involved in promoting the family's historic legacy in California and was also an active supporter of Native American rights in California.[26] The Bandinis called upon Greene and Greene to design for their family and guests a residence that would allow them to rekindle the romance of early-California pueblo and rancho life. This was a new challenge for the Greenes, who had become accustomed to convincing transplanted Midwestern clients of the need to reject exotic historical forms. Here, by contrast, were clients with deep roots in California's history inspiring them to draw from the regional paradigm to create a home that was uniquely Californian. In some respects, this was exactly what the Greenes had been implicitly searching for since they had arrived in Pasadena a decade earlier.

40

They began with the plan of a typical colonial-era *casa de rancho*, or *casa de pueblo*, a U-shaped plan with covered verandas, or *corredores*, on each of the three sides of the house that faced a central courtyard. In early California, the U-shaped adobe was the typology of choice. The courtyard hosted family gatherings, meetings, and entertainment that were the staples of rancho or pueblo life. Interest in the state's colonial lifestyle of the early nineteenth century had boomed following the publication in 1884 of the novel *Ramona: A Story,* by Helen Hunt Jackson. A large part of the story's romance was the carefully described domestic environment in which the story was set, a rancho house with an open courtyard and covered verandas designed for mainly outdoor life.[27] Like Helen Elliott Bandini, Helen Hunt Jackson was also a serious promoter of Native American rights. Indeed, Jackson's impetus for writing *Ramona* stemmed from a desire to

41 **Arturo Bandini house, Pasadena, 1903 (demolished).**
Posts supporting the shed roof of the *corredores*
(covered verandas) were placed on sunken stones,
Japanese style.

42 **Arturo Bandini house.**
Plan of house and courtyard. Pencil and watercolor on
tissue.

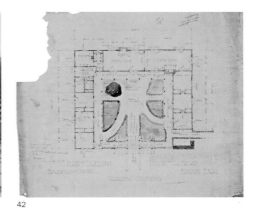

41 42

bring the neglected plight of Indians, especially in California, to national attention. In view of the natural affinity between Helen Elliott Bandini and the author of *Ramona,* and the Bandini family's rich history in colonial California, the U-shaped plan may have been chosen to honor not only the spirit of the state's architectural heritage but Jackson's fictional heroine as well.

The Greenes' design perpetuated the essential communal aspects of a classic *casa de rancho* plan while adapting specific spaces and details to the needs and materials of modern California. First, the Greenes chose upright boards and battens instead of the massive walls that were necessitated by the use of adobe. The traditional atmosphere of colonial hospitality was maintained by placing the open end of the courtyard at the front. A pergola was added at the mouth of the court to formally mark the entry and provide a modest degree of privacy to the courtyard. This pergola structure not only marked the courtyard's major entry axis, but also led to the minor axis of a path that led toward a side garden. Beyond the court, the house itself remained shaded behind the deep recesses of the *corredores* that lined the length of the three wings of the house. The *corredores* were sheltered by shed roofs supported by posts that sat on partly sunken stones, representing an ingenious melding of the Hispanic model with a traditional Japanese building method. While the Bandini house was under construction, Charles Greene bought a copy of Edward S. Morse's influential book, *Japanese Homes and Their Surroundings*, which included illustrations of Japanese covered galleries, or *hisashi-no-ma*.[28] The striking resemblance of these covered galleries to the work he was undertaking for the Bandinis must have seemed prophetic, and he wasted no time converting the idea from the pages of Morse to his current project.

In the California tradition, the Bandini courtyard would serve as an alfresco reception area, and under the shelter of the verandas the ceremonial life of the courtyard could be carried out even in inclement weather. A winding path led past a rock-lined pool to the far end of the court, where three pairs of glazed doors—"French Windows" on the plans—opened to the interior public spaces. The bottom of the plan's U was a nearly continuous great room with a minimal partition wall with folding doors to merely

suggest the separation of the dining area from the living area. Guest bedrooms were located in the wing off of the living room, while family chambers were closer to the kitchen, porch, and bath, shared with servants. While it was possible to move from one end of the house to the other without going outdoors, to do so would be to miss the point of the design. Circulation was intended to involve crossing the courtyard, or using the *corredores,* when necessary. Because of the inherent simplicity of the plan, and the equally simple treatment of materials, the cost of the house was low. The estimated contract price of $2,800 was significantly less than even the simplest of the more traditional houses the Greenes designed during this period.[29] Despite the low cost to build the Bandini house, however, the high value of the land it occupied made it an unaffordable real estate option for most clients. As a result, the courtyard plan would have an impact on the Greenes' future designs primarily for their wealthier clients.

Nearly simultaneous with the design of the Bandini house were house designs for Samuel P. Sanborn—a former client from 1899—and Dr. Francis Fenelon Rowland. The Sanborn house was a fascinating amalgam of ideas that would prove central to the Greenes' later work but in 1903 were still in the development phase. Most important among these ideas was the oblique-angle plan. First explored in the White sisters' house, the angled plan would emerge as a preferred form for the Greenes for many years. Its benefits were both aesthetic and practical, since more interesting spaces could be created when oblique angles were involved, and natural light and air currents could be exploited to better advantage without the inherent constraints of the right angle. An oblique-angled plan was also a logical alternative to the inherent space inefficiencies of the Bandini courtyard plan. A V-shaped plan, for example, could give a modest feeling of embracing the land without requiring quite so much of it to embrace as the U-shaped courtyard needed. Second, the Greenes were beginning to recognize the desirability of greater light and air circulation as their overhanging eaves deepened "to cast such beautiful shadows," as Charles would describe in a letter to Mrs. Garfield. Thus, in the Sanborn house, twenty-eight casement windows form a nearly continuous band on the upper level's front elevation to promote light and air circulation. A more elegant aesthetic solution to so

43 Illustration from *Japanese Homes and Their*
    Surroundings, by Edward S. Morse (1895), showing
    exterior posts on partially sunken stones.

44 **Arturo Bandini house, Pasadena, 1903 (demolished).**
    Combining living and dining rooms, this rustic great
    room could be partitioned using folding doors.

45 **Samuel P. Sanborn house, Pasadena, 1903.**
    First floor plan. Ink-on-linen presentation drawing.

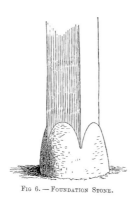

FIG 6. — FOUNDATION STONE.

43

44

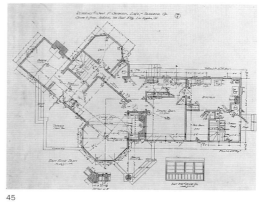

45

many windows would come later, but the concept was established here and the Greenes would continually refine it for future use.

The house for Dr. Francis Fenelon Rowland was another example of a somewhat rustic house for a wealthy and discerning client. Rowland was a medical doctor, a sportsman, and a founder of the Valley Hunt Club. Like the Greenes, he was a Twilight Club member and a friend of Arturo Bandini. For Dr. Rowland's house the Greenes borrowed the broad gable idea from the Darling residence in Claremont, but they positioned Rowland's family entry on the short end of the plan, hidden under the low eaves. His office was to be adjacent to the living quarters, so a separate patients' entrance was placed on one of the long, gabled elevations so as to be easily visible from the street. The patient reception area was distinguished by a double-height ceiling, a treatment mirrored on the opposite corner of the house where the kitchen rose to a two-story height, sending cooking heat and fumes up to vents near the exposed rafters. "Special-run" Oregon pine was specified for ceilings, and split shakes, "eleven inches to weather," gave texture to the long, broad slope of the roof. In 1912, the Rowland house was cut in half, moved from South Marengo Street, and reattached on its present site on State Street.

Immediately following the Greenes' contract with Dr. Rowland, another physician came to them with a request to design a one-story house with attached laboratory. Dr. Edith J. Claypole was another client who may have come to the firm by way of the Twilight Club, where her father was a member. On Ladies' Night, May 1902, Edith and her sister gave a presentation entitled "The Debt of the World to Pure Science." (Charles Greene had delivered a talk to the club the previous month entitled "Color in Art and Architecture.") The house the Greenes designed for Dr. Claypole had a simple plan that incorporated few luxuries but still included thoughtful planning and charming details. Oversized cobblestones supported the corners of the house and the tiled front porch, and an overhead trellis for climbing vines shaded the subsidiary porch off the dining room. The primary spaces for living and entertaining—the living and dining rooms—were contiguous, similar to the Bandini plan, separated only by a pair of leaded french doors. The generous-sized living room had the only fireplace in the house, but the main bedroom had interior casement windows

that allowed warm air to circulate from the living room. Otherwise, all windows were less expensive double-hung sashes. Period photos of the Claypole house show netting attached to the shed roof over the entry porch for vines to creep up to the roof. House vines were a common sight in Pasadena, where residents were proud to perpetuate the perception of a climate that allowed blooming flowers to thrive year-round.

In February 1904 the Greenes embarked on a commission that would further advance their confidence in designing furniture and decorative arts. Hired by Mrs. Jennie A. Reeve, the mother of their prior client Mary Reeve Darling, they were asked to design and partially furnish a four-bedroom, two-story house near the ocean in Long Beach, twenty-five miles south of Pasadena. Jennie Reeve was an important civic leader in Long Beach, a founder and supporter of the public library, and an activist for progressive women's issues. Thanks to the timing of the job and to the client's receptivity, the house would integrate many elements of the Greene and Greene firm's quickly growing architectural vocabulary. Charles, especially, had been refining these elements since the design of the White sisters' house the year before. This vocabulary would encompass not only the architecture of the dwelling itself but also its furniture, lighting fixtures, leaded-glass designs, decorative woodcarving, and landscape features.

It was the Greenes' most ambitious attempt yet to design a total domestic environment. The Reeve house was distinguished by a gabled design with deep, overhanging eaves that threw strong shadows across the planes of the house. Projecting bays with banks of casement windows on the west-facing front elevation and on the south allowed light to enter and air to circulate inside.[30] Indeed, additional sunlight was a desirable benefit in the seaside environment of Long Beach, where foggy summer mornings and cool ocean breezes were common. The projecting window bays, along with an entry portico of robust timber brackets, added depth and character to the otherwise cube-like main mass of the house. The modest landscape plan included a simple post-and-rail fence along the property line and a low gate at the path from the sidewalk. Details of the masonry foundation, entry steps, and the original footpath that connected the front porch to the side porch and service entrance were again similar to those illustrated in the Morse book.[31]

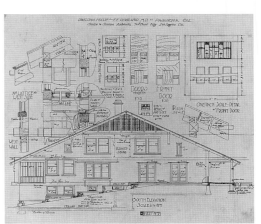

46

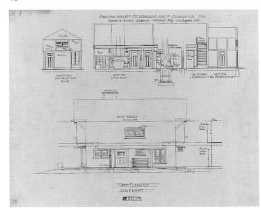

47

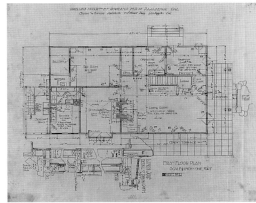

48

Inside the Reeve house, a square entry hall gives access to the living room on the right and to a short passage at the foot of the stairway, which leads to the dining room on the left. At the foot of the stairs a tall, leaded art-glass panel was set into a fixed sash that looked as though it had intended to be a door. Functionally, it provided borrowed light to the foot of the stairs, the entry hall, and the upper-level landing. Aesthetically, its landscape scene was an elaboration of an earlier design for James Culbertson. Like the Darling house, the Reeve entry included a carved panel in cedar and a screen for privacy on the stairway. The heart of the interior plan is the massive chimney that services three fireplaces on the first level. In the living room, an intimate inglenook was conceived as a space apart: three enclosed sides, and hearth bricks extending to fill the floor area create a miniature retreat to welcome fireside conversation and radiate warmth to the living room beyond. Behind the bench opposite the fireplace, a built-in cabinet was fitted with glass doors, leaded with flowing lines that suggest abstracted mountain peaks, trees, and wildflowers. The same thematic elements were incorporated into the hanging lanterns. Mrs. Reeve also commissioned movable furniture and built-in pieces. Both blend with the surrounding architectural environment so completely that in at least one photograph it is difficult to tell whether the built-in dining-room sideboard isn't actually freestanding, so convincingly does it give the appearance of an eight-leg case piece placed on a diagonal in the corner of the room. The details of the Reeve furniture are similar to those of the Greenes' built-in pieces for Mary Darling, with pegs and tenons proud of the surface. Its form was based on its structure, and so adhered to Gustav Stickley's early 1903 credo.[32] There was a subtle refinement to the proportions of the Greenes' work, however, and more subtlety in the grain of the woods that were selected. It amounted to a greater delicacy that reflected the personal artistic sensitivities of the Greenes themselves contrasted with the more production-oriented work of Stickley's United Crafts.

The Greenes had taken Stickley's message and turned it to their own uses. In addition to furniture, elaborate metal and art-glass lighting fixtures were designed for Jennie Reeve, and included the first hanging lanterns to be constructed to Charles's design specifications.[33] Lack of experience

52

49

50

51

probably explains why the lighting took so long to complete. Apparently contrary to promises made by the Greenes, by November 1904, ten months after start of construction, Mrs. Reeve could not yet use her house. Adelaide Tichenor, a close friend of Mrs. Reeve's with whom she had traveled around the world during the previous two years, became personally involved in the issue of the finishing of the house since it was to be the venue of a reception Mrs. Tichenor was helping to organize. Charles bore the brunt of Mrs. Tichenor's blunt criticism, since it was his lighting fixtures that were the cause of the delay. She wrote a blistering two-page attack, ending with: "Why you have left this lighting business undone is beyond any comprehension....We all feel very hard towards you as we do not see what we can do at this late date."[34] With Charles increasingly involved in designing and supervising decorative arts for his clients, this kind of sharply worded epistle would become all too familiar to him.

When finished, the Jennie Reeve house combined many of the architectural elements associated with the Greene and Greene style, but the integration of these elements into a truly progressive architectural statement remained elusive. With the exception of the diagonal fireplaces and hearths, the Reeve plan was still a tight, right-angled composition, not even as open or flexible as the V-shaped plan of the 1903 Sanborn house. Nor did the exterior reveal anything particularly experimental, such as Charles Greene's Arroyo View Drive house had done with its octagonal studio tower. Money may certainly have been a factor, and the practical constraints of the Cedar Avenue lot left little room for a more inventive and open floor plan.[35]

It seems also, however, that within the Greene and Greene firm the talents and contributions of the two brothers could still be isolated, showing that the brothers had not yet achieved the symbiosis of purpose and effort that would culminate in the beautifully orchestrated designs from 1906 to 1910. The lighting designs for Jennie Reeve, for example, were most likely designed by Charles Greene. This is not only suggested by Mrs. Tichenor's letter but by their design, which shows a fluidity of line in the leading the likes of which Charles loved and Henry resisted. The plans and elevations for the Jennie Reeve house, however, seem to have been more influenced by Henry than by Charles. They share the linearity and crispness of the house

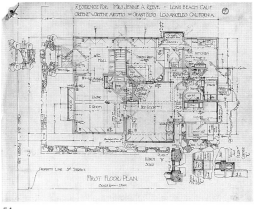

54

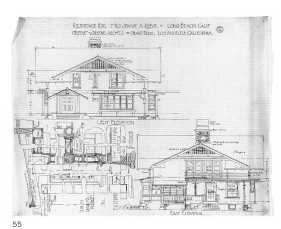

55

53

that Henry designed later the same year for his mother-in-law and his own family, a design that is documented as his. Over the next two years, a greater interweaving of the brothers' talents and thoughts would make such distinctions much more difficult to recognize.

Immediately following the Jennie Reeve commission, Charles Greene sketched an elaborate project identified only as "Sketch of a Dwelling Place by Chas. Sumner Greene, Architect, Pasadena, for W. B. T. Esqr. near Pasadena." The client was probably William B. Tomkins, for whom the Greenes had designed a house in 1898. Charles exhibited the sketch at the Louisiana Purchase Exposition in St. Louis in 1904 under his name alone, not under the firm's name. It included a dwelling divided into two separate structures, each with two levels, and an extensive landscape plan. Indeed, it is the scale of the project that is most striking, as it shows Charles Greene's developing ability to conceptualize architecture on a monumental scale, a scale with which the Greenes' work was as yet unassociated. Two dwelling structures are shown situated at right angles to each other, connected by an outdoor path. The public spaces wing consists of a large living room with a monumental fireplace and inglenook, a dining-room pavilion at an oblique angle to the rest of the floor plan, and an octagonal-bay breakfast room that projects into the courtyard. In the secondary wing, a library anchors one end, while bedrooms and baths complete the plan. The landscaped courtyard design, unlike the Bandini court, is stiffly formal. A long peristyle on one side, and a paved walk at right angles to it are opposite the L-shaped plan of the main structures, which taken together form an encircled compound. The structures were apparently conceived as having a stucco-type finish rather than wood, and its overall design is influenced by the California missions, especially in its use of arcades for outdoor passages. Charles Greene was fascinated by the missions, a few of which he had painted in watercolors. He had included at least one photo of the Santa Ynez mission in his scrapbook at about the time of this project. Plant materials figure into the drawing, too, with mature oaks and vine-like plants in abundance. The romantic and elegant design for W. B. T. was never executed, but Charles borrowed ideas from it that would emerge in his future work. There is a similarity, for example, in the juxtaposition of the motor court to the house and grounds at

56 Charles Sumner Greene, "Sketch of a Dwelling Place...
   for W.B.T. Esqr. near Pasadena," 1903 (project).

57 **Edgar W. Camp bungalow, Sierra Madre, 1904.**
   South elevation and plan. Ink-on-linen presentation
   drawing.

58 **Edgar W. Camp bungalow.**
   Living-room fireplace.

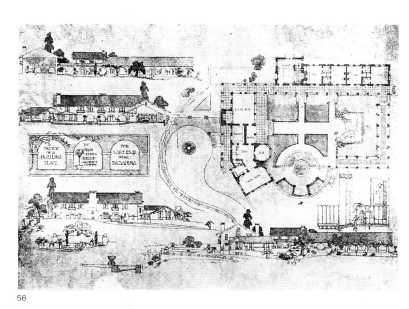

56

the Fleishhacker estate in Woodside, California (1911–12), and the arcade passages resemble the arched garden wall of Charles Greene's Carmel studio (1923). But more than this, the sheer scale of the W. B. T. project shows that Charles was preparing himself for much larger work. If it came along he would be ready. By the time the W. B. T. drawing was exhibited again, at the Los Angeles Architectural Club annual show in 1911, the Greenes had proven themselves on large-scale projects several times over.

An opportunity to attempt a more modest and modified *casa de rancho* plan in the spirit of the Bandini house presented itself in the late summer of 1904 with the commission to design a hillside house in Sierra Madre for Edgar W. Camp. It was another opportunity to adapt that spirit even more closely to present-day California life. The rough materials, charmingly composed in a straightforward way without decorative adornment, make it one of the Greenes' finest architectural understatements. It is the very picture of the deceptively simple house that the Greenes had been refining since the second Bolton house. The living room recalls the great room of the Bandini house of the previous year, and the overall composition prefigures the classic California ranch house typology of the mid-twentieth century. The simple board-wall construction and post-and-shed-roof terraces presage William Wurster's Gregory farmhouse (1928) in California's Santa Cruz Mountains.[36] The low profile and rambling circulation of the Camp bungalow also bear a resemblance to the ranch house floor plans (if not the adobe building material) of architect Cliff May's work of the 1940s and 1950s. Coming full circle, May's houses recall the hacienda plans on which the Greenes' Bandini house was based.

The Camp house does not represent a radical departure from the Greenes' previous work so much as a logical evolution from it. The plan's basic oblique-angle shape resembles that of the 1903 Sanborn house and is more practical than the Bandini concept of courtyard circulation. In the Camp house, bedrooms are accessible directly from internal living spaces without the need to venture outdoors in bad weather, or to invade other bedrooms, as was the case in the Bandini plan. The Camp furniture evolved from the Stickley-like pieces published in *Academy Architecture* that Charles had designed for the Mary Darling house (as well as from the

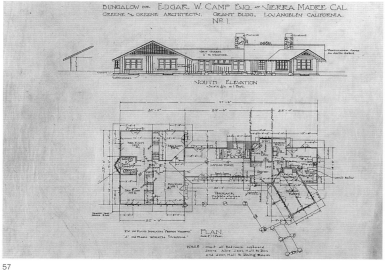

57

58

59 Desk designed for Edgar W. Camp bungalow, Sierra
Madre, 1904.

60 **Charlotte A. Whitridge house, Pasadena, 1904
(demolished).**
View from the northeast. Henry Greene designed this
house so that two households, his mother-in-law's
and his own, could function independently under the
same roof.

61 **Charlotte A. Whitridge house.**
Garden path.

59
60
61

furniture designs executed for Jennie Reeve). Though the designs are
indebted to Stickley, the Camp pieces show a higher level of refinement. The
Camp desk, in particular, is similar to one illustrated in the 1903 United
Crafts pamphlet, but with greater refinement. Finally, the Camp design
improves on the monumental treatment of masonry in the Bandini fireplace
and chimney by bringing the hearth's paving stones even further into the
living space, and by projecting massive boulders at the base of the fireplace
into the room to create inglenook seats on each side. Perhaps most important,
a broad range of evolutionary improvements within the Camp design for
house and furnishings represented higher levels of integrated skill and
coordinated aesthetics coming from the Greene and Greene firm.

Henry Greene's mother-in-law, Charlotte A. Whitridge, was a formidable
personage. She wished to stay close to her daughter's family, partly because
she was concerned for Emeline's fragile health. She was strong-willed and
generally accustomed to seeing her wishes come true. In early 1904 she
began looking for either a house or a lot to build on. After searching the
surrounding area, Mrs. Whitridge chose a sloping site in Pasadena that
commanded a view of the San Gabriel Mountains to the north and the San
Gabriel Valley to the south. She purchased the property and paid for the
construction of the house that she would then share with her daughter, her
daughter's husband, and their three-year-old son. It would be a house of her
son-in-law's design, but would remain her property.

There were many reasons why Henry could argue in favor of a return to
Pasadena, even though it meant sharing a house with his mother-in-law.
Most of the firm's work continued to be located there, and seemed likely to be
so for the foreseeable future. Henry may have hoped for closer family ties
with Charles, too, especially since Emeline and Henry had started a family.
Visits to grandmother and grandfather Greene could also be more frequent.
It must have seemed trying at times to share the governance of his family
home with his mother-in-law, but Henry bore it without complaint, as he did
similar challenges in life.[37]

The original plan of the Charlotte Whitridge house reflected the
relationship between the two sides of the family that was to occupy it.
Functional areas overlapped almost not at all: redundant living rooms, dining

rooms, and kitchens allowed each side of the household to maintain a
separate existence from the other, while still being in physical proximity.
Apart from the public spaces on the lower level, Henry's family's side
included two bedrooms on the upper level, while "Nanna" Whitridge occupied
the third. Downstairs, she had her own sitting room and a music alcove,
raised one step above her living room. Despite the separate functional areas
on the interior, the exterior aspect was that of a spacious, single-family home.
The house rambled down a gentle slope toward the southern end of the long,
narrow rectangular lot. The four sides of the house bristled with boldly
expressed architectural features: deep overhangs to protect interiors from
excessive sun, clapboard siding whose edges cut crisp lines of shadow across
the facade, and exposed structural elements such as the heavily bracketed
balcony over the recessed entry. A complex system of roofs—three gables on
the lower level, four on the upper level—intensified the impression that the
house was linked, room by room, to the subtle grading of its sloping site. A
later addition of bedrooms accommodated Henry and Emeline's growing
family: William Sumner and Isabelle Horton arrived in 1906 and 1907,
respectively, and the youngest, Elbert, was born in 1910. Over the years,
Henry also designed and constructed fences, pergolas, and stone paths to
enhance the garden in which his children loved to play. Now demolished, the
house was a direct statement of Henry's straightforward personal aesthetic,
and it showed how significantly this aesthetic differed from his brother's.
Where Charles loved to experiment with artistic design ideas, Henry
preferred inventing rational solutions to specific architectural problems. Both
approaches could achieve beauty in the process.

In March 1904, Mrs. Garfield revived the project for a winter home for
herself in South Pasadena. This time the house proceeded to completion,
though only after a series of delays and compromises by client and architect
alike. Mrs. Garfield's son, Abram, a Cleveland architect, and her daughter's
husband, Mr. J. Stanley Brown, weighed in on many of the design issues from
the beginning; their points of view can be detected in correspondence
between Mrs. Garfield and Charles Greene. Perhaps hopeful of gaining
concessions, she would begin her letters with sincere but diplomatic praise:
"I have submitted the plan I brought home, and it meets with general

62

approval, and my architect son likes your treatment of the roof....I would like better only two windows in the wall between the living room and the south porch, instead of the four....Then, on studying the plan more, I think the wall between the hall and living room should be extended to the north line of the dining room, and the wall taken away from the west side of lower landing....”[38] Charles Greene writes back, “I will arrange the windows in the living room and the stairs as you suggest; the latter will be much improved by the change.”[39] A few days later he writes to her again: “I … will at once proceed to make the changes suggested. This will cause some delay and expense as the working plans have all been figured … in fact we shall have to begin over again....”[40] Both Mrs. Garfield and Charles Greene were knowingly engaged in a friendly battle of the wills to get what they wanted out of the project. Each recognized that compromise, flattery, and the threat of higher costs (or lack of funds) were essential weapons in the negotiating arsenal.

On the important issues, however, Charles appealed to Mrs. Garfield’s aesthetic sense to help bring her around to his point of view: “The reason why the beams project from the gables is because they cast such beautiful shadows on the sides of the house in this bright atmosphere. Of course if you particularly wish to have them cut back I will have them so.”[41] The projecting gables remained, but Charles lost other battles. The knee braces on the entry portico that were originally meant to be angled to echo those on the corners of the house supporting the purlins were to be the subject of no compromise for Mrs. Garfield. She pointedly expressed her opinion while reasserting her overall authority as client: “I like so much better the perpendicular post that even if it is not as much in keeping with the general construction it will please me much better, and I must decide to have the upright posts or nothing at all.”[42] The subject of money had also been used as a carrot-and-stick method prior to the cancellation of the work the previous fall: “The difficulty of raising money just now has decided me to postpone a little longer. This will give time to reconsider its construction with regard to cost....Ten thousand nine hundred and fifty five [dollars] … will bring the cost of the house quite beyond any price I feel like considering and I must now see wherein to curtail expense.”[43] She writes a week later,

“[c]annot a cheap pine be substituted for the cedar called for in some of the finishing?”[44] Charles’s reply is sympathetic, though he stretched credibility to get his point across: “I shall be glad to try to reduce the cost and will restudy the plan. The difference between pine and the cedar we have specified would not amount to forty dollars altogether. It is the size of the house that counts most in this case … there is nothing extravagant about it, in fact it is very simple in every way.”[45]

Mrs. Garfield continued to propose changes, and almost insisted upon a complete overhaul of the roof to eliminate the east-west gables in favor of a single, north-south roof line. Charles managed to stand his ground, however, since the house as it was finally built conforms largely to the original plan. Charles was right that the sheer size of the six-bedroom house made the cost higher than the bungalow she may have imagined she was getting, but such appointments as the leaded art-glass lanterns and artistic masonry of the chimney and retaining walls hardly made the house “very simple in every way.” From the front, the full mass of the three-story structure is partially hidden because it sits on the edge of a hillside. On the back, or downhill side of the house, are the kitchen, laundry porch, and servants’ rooms suitably invisible to the upstairs household. Also at the back, facing south, banks of casement windows figure prominently in the design of the public spaces. As a result, while the exterior is a high and somewhat brooding chalet form, the interior of the Garfield house is light and airy, in contrast to the reputation the Greenes sometimes have for dark interiors. The dining room, breakfast alcove, and sun porch with interior windows to the living room enjoy an almost continuous wall of light on the south. Mrs. Garfield occupied her house in October 1904, a year and a half after engaging the Greenes.

That summer the firm had also designed a small speculative cottage in Long Beach for former client Jennie Reeve, and in the fall, Mrs. Cora C. Hollister, with her husband, the Greene’s former client Charles W. Hollister, commissioned a house in Hollywood.[46] As a courtyard design, the second Hollister house (now demolished) would broadly repeat the footprint of the Bandini house, but with the U-shaped plan facing away from the street. The result was a low, severely horizontal front elevation, with only an

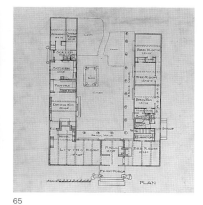

63   64   65

open trellis structure over the entry porch to break its strong linearity. The organization of interior space was more compartmentalized than the Bandini house, and included an interior hallway to connect the bedrooms along one wing of the plan. A charming inglenook with built-in benches was the focal point of the living room. The narrower courtyard functioned more nearly as a secluded family garden than a reception area, and lacked a *corredor* along one wing. These deviations from the Bandini plan may have been due to a slightly smaller lot size, but the courtyard concept satisfactorily responded to so many of the characteristics of Southern California life that, in spite of minor modifications, the basic form was used for the Hollisters and other future clients with sufficient land.

Also in 1904 a two-story, five-bedroom house (demolished) for Roger Henry Carleton Green in Vancouver, British Columbia, was drawn up in elevation and plan by Greene and Greene, with construction details to be supervised locally by others. The English-style half-timbered exterior treatment was a recapitulation of the Culbertson house, and was indeed more appropriate to the colder and rainier northern climate. A single-level octagonal conservatory with a standing-seam copper roof projected pavilion-like from the side of the house. Similar to the Garfield house, the R. Henry C. Green house plan allowed for a clear sight line from the reception hall through the drawing-room windows to the rear veranda, a precursor to the close connection between entry and rear garden that the Greenes would routinely establish in their largest designs, including the Blacker, Gamble, Pratt, and Thorsen houses. Also prescient in the design for the R. Henry C. Green house was the square-cross plan of the drawing room, which, like the Gamble House (1907–09), divided the room into functional subsets, with an inglenook facing a square bay of windows.[47]

Though it would not be completed until the end of the following year, the firm's next design project was for a large oceanfront house for Adelaide Tichenor of Long Beach. Adelaide Alexander Tichenor is known even today as "the Mother of Long Beach" for her energetic pursuit of initiatives and institutions that brought culture, progress, and dignity to her city. A native of Ravenna, Ohio, she came to Southern California in 1878 to teach. She met and married lumberman Lester Tichenor in Redlands in 1885, and,

following his death in 1892, moved to Long Beach in 1895 and continued to manage his business interests. By 1896 she had established the Long Beach Ebell Club, the city's oldest women's service organization, and with her friend, Jennie Reeve, she soon helped to establish the Long Beach Public Library by donating money and art books. She was known nationally as a leader in the fight for women's suffrage.[48] The sometimes stormy working relationship between Charles Greene and Adelaide Tichenor nonetheless ultimately produced a house that not only pleased the client but was of pivotal importance to the firm.[49]

The significance of the Tichenor house stems largely from the timing and broad scope of the project. Mrs. Tichenor came to the Greenes in 1904, at a time of the firm's growing confidence in accepting commissions for larger houses with furnishings, hardware, and lighting fixtures. Mrs. Tichenor asked Charles Greene for his help in selecting decorative objects, too, for her house-in-progress. In some ways, Mrs. Tichenor was the ideal client: intelligent, decisive, well traveled, willing to take risks, and wealthy. Work was to have begun during the spring of 1904, but Charles was still fully engaged in his work for Edgar Camp, Lucretia Garfield, and Jennie Reeve. Henry Greene also had a full complement of work, including the design and construction of his mother-in-law's house.[50] Consequently, it is unlikely that Charles had had time to work on the design of Mrs. Tichenor's house when he received a letter from her imploring him to travel immediately to St. Louis to join her at the Louisiana Purchase Exposition.[51] There were several reasons Charles would have obliged. As previously mentioned, the Greene and Greene firm had entered photographs of the James Culbertson and George Barker houses in the exposition's architectural competition, and Charles had independently entered his sketch for the "Projected Dwelling for W. B. T. near Pasadena." He was also well aware of the value of such expositions to his professional development, having benefited from visiting fairs in Chicago (1893), San Francisco (1894), Glasgow (1901), and Buffalo (1901). Mrs. Tichenor wrote to Charles on June 10, 1904 (on exposition stationery from the California State Building), insisting that he drop whatever he was doing to join her. She cajoled and pleaded, even to the point of mentioning something that might particularly entice Charles: "I do not want you to go on with my home until

66 **Adelaide A. Tichenor house, Long Beach,
1904–05 (altered).**
Overhead view taken from the north after addition of
the garage in 1916.

67 **Adelaide A. Tichenor house.**
Early view of front (south) facade prior to enclosure
of the second-floor balcony.

68 **Adelaide A. Tichenor house.**
Garden.

66

you see [the Fair] ... you will be able to get so many ideas of woods and other things for finishing what you now have on....It will be impossible for me to describe to you the effect of the woods...." Her repeated mention of the "woods" is of interest. Was she referring to a particular exhibit? If so, it may well have been the so-called Bellevue in the Japanese Imperial Garden, an exhibit composed of "many different kinds of woods, no two pieces from the same species of tree."[52] Or, she may have been making a more general comment designed to arouse Charles's known passion for wood. In any event, the persuasion was sufficient to draw Charles away from his other clients, and he boarded a train for St. Louis.

Charles Greene's scrapbook of the period contains numerous magazine clippings of illustrations taken from the exposition.[53] First among these are views of the Japanese pavilions in the Imperial Garden compound. Mrs. Tichenor's travels with Jennie Reeve had recently exposed her to Asian architecture, and the St. Louis fair had the most extensive and authentic representation of Japanese architecture ever seen in America, more than at Philadelphia in 1876, or even Chicago in 1893. Charles's own interest in Japanese architecture had recently been engaged in a very real way through the Edward Morse book. He exercised his specific knowledge in the plain board walls, exterior post treatments, and covered galleries of the Bandini and Hollister houses, and the artistic stone walkways and hanging exterior lanterns of the Jennie Reeve house. Accordingly, the stage was set for a more thorough integration of Japanese design elements into a house for Mrs. Tichenor.

The Tichenor house consists of a two-story block with two single-story wings attached to form a U-shaped structure sheltering a courtyard garden. The general massing of the house, the sheltered, upper-level gallery, and the garden bridge evoke authentic Japanese forms. There is nonetheless something essentially familiar about the house relative to the firm's previous work. Its clinker-brick-filled half-timbering on the lower level recalls their fascination with historic English architecture, and the U-shaped plan echoes the nineteenth-century California *casa de rancho*. The formal entry is on the south end of the house, near the edge of the bluffs facing the ocean, as far as possible from the main street.[54] Visitors could approach only by way of First

68

69 **Adelaide A. Tichenor house.**
Early view of courtyard garden taken from the original teahouse structure (demolished).

70 **Adelaide A. Tichenor house.**
View from living room toward the inglenook and doors to the garden.

69

70

Place, a quiet cul-de-sac parallelling the east side of the house. As Randell Makinson has noted, Charles Greene may have designed this two-story portion of the house with reference to the main pavilion at the Japanese Imperial Garden in St. Louis.[55] Its modified *irimoya* tile roof has also been noted by historian-architect Clay Lancaster, and overt Japanese inspiration was cited as early as 1909 by Aymar Embury in his *One Hundred Country Houses*.[56] As focal point at the back of the garden a small tile-roofed teahouse—another Japanese-inspired element—was placed with the back of its rear wall to Ocean Avenue. Inside, the great-room concept, also borrowed from the Bandini house, was employed in the contiguous reception, living, and dining areas. The dining room actually occupies a raised platform, two steps higher than the level of the great room, creating a somewhat more compressed, intimate space for dining. The furnishings reflect an Asian influence as well. A crude interpretation of the Chinese "lift" appears repeatedly in the Tichenor drawer pulls, a precursor to the highly refined use of the same device in the Greenes' later work.

Whether despite or because of Charles Greene's earnest attempts to combine his interpretation of Mrs. Tichenor's initial wishes with her later demands, the house cannot be considered an unqualified success. The strong-willed Adelaide Tichenor did not allow her architect to do as he pleased during the design process. One alteration in particular—her insistence on enclosing a portion of the open balcony on the upper level—compromised the compositional balance of the ocean elevation.[57] The heavy, box-like mass of the two wings, with their relatively scarce window area, also does not convincingly resonate with the carefully composed two-story portion of the house. Relatively speaking, Charles Greene had only recently begun to explore combining oriental and occidental design elements. He appreciated the implications of California's shared position on the rim of the Pacific Ocean and he increasingly looked to Japan for inspiration in developing a new, regionally appropriate idiom. It would be another two years, however, before this interest matured to the point of broadly defining the identity of the firm's work.

While Charles juggled the demands of Mr. Camp, Mrs. Garfield, Mrs. Reeve, and Mrs. Tichenor, the firm was separately pursuing another vision of California domestic design. A previously unknown set of drawings and specifications identified as "A California House" are among the surviving documents from the Greene and Greene firm.[58] Several interesting theories are suggested by these drawings and specifications. Though undated, they appear to be from late 1904 or early 1905, based on stylistic similarities to other houses designed by the firm during that period. The Grant Building office address is shown on the drawings, definitively dating them between February 1903 and March 1906, but the style of drafting and design is most similar to drawings dated 1904 and 1905.[59] "A California House" is most likely the independent concept of Henry Greene, since it shows several similarities to other designs of that period that are most likely his. But we also know that Charles Greene opposed speculative design, even though the firm, though probably under Henry's direction, occasionally engaged in it.[60] If "A California House" was Henry Greene's initiative, what was his reason for designing it? Could it have been a response to the high volume of work coming into the firm and the attendant need to deal more efficiently with the load? In particular, a standarized design might have been attractive to those of the Greenes' clients who were real estate speculators, such as Josephine van Rossem or Jennie Reeve, who commissioned a speculative house and a small cottage after her primary residence. Henry may also have been motivated by frustration at the firm's inability to get through the design process more quickly. A standardized design could speed this phase, providing a point of departure for design discussions. Henry was certainly aware of the lengthy and sometimes contentious debates that slowed the Garfield and Tichenor projects, and while some clients needed kid-glove attention, some did not. "A California House" seems tailor-made to answer the needs of a clientele that might otherwise have purchased a high-end builders' pattern-book house. It also represents Henry Greene's idea of the basic requirements of upper-middle-class homebuilding.

"A California House" was designed as a two-story house with three bedrooms, a sewing room, and one bath upstairs. Downstairs, a generous living room, twenty-six feet long by thirteen feet wide, opens onto a porch through french doors. The twenty-by-fifteen-foot dining room was placed at right angles to the living room and was designed to include a built-in

71 "A California House," c. 1904 (project).
First floor plan. Ink-on-linen drawing.

72 "A California House."
Second floor plan. Ink-on-linen drawing.

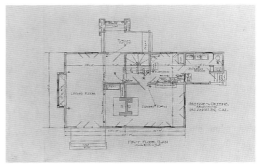

71

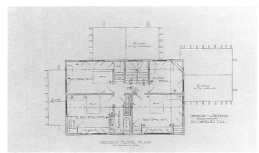

72

GREENE & GREENE

sideboard and two banks of casement windows. Two of the upstairs bedrooms show built-in window seats the entire length of the casement-windows. The typed contractor's specifications are similar to those for other Greene and Greene jobs of the period, but the design and proposed construction details boast no expensive options or materials, and could be honestly described as "plain." Nevertheless, the drawings and specifications are nearly as detailed as they would normally have been for a specific client, suggesting that "A California House" was not considered an idle, hypothetical exercise in design but a thoughtfully considered plan ready to adapt on short notice. The specifications indicated at the outset that the house should be situated on a "southwest corner of intersecting streets on a level lot." The foundation was to be of cobblestones, "pointed with dark cement mortar, well back of face." The roof and siding were to be of unstained cedar shingles, but, "all trim, casings, etc. stained with Cabots Creosote, one brush coat." Framing and interior wood was to be Oregon pine; "[i]nside woodwork all stained and filled [with paste filler] and rubbed off, and one coat of boiled oil well rubbed off." Doors are specified to be stock sugar pine, except the front door, which was to be "mill-made to detail."[61]

Sadly, "A California House" was never built exactly as it was designed, though several Greene and Greene houses of the period were clearly influenced by it. The very existence of the design, however, indicates a recognized need for basic, dignified, and cost-effective housing during a builder's market.

The second house design for Josephine van Rossem most closely resembles "A California House." Her purpose was real estate speculation, and the cost-conscious aspects of the design were no doubt attractive to her. In the van Rossem version (1904), the plan's orientation of living room to dining room is essentially a reversed, mirror image of "A California House." The massing of volumes and organization of windows is similar, and the pitch of the roof is identical in both designs. Some differences aside, the second van Rossem house best reflects the firm's attempt to enter the high end of the mass-housing market. Its cost, however, was $5,100, a sum significantly greater than most three- or four-bedroom houses being built in Pasadena at that time. "A California House," however laudable, was unable to compete.

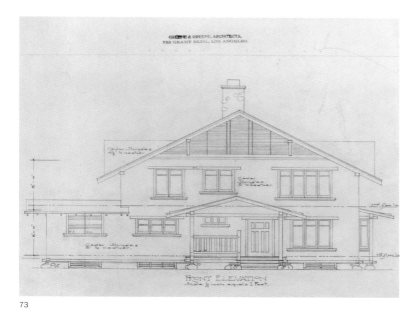

73

73 "A California House."
Front elevation. Pencil-on-tissue.

74 Josephine van Rossem house #2, Pasadena, 1904.
This design came closest to the Greenes' concept for
"A California House."

74

4

Stones of the Arroyo

1   Page 72:
West portal, Oaklawn Residential Park, South
Pasadena, 1904–05.

2   Kate A. White house, South Pasadena, 1904 (altered).
South facade.

3   Rev. Alexander Moss Merwin house, Pasadena, 1904.
South facade.

2   3

GREENE & GREENE

Two days before Christmas of 1904, a Pasadena newspaper announced a $3,085 contract between the South Pasadena Realty and Improvement Company as owner, Greene and Greene as architects, and Peter Hall as contractor. The contract was for two stone-and-iron-entrance gateways, and 1,220 linear feet of fence to surround the as-yet undeveloped Oaklawn tract of home sites near the fashionable Raymond Hotel.[1] More important than the contract was the contractor. During the first ten years of their architectural practice, the Greenes had worked with a variety of Pasadena and Los Angeles builders, including W. S. Plant and James P. Dawson on the Winthrop B. Fay house, Arthur Gourlay on the Howard Longley house, John Erickson on the James Swan house (and Charles Greene's own house), Charles N. Stanley on the James Culbertson house, David M. Renton on the second Josephine van Rossem house, and August C. Brandt on the Charlotte Whitridge house.[2] There is no evidence to suggest that the Greenes were unhappy with any one of these contractors, but they might have wished for the greater consistency of quality that might come from a close association with one, rather than many. In the summer of 1904, a Swedish man named Peter Hall had built a cottage to their design for Kate White in South Pasadena. He returned in December to build their house for the Rev. Alexander Moss Merwin.[3] Kate White's was a simple bungalow, a recycled version of the 1903 floor plan for Dr. Edith Claypole, and as a result was unlikely to have put Peter Hall and Charles Greene in close working contact with each other. Rev. Merwin's house appears to have been the work of Henry Greene.[4] With the Oaklawn portals, however, came the best opportunity yet for Charles to assess the skill of this promising builder, a man just one year older than he.

Peter Hall (1867–1939) and his brother, John (1864–1940), were born Peter and John Jonasson in Stockholm, Sweden. They had immigrated to America as children, their parents changing their last name, as many immigrants did, to convey a more neutral ethnicity. Peter was nineteen when he arrived in Pasadena to work as a stair builder.[5] After taking a temporary building job in Port Townsend, Washington, he returned to work with his older brother, John, at the Pasadena Manufacturing Company. The more entrepreneurial of the two siblings, Peter quit the company in 1900

and began his own contracting business. John had become a skilled cabinetmaker and elected to remain with the Pasadena Manufacturing Company, serving as a foreman until 1906.[6]

Charles Greene's presence at the Oaklawn site was probably frequent during construction of the portals in January and February 1905. He had carefully indicated the size and shape of each of the portals' stones on the presentation drawings, and he would develop a reputation for closely supervising his masonry work.[7] Growing up as young boys in Sweden, Peter and John Hall probably learned woodworking like most other boys in Sweden, in the *sloyd* tradition of home instruction whereby children would learn from their elders how to carve wood into useful objects, sitting around the hearth during the long winter evenings. This native tradition might have seemed quaint to the Greenes, whose highly structured, bench-work education at the Manual Training School in St. Louis was in marked contrast. Ultimately, it was the quality of the work that mattered most to them all, and from that point on, the two pairs of brothers would collaborate on some of the finest achievements of the American Arts and Crafts movement.[8]

The newly announced Oaklawn housing tract was advertised to "those who want the best in every particular and will appreciate living in the most exclusive Private Residence Park in the midst of Pasadena's best improvements."[9] This was certainly boosterism, but not far from the truth: the first house to be constructed in the tract would cost $30,000, a large budget for the day. Charles Greene's preliminary conceptual sketch of the Oaklawn portals shows two pairs of pillars, carefully fashioned from piles of arroyo stones. The largest boulders were placed at ground level, with increasingly smaller cobbles toward the top, terminating in a series of clinker-brick platforms at varying heights. Each pair of pillars was connected by a timber and tile roof sheltering a brief passage through wrought-iron gates that spanned the gap between the pillars at the sidewalk. For the roof, Charles Greene specified on the drawing Ludowici tiles, "glazed, of moss-green color, all to be approved by Architects." They were similar to those he would specify for the roof of the Tichenor house, which had been in the design phase since the fall of 1904 but was still three

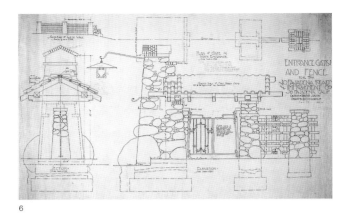

4

5

6

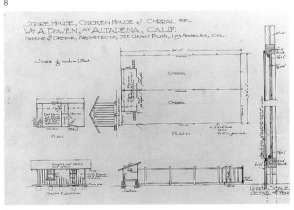

7

8

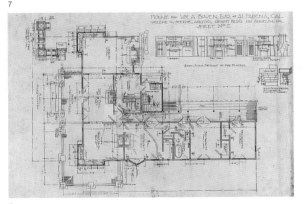

9

4 Peter Hall (1867–1939), c. 1905.

5 John Hall (1864–1940), c. 1920.

6 **Oaklawn Portals, South Pasadena, 1904–05.**
   Portal elevation and details. Ink-on-linen drawing.

7 **William A. Bowen house, Altadena, 1905.**
   East (front) facade.

8 **William A. Bowen house.**
   Plan with section details. Ink-on-linen
   presentation drawing.

9 **William A. Bowen storehouse, chicken house, and
   corral, Altadena, 1905.**
   Plans and elevations. Ink-on-linen presentation
   drawing.

months from start of construction. The tiles may have been ordered simultaneously.[10] Metal lanterns with glass panels and broad-brimmed hoods were designed to hang from tendril-like iron hooks projecting from the pillars over the roadway. These, however, were probably never made, since none of the surviving photographs from the period shows them in place. The fence, which bordered much of the housing tract, consisted of stone pillars with brick caps—miniatures of the portal pillars—with the intervals between the pillars spanned by lath strips in a simple crosshatch pattern. The overall effect of the gateways and perimeter fence—not to mention the charming oak-tree-shaded sitting area in the center of Oaklawn Avenue—was to create a naturalistic and harmonious theme for the tract. While the job was under construction, one newspaper journalist generously conceded that "the artistic effect is all that the designer could possibly have anticipated."[11] The new architect-contractor alliance was successful, and ushered in a decade of sophisticated millwork, construction, and custom cabinetry and furniture making that would fundamentally alter how the Greenes' work would be executed and perceived.

While Charles worked on the Oaklawn project, the firm also designed a ranch house and outbuildings for William A. Bowen in Altadena. As it was ultimately built (the client rejected the first scheme), the house had the outward appearance of the front elevation of the Cora Hollister house: a low roof parallel to the street, with a simple trellis structure over the entry and front terrace. All bedrooms had direct access to the outdoors, and due to the lack of an interior hallway (as in the Arturo Bandini plan) only one of the three bedrooms communicated internally with the rest of the house. The implications for outdoor living could not have been more blunt. The symmetry of the front elevation was broken by a terrace on one side, its railing supported, like the Oaklawn fence, by cobblestone pillars capped with dark bricks. Two fully glazed bays projected from each of the corners at the front of the house, promoting interior light and air circulation. A corral, storehouse, and even a chicken coop completed the Greene and Greene design for the Bowen *ranchita*.

Returning to the Park Place tract that winter, the Greenes designed a house for Mrs. Louise T. Halsted and her husband, S. Hazard Halsted, who

10 **Louise T. Halsted house, Pasadena, 1905.**
South facade.

11 **Louise T. Halsted house.**
Living room.

10   11

was president of the Pasadena Ice Company. It was the seventh Greene and Greene house to be built in or near Park Place in three years. The character of the neighborhood had been fundamentally skewed toward the Greenes' woodsy aesthetic.[12] The Halsted house was a one-and-a-half-story bungalow (one bedroom and a sun porch upstairs) that continued in the tradition of the Greenes' smaller, well-built houses.[13] The deep overhang of the eaves along the front elevation of the house created a dark void for shaded privacy on the front terrace (similar to Dr. Rowland's house and office of 1903). Roof purlins projected farther beyond the verge boards than they had previously, giving a marked distinction to the gable ends. In the tradition of the Greenes' plans that honored a dictum of architect Ralph Adams Cram, the living room was by far the largest single space in the house.[14] A fireplace and inglenook bench provided focus for the room, which was further enlivened by a ceiling patterned with bands of dark-toned wood. As was typical in their smaller houses, the Greenes separated the dining room and living room with double glass doors to give the option of having a continuous open space from one end of the house to the other.

The small house had a limited future in the Greenes' office. Increasingly large structures were being commissioned by wealthier clients, eclipsing their ability (if not willingness) to accept smaller house designs. In mid-1905, the Alta Planing Mill Company was hired to build a five-bedroom house designed by the Greenes for their client Dr. Arthur A. Libby. Though this house signaled the growing scale of the Greenes' work, its cube-like form has some of the earmarks of their smaller "California House." The design for Dr. Libby returns to the concept of the single-ridge roof with a large, unifying gable. Unlike the Darling and Rowland designs, however, the Libby roof was elevated to allow for a full-width upper level and full-height windows along all four elevations. Even so, the eaves were made deep enough to cast shadows over the house to shield the interiors from the sun. The Libby house (before its demolition in 1968) sat well back from the street, as if on a tiered pedestal: the first stage was bermed earth, the second stage a raised porch along two sides of the house. The timber porch railing was punctuated by brick pillars, and a large trellis sheltered the porch alongside one corner of the house. In the rear, a paved auto court with

a dramatic porte cochere defined the area between the house and garage. From the street, the form of the Libby house was that of a larger-than-life chalet related more closely to Adirondack camps, such as William West Durant's "Sagamore" on Raquette Lake (1897), than to the authentic Swiss progenitor. Also beginning to emerge in the Libby design, however, were features of the Greenes' later, better-known houses: deep eaves, expressed joinery, the bedroom balcony (later identified as sleeping porches), and the porte cochere, which reappeared with spectacular effect in the Blacker house of 1907–09.

In 1904, the Greenes had designed a house for Judge Charles J. Willett, who had served as the attorney for Alice Greene and her sisters in their father's probate case, and who also owned property on Arroyo Terrace (known as Arroyo View Drive until late 1902) in Park Place. The design, which was never built, had characteristics of Charles and Alice Greene's own house four lots to the west, including an upper-story octagonal tower, which on the judge's plans was transformed into bedrooms on both levels. Why the house was not built is unknown, but Judge Willett returned to the Greenes in 1905 to ask them to design a rental property for his Park Place lot. Similar to the recent plan for the Halsteds, and nearly a mirror image of the Kate A. White plan, the Willett scheme was modified slightly to project the dining room forward from the plane of the living-room elevation, and to place a servant's bedroom on the half-story space above. The low-lying, charmingly proportioned form of Judge Willett's rental house was often reproduced in national publications, and served as a model for other small dwellings.[15]

That spring the Greenes also designed a house for Lucy E. Wheeler in Los Angeles. Ms. Wheeler ran a stenographic business whose services Greene and Greene routinely used to draw up contractor's specifications for their jobs. The house she commissioned was for her mother and sister as well as herself, and though her budget was not extravagant, it was sufficient to produce a well-built, four-bedroom house. Created for an urban lot, the plan is narrow and long compared with the generously scaled parcels the Greenes normally worked with in Pasadena, even for their smaller houses. Their increasing tendency toward designing low, horizontal elevations and casual, rambling plans would not work here. The design solution was to return to the

12 **Dr. Arthur A. Libby house, Pasadena, 1905** (demolished).
View from the southeast.

12

13 Judge Charles J. Willett house, Pasadena, 1904 (project).
First floor plan. Ink-on-linen presentation drawing.

14 Judge Charles J. Willett house (altered).
View from the northeast.

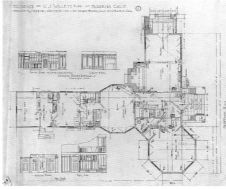

13   14

two-story block of the "California House" prototype with modifications to shape it to the narrow urban lot. Constraints on all four sides challenged the design. The resulting plan operates with tight efficiency, especially in the service area, which manages without crowding to include kitchen, pantry, screened laundry porch, and watercloset, all in less space than is occupied by the living room alone. Its efficiency and sober form have the earmarks of Henry Greene's involvement, though the color scheme, including a bright blue bedroom, speaks of Charles's touch, too.

Though construction did not take place for nearly a year, the next job to come into the Greenes' office was the design of a third residence for Josephine van Rossem. This would be her own home, not a rental as before, so the strict cost considerations that applied to her speculative houses were somewhat relaxed. Mrs. van Rossem woud spend half again as much on her own house as she had on the more expensive of her two earlier houses. Mrs. van Rossem chose her own contractor, Christian M. Hansen, who had never worked for the Greenes before. The building site was on the Orange Grove Avenue side of Park Place, on the streetcar line near the Greenes' growing cluster of houses on Arroyo Terrace. Sited on one of the busiest streets in Pasadena, the house under construction could serve as a community billboard for the Greenes' architecture. For the first time since the Edgar Camp house more than a year before, the Greenes returned to the obliquely angled plan to take advantage of the shape of the lot, its sloping topography, the mountain views, and the courtyard ambiance that a V-shaped plan promised to give the rear of the house. Glazed doors from the living room, the hallway, and three of the four bedrooms opened directly out to the garden. A massive foundation of arroyo cobblestones and boulders raised the living quarters—sheathed in spilt redwood shakes—above the noise and dust of the street and allowed for construction of a full cellar above grade. The bedroom wing was angled to the northwest, away from the street side of the plan that was occupied by the dining room, living room, and hall. The van Rossem interior was striking for its use of broad redwood boards in the living room and artistically perforated Oregon pine paneling in the dining room. The paneled and beamed ceilings added to the impression of rusticity, and the batten-door, Oregon-pine sideboard that the Greenes

designed for the room the following year helped to unify the house with Mrs. van Rossem's eclectic furnishings.

In the foundation, facing Orange Grove Avenue, the Greenes' design called for a small, arched opening, set in brick and stone. This simple design, first used here, became a life-long theme especially for Charles Greene. The arched niche form of about this proportion would be expressed by Charles in different materials over the years—including wood, brick, stone, or plaster—and in different sizes, sometimes small, as here, or monumental, as in the Mortimer Fleishhacker water gardens of 1927–28. Charles's use of the form would always be a gracefully proportioned and romantic architectural gesture.

In May 1905, one month after construction began on the Lucy Wheeler house, a speculative house of the Greenes' design was underway for Iwan Serrurier on East California Street. The attractive, unified aspect of the Greenes' exterior design, with its set-back front porch, large gable, and split-shake exterior, made it a favorite image in illustrated magazines.[16] There were unusual aspects, however. Uncharacteristically, a hall that spanned the length of the house from a rear porch to the living room, describing the major axis, was not expressed on the exterior. Rather, the L-shape suggested a dog-leg organization of space that was not borne out on the interior. The Serruriers rented the house as income property, choosing instead to live in the Greene and Greene house that had been built in Altadena for contractor August C. Brandt three months after the Serruriers' California Street house was completed.

In the summer of 1905, the Greenes, with Peter Hall, had undertaken alterations to a house for David Tod Ford, probably recommended to the Greenes by his son, Freeman, the vice-president of the Pasadena Ice Company. The senior Ford, president of the Youngstown Iron and Steel Company, had been a mentor to an up-and-coming Youngstown lawyer named Henry Mauris Robinson. Robinson had lived with the Ford family, and eventually married Mrs. Ford's cousin, Laurabelle Arms, heiress to another iron and steel fortune.[17] Robinson and his wife felt that a residence in the West would be beneficial to their financial and professional commitments: Henry had investments in the Tombstone Mining Company of

15 **Josephine van Rossem house #3, Pasadena, 1905–06 (demolished).**
View from the northeast.

16 **Josephine van Rossem house #3.**
View from living room toward the garden doors.

17 **Josephine van Rossem house #3.**
Garden (top) and street elevations. Ink-on-linen presentation drawing.

18 **Josephine van Rossem house #3.**
First floor plan. Ink-on-linen presentation drawing.

15

16

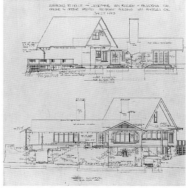

17

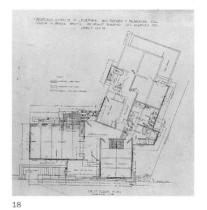

18

19 Iwan Serrurier house, Pasadena, 1905 (demolished).

20 Laurabelle A. Robinson house, Pasadena, 1905–06.
View from the southeast. In 1918 the Greenes converted the open porch on the south to an enclosed sunroom. Henry Greene designed a library addition in 1929 and a garden pergola in 1930.

20

19

Arizona and had also been appointed legal counsel for the Pacific Lumber Company in California. David Tod Ford persuaded the Robinsons to settle near him, in Pasadena, arranging for them the purchase of a sizable lot adjacent to property he had bought for his family's use.[18] The Robinsons hired the Greenes, putting them in complete control of designing a residence, its furniture, lighting fixtures, leaded art glass, metalwork, and landscaping. Plans were prepared in August 1905 and a building permit was issued later that month. "Mrs. L. A. Robinson" was the name shown on the linen presentation drawings, and while it was not at all unusual for architects to work with the wife of a married couple as the principal client, Laurabelle Robinson's active participation in the project was especially appropriate. First, her husband was busy incorporating the Pacific Lumber Company the very month the contract for the house was signed, leaving his wife to attend to the details. Also, Mrs. Robinson was undoubtedly paying for the work with some of her own sizable fortune, which served as a stabilizing presence against her husband's speculations in mining and lumber.[19] The Robinsons traveled extensively during the construction of the house, not arriving in Pasadena until it was completed in the summer of 1906. In February 1906, however, they reviewed and approved new drawings for a complete redesign of the living room's fireplace elevation.[20] The furniture drawings were prepared in October 1906 and the pieces produced over the following year.[21]

The Robinson's L-shaped parcel of land extended from South Grand Avenue to the bluff of the Arroyo Seco and down its escarpment, about a quarter of a mile south of the Park Place tract where the Greenes' bungalows had proliferated. Charles and Henry made the most of the site, choosing to position the house well back from the street, on the edge of the steep drop to the arroyo. The landscape plan was orchestrated to give ceremonial weight to the approach. Thirty yards from the street, a pair of tapered stucco portals flank the winding driveway. Lanterns with broad brims, similar to those designed (but never made) for the Oaklawn portals, top the imposing pillars. The drive originally continued through the heart of a grove of orange trees, a concept favored by Henry Greene. Henry's influence could be seen in the formality of the grove, which was calculated to evoke a civilized, romantic image of California.[22] At the edge of the roadway,

21 Laurabelle A. Robinson house.
Detail of living room, showing drop-front desk made
by John Hall to the Greenes' design.

22 Laurabelle A. Robinson house.
View from the southeast.

23 Laurabelle A. Robinson house.
Living room, view to the entry hall.

24 Laurabelle A. Robinson house.
Detail of den. The Greenes designed most of the
Robinsons' furniture, including the red oak desk
and lamp pictured.

22

21

23

24

the entry drive is punctuated by low stucco pedestals for planters to act as a visual buffer to the orange trees behind.

The striking mass of the house gradually appears, as surprising for what it is not as for what it is. The Robinson house is not the elaborate lodge of split shakes and boulders that one might reasonably have expected at this juncture in the Greenes' careers. Unlike Dr. Libby's chalet, or Edgar Camp's rambling bungalow, the Robinsons' house had the proportions of an estate, and was designed to impress. The material was stucco and half-timbering, used by the Greenes only sparingly. The influence of Japan resonates in the exposed structural posts and profiled beams that support the flat roof of the balcony to the left of the entry, but there are other affinities as well. The bold half-timbering resembles Germanic tradition as much as English. The tapered, stucco buttresses on the exterior may have been suggested to the Greenes through Charles's familiarity with the work of C. F. A. Voysey, who used the device often. (Voysey's work appears tipped into one of Charles's scrapbooks.) Another possible influence—the adobe buttresses of early Spanish mission architecture of the Southwest—also bears investigation. Originally painted an earthy ochre, the exterior hue of the Robinson house was more akin to natural adobe than to Voysey's whitewashed roughcast, and blended more compatibly with the arid hillsides of the Arroyo Seco. Hints of American Indian influence appear, too, especially in the pavilion-like den. The flat roof construction, with beams that projected from above the band of windows on the front elevation (before an extension was added in 1929), resembled pueblo structures with timber vigas that extended beyond the surface of exterior walls in traditional construction. Prominent buttresses, supporting the exterior corners of the main volume, also distinguish the Robinson den; they hint of the buttresses used to strengthen the thick walls of adobe structures.

The Greenes could have been exposed to Southwest themes in any number of ways. In 1905, along with their clients Arturo Bandini, Adelaide Tichenor, and C. J. Willett, the Greenes joined the Southwest Society of the Archeological Institute of America, a chapter formed by Charles Fletcher Lummis to protect and promote the region's native traditions.[23] The pages of *The Craftsman* magazine frequently published articles on Native American and Spanish Colonial themes, and scores of lectures were given locally on

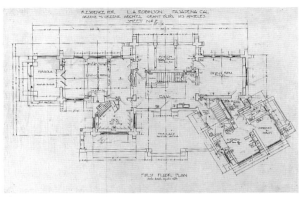

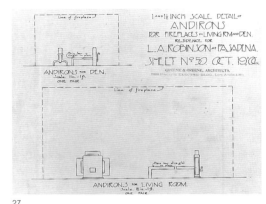

26   27

26 **Laurabelle A. Robinson house, Pasadena, 1905–06.**
First floor plan. The service wing appears as an
angled appendage on the north end of the house.
Ink-on-linen presentation drawing.

27 **Laurabelle A. Robinson house.**
Detail of den and living -room andirons.
Ink-on-linen sketch.

28 **Laurabelle A. Robinson house.**
A re-creation of the Robinson dining room, this space,
which contains the original furniture and ceiling
chandelier, is part of the Greene and Greene
Exhibition in the Virginia Steele Scott Gallery of the
Huntington Library, Art Collections and Botanical
Gardens, San Marino, California.

Southwest and American Indian subjects during this period. As early as 1897, Adam Clark Vroman delivered a lecture to the members of the Twilight Club devoted to the New Mexico pueblo of Acoma.[24] Indeed, the massive south chimney of the Robinson house resembles the tapered form of the large adobe buttresses that support the walls of Acoma's San Estevan del Rey, the Spanish mission built with Indian labor. Details in the Robinsons' den resonate with Native American design themes, too, including the stylized feathers depicted in the leaded art-glass casement windows, and a table lamp of red oak, designed in 1906, that contains an Indian swastika design. Antique Southwest tribal baskets were used to further decorate the room.[25]

The main stairway dominates the Robinson entry, exhibiting a complex construction in cedar that is worthy of Peter Hall's reputation as a stairbuilder. Rising to an upper-level balcony that surrounds the open well of the double-height space within the hall, its vertical panels are interrupted by short, horizontal cross members that create a decorative rhythmic pattern. Through the entry past the foot of the stairs, the original beam-ceilinged, open porch (since enclosed) offered fresh air and views of the arroyo below. In the living room, a wide picture window was placed on axis with the fireplace to take advantage of the same vista. From the living room, glazed doors led to a pergola terrace that was altered in 1918 by Charles Greene to become an enclosed sun porch with delicate, symbolic carvings showing sun and moon, mountains and sea, clouds and stars. The original treatment of the dining room, located on the northwest corner of the plan, relates more closely to the Greenes' earlier work, but the quality of construction details and furniture design and manufacture were far more refined than in previous houses.[26] The decorative aspect of the dining room derives primarily from the quality of the soft satin finish of the Port Orford-cedar trim, the earthy greens of the painted plaster, and the construction details—butterfly joints that connect bands of wood trim in the baseboards and chair rails along the walls, and blocked scarf joints that connect lengths of picture rail at the frieze level.

The Robinson dining-room and living-room furniture is where one can best appreciate the significantly more refined work that was now being

contributed by the Hall brothers. These pieces should be compared with the Greenes' pieces for Adelaide Tichenor, which were being made at about the time the Robinson house was in the design phase, though the Robinson furniture probably dates to early 1907.[27] The Robinson dining chair design is derived from early Ming Dynasty furniture: a gentle bow in the crest rail and a "lift" in the bottom stretchers. Corner brackets derive from Japanese construction and were pictured in the book by Edward Morse that Charles bought in late 1903. The crest rail is designed as a flowing line, continuous with the upright members. Other pieces are detailed with traditional mortise-and-tenon joinery, though without direct expression. The sleek simplicity of the chairs is echoed by the two sideboards (the larger designed in 1906 and the smaller in 1910), which are neither Ming nor Japanese, but neoclassical in mass, with only hints of Chinese influence in the flowing bands of a "lift" motif in relief across the cabinet doors, and Japanese influence in the brackets, similar to those used in temple construction. By contrast, the dining table expresses its construction directly, by way of protruding tenons in the pedestal structure, rivet-like pegs that conceal screws that attach the edge to the top, and visible butterfly joints that join the mahogany slabs of the tabletop. The shape of the top relates to the Japanese *tsuba*, sword-guard shapes collected by Charles Greene. A radical transformation had taken place since the designs of the relatively four-square Tichenor furniture. The shapes had become softer, the wood more subtly grained, and the construction far superior. The working relationship between the Greenes and the Halls had sparked a higher level of design and manufacturing. The designs demanded fine craft, but the new availability of craft expertise probably suggested to the Greenes designs they would not have attempted otherwise.

The design and construction of leaded art glass for the Robinson house was further evidence of a dramatic evolution in the Greenes' work. It was at about this time that the Greenes began to contract with Emil Lange, a German-born art-glass craftsman who had relocated to Los Angeles from Burlington, Iowa, in 1904, following a stormy separation from his wife. Lange's Iowa business was mainly in ecclesiastical windows, for which he was responsible for design as well as manufacturing. In Los Angeles he went

28

29 Henry and Emeline Greene, with son Henry Dart
   Greene, on the beach at La Jolla, Calfornia, in the
   summer of 1905.

30 **Louise Bentz house, Pasadena, 1905–06.**
   East (front) facade.

29

into business with Harry Sturdy, and their firm, Sturdy-Lange, was soon known for superior work in art glass. The decorative glass in the Robinson house appears similar to the work of Emil Lange and is most stunningly illustrated by the adjustable-height dining-room chandelier.[28] The design is a detail of a cherry tree, its fruit hanging in pairs from spreading branches. Unlike Charles Greenes' earlier designs in leaded glass, which were either broadly scenic or depicted highly focused details abstracted from nature (a single flower or leaf), the Robinson designs for the chandelier and the entry doors are like middle-field snapshots of identifiable natural elements, such as most of a tree or a length of vine. This was an important choice by Charles Greene that distinguished his leaded art-glass designs from those by other architects, and may have been made possible by Lange's expertise. Charles did not completely abandon the more tightly focused glass compositions, however, and the stylized feather design in windows for the Robinson den and upper-level hall are close to Prairie School designs in their abstraction and detail.

Although the firm was very busy the summer of 1905, Henry carved out time to take his family on a well-deserved vacation to La Jolla, a resort town north of San Diego, where they stayed at the Green Dragon Inn and played in the surf. Back in the office in the early fall, the Greenes designed a modified version of Henry's "California House" as a two-story residence for Mrs. Louise Bentz and her husband, who had commissioned the Greenes to design their retail shop in 1901. The house would not be constructed until the summer of 1906 (and would benefit from additional refinements in the Greenes' designs as a result), but the office's job number that was assigned to it places the origin of the commission in 1905. The house shares some characteristics with the second Josephine van Rossem house in plan and elevation, though the Bentz design opens more to nature in its fenestration and terraces. The interior appointments are not elaborate, but show a studied effort to bring a distinctive sense of hospitality to the environment. The entry hall opens directly to the spacious living room, where a bank of casement windows lights the southwest corner and allows for good circulation of air. Access to the side terrace was provided for through a trio of french doors on the south. The stairs begin at the back of the entry hall, effectively de-

emphasizing the family quarters and making the public space of the living room immediately inviting. The intimate dining room is secluded behind a panel door immediately to the right of the entry. An Oregon-pine sideboard, designed by the Greenes, is a commodious case piece with batten doors and keyed tenons. On the inside of its cabinet doors, the screw-head slots are aligned with each other, an obsessive detail common to the Greenes' work of this period. John Bentz was an investor in the Prospect Park development, and he hoped the house would serve as a model for the development, though this expectation was not met.[29] Though the premise of the "California House" was challenged by its lack of proliferation in Prospect Park, the design was used successfully elsewhere, always in modified form, as late as 1912.

Late in 1905, the Greenes developed project drawings for a second house for Iwan Serrurier, and designed an urban house for Mrs. L. G. and Miss Marion A. Porter in Los Angeles (now demolished). This design included a sleeping porch, treated as an outdoor room above the living spaces of the lower level. They also produced drawings, reminiscent of the Libby design, for a two-story, broad-gabled house in Santa Barbara for Mr. T. Stewart White. Like the second Serrurier house, it was never built.

Dr. William T. Bolton, a former client for whom the Greenes had designed two earlier houses, returned to them in the spring of 1906 for the design of another residence. It was to be built on Elevado Drive (now Del Mar Avenue), near the fashionable section of South Orange Grove Avenue. The commission included a full range of furniture. Dr. Bolton died before the house could be occupied, however, with only the dining-room furniture completed. His widow rented the house, partly furnished, to Mrs. Belle Barlow Bush, who continued as the Greenes' client, commissioning the remaining funiture for the house.[30] The Bolton floor plan describes a somewhat narrow rectangle, with the roof ridge positioned lengthwise to emphasize the length and horizontality of the mass of the house, all somewhat reminiscent of Henry Greene's design for the Merwin house (1904), minus the classical portico.

The Bolton house was originally distinguished by a bay of tall stairwell windows on the north elevation, studio-like, where a good amount of light and a minimum of direct sun could enter.[31] To the right of the original tall-window bay was a lancet window to light the service staircase. Casement

31 **Louise Bentz house, Pasadena, 1905–06.**
Detail of stair-hall.

32 **Louise Bentz house.**
Detail of dining-room sideboard crafted of Oregon pine.

33 **Louise Bentz house.**
Early view of house shortly after construction.

34 **Louise Bentz house.**
Elevations and section of dining sideboard.

35 **Mrs. L. G. and Miss Marion A. Porter house,
Los Angeles, 1905 (demolished).**
Details of leaded-glass lighting fixture. Pencil-on-tissue
drawing.

36 **T. Stewart White house, Santa Barbara, 1905 (project).**
Side elevation. Pencil-on-tissue drawing.

31

32

33

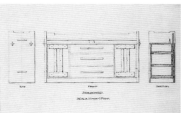

34

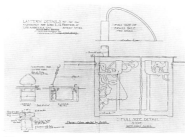

35

36

37 **Dr. William T. Bolton house #3, Pasadena, 1906 (altered).**
Entry portico on the north facade.

38 **Dr. William T. Bolton house #3.**
Detail of interior showing original furniture designed by the Greenes.

39 **Dr. William T. Bolton house #3.**
Furniture designs. Ink-on-linen presentation drawing.

40 **Dr. William T. Bolton house #3.**
South (rear) facade.

41 **Dr. William T. Bolton house #3.**
Front facade, view from the northwest.

37

38

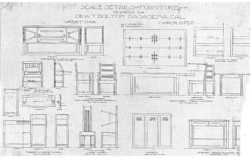

39

40

41

windows in an unusual variety of shapes and sizes answer to the specific interior functions and give the house a unique character. Designed in March 1907, the furnishings evolved from the sleek and restrained Robinson dining pieces, though the Bolton dining chairs lack overt Chinese reference. The "lift" motif (here inverted) was used only as a streamlined abstraction. Delicate inlays were indicated on the sideboard and server, showing how quickly the Greenes began to appreciate the woodworking skills now available to them through Peter and John Hall.[32] The Bolton hall chairs particularly show the proto-modernist linearity of Frank Lloyd Wright's designs of the period, but with a distinct scuptural grace. In the Bolton designs, the Greenes introduced small squares of decorative ebony inlay on the facing panels of the dining-room sideboard and server drawers. These squares, in groups of twos and threes, evolved into stand-alone square plugs that hide brass wood screws, a signature motif of the Greenes' classic furniture and interior paneling from 1907 to 1910.

While the Greenes' busy careers were progressing successfully, they also had their share of disappointments. In the spring of 1906, they designed a bridge for the Oaklawn housing tract (for which the Greenes had designed the portals and a fence). The bridge was required to connect the private Oaklawn Place roadway with Fair Oaks Avenue, a busy public thoroughfare, by crossing over a depression that contained several rights-of-way: the Atchison, Topeka and Santa Fe railroad line; the newly completed San Pedro, Los Angeles, and Salt Lake City tracks; a cycleway; and a private roadway. The initial design—an undistinguished trestle-type bridge—was discarded in favor of a more elegant crossing to consist of five gently arcing, shallow-radius spans totaling 340 feet. The form was reminiscent of a Palladian-inspired bridge that Charles Greene had seen in England while visiting the gardens at Stourhead during his honeymoon with Alice in 1901.[33] The approved design was engineered by Michael de Palo, who had a recognized history in bridge building. The general contractor was Carl Leonhardt, also a competent professional. The Greenes had worked with neither man before, however, and problems soon emerged. A waiting station was designed at the east end of the bridge to complement the Greenes' portals on the north end of the Oaklawn development, and small stone

42 **Turf bridge at Stourhead gardens, Wiltshire, England.**
Charles and Alice Greene visited these famous gardens
during their 1901 honeymoon.

43 **Oaklawn bridge and waiting station, South Pasadena,
1906** (altered).

GREENE & GREENE

42

43

44 **Oaklawn bridge and waiting station.**
South pier of waiting station, with obelisk beyond.

45 **Oaklawn bridge and waiting station.**
South side of bridge. The center pillar was added
when cracks appeared shortly after construction.

46 **Oaklawn bridge and waiting station.**
An eighteen-ton stress test performed after the bridge
was completed in 1906 produced a deflection of
three-sixteenths of an inch in the main span.

44

45

46

pillars, also meant to complement the portals, were originally to stand at the Fair Oaks end of the bridge. The idea for the portals was replaced with a design for a single obelisk, a severely modern design in keeping with the simplicity of the concrete spans.

Construction began inauspiciously when it was discovered that the developer lacked official city permission to proceed. South Pasadena's superintendent of works was instructed to halt the project. At a special meeting, urgently called by the city's board of trustees, agreement to the plans was finally reached and work resumed.[34] When the bridge was completed, and the wooden bracing removed from the steel-reinforced concrete structure, fissures of up to one-quarter-inch appeared in the arches of the bridge. As a stress test, a dead-weight load of eighteen tons was positioned at the top of the long span. This revealed a deflection of three-sixteenths of an inch, an acceptable amount from an engineering perspective. This was not sufficiently comforting to the railroad executives, however, who worried about the potential threat to the trains that would travel under the span. They insisted that remedial action be taken immediately. An extra pillar, conceived by committee after the fact, was inserted into the design, clumsily bisecting the graceful arc of the main span and ruining the purity of the design.[35] A few months later, a critical article apppeared in *Architect and Engineer* suggesting that it was not the architectural design that was at fault but the engineering specifications—in particular the faulty placement of reinforcement bars—that caused the cracking.[36] The damage to the Greenes' reputations and self-esteem, however, was done. Henry Greene's daughter later recalled her father saying that he "really went through hell" with the Oaklawn bridge, and indeed, it was the last bridge Greene and Greene would design.[37]

Also during this period, the Greenes designed a house near the Arroyo Seco on West California Street for Caroline de Forest, a first cousin of Lockwood de Forest Sr., the designer and business partner of Louis Comfort Tiffany, who had married into the de Forest family.[38] Caroline de Forest lived with a companion, Mary Callender (and eight servants), in an apartment at the Tiffany mansion at 27 East 72nd Street at Madison Avenue in New York City, where they were known for their Sunday afternoon musicales.[39] The Pasadena house that Miss de Forest had commissioned from the Greenes, then, was a seldom-used seasonal resort cottage. The modest square footage of the house is skillfully organized into generous spaces by exploiting the hillside topography and distant views, and by manipulating fenestration to lengthen sight lines and protect privacy.

The house sits on an incline—steep toward the south and more gradual toward the west—resulting in fine views in several directions. The broad gables are positioned on the side elevations, parallel to the north-south alignment of the major axis of the house and perpendicular to the street. The sweeping shed of the roof, with a small balcony cutout to give light to the upstairs bedrooms, faces the street, giving privacy to the interior in a way that recalls the F. F. Rowland house. The house is entered by following a path that winds gently down the slope from the sidewalk, along the east side of the house, past a shallow bay of casement windows, and up a short flight of steps to an entry porch. Three french doors open directly into the south-facing great room, a contiguous space based on the combined living-room–and–dining-room concept used by the Greenes where space was at a premium (the Claypole house), or expansive hospitality was the rule (the Bandini house). In the de Forest house, this space is filled with sun throughout the day due to a continuous band of casement windows along the south wall. The wide brick fireplace is flanked on one side by an inglenook bench and a narrow built-in bookcase is tucked into an alcove against the north wall. A glazed sun porch projects from the southeast corner of the living room like a transparent pavilion overlooking the steep hillside. A sitting room, bath, and kitchen occupy the street end of the plan, though they are secluded from view by the long shed of the roof. The small upstairs level—two bedrooms and a bath—is actually a half-story, attic-like space made compact by the low placement of the roof, a device that gives the house its intimate charm.

In mid-1906, more than twenty projects or jobs were in various stages of completion in the firm's office. One of these was the project that had apparently resulted from the publication of the James Culbertson house in the March 1906 issue of *Good Housekeeping*. By mid-April, the Greenes had furnished Louis K. Hyde, a banker living in suburban Plainfield, New Jersey,

47 **Caroline S. de Forest house, Pasadena, 1906.**
Bay window on the east facade.

48 **Caroline S. de Forest house.**
Living room.

49 **Caroline S. de Forest house.**
The sun porch projects from the living room over the garden .

50 **John Bakewell Phillips house, Pasadena, 1906.**
South (front) facade.

51 **Caroline S. de Forest house.**
Kitchen.

47

48

49

50

51

with a set of plans identical to the Culbertson house as it was built in 1902. Mr. Hyde's Greene and Greene house was never constructed, but the episode demonstrated how the appeal of the Greenes' work outside of California might have been limited to the more traditional styles in which they worked.[40] At about the same time, the Greenes designed a small winter retreat for Mrs. Jennie Reeve in the town of Sierra Madre, just east of Pasadena. Given the heavy workload in the Greenes' office at the time, the design of the $1,359 bungalow was probably taken on as a favor to their former client. When it was completed, Mrs. Reeve wrote to Charles Greene, saying that despite being a "small and cheap house," she found it to be "convenient and artistic … but [you] could not build even a chicken coop and not have it artistic."[41] A more typical client in 1906 was John Bakewell Phillips, who had a building budget of $10,000. Though generous by the standards of the day, this sum could produce only a spirited variation on the Greenes' generic "California House" design, probably because of the careful hand-finishing required by Peter Hall, who acted as contractor. The casement windows were the first to include a form of the Chinese "lift," an abstraction of clouds, in the horizontal muntins. This was an expensive detail that had previously been expressed only as a straight crossbar, though a suggestion of the lift had appeared in drawings for the Tichenor and Robinson doors. The stairways and halls of the three-level Phillips house form a centralized interior circulation core, thereby making the most of exterior wall surface to let light into the upper-level chambers. In a detail characteristic of traditional chalet construction, the upper two levels of the Phillips house are cantilevered slightly over the lower level on the front elevation, similar to the Garfield house and Josephine van Rossem's second speculative house. Ironically, while the Greenes' group of Arroyo Terrace houses was often referred to by writers and the general public as "Little Switzerland," it was the larger designs of the "California House" type—only one of which was in the Arroyo Terrace area—that had more in common with the traditional Swiss style of building. Even so, the resemblace was only skin deep. Elements that distinguish traditional Swiss architecture— decoratively carved verge boards and elaborate balusters and brackets— appear nowhere in the Greenes' work. Indeed, exotic influences that came to

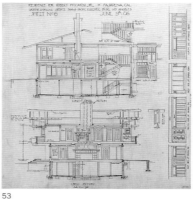

52

53

52 **Robert Pitcairn, Jr., house, Pasadena, 1906.**
   South (front) facade.

53 **Robert Pitcairn, Jr., house.**
   Sections and interior elevations. Ink-on-linen.

54 **Josephine van Rossem house #1, as altered for
   James W. Neill, Pasadena, 1906.**
   North (front) facade.

55 **Theodore Irwin, Jr., house, Pasadena, 1906–07.**
   West (front) facade.

bear on the Greenes' designs were not expressed literally, but as streamlined derivations made relevant to California's climate and topography, and the Swiss references were no exception.

In mid-1906, the Greenes' domestic designs began to express more distinctly a vocabulary of architectural detail—especially in wood— that would characterize their finest houses. They also began to manipulate indoor and outdoor spaces to take better advantage of the mild regional climate. The commission for Robert Pitcairn, Jr., the son of a wealthy and prominent Pennsylvania Railroad executive, was the first to involve the application of this vocabulary and spatial manipulation in a thoroughly coordinated way. The Pitcairns had become familiar with the Greenes' work through living in the house designed by them for Anna Hansen.[42] If the Robinson house hints at the future of the Greenes' mature vocabulary of detail, the Pitcairn house is a lexicon of their mature design elements. In massing, scale, materials, and detail, the Pitcairn house can be accurately viewed as a dress rehearsal for the Greenes' largest and most elaborate houses, since it broadly expresses the architectural identity and spirit for which their work became best known. The house combines a broad array of classic Greene and Greene devices: a shingled exterior; a roof pitch of three feet, ten inches in twelve feet; major structural timbers expressed both on the interior and exterior; deeply overhanging eaves; exposed rafters, purlins, and beams that project significantly beyond the eaves; "Malthoid" roofing that integrates rain gutters with the roof; a subtle upward sweep, or "lift" built into the ends of the ridge beam; green terra-cotta Chinese blocks set into the foundation for basement ventilation; and casement windows employed almost exclusively throughout. Most important, however, are the terraces and sleeping porches that break away from the interior floor plan to extend living space outdoors on the upper level. The Pitcairn house is the product of Peter Hall's workmen, whose distinctive finishes and careful attention to detail are evident throughout.[43] The house also displays the Greenes' continuing interest in expressing structure by adapting Japanese construction themes to regional conditions and their own aesthetic sense. In the Pitcairn house, the Greenes and Halls refined the use of the keyed scarf joint, similar to the Japanese *kanawa-tsugi*, to decoratively join, and

functionally strengthen, in-line timbers of significant length. The principle of using wedges to fix rails to posts, similar to the Japanese *kakezukuri* construction, is used here for the first time. It was also here that they pioneered the artistic use of robust wrought-iron straps to bundle posts and corbels.[44] At no time previously had all of these devices, themes, and details been employed by the Greenes in a coordinated architectural statement.

In the presentation drawings at least, an American Indian theme is also present. The original design for the front elevation shows an entry door with an anthropomorphic arrangement of paneling, with geometric arms, legs, and a head, with a leaded art-glass design that suggests the feathered headdress worn during ceremonial Navajo dances. It was intended that the "head" portion of the design be carried over to the casement windows as a repeating motif, but like the front door, this detail was discarded in favor of a simpler, less expensive treatment.

The Greene and Greene firm was hired soon after the Pitcairn house was under construction to design major alterations to expand and update the first of Josephine van Rossem's speculative houses. Its new owner, James W. Neil, a mining engineer, wanted the clapboard siding replaced with shingles, a porch added to the east side, and an entry portico on the north. The living room was expanded to incorporate the space previously used by the entry walk, and a pergola was extended over the driveway. An elaborate brick-and-boulder retaining wall with immense, buttressing piers was constructed along the sidewalk, joining it thematically to the other Greene and Greene houses along Arroyo Terrace. A narrow wooden gate set with green terra-cotta Chinese tiles was another prominent feature of the masonry screen at the sidewalk. It was as different a house as it could be from its original form, an example of the dramatic evolution in the Greenes' style over the previous three years.

At the same time, a design project was underway for Frank W. Hawks, a native of Goshen, Indiana, who had purchased the property next to the van Rossem–Neil house. Hawks was comfortably well-off, descending from the leading industrial family of Goshen and having married the heir to a Neenah, Wisconsin, paper fortune. Like so many others whose roots were in Indiana, the Hawks came to Pasadena to assume the area's relaxed lifestyle

54

55

and partake of its social and cultural benefits. The Greenes' original concept for the Hawks house combined the U-shaped plan of the second Hollister house (a veranda on one side of the courtyard) with a double-height living room, massive stone and brick fireplace, exposed king-post trusses, and iron straps to fasten timber corbels. It would have been a magnificent embellishment on the *casa de pueblo* concept behind the Bandini house, and surely would have been constructed with the great care for detail and hand finishing that the Greenes' houses of that period enjoyed. The courtyard house was never built, but the drawings leave a tantilizing clue to the adventurous thinking the Greenes were capable of in this phase of their careers.

The next project to occupy the firm was the deceptively simple idea of altering and adding to a one-and-a-half-story house. The design program and budget would allow the Greenes to draw on their burgeoning vocabulary of wooden structure and detail, but at the same time it challenged their ability to manipulate traditional, pre-existing spaces into dramatic and progressive architecture. The result was simultaneously elegant and quirky—a charming anomaly among the Greenes' houses that successfully exploited their knowledge of Japanese design, Arts and Crafts theories, and their own ability to conjure the greatest degree of beauty and serenity from a given space. It is undoubtedly one of their finest houses. The client was Theodore Irwin, Jr., the son of a wealthy industrialist and art collector from Oswego, New York. "Theo," as the younger Irwin was called, was a priviledged young man. He attended Union College in Schenectady, was a member of the Sigma Phi Society, the oldest "national" fraternity in America, and by age twenty-five had married Molly Hilliard of Anchorage, Kentucky, with no worries as to how to provide for his family. They had two daughters, Nanine and Louise. Living near the family patriarch, Theodore Irwin, Sr., Theo and his family enjoyed high social status and a comfortable, leisurely life in Oswego. Approaching middle age without yet having established a profession, however, Theo attended the Medical College of Syracuse University from 1899 to 1902, graduating at age forty-four. His father's death later that year left him with a large fortune, and rather than pursue a medical career he elected to spend his time managing (and spending) his

inheritance, and acting as curator of his father's notable library and art collection. Irwin lived in high style himself, but made an equally happy life for Molly and their two daughters.[45]

In the summer of 1901, Pasadena dressmaker Katherine Mohn Duncan moved a small house onto a lot she had purchased in Park Place at the corner of North Grand Avenue and Arroyo View Drive, becoming one of the neighborhood's earliest residents. The house was insufficient for her needs, and she expanded it, adding six rooms in 1903.[46] In January 1905, the Irwins traveled to Pasdena by rail, at which time it was their custom to reserve "two drawing rooms on a Pullman car on the first section of the fastest train out of Chicago." Once in Pasadena, they stayed at the Hotel Maryland and ultimately rented Katherine Duncan's house at 240 North Grand Avenue.[47] This was the house they would purchase, not so much for the cottage as for its spectacular site near the edge of the Arroyo Seco and for its proximity to their Chicago friends James and Nora Culbertson, who lived across the street. Probably with a referral from Culbertson, by the summer of 1906 Theodore Irwin had called on Charles and Henry Greene to redesign Katherine Duncan's house to suit his family's needs. Having already grown once before to double its size, the house would now be expanding as much again and in the process shed all trace of its former modest aspect. By early 1907 it was ready for occupancy, utterly transformed.

The Greenes' design for Mr. Irwin evokes a Japanese-inspired house made for America. In the Japanese tradition, landscape, terraces, and walkways are carefully composed to harmonize with the house and with one another. A Japanese stone lantern on the west entry walk echoes the source of influence, were there any doubt. Timber structural members are exposed here more extensively than in any previous Greene and Greene house. The brothers had seen examples of this tradition in Japanese building only in books, and at the various world's fairs they had attended, but they adopted the idea for the Irwins with characteristic confidence and a style of their own. Massive wood posts are secured to a series of timber trusses with mortise-and-tenon joinery to support the deep overhang of the upper-level balconies that shelter the northwest terrace. Supporting the terrace is a brick-and-stone serpentine wall, a Jeffersonian invention taken to its

56 Theodore, Jr., Molly, and Louise Irwin on the terrace
of their Greene and Greene home, Pasadena,
c. 1910.

57 **Theodore Irwin, Jr., house, Pasadena, 1906–07.**
First floor plan. Ink-on-linen presentation drawing.

58 **Theodore Irwin, Jr., house.**
Second floor plan. Ink-on-linen presentation drawing.

56

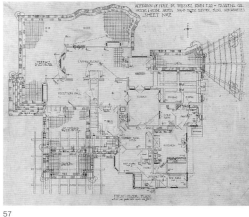

57

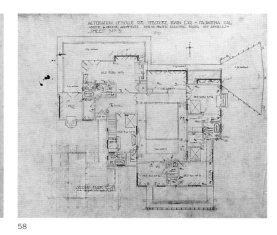

58

naturalistic extreme. On the upper level, casement windows, balcony railings, rafter tails, and protruding beam ends establish the horizontal line on the north elevation of the house. Compositional tension intrudes on the west elevation where the horizontal forces meet the vertical, two-story gabled tower and massive brick-and-boulder chimney stack. Balance is restored by the extension of the southwest terrace and pergola, an elegant massing of clinker bricks and timbers under the shade of the still-standing, original eucalyptus tree.

The various entrances to the house (there are five) were initially so unassuming that Irwin asked the Greenes to return in July 1908 to mark a more formal entry on the southwest by adding a portico and door, and to create a more welcoming and obvious pedestrian entrance by adding steps from the walkway to the terrace. Irwin was a lover of the automobile (in 1906 he had purchased the first Packard sold in Los Angeles), and so the family routinely entered from the motor court, under shelter of the dramatic, fan-shaped porte cochere near the end of the winding driveway.[48]

Entering the house under the added southwest portico and existing reception room, the visitor approaches the broad raised hearth and fireplace of the living room, where a nearby built-in window seat adds to the image of warmth and domestic comfort. Owing to the heavily trussed overhangs on the exterior, the views of the Arroyo Seco and San Gabriel Mountains can be enjoyed through a broad plate-glass window without interruption from vertical posts. As documented in a series of early photographs taken by Theodore Irwin, himself a skilled amateur photographer, the public spaces were appointed with Gustav Stickley's Craftsman line of furniture. It was a natural choice, probably suggested by the Greenes as a fitting complement to the house and to the Irwins' collection of Asian and Native American objets d'art. Indeed, the Greenes and their client painstakingly created a classic American Arts-and-Crafts environment, seemingly from (or perhaps for) the pages of *The Craftsman* magazine.[49] The Duncan-era staircase, which had terminated in the middle of the living room, was sealed by the Greenes above the first landing, resulting in a charming alcove, a kind of raised seating area. After living with this arrangement for a short time, however, the Irwins had it removed, possibly considering it to have

been too disruptive as it jutted into the main space of the living room.[50] At about the same time, probably in 1908, the opposite wall was also shifted approximately three feet north to widen the living room. Despite this, and despite the greater size of the house overall, the individual rooms within the structure still have the intimate feel of a smaller house, like the structure for which they had originally been proportioned. No imposing stair-hall or elaborate reception room was added, nor was any other architectural gesture employed on the interior to unduly impress. To the contrary, circulation within the house can be a somewhat forbidding experience to the visitor, partly because of the ambiguity of multiple entrances and the fact that the stairs are hidden in the dim of a back hallway. For residents, however, the solution to comfortable circulation is concealed in the heart of the house, in the form of an intimate fountain court that gives flexible logic to the plan. In this central space, open to the sky, the Greenes set the upper level back, both to create an exterior balcony on the upper level and to cause sunlight to filter down (through a lattice canopy) to the sheltered room-like courtyard below. French doors on all four sides of the court's patio (when left open on fine days) promote easy circulation to other areas on the ground floor, while the balcony above gives similar access to the upper rooms. More than a decade after proposing the idea for the unbuilt "Job No. 11" (1896), the Greenes returned to the concept of the interior court, open to the sky, as a means to lighten interior spaces, improve circulation, and blur the line between interior and exterior.

Just beyond the family's vestibule, with its access to the interior court, the dining room stands as the logical terminus of the visitor's journey from the North Grand Avenue walkway to the entry portico, and through the public interior areas. On the east wall of the dining room is the Greenes' first actual use of Grueby tiles in their architecture.[51] Surrounding the fireplace is a mantel, consisting of a built-in platform structure with independent supporting posts connected to the wall with expressed mortise-and-tenon joinery. Decorative bands of cedar in varing widths are composed symmetrically over the mantel in a variation on traditional Japanese interior treatments, while wood banding on the ceiling surface echoes the exotic reference. Eleven bell-shaped bulb-shades suspend whimsically from

59

GREENE & GREENE

60

61 **Theodore Irwin, Jr., house.**
Second-level gallery, chimney niche

62 **Theodore Irwin, Jr., house.**
Second-floor gallery, view to the east toward balcony.

63 **Theodore Irwin, Jr., house.**
Staircase with lancet window and transom.

62

61

63

65

64

swagged bronze chains to make up the chandelier. Wall space not occupied by casement windows is lined with plate railing supported by cedar molding and finished with a pegged lap joint. All surfaces are rounded and smoothed in the tradition of Peter Hall, who served again as contractor to the Greenes. A spacious service wing, a guest suite, and a separate garage structure with chauffeur's living space completes the lower level. The upstairs was inteneded primarily for family access judging by the narrow flight of stairs originating in the back hall. The blond softwood in the upstairs bedrooms was originally painted, though Irwin's study, and the glazed "gallery" with its exposed Oregon-pine trusses overhead, were stained dark.

Like the Robinson and Pitcairn designs, an American Indian subtheme emerges along with the more overt Japanese references, particularly in the pattern of the Grueby fireplace tiles in the northeast bedroom, which resemble the stepped or serrated-diamond design found in *saltillo sarape* textiles of the Hopi tribe. The Greenes' work continued to draw on a variety of traditions for inspiration, but rather than imitating historical designs, their interpretations merely resonate with the many forms that the brothers believed had natural relevance to Southern California.

The Greenes' design that was ultimately built for Frank W. Hawks and his family was on the boards when the major Irwin alterations were being designed. Having rejected the more elaborate earlier plan, Hawks requested a near copy of the Bentz house, which had been meant to inspire other homes in Prospect Park. The Hawks house differs in one significant respect, however, in that it includes a deep covered porch that is oddly out of proportion to the need for shelter on the shady, north-facing front elevation. The interesting result is that rather than casting shadows on a sunny surface, the projecting beam ends catch and reflect the sunlight and contrast with the profound darkness within the deep porch. The special charm of the design, however, is in the landscaping, which is executed in materials sympathetic to the neighboring houses. The brick-and-pebble-stone driveway simulates a natural creek bed meandering from the direction of what was the city's reservoir on the hill above. The middle of the driveway comes to a noticeable crest, both for drainage and aesthetic effect:

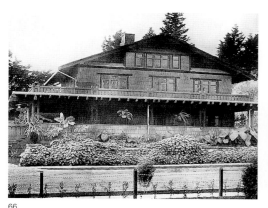

66

67

68

the roadway appears to have been worn by centuries of use. The Greenes' signature arroyo-stone pillars, with a brick cap, flank the mouth of the driveway at the sidewalk. In later years, additional courses of bricks were added and topped by lanterns inspired by Greene and Greene designs.

Between July and September 1906, Greene and Greene were busily engaged in a high volume of work. The Bolton and Pitcairn houses were under construction; one of the Pasadena Ice Company clients, Freeman A. Ford, had requested a house design that would not be settled on finally until a year later; the Bentz house, a design project begun in 1905, was now in construction; and the firm had designed two houses for Frank W. Hawks, the second of which had been accepted and was under construction by the end of August. Added to this, Charles Greene was about to begin the second-level addition to his own house, and the Robinsons' furniture would be under way soon. It was at this juncture that a commission came from Mrs. Mary E. Cole and her husband, John, who had only recently moved to Pasadena from Rochester, Minnesota. John Cole was the president of the Pasadena Milling Company, whose new building produced flour and other wheat products. Mary Cole wanted a house for her family that suited their social and business standing in the community. The lot was on Westmoreland Place, next to the home of Mrs. Cole's sister, who had married John Willis Baer, the president of Occidental College. Westmoreland Place is a short, private street whose south end abuts Arroyo Terrace. It was designed for only six private homes, whose design and construction was tightly controlled by a covenant of restrictions. The Greenes' first design for Mrs. Cole was begun about September 1906. It was thought to be too large, and so was altered to delete the den (a library was retained, however). Construction did not begin until May 1907, but the design was established in the fall of 1906. Interestingly, the accepted first-floor plan bears a resemblance to the organization of functional spaces in Hunt and Grey's plan of the proposed Robert R. Blacker house for the Oak Knoll neighborhood, under development across town. The Blacker plan had been published in *Architectural Record* in October 1906, and though the Greenes would later win the Blacker commission away from Hunt and Grey, they retained the essential features of the original U-shaped floor plan.

The Greenes' plan for the Cole house is essentially an H-shape, but the grouping of spaces is similar to the published Blacker plan by Hunt and Grey. The dining and kitchen areas are separated from the living room and library wing by a transverse stair-hall that overlooks the garden through doors directly opposite the entry. The Cole plan also called for a prominent porte cochere on the front of the house (a concept that the Greenes later added to the Hunt and Grey plan for the Blackers). If general features for the Mary Cole house had been suggested to the Greenes by the published Hunt and Grey plan, the execution of the final design and its details were thoroughly Greene and Greene and the work of their favored contractor, Peter Hall. With the Greenes' structural and material conventions established in the Robinson, Pitcairn, and Irwin house designs, the Cole commission allowed the Greenes to focus increasingly on decorative treatments. Rookwood tiles were specified for selected fireplaces: green for the living room, green and dark blue for the dining room, blue-grey for one of the bedrooms, and light cream for another.[52] Most notably, the Greenes indulged their famously artistic interest in arroyo boulders, both for the pillars that support the porte cochere and for the monumental chimneys that rise through the eaves on the north and south elevations. The half-architectural, half-sculptural chimneys rely equally on normal building principles and a bizarre reverse physical logic. The massive boulders look as though they had been dropped from the sky, in the way that sand castles are created at the beach by dripping wet sand from above. Indeed, at a certain level, the chimney's stones appear to "float" in a background of stucco, as if caught in mid-fall. Significantly wider at the bottom, the stack of rocks eventually gives way to dash-coat stucco and a brick cap, over which a more slender, stuccoed stack is whimsically embossed with two "eyes" that cause the tops to resemble the heads of American Indian dolls in the Hopi Kachina tradition.[53]

Inside, the spaces are proportionally well balanced and sober, and exquisitely hand finished in the best tradition of Peter Hall's craftsmen. The oak library, with its angled fireplace of carefully shaped brick, lies inside the entry to the left, echoing the Robinson den. In the living room, a pair of inglenook benches with brass and wood inlay originally flanked the

69 **Mary E. Cole house, Pasadena, 1906–07 (altered).**
West and south elevations. Ink-on-linen presentation
drawing.

70 **Mary E. Cole house.**
First floor plan. Ink-on-linen presentation drawing.

71 **Mary E. Cole house.**
South chimney built with massive Arroyo Seco boulders.

72 **Mary L. Ranney house, Pasadena, 1907 (altered).**
East (front) facade prior to addition of the
northwest wing.

73 **Charles W. Leffingwell ranch house, Whittier, 1907
(demolished).**
This ranch-hand bunkhouse and office, whose
massing recalls the Bolton house of 1906, was
designed by Mary L. Ranney in the Greene and
Greene firm.

74 **Mary L. Ranney house.**
Contemporary view with 1912 addition.

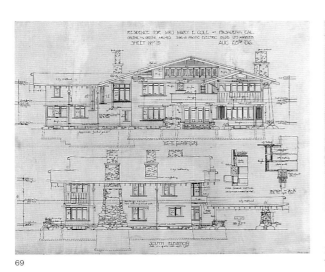

69

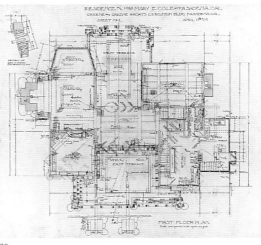

70

71

fireplace, where above the mantle was carved the motto "Home Keeping
Hearts are Happiest." A glazed bay at the west end of the room provided
views of the arroyo. A tiled terrace, now enclosed, was conceived as a
sheltered outdoor room, also with views to the west. In various parts of the
house, leaded art-glass panels depict abstracts from nature in close-up:
portions of grape vines are shown in the stair-landing transom, and in the
dining room, five leaded-glass panels, now removed, depicted a branch of
cherry-red blossoms.[54] With so many decorative and artistic additions to
their architecture, however, the Greenes crossed a subtle but symbolic line.
Metal, leaded art glass, and decorative tiles were now being used not merely
as color and texture, but as canvas for Charles Greene's artistic impulses.
The rapid refinement of the Greenes' architectural designs had just as
suddenly led to a high-art sensibility in decoration. Nor were they alone in
the elevation of Arts and Crafts ideals to a new decorative level. Harvey
Ellis had begun introducing his stylish inlays to Gustav Stickley's furniture
designs in 1903, and one could argue in any event that this tendency had
come from England, the birthplace of the movement, even earlier. The
Greenes' designs were less stylized in their representation of nature,
however. In his decorative designs for the firm, Charles Greene did not
consult conventional grammars of ornament. His inspiration came from the
land and sky around him. He sketched from direct observation, the blossoms
and branches for his decorative inlays modeled by those he came upon while
wandering through the parklands of the Arroyo Seco, or occasionally from
photographs of nature in the many books and magazines he kept.[55] A lively
new muse was at work for the firm, bringing fine art to craft in the building
and decorative arts.

It continued to be a period of intense activity for Greene and Greene,
and the office staff swelled to keep pace with the workload. Between 1906
and 1908, talented apprentices, some of whom were on summer break from
their formal architectural educations, joined the firm to learn what they
could, much as the Greenes had done in Boston fifteen years before.
The office was an invaluable proving ground, and as one former acolyte in
the firm reminded the Greenes in 1948, "just about every architect in
Pasadena got his start in your office...."[56] There was an air of instruction as

72

73

74

well as duty, judging by the pithy saying that was posted on an office wall for the edification of the drafting staff: "If you don't do any more than you get paid for, you will never get paid for any more than you do." Among the office staff who worked for the Greenes were Sylvanus Boardman Marston, John Cyril Bennett, Mary L. Ranney, Margaret Armstrong, Samuel B. Morris, Philip Hubert Frohman, Deland W. Harris, Leonard W. Collins, Roy Parkes, Joseph Lippiatt, Leslie Lippiatt, John Vawter, and Huntington Barker.[57] Some of these, including Marston, Bennett, Frohman, Vawter, and Harris, became noted architects. Others, such as Mary Ranney, abandoned architecture altogether to pursue a career in other fields. Leonard Collins remained with the Greenes as a draftsman for many years. Most of the Greene and Greene office staff, however, remain nearly anonymous, known only by the penciled initials that appear on architectural tracings that survive from the office records.[58]

Before going on to establish Pasadena's Westridge School for Girls in 1913, Mary Ranney proved to be the most talented draftsperson and designer working for the Greenes. She was allowed to claim official credit for at least two of the designs she executed in the office, a rare honor for a non-principal in a firm of the period. Miss Ranney's own house was the first of these, and the last of the Greene and Greene designs in Park Place.[59] The house was a simple, two-story rectangular block that nonetheless exhibited many of the signature characteristics of the firm's work: wooden construction, structural expression, asymmetrical fenestration, clinker-brick foundation walls, and a highly restrained approach to decoration. Whereas the terrace areas close to the house are regular and linear, the composition of the walkway and short flight of steps to the sidewalk has some of the sculptural quality of Charles Greene's more skilled masonry designs. According to the inscription on the drawings, the house was "designed by Mary L. Ranney in the office of Greene & Greene, Architects."

Ranney was soon chosen again to execute a design for the Leffingwell Rancho, an office and bunkhouse attached to a citrus-growing ranch in Whittier, California, twenty miles southeast of Pasadena. The client, Charles Warring Leffingwell, was the son of an Episcopal rector from Knoxville, Illinois, who had come to Southern California during the building boom of

the 1880s and purchased five hundred acres of arable land near Whittier. For years he struggled; the lemon groves he planted became diseased. Water was scarce. Putting his son in charge of the operation, Leffingwell financed new plants and irrigation, and the ranch began to turn a profit. In 1899, the younger Leffingwell married Virginia Preston Rowland, daughter of the Greenes' 1903 client, Dr. Francis Fenelon Rowland. By 1907, the lemon groves had become successful and Leffingwell hired his father-in-law's architects to improve the rancho with a new office and bunkhouse block. The Leffingwell Rancho was a two-story, shingled design with modest asymmetry and a vast sheltering portico supported by substantial timbers. Like Miss Ranney's own house, the simplicity she envisioned became its finest quality. If Ranney had had a mentor in the office it was probably Henry Greene, whose work consistently exhibited the same keen eye for reduction. Charles, by contrast, was on the brink of exploring more elaborate artistic avenues in his architecture and furniture designs.

5

The Tree of Life

There is in wood something that stimulates the imagination, its petalous sheen, sinuous grain, delicate shading that age may give to even the commonest kind.
—Charles S. Greene [1]

1 Page 104:
David B. Gamble house, Pasadena, 1907–09.
Stair railing and leaded art-glass entry doors.

2 Robert R. Blacker estate, Pasadena, 1907–09.
North (front) facade of main house, with covered terrace to the east (left) and porte cochere to the west (right).

2

Early in 1907, the Greenes entered the most demanding phase of their careers. News of their home designs had circulated widely in national magazines since 1902, and potential clients of exceptional discrimination and significant wealth continued to arrive in Pasadena each winter to stay at the resort hotels. Many decided to build homes, either for winter use or retirement. Several factors were conducive to the Greenes' success during this period. At thirty-eight and thirty-seven, respectively, Charles and Henry were at the height of their combined creative energies. Charles had significantly refined his approach to designing furniture, lighting fixtures, and other decorative arts, and Henry made certain that the drafting staff in the office could reliably reinterpret the challenging conceptual sketches produced by his brother. These were then converted into precise, dimensioned drawings that guided the various craftsmen in their work. Henry also shepherded the less elaborate commissions in and out of the office with skill and efficiency, helping to keep finances afloat.

The Greenes had been working with Peter Hall since 1904, and the relationship had become stronger through the next two years. Charles Greene had hired Peter Hall to execute the alterations to his own house on Arroyo Terrace, and by late 1906 the Greenes had come to enjoy and expect a high level of professionalism and craftsmanship from the men employed by Hall. Peter's quieter brother, John, a cabinetmaker, offered the Greenes the competence and continuity to reliably execute the furniture designs they submitted. But more than that, it seems that the Halls had also given the Greenes the confidence to design with greater freedom. Charles's dreams were no longer constrained by the technical limitations of inconsistent or inaccurate execution, as they had been in the past. This allowed him, as lead designer for the firm, to search his own creativity to an even greater degree. Increasingly progressive and artistic designs resulted, stimulated largely by the individuals that Charles and Henry Greene counted on (especially the Halls and Emil Lange) to transform their sketches and specifications into houses and objects of remarkable beauty and soundness.

Robert Roe Blacker, a native of Brantford, Ontario, moved to Manistee, Michigan, by the age of twenty-one and made a fortune in the booming lumber industry during his nearly forty-year career.[2] His second wife, Nellie

Celeste Canfield Blacker, was also wealthy, being the eldest daughter of John Canfield, another successful Manistee lumber baron. In 1906, at age sixty, Robert Blacker and his wife retired to Pasadena, where they commissioned the nationally known team of Myron Hunt and Elmer Grey to design a large residence for them on five-and-a-half acres of land in the exclusive, but as yet sparsely developed Oak Knoll tract. Oak Knoll had been subdivided in 1886 during the land boom that followed the opening of rail service from the Midwest. It had been the first Pasadena neighborhood with streets laid out relative to the natural contours of the terrain, an idea pioneered by Frederick Law Olmsted in the Chicago suburb of Riverside, Illinois.[3] The land boom was followed by a slump, however, before any Oak Knoll parcels were sold. Oak Knoll stood empty—save for grazing sheep— until 1905, when real estate developer William R. Staats joined railroad magnate Henry E. Huntington to try again, this time during a stronger land market. Blacker was one of the first to purchase along the winding, tree-lined streets. His was the most prominent site, a peninsula jutting into the middle of the development surrounded by the tract's principal streets. In February 1907, in its twenty-second annual exhibition catalogue, the Architectural League of New York published a perspective rendering of the proposed "Residence and Garden for Mr. R. R. Blacker," submitted by Hunt and Grey. As viewed from the southeast, it depicts the rear elevation of a large, stuccoed villa surrounded by formal walled gardens with pathways, a pond, and even a mission-style arch over a stile that was to give access to the east lawn. The interior plan of the first floor had been published in *Architectural Record* as early as October 1906.[4] By the following month, however, the Greene and Greene name appeared on the survey sheets, indicating that Mr. Blacker had released Hunt and Grey and named new architects for the project.[5]

The Blackers' site, like the Robinson site, was far bigger than those to which the Greenes were accustomed. Charles Greene had dreamed of creating an estate on this scale, as evidenced by the "Proposed Dwelling for W. B. T." he submitted to the architectural competition at the 1904 Louisiana Purchase Exposition in St. Louis. The Blacker project was real, however, and would give the Greenes many opportunities to push their

3

4

5

talents to a new level. They chose to site the house in the northwest quadrant of the property, on high ground near the corner of Hillcrest and Wentworth avenues, west of Hunt and Grey's originally proposed site. The Greenes' positioning allowed for sweeping views down from the house toward the lower reaches of the lot, and presented numerous opportunities for dramatic landscaping. Most notable was the Greenes' plan to create a rock-lined pond—complete with a footbridge to a small island—planted generously with lotuses, papyrus, lilies, and other water-loving plants. Indeed, the Indian lotus (*Nelumbium speciosum*) would become the decorative thematic identity within the main residence itself.[6] The initial landscape scheme introduced fully mature trees as well as new plants, striking a balance that created a showcase garden from the beginning, and the Blackers' landscape was a visible feature from nearly every part of the house. The front entry was placed on axis with clear-glazed french doors at the far end of the entry hall, so that the view to the south was immediately seen upon entering the house. Along this line of sight, native palm trees and low shrubs flanked a swath of grass that terminated in a distant crescent of trees at the bottom of the lot. To the right, a wisteria-laden pergola filtered the view toward the garage structure, a two-story outbuilding (now enlarged into a private residence) that was linked by a second pergola to a keeper's cottage, which was shrouded in climbing roses. Beyond that, a delicate lath house, since demolished, was placed near the southwest corner of the property to supply plants for the vast grounds. A third pergola, in the northeast sector of the property, was designed and constructed in 1910 as a free-standing garden retreat, and acted as a focal point along the cypress-lined axis projecting east from the living-room terrace of the main house. In total, the grounds comprised four distinct sectors: the house, with its distinctive porte cochere, adjacent terraces, and sheltered rear courtyard; the formal allée of palms and adjacent pergolas and outbuildings to the south; the naturalistic pond area with its free-form island, exotic plants, and nearby pergola; and finally, the open, grassy, park-like area sloping to the southeast. Subdivided for housing following Mrs. Blacker's death in 1947, the extensive original gardens can be seen now only in photographs, and few remnants of the original plantings remain.

Construction of the main residence commenced in late spring of 1907, following completion of the outbuildings. Building contractors Dawson and Daniels had been hired to construct the outbuildings and frame the main house. It was the only time they would act as contractors to Greene and Greene. This firm, however, appears to have subcontracted with many of Peter Hall's laborers, since the surviving wage log for 1907 shows William Issac Ott—an associate of Peter Hall—as working on the Blacker site. Throughout April 1907, John Hall is also listed. Ott supervised an average weekly workforce of about a dozen men, including his son Leslie, but during the busy week of April 13, 1907, a total of twenty-eight men worked full-time on the construction site under Ott's supervision. Nine carried the title of carpenter, the balance being masons, plasterers, plumbers, and laborers.[7] The grading, foundation, sewer lines, framing, and exteriors occupied the better part of a year to complete, after which Peter Hall was formally engaged to execute the Blacker interiors. John Hall had also opened an independent workshop in 1907 to accommodate the Greenes' furniture commissions, but he would not be building the Blacker furniture until 1909, following completion of the Robinson, Bolton, and Gamble pieces.[8]

In scale and quality, the Blacker house was unlike anything the Greenes had ever undertaken. At their disposal was a seemingly limitless budget.

6

7

8

9

7 **Robert R. Blacker estate, Pasadena, 1907–09.**
Main pier and timber structure supporting porte cochere.

8 **Robert R. Blacker estate.**
Detail of iron straps and wedges that bind major beams
on north facade.

9 **Robert R. Blacker estate.**
Southeast wing comprising master suite and balcony
above, and guestroom below.

10 **Robert R. Blacker estate.**
Entry hall.

10

11

12   13

Equally important were Mr. Blacker's connections within the lumber business, which made it possible for the Greenes and the Halls to have access to the finest quality woods for framing, interiors, and furniture. This was critical to the future of the firm, since the Greenes had had a potentially embarrassing problem with twisted timbers on the entry portico of the Robinson house. With the fundamental requirements on the Blacker house assured, the Greenes set about designing the most elaborate masterpiece of their classic style. The elevations drew on basic forms they had developed in earlier drawings for the Pitcairn, Ford, Irwin, and Cole houses, and Charles Greene's own house had provided further opportunity to refine the specific wood vocabulary to be used in the Blacker house. What distinguishes the exterior most visibly is the porte cochere, a titanic structure that rakes acutely toward the street, throwing off balance the otherwise rational symmetry of the main mass. The pier supporting the end of the porte cochere is again resonant with Hopi Kachina forms with timber "arms" and clinker-brick "body" and "legs." Balancing the porte cochere is the northeast terrace, with an overhang that extends from the corner of the east gable into the garden. Both the porte cochere and the terrace roof are deep projections echoed in the overhangs of the eaves around the perimeter of the house. Exposed rafters, purlins, and beams cast shifting shadows along the exterior walls. On the rear of the house, the west balcony on the second level promoted enjoyment of the garden views, though it was enclosed in 1914 to create a year-round interior space. Because of the visible position of the house within the Oak Knoll tract, no one elevation could be considered less important than another; the service porch, for example, was designed with detailing and sensitivity equal to the other elevations. Mortise-and-tenon joints, scarf joints, butterfly joints, iron straps and wedges, profiled beam ends, and sculpted copper downspouts are all placed and executed with due respect for their contribution to the total design, regardless of location.

One is prepared for the entry into a dimmer environment by the passage under the robust timbers of the porte cochere. Past the leaded art-glass doors, whose design suggests the rays of the sun, the teak-paneled entry hall is subtly divided into three distinct zones. Each is marked by a change in ceiling height or a change in the orientation of overhead beams. In the first zone, the low ceiling and dim, golden ceiling light create an intimate and comfortable transition to the second, a small reception area. Here, Greene-designed furniture—a teak bench, a cabinet, and a hanging mirror—were originally placed to serve family or visitors entering or leaving the house. Distinct from this is the third zone, the main body of the hall, where the overhead beams are at ninety degrees to those in the initial entry area. For the Blackers, the main hall served as a vast, light-filled sitting room with a full complement of furnishings, including a second cabinet surmounted by a telephone box, a settle with an adjustable back, "Morris" chairs, a library table, and small footstools. A tall, pagoda-like teak lantern with panels of intricately leaded iridescent glass hangs from the center of the hall, while its smaller counterparts hang from beams in the corners, all casting a soft glow. From here, the view of the palm allée to the south could be enjoyed.[9]

On the east side of the hall, the main staircase rises to a landing alongside a triple-thickness baseboard panel whose gentle arcs flow from riser to riser like a cascading stream. At the landing, a leaded art-glass oriel window borrows exterior light through the design of a grapevine that rises through a dense trellis structure in the lower panels and climbs free of it in the upper casement panels. Behind the east wall of the stair-hall lies the living room, a mahogany-paneled space from which a rich palette of colors glows. The fireplace is surfaced with Grueby tiles in mauve, accented with burnt-red tile chips in a modified *tsuba* shape. Six leaded art-glass and mahogany-frame lanterns depicting lotuses and lilies hang by leather straps from box beams on the ceiling. Golden lotuses and lilies on the ceiling catch reflected light from the lanterns, contrasting with the matte olive-brown earthtone of the ceiling's background color. Surrounding the room, a sculpted-relief frieze of lotuses is covered entirely in golden metal leaf. Mahogany brackets and truss-like trim pieces are applied to the course of the frieze as if to bring a pergola-like structure indoors.[10] A bronzed "old copper" fire screen, designed in 1914, is also embellished with lotuses, and with handles cast in an abstracted cloud design similar to that illustrated in the pages of Morse's *Japanese Homes and Their Surroundings*.[11] A richly

14 **Robert R. Blacker estate, Pasadena, 1907–09.**
Detail of teak staircase post and mahogany lantern
in entry hall.

15 **Robert R. Blacker estate.**
Living-room frieze relief depicting lotuses, the
symbolic device of the house.

16 **Robert R. Blacker estate.**
First-floor guest bath.

14

15

16

inlaid desk (1908), music cabinet (1909), and table lamp (1912) were designed for the room, along with sufficient chairs and sofas to fill the large space.

To the east of the living room, a broad terrace extends the living space outdoors. Illuminated by large copper lanterns paneled in iridescent glass, the terrace is paved in eight-inch terra-cotta tiles and edged with clinker bricks. Overhead, large posts, beams, and trusses of Oregon pine support a balcony roof above, and create a shaded outdoor room beyond the northeast corner of the house. In the days when the original gardens were intact, this terrace was one of the departure points for visits to the east gardens, including the free-form lotus pond and the pergola structure that lay beyond an avenue of lawn marked by potted topiaries. Through a narrow passage from the living room is situated the formal guest room, a one-story pavilion with windows on three sides for views of the pond, south garden, and inner court. Leaded art-glass and mahogany lanterns and sconces shed soft, golden light through a design of stylized flowers on the sides and an abstracted step-pyramid on the front panels. A full, tiled bath includes an elaborate shower appliance and leaded, opalescent art-glass windows to shed artistic, soft light and provide privacy. The Blackers, who later became important benefactors of the California Institute of Technology, would often accommodate visiting lecturers and professors in this guest suite.

On the opposite side of the house, the dining area occupies the lower level of the southwest wing. Extending like another pavilion into the garden, these rooms receive daylight on three sides. Removable glass doors separate the breakfast room from the formal dining area without blocking light from one to the other. For large groups, the doors could be removed and the breakfast and dining tables joined to seat twelve. Leaded art-glass casement transoms in an abstracted sun-with-clouds design enhance the intimate space of the breakfast room, while bookmatched, vertical grain panels of mahogany line the dining area. Originally, cherry blossoms were painted onto the canvas frieze (now missing), bringing a vision of nature indoors. In both the dining and breakfast room, chandeliers of delicately perforated mahogany with stained and leaded art-glass panels were suspended from leather straps blocked with mahogany medallions in *tsuba*

shapes. Abstracted cloud, fish-scale, and butterfly forms decorate the bottom panels. The dining furniture, like that of the living room and entry hall, has a distinct identity. A vertically oriented, carved pattern of waves carries through chairs and sideboard, and square-plug inlays of ebony, with vine-like twists of mother-of-pearl and metal wire, stand proud of the surfaces. Echoes of these motifs appear in the breakfast table and servers. The sideboard's drawer pulls float like clouds on a background of wispy mahogany grain. Dark-green Grueby fireplace tiles are accented with smaller rust-red and golden-yellow squares. In the upstairs guest bedroom, Rookwood field tiles with decorative fragments of Grueby tile depict a climbing vine in the fireplace. A riveted copper hood is chased in a design of cloud-like smoke that rises in volcanic plumes from above the fire box below. Throughout the house, the repetition of motifs symbolizing the elements—earth (vines), water (clouds and waves), and fire (sun-like shapes)—became fundamental to the decorative order that emerged in the Greenes' work in 1907. The symbols would gain increasingly deep spiritual significance for Charles Greene, and would continue to appear in his work in the years to come.

While the Blacker outbuildings were under construction, the Greenes were attempting to resolve a nearly year-long project to design a house for Freeman A. Ford, vice-president of the Pasadena Ice Company. Ford had come to the Greenes in the summer of 1906 to commission a house to occupy a site north of his brother's property and immediately south of his long-time family friends, Henry and Laurabelle Robinson. In September 1906, the Greenes had presented their plans for a distinctive courtyard house with a stucco finish and half-timbering on the exterior walls of an upper-level sleeping porch, a treatment that would have complemented the Robinson house exterior very well. Ford requested another scheme, however, which was not presented until May 16, 1907. The delay was probably the result of the substantial previous design commitments the Greenes had made to the Blackers, the Coles, and other clients. By then, the Greenes had made significant progress toward the mature state of their signature wood style, and their second design for Mr. Ford exhibited a more even balance between horizontal and vertical masses, and the articulation of structural wood that had become their trademark style.

17

18

19

17 **Robert R. Blacker estate.**
Second-floor guest room fireplace with hand-hammered copper hood depicting plumes of smoke.

18 **Robert R. Blacker estate.**
French doors open from the living room to a sheltered terrace on the east side of the house.

19 **Robert R. Blacker estate.**
Living room table lamp designed by Charles Greene, 1912. Long thought to be lost, this important piece, demonstrates the dramatic evolution in the Greenes' decorative arts when compared with the Robinson table lamp of 1906 (see fig. 24, p. 81).

20 **Freeman A. Ford house, Pasadena, 1906–08 (altered).** Contemporary view of courtyard, pool, and entry door.

21

Freeman A. Ford house. View of courtyard showing original double-height, gabled construction over entry, c. 1914.

22

Freeman A. Ford house. East facade as viewed from auto court. Steps at right lead to courtyard entry.

23 **Freeman A. Ford house.** The anthropomorphic structure of the entry door and feather design of the art glass suggest a Native American ritual dancer.

20

21

22

The design differed significantly from the Blacker and Cole houses, however, because of the dramatic site it was to occupy high above the Arroyo Seco. The interim Ford design focused on maximizing opportunities to appreciate the beauty of the arroyo by giving views to most of the interior spaces on the west side of the house. On this elevation, the Greenes designed the rooms with wide plate-glass windows, bands of casements, and broad, deep balconies. This visually dramatic approach was rejected, however, and the original, single-level courtyard scheme was ultimately approved with only minor revisions.[12] As constructed, the house is unique within the Greenes' work. The plan relates nominally to the 1903 Bandini courtyard house, but there is far greater formality in the Ford design. The organization of the courtyard space suggests a focus on privacy, rather than easy circulation or hospitality. Opportunities for access from the interior to the courtyard are more limited than in the Bandini plan (or compared with historical *casa de campo* antecedents). The Ford house sits well away from the street on the eastern edge of the arroyo's escarpment. The driveway winds toward the high point of the site and curves gently to meet the wide, brick entry stairs flanked by jardinieres and planter boxes. Just past the top of the stairs, a covered pergola connects the south wing of the house to the north, giving the visitor a sense of entering the privacy of an inner court. As originally conceived, the materials of the courtyard were hard and finished in light earthtone colors, the ensemble producing an austere yet bright and open space.[13] The low surface of the original grey malthoid roof echoed the reflective expanse of hardscape: tile pavers, brick steps, and planter platforms, stucco exterior walls, and a pebble-dash fountain. The sheltering form of the deep eaves and exposed rafters, and the jeweled color of the entry door, however, transformed the shady edges of the court into an inviting sanctuary.

The distinctive ambience of this court may have been suggested by a building that Charles Greene had seen during his visit to the St. Louis Fair in 1904. A photograph of the German pavilion, designed by Joseph Maria Olbrich, was one of the first entries Charles made in the St. Louis portion of his scrapbook, and shows an interior courtyard fountain that compares closely with the Ford courtyard. Several more illustrations of the interiors

24 Dining tabletop from Freeman A. Ford house,
    Pasadena, 1906–08. The top, almost imperceptibly
    oval-shaped, shows a delicate inlay of contrasting
    woods in a design of creeping vines.

25 Serving table for dining room, Freeman A. Ford house.
    Photographed in the workshop of John Hall, c. 1907.

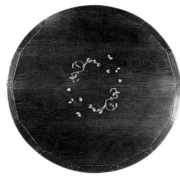

24

25

were included on the following scrapbook pages.[14] Beyond the Ford court, through the front door, an intimate entry hall acted as a small transitional space. A rich palette of bright blue, green, and cream-colored glass is arranged around the inner wooden members of the entry door in a peacock-feather design that extends to the transom lights. These inner wooden members are in the form of a stylized human figure, so that the panel of wood and glass together depicts a feathered, anthropomorphic figure reminiscent of American Indian ceremonial dancers. The Hopi tradition of the Butterfly Dance, in particular, involves participants wearing a *tableta*, or flat headdress adorned with feathers.[15] Behind the entry, a study was originally reached by way of a passage on the right, from which a flight of stairs led to a loft space. The loft and stairs were later removed and the ceiling lowered to eliminate the study and create a deeper, but lower, entry hall. To the left of the entry, steps lead down to the living room, which is paneled in Port Orford "white" cedar. A smooth, brick fireplace and secluded inglenook area are immediately to the right, in a windowless corner lighted by one intricately leaded art-glass and mahogany light fixture mounted flush to the ceiling. Additional hanging lanterns in metal and glass also bring soft light to the dim recesses of the room. Beyond the fireplace area, large windows and a balcony give spectacular views of the ravine below and hills to the west.

On the south wall, steps up to a long passage communicate with the family bedrooms. Moving from west to east, each room projects successively further beyond the main mass of the house to allow for corner windows, improved air circulation, and views. A nursery, located at the end of the hall on the left, is accessible directly from the courtyard, and a narrow flight of stairs leads from the hall to a second-level sleeping porch, originally echoing the loft over the entry. This was a typically spirited gesture, probably designed by Charles Greene, to attempt to amplify the possibilities of outdoor living for his clients. On the opposite wing of the house, the dining room, like the living room, has a dim zone just inside and a brighter zone beyond, where casement windows on the northwest corner of the room give more views of the arroyo. Probably to mitigate the dimness, Charles Greene had wanted to apply 256 square feet of gold leaf in the living room and

dining room—similar to the decorative frieze and ceiling in the Blacker house—but the Fords declined.[16] The pantry, kitchen, side porch, and servants' quarters complete the north wing, behind which is the garage, set back to the east.

While the essential concept of the Ford house dates from the fall of 1906, its construction took place from July 1907 to March 1908.[17] The chronology of commissions during this period is significant, since it establishes not only the large quantity but also the high quality of activity in the Greene and Greene office. The Blacker outbuildings were begun in April 1907; construction began at the Cole house in mid-May; the two design revisions for Freeman Ford were presented in May and June; and furniture was being crafted from the Greenes' designs for the Robinson and Bolton houses. There was also a suite of living-room and dining-room furniture to be designed and produced for Freeman Ford. The Ford furniture included an unusual round dining table, with host chairs and side chairs in dark mahogany. A design of leafy stems and flower petals inlaid with contrasting woods decorates the tabletop. The dining server is plain, and has the proportions and simplicity of the Greenes' most austere work, lacking inlays or elaborately expressed joinery. Small square ebony caps, arranged with no discernible decorative pretense, cover the brass screws that secure the components of the base. Ebony splines join the table slab to its ends. The thin, broad top cantilevers beyond the rails and stiles of the base, producing a serene horizontal line. The living-room furniture included an upholstered couch that resembled a similar piece for the Robinson house, and a wingback chair with deep side panels. Some pieces merited Charles Greene's more fanciful treatments, such as a tabourette with silver wire inlay in the top surface depicting a twisted vine running through thin, straight lines that suggest cloud abstractions. Because of the Fords' ultimate rejection of the second house design, and the return to the 1906 concept, the resulting house had evolved into a hybrid of the Southwest adobe-stucco aesthetic of the Robinson house, and the articulated wood construction of the newer designs for the Coles and the Blackers. It was this wooden building language that would consume the Greenes' professional practice for the next three years.

26 David B. Gamble house, Pasadena, 1907–09.
Deep overhanging eaves shelter the upper-level
sleeping porches on the west facade.

27 David B. Gamble house.
View from the northwest (from the garden).
Numerous porches and terraces extend toward the
surrounding grounds and provide views of the natural
landscape beyond.

26

27

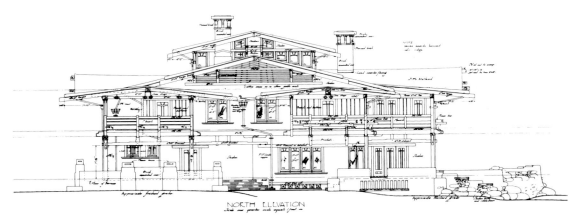

NORTH ELEVATION

28

David Berry Gamble was one of ten children of James Gamble, a co-founder of the Procter and Gamble Company, the highly successful soap and tallow concern based in Cincinnati, Ohio. In the early years of the new century, David Gamble and his wife, Mary Huggins Gamble, had come with their three sons and Mary's sister "Aunt Julia" Huggins to Pasadena to stay in the city's famous resort hotels during the winter seasons. In May 1907, they decided to purchase the largest parcel along Westmoreland Place, two lots north of Mary Cole's Greene and Greene house, for which ground had just been broken. The Cole house and the Arroyo Terrace enclave of Greene and Greene houses were easily within view to the south, and must have made a strong architectural impression on the Gambles. Within days of the purchase of the land the local newspapers announced that the Greenes had been commissioned to design the Gambles' new house.[18] Mature eucalyptus trees shaded the high point of the site, from which fine views of the riverbed and the mountains beyond could be had. This is where the Greenes chose to place the house, not only for the views and shade, but for the cooling breezes that came down the arroyo. The first design the Greenes presented to the Gambles was for a house of U-shaped plan, with a garage and service wing appended. It was a plan for a relaxed, informal lifestyle, designed to fully exploit the views and natural features of the site. Perhaps too informal, the concept was rejected in favor of a second scheme that proposed a more traditional and compact floor plan, positioned at an angle to the street. The plan itself was adopted, but the convenant of restrictions governing Westmoreland Place stipulated that the front elevation of all houses had to be parallel to the street. The footprint of the house had to be shifted a few degrees clockwise. Similar to the situation of the Blacker house plan inherited from Hunt and Grey, the Greenes had once again been challenged to work creatively through unforeseen external requirements. The design process for the residence was largely completed by February 1908, and a construction permit was issued on March 9, 1908. Fixtures and furnishings would be designed and executed over the next two years, but the Gambles were able to occupy the house during the 1909–10 winter season.[19] The Gambles made their wishes known with regard to design details (Charles Greene's notations about Mrs. Gamble's specific requirements survive on

scraps of yellow paper), but overall, the Gambles had sufficient confidence in their architects to depart for an extended tour of Asia while the house was under construction.[20]

The aspects of the house that are most notable from the street are two elements in contrast: a traditional gabled elevation on the south, and a deep terrace with a heavily timbered sleeping porch on the north, jutting away from the primary mass of the house to claim a central aesthetic role in the overall design. The two disparate elements are unified, however, by the shared horizontal line of deep eaves and exposed rafters and beams, and by the simple rhythm of the split-redwood-shake surface. The broad mass of the first and second levels is given height and balance by the one-room, third-level attic space. The attic idea had been borrowed from the second residential design scheme for Freeman Ford, who had rejected it just weeks before the Greenes began design work on the Gamble house.

The driveway, of bricks laid in a chevron pattern, was designed to disappear behind the sculpted half-ellipse of lawn separating the house from the sidewalk. The separate garage structure, embedded along the north property line of the site, resonates with the design of the house. As on the garage the Greenes had designed for the Blackers, a series of massive iron strap hinges were shaped with respect to the structure, creating a harmony between the materials that is echoed in the iron details of the main residence.

The north and rear elevations of the house are devoted to outdoor life. Each of three sleeping porches—screenless outdoor rooms defined by robust timber posts and railings, board-and-batten paneling, and dramatically deep eaves—challenges the distinction between interior and exterior on the mid-level of the house. These porches, in turn, shelter the recesses of the terraces below: large expanses of terra-cotta mission tiles with edges, steps, and paths in contrasting fire-brick. The terraces are elevated behind imposing walls: a brick foundation wall coated with pebble-dash on the front and north elevation, and a delightfully sinuous and seemingly random clinker brick and arroyo-stone retaining wall on the rear. The naturalistic shape of the west terrace, originally appointed with woven willow furniture and Persian rugs, is artistic and anti-architectural enough to create an

29

30

appropriate buffer between the linearity of the house and the graceful undulations of the middle landscape, also designed by the Greenes. Stepping stones emerge above the water's surface in the terrace's pond, a concept adapted from Japanese landscape traditions. The same influence continues where a rock path, embedded in the lawn, leads to the bottom of the garden.

The broad entry, which stands beyond a run of brick steps, consists of a large, leaded art-glass central door, two narrower side doors with screens, and a series of leaded transom lights, all within a massive teak frame. The leaded-glass design in the doors can be only partly discerned from outside; it is from within the entry hall, looking back, that its full impact is appreciated. Inspired by the California Live Oak, designed by Charles Greene, and executed by glass craftsman Emil Lange, the Gamble entry must be counted among the most transcendently beautiful domestic spaces in America. Early-morning light casts a green and golden glow on the oak flooring, Persian carpets, and Burma teak paneling. Just inside, the right angles of the main staircase create a deep alcove fitted with a built-in bench seat and a marble-top stand for potted plants. The plan of the house is tripartite: guest bedrooms, dining and service spaces, and Aunt Julia's chambers are arranged in the south rectangle; the stair and hall circulation core is in the hyphen-like midsection of the house; and the den and living room occupy the northerly portion, with the immediate family's bedrooms and sleeping porches above. From the entry, the visitor's eye is drawn to the light of the west terrace doors at the end of the hall. A Chinese "lift" design, the traditional stylized cloud, is visible in the mullions, and angled rays, symbolizing the sun, emanate from the top of the lift motif. This was not new decorative territory for the Greenes, but rather a subtle evolution from the elemental references of earth, water, and fire in the Blacker house. Indeed, with the symbolized sun as fire, the other elements could be witnessed beyond the door: water in the pond and earth in the soil of the garden.

For the hallway, Mrs. Gamble became involved in the furnishings. Charles Greene recorded her suggestion that the chairs be designed "not like Mrs. Bush's [chairs, whose] backs [are] high but not narrower at top," referring to the severe tapering that the Greenes had designed the previous

31 Previous pages:
David B. Gamble house, Pasadena, 1907–09.
East (front) facade. The brick driveway hides behind
a mound of lawn, creating the impression of a
continuous flow of greenery.

32 **David B. Gamble house.**
The Tree of Life design on the leaded art-glass entry
pays homage to the principle material used in the
construction of the house.

33 **David B. Gamble house.**
Dining room.

32

33

year in the hall chairs for Mrs. Belle Barlow Bush, the tenant renting the
William T. Bolton house. The Greenes complied, producing a wider seat and
back for Mrs. Gamble. In the top rail of the Gamble hall chairs are hand-
holds that resemble the bird-like shapes in the top rails of Charles Rennie
Mackintosh's chairs for his own house, though the resemblance could be
coincidental.[21] Charles Greene's notations also indicate that originally there
was to be a hanging clock in the hall, with an abalone-shell inlay depicting
swans on the water, "to brighten" the space, according to his notes. No actual
drawings exist of this piece, however, and it was never executed.[22] A
mahogany hall table with ebony-trimmed drawers stands on the south wall,
a copper and shell lamp (probably designed by Frederick H. W. Leuders
around 1910) shedding soft light on its satiny surface.[23]

Through a broad, cased opening near the west end of the hall, the living
room extends toward the north. In this space, more than any other in the
house, can be seen the Greene and Greene manifestation of
gesamtkunstwerk, the concept of comprehensive artistic design of a living
environment. As with some of the interiors designed by Charles Rennie
Mackintosh and Charles Francis Annesley Voysey, the Greenes let no detail
escape their artistic control in this space. Furniture, light fixtures, rugs,
andirons, fireplace tools, metal hardware, and built-in features all express
the spirit of the Greenes' design vocabulary as it was envisioned for the
Gambles. Every aspect was scrutinized, no sight line was neglected, and the
placement of every object, including the piano and even a table lamp, was
carefully considered and committed to the drawings for the room. The
square-cross plan of the living room allows for convenient zoning of the
space into compact functional areas, each defined by beams and trusses
overhead, as well as by five separate rugs woven to Charles Greene's
watercolor designs.[24] The inglenook space is dominated by a broad hearth
and fireplace in olive-green field tiles with yellow and buff decorative chips
arranged to depict a creeping vine. The fireplace is cased in richly burled
teak and flanked by recessed bookcases concealed behind leaded art-glass
cabinet doors. The entire room is encircled with a series of clear-redwood
panels installed at the frieze level. Each is hand-carved with scenes from
nature, as if to give a view onto an idealized landscape as traditionally

34

34 **David B. Gamble house.**
   Detail of guest-room writing desk and chair.
   A silver-handled letter box could be removed from
   its pedestal to be used elsewhere in the house.

35 **David B. Gamble house.**
   Living-room inglenook bench and leaded art-glass
   book cabinet door. Finger joints are used to connect
   wood at outside corners. Overhead reading lights
   were designed to be "not too subdued."

expressed in Japanese homes using decorative *rammas*.[25] As executed, the living room is remarkably faithful to the Greenes' earliest conceptual sketches, though the lighting fixture designs evolved as the project progressed. Concerned that Mr. Gamble have a light bright enough to read by, Mrs. Gamble requested "bright" lights, "not too subdued." Charles's notes to himself also say: "Fixtures electric, slender, not too woody. Lantern something like Mrs. R. R. B[lacker]'s." Mahogany and iridescent art-glass lanterns hang like pagodas over the inglenook seats, but it is not known if the light was considered by Mr. Gamble to be strong enough for reading. The originally conceived pine-branch design, however, was deleted in favor of another of Charles's increasingly spare abstractions of vines, variations of which appear throughout the house.[26]

Across the hall, at the southwest corner of the house, the dining room projects into the garden like a pavilion, surrounded on three sides by the rear terrace and nature. A pair of pocket doors, with art-glass panels in a segmented cloud design, can be closed to give privacy to the room. The room is paneled in Honduran mahogany, creating a darker and more formal environment than the teakwood living room and hallway. A massive, built-in sideboard on the south wall is the focal point of the room. Cabinets and drawers, with panels chosen for their beautiful grain patterns, are symmetrically arranged under a T-shaped group of golden-yellow opalescent-glass windows in a design of a blossoming vine with blood-red flowers. A hanging leaded-glass chandelier, framed in mahogany, casts a soft, golden light on the table, itself a masterpiece of engineering and further evidence of the Hall brothers' significant contribution to the design evolution of the Greenes' work. Compared with the Blacker dining furniture, and even the earlier Bolton pieces, the Gambles' dining-room suite is sober, though this had not been Charles Greene's intent. His sketches show that he had envisioned the chairs and table with elaborate inlays of metal wire and contrasting woods. The Gambles may have felt that it was too much of a display (or that they would be without dining-room furniture for too long, waiting for it to be completed); ultimately they confined the decorative inlays to the guest-bedroom and master-bedroom furniture. There the Greenes excelled, and the guest-bedroom pieces rank

35

36

37

38

39

36 **David B. Gamble house, Pasadena, 1907–09.**
Bronzed metal entry hall lantern depicts the rose and crane of the Gambles' heraldic crest.

37 **David B. Gamble house.**
Entry-hall table, designed with horizontal emphasis similar to the Freeman Ford serving table (see fig. 25, p. 114).

38 **David B. Gamble house.**
Dining-room wall sconce of mahogany and iridescent leaded glass.

39 **David B. Gamble house.**
One of two octagonal ceiling fixtures in the master bedroom, this wooden "basket"-design lamp hangs from leather straps and is embellished with abalone shell inlay.

40 **David B. Gamble house.**
Living-room inglenook with Burmese teak queen-post trusses.

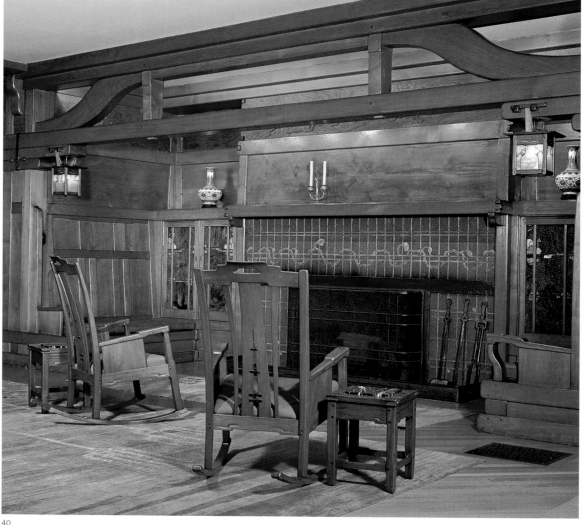

40

41

41 **David B. Gamble house.**
    Detail of carved living-room frieze with adjacent
    boards, blocks, and iron straps—decorative elements
    that mimic functional features in other areas of the
    house.

42 **David B. Gamble house.**
    View of kitchen looking south toward the service porch.

43 **David B. Gamble house.**
    Two opalescent-glass doors transform a dim corner
    at the back of the second-level hallway.

among the most exquisite they created. Indeed, the guest-room writing desk
was a favored form for Charles; he re-created it later in rosewood, with a
different, more elaborate inlay detail. The guest-room wall sconces are
remarkable, not only for their intrinsic beauty—delicate art-glass roses
leaded into flared mahogany frames—but for the contrast with the frosted-
glass shades originally used in every other bedroom in the house.

The upper, family bedroom level of the Gamble house takes on a more
relaxed ambience than the public spaces downstairs. Color and surface
contrast play a larger role than wood, and each room has plaster walls
painted a different muted earthtone. Port Orford cedar, a soft wood with an
even, satin-like reflective quality, is the dominant trim and door material,
though its subdued grain gives it a monotone appearance compared with the
exotic hardwoods of the public spaces. Stickley's Craftsman furniture was
specified for the boys' bedroom and the family guest room, but the master
bedroom and Aunt Julia's room merited the Greenes' furnishings. The master
bedroom pieces, especially, create a compositionally balanced and coordinated
environment similar to that of the living room. Three rugs, each with a
simple geometric design, set off the functional areas of the room. These
include the entry; the fireplace area, with an inglenook space and a day-bed
bench (an overhead light is bright enough for Mr. Gamble to read by); and
the main body of the room, with two beds, chiffonier, dressing table, and desk.
Throughout the house, but especially in the master bedroom, it is the
sparseness of decorative detail that imbues the space with particular beauty.
Restrained and subtle decorative inlays grace the furniture: tiny bits of semi-
precious stone, vermilion, and fruitwood, depicting plant fragments on fields
of black walnut.

The single-room space for the third level was originally labeled "attic." On
the final presentation drawings, the space was incorrectly renamed "billiard
room." The Gambles, who were a sober Presbyterian family that did not
believe in such idle amusements, used it for storage. Despite this, the attic is
a superb example of structure put to use, both functionally and aesthetically.
The Greenes exhibited a convincing ability to do this, but it is in the
simplicity of an undecorated space that structure can best preside as beauty.
Two king-post trusses support the roof, each Oregon-pine timber selected for

42

43

44 **David B. Gamble house, Pasadena, 1907–09.**
Living room. Each piece of furniture in the living room was designed to occupy a specific location within the space.

45 **David B. Gamble house.**
Living-room lantern. This mahogany and art-glass vessel of colored light hangs by leather straps from a ceiling plate of Port Orford cedar.

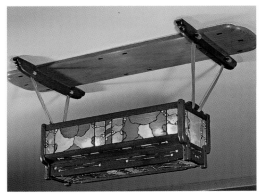

45

46

47

its clear, straight grain, lack of defects, and appropriate seasoning. All edges were milled to a radius that produced a softened appearance—perhaps to suggest ages of gentle wear—and hand-sanding and oiling enhanced the details and natural characteristics of each piece of wood. Each post and beam, each rafter and corbel, is treated with precisely equal respect, making for a unity of effect that belies the labor-intensive construction. The iron straps and wedges that bind the truss systems are functional, the pragmatic counterparts of the analogous decorative straps in the living room. In the final analysis, function and analogy are both means to an end: beauty.

Simultaneous with the Gamble house, the firm was also involved with alterations to Dr. William Bolton's house for its tenant, Mrs. Belle Barlow Bush; the addition of a bath and closet to the Theodore Irwin house; alterations to the interior of an Oaklawn house for architect G. Lawrence Stimson; and dining-room alterations and bookcases for the West California Street house of Mr. Lon F. Chapin. On November 19, 1907, it was reported in the *Pasadena Star* that Charles Sumner Greene had offered to contribute his design services for the erection of a "casino" on Pasadena's Monk Hill (Charles's drawings more picturesquely describe it as a "Shelter for Viewlovers"). In a design spirit similar to the Oaklawn waiting station (1906), the robust stone-and-timber shelter was designed to seem like a natural outgrowth of the hilltop, looking from the moment it was finished as if it had always been there. It was adopted by the community, and locally became the site of the annual Independence Day picnic. The structure was demolished in 1923 to clear the site for a school. Charles Greene likely spent much of the spring of 1908 on the building sites of the Gamble and Blacker houses. The commission to design a house for William J. Lawless, which also came into the office during this period, likely fell mostly to Henry. It was a relatively modest residence compared with the estates on which the brothers were spending so much of their time, and the uncomplicated but inventive design (now significantly destroyed) recalled the Greenes' simpler work of 1904 and 1905. Spacious porches and balconies were more prominent than on their earlier houses, however. A long terrace of stone and wood crossed the breadth of the front elevation, and the depth of the overhanging eaves and distinctive profiling of the beam ends were carried out using the newest

48

46 **David B. Gamble house, Pasadena, 1907–09.**
Detail of family guest room, second level, showing lavatory and medicine cabinet behind a closet door.

47 **David B. Gamble house.**
King-post truss in third-floor attic space.

48 **David B. Gamble house.**
Detail of Mr. Gamble's den, showing unusual vertical orientation of fireplace and chimney breast.

49 **David B. Gamble house.**
Detail of functional straps and wedges that bind Oregon Pine corbels in the third-floor attic.

50 **Charles M. Pratt house, "Casa Barranca," Ojai, 1908–11.**
Front facade, view from the southwest.

49

50

Greene and Greene design and construction methods. Lawless was happy with his house, and in November 1908 persuaded his neighbor and friend, George H. Letteau, to allow the Greenes to design and supervise the construction of a pergola and brick walk to connect their adjacent houses.

In the late spring of 1908, the Greenes were asked to develop a series of sketches for a winter residence in the resort town of Nordhoff, in the idyllic Ojai valley north of Los Angeles.[27] The clients were Charles Millard Pratt and Mary Seymour Morris Pratt, of Brooklyn, New York. Like his father, Charles Pratt, Sr., the younger Pratt was an officer of the Standard Oil Company, which had purchased the Charles M. Pratt Company, developer of the internationally successful lighting kerosene "Astral Oil."[28] The senior Pratt had cultivated in his family a love of wood architecture in the wild by building one of the first rustic "camps" in the southwest Adirondack Mountains in 1870.[29] The family vacationed at the cabin every summer until 1905, and in 1909 the younger Charles Pratt purchased his own "camp" on Little Moose Lake in the Adirondack League Club preserve near Old Forge, New York.[30] He and Mary also owned a farm in Connecticut, a city residence on Clinton Avenue in Brooklyn, and a Shingle Style vacation house called "Seamoor" (a play on his wife's middle name) on one thousand acres near Glen Cove, Long Island. The younger Pratt maintained his father's honest affection for wood architecture in spectacularly beautiful settings, and when the son announced his intent to build in "the Ojai," his chosen architects could be assured of a serious and appreciative client. Under what circumstances the Greenes were chosen is not precisely known but the Pratts may have seen their work on their occasional visits to Pasadena. It is also interesting to note that Mrs. Pratt was a Vassar College classmate (1880) of Caroline Canfield Thorsen, a soon-to-be Greene and Greene client and sister of Nellie Canfield (Mrs. Robert R.) Blacker.[31]

Unlike the Blacker and Gamble houses, the fourteen-acre site chosen by the Pratts for their home had no near neighbors and no artificial conditions governing its development or the design of the house to be located on it.[32] Further, there were abundant natural features to which the actual positioning of the house could be related. If the Blacker and Gamble houses represented the high art of suburban domestic architecture of the period,

the Pratt house and grounds signify their rural counterpart, with an altogether less formal design program for the house and furnishings that reflected, in design and decoration, the open countryside on which it would be built. The principle defining characteristic of the property was a steep ravine, or *barranca,* that ran from the foot of the Topa Topa mountains to the valley below, and gave the house its name, Casa Barranca. Preliminary sketches for the house, drawn in June 1908, show a rigid, L-shaped plan, with a small, one-story sleeping porch appended at a forty-five-degree angle onto one end of the house. The Greenes soon recognized, however, that the views and the hilly topography on the edge of the property's ravine were conducive to a more informal plan.

By September 14, 1908, the basis of the Greenes' final design had been worked out. It featured a radically informal, V-shaped plan (that maintained the original angled porch) and interior volumes of various heights, all under a constantly changing roofline that echoed the rise and fall of the mountains behind it.[33] The chimneys and foundation would be constructed of the sandstone boulders that comprised the local geology, and the exterior of the house would be sheathed in stained split-redwood shakes. Since Charles Pratt had become part-owner of the nearby Foothills Hotel, he and his wife took most of their meals and entertained there. Accordingly, they did not require spacious public rooms for socializing in their new house. Indeed, they reportedly used the house only as "sleeping quarters."[34] A single room served as entry hall, reception area, and living room at the pivot point of the V-shaped plan. The beamed ceiling of the seven-sided room, and the light-colored, maple flooring, give the space the informal feel of an Adirondack "camp," minus the rustic hickory bark typical to the idiom. Similar to the Cole and Blacker houses, the entry also serves as a direct passage to the rear terrace through a bank of french doors opposite the front doors. Also like the Blacker entry hall, the space takes on a sitting-room atmosphere, heightened by the inclusion of a fireplace and built-in inglenook bench in the northwest corner. Immediately to the right of the entry, the near-cubic space of the dining room is taller than the other rooms, but compact in area, and clearly expressed on the exterior by a raised portion of roof. The dining room's paneling above the picture rail is redwood, stained subtle hues of red

51 Mary Seymour Pratt, a 1880 Vassar College classmate of Mrs. Blacker's sister, Caroline Canfield Thorsen, herself a soon-to-be client of the Greenes.

52 **Charles M. Pratt house, "Casa Barranca," Ojai, 1908–11.**
Garden view of house showing how the V-shaped plan embraces the rear terrace.

53 **Charles M. Pratt house.**
First floor plan. Ink-on-linen presentation drawing.

54 **Charles M. Pratt house.**
In classic Greene and Greene fashion, rafters and beams extend beyond the eaves to catch sunlight and cast shadows.

51

52

and green and softly lighted by a tall, octagonal chandelier of mahogany and frosted glass with a delicate vine design trailing through its panels. The pattern of chevrons in the fireplace bricks evokes American Indian textile designs, and is faintly echoed in the chevron of the maple floorboards.

The two-story wing on the north contains four bedrooms, each with a sleeping porch, balcony, or other independent access to the exterior. The guest bedroom—a small chamber behind the chimney wall of the living room—is elegantly distinguished by a pair of leaded-glass transom windows that borrows enough light from the hallway to show the design of a branch, green leaves, and ruby-red and pink blossoms on a field of green and yellow streaks. The design of the fireplace, normally a symmetrical feature in the Greenes' houses, is set off-center to maximize the efficient use of flue space within the chimney stack that serves the bedroom and the living room. Farther along the hallway, a pair of french doors, designed and installed by Henry Greene early in the life of the house, were added to replace the original casement windows, thereby correcting a defect in circulation logic that had not allowed for access to the rear terrace from the bedroom wing of the house. (More recently, french doors have been added to the kitchen for the same reason.) On the north end of the plan, the charming lower-level sleeping porch, originally without walls or screens, angles to the east to provide privacy from the motor court on one side and take advantage of the mountain views on the other. The roof of the bedroom wing provides adequate shade to the upper level but also gave the Greenes an opportunity to expose an elaborate structure of tenoned-and-pegged queen-post trusses on the interior of the northerly, upper-level bedroom. On two sides of the room, the white-cedar ceiling slopes with the drop of the roof, creating an intimate cabin-like ambience.

Mr. and Mrs. Pratt occupied the finished house for the first time during the winter of 1911, and the dining-room furniture was delivered personally by Peter Hall in February of that year.[35] Carefully scaled to complement the room sizes, the furniture is noticeably more compact, and less formal, than the corresponding Blacker or Gamble pieces. Reflecting the size constraint of the room itself, the table was not designed to expand. Living-room furniture was not designed until in 1912, and reflects the Greenes' increasingly

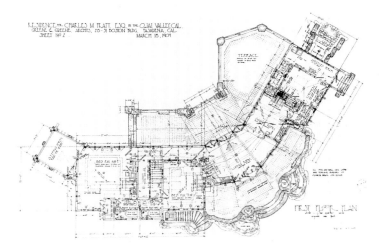

53

54

decorative design vocabulary.[36] In contrast to earlier pieces, the living-room chairs are wider, more accommodating, and less rigid than the chairs for the Gambles and the Blackers. And, if possible, they are more sumptuous in their use of materials. An eight-sided library table—small compared with others they had executed—was designed and constructed with exceptionally beautiful pieces of fiddleback mahogany in the top. An exquisite drop-front desk, also for the living room, was decorated with inlays of contrasting woods in the form of a venerable and gnarled oak tree, and was considered worthy of a rare detail photograph by Leroy Hulbert, who was commissioned by the Greenes in about 1915 to document their most important work. The desk's chair nominally relates to the simple formality of Charles Rennie Mackintosh's ladderback pieces for Windyhill (1901), but its silver inlays and wave-like perforations give it a design identity that is comparatively more decorative than architectural.[37]

Though Charles Greene's hand was clearly at work in the design of the Pratt house, Henry Greene and Peter Hall were left to see that the house was built according to plan. Charles departed for England just prior to the beginning of construction, though even after his return, and for many years following, his brother was the one to return to supervise the ongoing maintenance of the house, quietly tending to its needs.[38]

The last of the large and elaborate wooden houses designed by Greene and Greene, the William R. Thorsen house in Berkeley, California, was produced nearly simultaneously with the Pratt house—the presentation drawings were dated only two weeks apart in March 1909. The Thorsen house was designed for an urban lot that offered virtually none of the siting possibilities that the Greenes had been able to choose from while planning the Pratt's Ojai house. It also offered fewer options than were typically available to them even in Pasadena. The client was William Randolph Thorsen, a lumberman who had married the daughter of his employer, and the sister-in-law of his colleague, Robert Blacker. Like Nellie Canfield Blacker, the younger Caroline Canfield Thorsen, known as "Carrie," had inherited a comfortable sum from her father's lumber business in Manistee, Michigan, which, ironically, had been founded by William Thorsen's father, John. A native Norwegian with a strong love of the sea, John Thorsen had

incorporated the Stronach Lumber Company in Manistee in 1872 and had hired John Canfield as its president. His young son, William, served as secretary-treasurer.[39] By the 1890s, the Michigan timber business was slowing down, and by 1900 William Thorsen had left for California to establish a new concern, the Westside Lumber Company, near the town of Tuolumne in the goldmining region of the remote foothills of the Sierra Nevada range. He began to reap the benefits of the West's building boom, and in 1903 built for his family a 4,200-square-foot house designed by New York architects Emory and Emory. Called "Thorwald," the house (extant today) is strikingly similar to a Long Island bungalow designed by K. C. Budd that Thorsen may have seen illustrated that year in a popular magazine.[40] It is difficult to imagine that Carrie Thorsen could be fully content with outpost life, after having become accustomed to a high level of social activity in Michigan. After a few years, Thorsen transferred his company's headquarters to San Francisco, and in 1908 he purchased property for a home in Berkeley, near the University of California. It was a corner lot on fashionable Piedmont Avenue, a broad, tree-lined thoroughfare that had been planned by Frederick Law Olmsted in 1865.[41]

The choice of Charles and Henry Greene to design the Thorsens' Berkeley residence may seem unusual on the surface. This quiet, bayside academic community had developed an enviable and justified reputation for artistic and progressive housing, much of it for the university's professors. Berkeley favored such well-respected, locally based architects as Bernard Maybeck, Louis Christian Mullgart, Julia Morgan, John Galen Howard, and Ernest Coxhead. The desire to bring the Greenes four hundred miles to the north to execute a complex residential commission was almost certainly driven by sentiment (and possibly a desire for enhanced social standing). The will, and the financial resources of Caroline Thorsen, moved the project ahead. Mrs. Thorsen was aware of the Greenes' work in designing and building her sister and brother-in-law's house in Pasadena's Oak Knoll tract. Family and professional ties between the Thorsens and the Blackers were quite strong, and one way to demonstrate and honor that closeness was for one family to emulate the other's living environment. It also seems more than coincidental that Caroline had graduated from Vassar College in 1880

55 **Charles M. Pratt house, "Casa Barranca," Ojai, 1908–11.**
Leaded art-glass windows allow an exchange of light
between hallway and guest bedroom.

56 **Charles M. Pratt house.**
Living-room ceiling light fixture in mahogany and
frosted glass.

57 **Charles M. Pratt house.**
Living-room ladder-back rocking chair, 1912.

58 **Charles M. Pratt house.**
Living-room drop-front desk in mahogany with oak and
fruitwood inlays, 1912.

59 **Charles M. Pratt house.**
Living-room library table with fiddle-back mahogany top
and silver inlays, 1912.

60 **Charles M. Pratt house.**
Living room.

55

56

57

58

59

60

GREENE & GREENE

61 **Charles M. Pratt house.**
Dining room.

62 **Charles M. Pratt house.**
Dining side chair in mahogany.

63 **Charles M. Pratt house.**
First-floor guest room.

61

62

63

64 Craftsmen pose with Charles Greene (second from right, partially hidden in rear) on the rear steps of the William R. Thorsen house during construction, probably in December 1909. William Issac Ott, supervising contractor for Peter Hall, stands fourth from the left. His son, Leslie, is at the far left.

65 **William R. Thorsen house, Berkeley, 1908–10.** Garden view showing timber bridge from main residence to garage.

66 **William R. Thorsen house.** Garden view from the southeast.

64

65

66

with Mary Pratt, and that within months of each other, twenty-eight years later, they would both become threads in the web of client connections that fueled the Greenes' classic years of production.

Although the design of the house seems to have been a collaboration of the two brothers at the height of their classic period together, the Thorsen house is visually distinct from the Pasadena houses of the same period.[42] This is primarily because of radically different local conditions in Berkeley that dictated how its form would need to function. Cool weather and foggy skies, generated frequently by marine conditions, suggested for the house a steeper roof pitch, shallower eaves, and avoiding cantilevers that would cast deep shadows. This promoted a more vertical orientation of the main mass of the house as compared to the well-defined horizontality of the Pasadena houses. Sleeping porches were less practical in the cooler climate; in their place, the Greenes designed uncovered balconies for enjoying the spectacular westward views of San Francisco Bay and the Golden Gate. Stairs, not a formal drive, proved to be the appropriate approach to the front door in the pedestrian-based, urbanized setting of Berkeley, and the garage was hidden from arriving visitors, beyond the service wing on the north property line. But despite these fundamental differences, the house is unmistakably the Greenes' work. The articulation and softening of timbers, the "lift" motif in the windows and doors, and the distinctive use of clinker bricks as a bold foil for the exterior of split redwood shakes, are characteristics of their finest Pasadena work that easily and effectively migrated to the north. The Thorsen house stood out among its mostly stucco neighbors, though especially next to the concrete house immediately to the south, which had been designed by Julia Morgan in 1905 (now the heavily remodeled Chi Psi fraternity chapter).[43] Even if it had been built in the North Berkeley hills, where more of Bernard Maybeck's unstained-shingle houses could be found, the Greenes' design for the Thorsens would still seem out of place, posing as an elegant temple of high-art craft among the charming and quirky shingled cottages for which the city is better known. Charles Keeler's book, *The Simple Home* (1904), had suggested home-building and decorating guidelines for Berkeley hill dwellers that were based on the use of uncomplicated local materials and a palette of hues

taken from the surrounding land. The Greenes chose to put precious materials in the service of polished craft, a significantly different approach to arrive at an Arts and Crafts aesthetic. For this reason, the house was, and still is, a local paradox, but one that underscores the broader theoretical distance that existed between the work of mainstream Arts and Crafts practitioners and the Greenes' renowned structures from 1907 to 1910. It is a paradox that continues to challenge the definition of Arts and Crafts architecture.

The L-shaped plan of the Thorsen house was dictated by the shape of its corner lot and by the desire for a private and sheltered garden space. Such a plan had the added benefit of creating a natural separation between the family's chambers and the service areas of the house, an important feature in the Thorsens' formally run household. The shape of the plan nestled into the right angle of Piedmont Avenue and Bancroft Way at the low end of the sloping lot. So the house would not loom too large on the west property line, and to avoid significant excavation of soil on the east end of the property, the Greenes limited the wing on Piedmont Avenue to two stories in height, then set the facade back from the street some thirty-five feet. This still produced an imposing mass to the passerby, but one that belied the 9,200-square-foot interior space. The elevated bulk of the west wing was also visually lightened by fitting the facade with large picture windows. Raised planting beds on either side of the massive brick entry stairs beautify the buffer between the house and the sidewalk and promote an ambience of seclusion. The entry stairs are far more complex than originally presented on the final drawings, which showed a straight run of steps to the door. Charles produced an alternate design, but not until March 1910, a year after the beginning of construction. At the top of the stairs, a deep timber portico, fitted with a broad leaded art-glass lantern, both marks and shelters the entry. The north side of the L-shaped plan is mainly comprised of the service areas of the house in the rear, with the dining room and guest bedroom facing Piedmont Avenue on the front. This wing was developed as a full, three-story gabled elevation, complete with service entrance (with separate address) on Bancroft Way. On the west end of the wing, the guest bedroom opens to a spacious balcony over the projecting bay of the

67 **William R. Thorsen house.**
West (front) facade. The urban embodiment of the
Greenes' predominantly suburban language is
reflected in the lack of automobile access to the front
door, an arrangement distinctly different from most of
the Greenes' work situated on the expansive home
sites of Pasadena.

67

68 **William R. Thorsen house, Berkeley, 1908–10.**
Early conceptual sketch of leaded-glass design for
entry door, side light, and transom. Pencil and crayon
on tissue.

69 **William R. Thorsen house.**
Profile of front elevation from the south, showing
northwest dining-room wing, second-level balcony,
and overhanging roof.

70 **William R. Thorsen house.**
Covered terrace facing rear garden.

71 **William R. Thorsen house.**
Entry hall looking west toward leaded art-glass door.
A built-in mirror and hat hook can be seen on the left.

72 **William R. Thorsen house.**
Detail of living room showing built-in drop-front desk
and glazed bookcases.

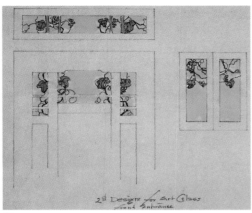

68

GREENE & GREENE

dining room below. At the top the eave is deep, but the descending verge boards rake back at an angle to further open the balcony space to the sky.

In late 1909, when the framing and sheathing of the house were completed and the interior was ready to be finished, Mrs. J. W. Beswick-Purchas wrote a letter to William and Caroline Thorsen, her brother and sister-in-law, to offer her impressions of the Greenes' work. She had recently paid a visit to Robert and Nellie Blacker at their new residence in Pasadena, and, in an apparent attempt to influence at least the interiors of the Berkeley house still in construction, she penned this no-nonsense critique:

"You will want to know what I think of this house, as that is the question uppermost in your minds at present. Well—I find the *outside* of the house and the grounds *very* pretty and attractive—but my impressions after moving through the various rooms was that this architect has let his fancy run riot in wood! There is so much wood about the outside that when one finds oneself encased in wooden rooms, wooden wall, wood ceilings, wood floors, wood fixtures for light—well, one has a little bit the feeling of a spider scrambling from one cigar box to another.

The hall is excellent—as that is a public room and can take the wood surroundings but my own feeling would run to more warmth of color and softer things. However, these are all individual tastes. Only I hope you won't have quite so much wood or people may say: Lumberman! hm! nothing like using up your own goods! I find the porches—the porte-cochere, etc.—most attractive. It is the bedrooms that suffer and seem a little cold in this handling. Two heavy beams transect the large guest room and broad bands surround this frieze. This idea, taken from the old English taverns, does not seem suitable to a bedroom. I am thinking of the architect, mind you; this is no personal criticism. All Mr. Green's [*sic*] woodwork is a delight for the softness of its finish. It is like fresh butter or paste squeezed out of a tube—so soft are the surfaces and the corners. As for the furniture, I find it very excellent for one or two rooms—such as the hall or dining room especially—but in my opinion it is too light in structure and too hard for living rooms. It is all in keeping with the style of architecture and the wall fittings but there is not a deep, soft chair or sofa in the house. It is all as the style of office

69

70   71

furniture though it is built on fine old English plain lines and beautiful work. But you see what I mean, don't you? It is studio furniture.

I am glad you are furnishing most of the rooms yourself and you will be glad for every bit of color in your rugs if Mr. Green gives you as much wood with a dull finish and sad color as he has here.

Nellie's rugs are very fine and very pretty. But too light and dainty in coloring for the somber wood colorings. One more point. Don't let Green light your rooms with lanterns of stained glass. They are very artistic in shape and coloring perceived in the daylight but as points of illumination they are rather negative and one finds oneself in a 'dim religious light' everywhere in the house.

This is a damper to a natural buoyant flow of spirits—a hindrance to work of any sort, and very expensive—as one has to turn on all the lights in a big room not to feel that one is in moonlight.

One more thing. Do have a plain electric light near the beds in your bedrooms and a table beside the bed where this light can stand to be switched on at will. It is rather a nuisance to get out of bed and walk across the room to see what time it is in these dark, early mornings.

I am afraid I will leave you with the impression that I like few things in Nellie's house but I have pointed out rather the faults which struck me unfavorably, that you might get another point of view when you are considering all these questions.

The dim lights may be grateful to two people with affected eyesight but I am sure they would spoil the ordinary healthy sight in trying to work in indifferent, insufficient light....Green is leaving today for Berkeley."[44]

While she left little doubt as to her feelings, it is difficult to say what impact, if any, the criticisms had on the Greenes' and the Thorsens' plans. The program for the public rooms, at least, emulates the Blacker house model in many respects. In both houses, the entry and stair-hall are paneled in teak, and the living and dining rooms are finished in mahogany. Even the dramatic grain of the eight-ply paneling is similar in both houses. As at the Blacker house (and against which Mrs. Beswick-Purchas had warned) mahogany and stained-glass lanterns hang by leather straps from the Thorsens' ceiling in the entry hall, stairway, and upstairs hall. Leaded art

72

73

74

73 **William R. Thorsen house, Berkeley, 1908–10.**
Detail of living-room fireplace with fire screen.

74 **William R. Thorsen house.**
Detail of painted frieze in living room.

75 **William R. Thorsen house.**
Entry hall and main staircase.

76 **William R. Thorsen house.**
Detail of south wall of dining room with original sideboard.

77 **William R. Thorsen house.**
Detail of east wall of dining room with original serving table and built-in china cabinet.

78 **William R. Thorsen house.**
Dining host chair, 1909, of mahogany with abalone shell and fruitwood inlay.

79 **William R. Thorsen house.**
Dining room.

glass for the house was executed by Emil Lange, who followed Charles Greene's design for a stout, gnarled grapevine that stretches its limbs from the side lights of the entry into the front door and transom panels.[45]

The living room is a long, light-filled space, with a broad window on the west, flanked by casements, and on the south, more windows angled out in a dramatic bay. In January 1910, possibly as a result of the Beswick-Purchas letter, the Greenes designed six recessed ceiling lights as substitutes for the solitary "eye-comfort" fixture that was originally designed to hang in the center of the room.[46] The built-in features of this room rival any among the Greenes' work. Built-in bookcases with glazed cabinet doors dominate the wall space, and a built-in fall-front desk is fitted into the east wall. Mauve Grueby tiles face the fireplace and hearth, and the polished-steel lintel, shaped in the "lift" design, is inlaid with a vine-like pattern in copper and brass. In 1914, Charles Greene designed a steel fire screen, whose image of birds, a serpent, and a bat amid flames, previews the symbolist direction his decorative arts designs would soon take. Gloomy, ebonized wall sconces with leaded art-glass panels shed dim light above the fireplace. Above these, paintings of delicate rose vines form a band of light above the mahogany trim, broken only by planter-shaped brackets from which the vines seem to grow. The exquisite trim detail and overall quality of construction is a tribute to William Issac Ott, who was sent north from Pasadena by Peter Hall to supervise the project. Indeed, the local firm of Hall and Ott was temporarily established for the sole purpose of building the Thorsen house.

Off the entry hall is a small den, originally used to display Mr. Thorsen's yachting trophies. Paneled in simple canvas stretched between teak-trim frames, its masculine aspect is reminiscent of Mr. Gamble's den. The dining room is approached from the side, the full view of it a surprise until the moment of entry through double, piano-hinge french doors. Daylight floods in from the west bay of windows, and at night, a fire in the fireplace, and two overhead leaded art-glass boxes, would cast a golden glow on the Greene and Greene furniture.[47] The dining suite was the only furniture originally designed for the house, though several pieces were commissioned later for other areas. The Thorsens purchased American antiques and Persian rugs for the other rooms in the house, but gave the Greenes

75   76   77

responsibility even for the rug in the dining room. All of the dining pieces—sideboard, server, table, and chairs—were conceptualized by Charles Greene on one sheet of paper. In this way, each piece could be carefully proportioned to the others, and it is arguably the most refined and successful furniture of the Greenes' careers. With the dining table fully extended to seat fourteen, the furniture comes into ideal scale with the room. Decorative inlay, depicting a delicate periwinkle design, is carried out in each piece (except the server) in abalone, oak, and fruitwoods. The chair backs employ a modified "lift" design in the splats, with tiny brass pins fastening ebony connectors to the mahogany uprights. Here also the frieze was painted with branches and blossoms on a trellis structure, bringing a hint of nature indoors.

    Port Orford cedar was used for built-in drawers and cabinets and for trim material in the upstairs halls and chambers. These included separate suites for Mr. and Mrs. Thorsen, a bedroom in the north wing for their two sons, a guest bedroom, a sewing room, and servants' quarters on the third level. In the basement, a space referred to as the "Jolly Room" was dedicated to stage performances and leisure activities for the boys. In all aspects, the Thorsen house was designed and built to the highest standards, and represents the Greenes at the height of their powers working together as a team. It would not last. With this commission, the door closed on the era of the "ultimate bungalows" and the coming years would never generate the same level of progressive design within the Arts and Crafts idiom.

78

79

6

The Elusive Client

1   Page 138:
    William Mead Ladd house, Ojai, 1913.
    Cellar door, west facade.

2   Charles Sumner Greene, c. 1905.

3   Charles Robert Ashbee in 1901, photographed by
    Frank Lloyd Wright.

2   3

In January 1909, Charles Robert Ashbee, the English architect, designer, and social reformer, came to Southern California with his wife, Janet. They had crossed the American continent presenting lantern-slide lectures and meeting with prominent figures of the Arts and Crafts movement. A promotional broadside for one of Ashbee's talks described him as "the direct successor of William Morris in England"—to be sure, a bit of calculated boasting designed to lure an audience, but not without basis.[1] Ashbee was indeed the most energetic Briton to champion the movement after the death of Morris.[2]

Ashbee's journal entries of the 1908–09 visit to America provide a glimpse of his hectic schedule as well as witty and insightful portraits of Americans seen through British eyes. He suffered no fools lightly, and his wry observations could be caustic and dismissive. At a luncheon in Los Angeles that he described as "noisy" and "indigestible," Ashbee noted that "guests arrived ... [including] a miscellaneous lady with yellow hair who asked inane questions," but he proceeded to describe Charles Greene, another arriving guest, as "the architect, who has built many beautiful houses in Pasadena."[3] A letter introducing Ashbee had been sent to Charles Greene by the visitor's Chicago host, Charles J. Morse, an engineer who collected Chinese and Japanese drawings.[4] In the ensuing days, the two noted architects had the opportunity to become better acquainted, and Charles Greene devoted time—apparently on two separate occasions—to showing Ashbee some of his work. Ashbee's journal entry about his visit with Charles Greene is one of the most effusive of his American journey:

"I think C. Sumner Greene's work beautiful; among the best there is in this country. Like Lloyd Wright the spell of Japan is upon him, like Lloyd Wright he feels the beauty and makes magic out of the horizontal line, but there is in his work more tenderness, more subtlety, more self-effacement than in Wright's work, and it is more refined and has more repose. Perhaps it loses in strength, perhaps it is California that speaks rather than Illinois, any way as work it is, as far as the interiors go, more sympathetic to me.

He [Charles Greene] fetched us in his auto again this afternoon and drove us about, then took us to his workshops where they were making without exception the best and most characteristic furniture I have seen in this country. There were chairs of walnut and lignum vitae, exquisite dowelling and pegging, and in all a supreme feeling for the material, quite up to our best English craftsmanship, Spooner, Barnsly [sic], Lutyens, Lethaby. I have not felt so at home in any workshop on this side of the Atlantic—(but then we have forgotten the Atlantic, it is the Pacific!). Here things were really alive—and the Arts and Crafts, what all the others are screaming and hustling about, are here actually being produced by a young architect, this quiet, dreamy, nervous, tenacious little man, fighting single-handed until quite recently against tremendous odds.

I noticed—'tis the old story—that the men who were doing the work were old men, some quite old. I talked with one of them—men who had still a traditional feeling for craftsmanship in woods, and who had learned their trade before the days of machine development and before the American wood crafts had become 'grand rapidized.'

After a visit to several of his houses in the Arroyo, Greene took us to tea with Mrs. Garfield, the widow of the murdered president. She was a bright, determined, keen capable little lady, a woman who had seen the world, felt its hardness and vanity, but still had the sun in her eyes. We looked out on the mountains and discussed single tax in the intervals of tea and fingering the surface of Greene's scholarly paneling. As the afternoon wore on a glorious sunset lit the snow on the mountains to rose red. I don't wonder the rich and great come to live in Pasadena—and it's certainly an education for them."[5]

Between the lines of Ashbee's account one senses the mutual enjoyment of collegial and kindred spirits. They even found time to discuss a Socialist political cause in Henry George's single tax. In the midst of a large volume of important and pressing work in the firm, however, it may have seemed odd to Henry Greene that his brother would one day take time to attend a "noisy" and "indigestible" social lunch and on two other occasions to chauffeur the visiting Englishman around Pasadena. Such a feeling may also have been compounded by the fact that Henry Greene's name, or any mention of his existence, is absent from Ashbee's journal entires. Henry apparently did not rate Ashbee's notice, nor was there any mention of a visit to the architects' offices where the drafting work would have been seen

4 72 Scarsdale Villas, London, where Charles Greene
   and his family lived during the spring and summer
   of 1909.

5 Charles Sumner Greene, drawing of Tintagel Church,
   Cornwall, England, 1909. Charcoal on heavy paper.

4   5

unexalted by three-dimensional form. Ashbee's encounter with Charles
Greene was intended (no doubt by both) as artist-to-artist, a chance for each
to validate the other's work, and one can easily imagine the two men
indulging themselves in an appreciation of the objects of their mutual
admiration as the afternoon slipped by. The timing of his visit was brilliant,
for the furniture Ashbee witnessed being made was the exquisite walnut and
lignum vitae pieces for David and Mary Gamble's bedroom.[6]

Back in the office, the drawings for the Pratt and Thorsen houses were
under way and would be completed within the next two months. Other work
was on the boards, too, but having had an opportunity to commune with the
wandering Ashbee, Charles Greene would soon crave for himself a similar
distraction from the daily pressures of the profession. Within sixty days,
Charles left to his brother the responsibilities of the firm and departed with
his family for an extended stay in England.[7]

For three guineas a week the Greene family leased 72 Scarsdale Villas,
one among a row of classicized townhouses off Earl's Court Road in London's
West Kensington.[8] During their six-month residence Charles and Alice
visited museums and galleries, shopped, enjoyed their children, and
generally relaxed. If he cared to, Charles may have visited the architecture
room at the Royal Academy of Art, where he would have seen drawings by
C. F. A. Voysey of Lodge Style at Combe Down, Bath, a somewhat eccentric
stone lodge with romantic historical references, the kind of thing that would
have appealed to Charles.[9] In May, the Greenes attended the Milton
Costume Ball in Piccadilly, and in July they left the children behind in
London—with Alice's sister, Jane—to visit the Cornish and Devonian coast
by themselves. Charles took his watercolors, and painted a view of the
church and ruined castle at Tintagel and hill-hugging houses in the
picturesque fishing village of Clovelly. Charles and Alice were not very
distant from where they had spent part of their honeymoon, and could relive
those happy days as they explored more of the area's romantic seaside
towns. For Charles, life had changed dramatically in the intervening eight
years. The firm had evolved rapidly from local acceptance to national, even
international, recognition. Greene and Greene had more work than they
could handle (though no one in the firm was getting rich), and yet Charles

sensed a need to step back, to diversify his creativity into other areas,
including painting and writing. If while he was in England he looked up his
recent acquaintance, C. R. Ashbee, there is no evidence of it. Nor did he
reach out to other figures associated with the Arts and Crafts movement
while he was in London. It was a missed opportunity, but shows the depth of
his ambivalence toward his profession.

From Clovelly, Alice wrote in a postcard to her sister at their London
address, "I am getting homesick for the children and will be quite ready to
board a train from Bude for London."[10] The ensuing months were a restful
period of reflection for Charles and little of a business nature occupied his
time, though he wrote to Peter Hall in July, and may have mailed his
conceptual sketches for the Thorsen dining furniture at about that time. In
August, Hall replied to his letter with an update on the various jobs in
progress, and reassured him: "The work is moving along finely....I hope you
are having a nice time and will be glad to see you back."[11] In early October
the Greenes visited Paris, where they saw Durand Ruel's private collection
of paintings by Claude Monet.[12] Returning to England, they sailed on the
S. S. Hanover from Liverpool to Philadelphia on October 27, 1909, and
returned to California via New York and Chicago. It was Charles Greene's
last trip abroad.

While his brother was in England, Henry oversaw the considerable
quantity of work already under way in the firm, including the construction
of the Pratt and Thorsen houses. From January through June 1909 he
prepared scores of drawings for a house for Henry K. Bradley comprising
five distinct designs. The most highly developed were the fourth and fifth
schemes, and a job number was optimistically assigned to the client in 1910,
but Bradley never went ahead with the work.

The principal new project that spring that did proceed to construction
was a house for Mrs. Margaret B. S. Clapham Spinks. The commission for
Mrs. Spinks and her husband, Judge William Ward Spinks, had first come
into the Greene and Greene office as a design project in May 1907, though
there is no evidence of any actual work taking place prior to 1909. Charles
had not yet left for London when the presentation drawings were completed
on March 31, 1909, but the configuration and details of the house suggest

6 **Margaret B. S. Clapham Spinks house,
Pasadena, 1907–09.**
Site plan. Ink-on-linen presentation drawing.

7 **Margaret B. S. Clapham Spinks house.**
Second-floor hallway and skylight, the latter a favorite
feature of Henry Greene's.

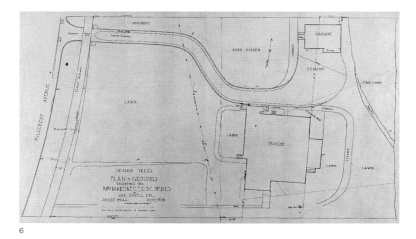

6

the primary involvement of Henry Greene. The contract was awarded not to Peter Hall, but to Will Taylor, a newcomer who had never worked with the Greenes previously. The permit to build the $11,000 house was issued on April 23, 1909.[13]

The Spinks house design is an elaboration of the rectangular, large-gabled form of the "California House" developed by Henry Greene in 1904–05. Benefiting from refinements made in the intervening years, the Spinks house has more character and variety than related earlier designs, thanks especially to a more adventuresome approach to the design of the porches and terraces. Characteristically, the siting of the house was dictated by the topography of the lot. Henry recognized that by placing the house just west of the slope into the canyon to the east he could take advantage of dramatic views from the rear of the house and an equally dramatic set-back from the street. In front, an expanse of subtly graded lawn rises nearly to the level of the entry terrace, but the formal path of entry is by way of the drive that skirts the lawn (and, originally, an orange grove) near the north edge of the property, eventually curving toward the house. Projecting from the extreme northwest corner of the structure is a distinctive portico. Five brick steps precede the entry terrace under a deep and broad timber overhang. Light from a broad-brimmed lantern illuminates the portico area. The front door is approached obliquely in the shaded recess of the terrace, whose area is figuratively carved from of the volume of the main block of the house. The interior is simpler than those of the elaborate houses designed for the Greenes' recent clients. Plaster walls with cedar trim replace the exotic hardwood paneling of the more expensive houses. A skylight, one of Henry's trademark architectural elements, illuminates the upper hall and staircase. A broad porch on the rear elevation allows outdoor access through french doors in the living and dining room. Judge and Mrs. Spinks lived in the house only two years, selling it in 1911 to Mrs. William F. West. Typical of many of the subsequent owners of other Greene and Greene houses, Mrs. West commissioned the brothers to design alterations so that they would be sensitively integrated with the original structure.

Also dated March 31, 1909, were the drawings for alterations to the entry hall and staircase of the James Culbertson house. At the request of

Mr. Culbertson, however, the work was not to be finished until after Charles had returned from England to supervise the decorative details.[14] Other projects came into the office, though most were put on hold until Charles's return. The same was true for the decorative details in the Pratt and Thorsen houses, which were supervised by Charles after his return.

The house that Henry Greene designed for Dr. S. S. Crow, and the gardens and outbuilding he later created for Edward S. Crocker, are among the most beloved commissions of the Greene and Greene firm. Designed and executed entirely under Henry Greene's direction, the house and grounds show the younger brother's mature ability that had been suppressed in the natural hierarchy of the sibling firm. A compact design compared with most of the Greenes' work of the same period, the Crow house nevertheless received much of the care and attention paid to their grander commissions. The single-story structure is arranged around a narrow courtyard in a U-shaped plan whose open end faces away from the street. While there is precedent for similar plans within the Greenes' work (e.g., the Cora Hollister house, 1904), the specifics of the Crow house differ. One wing of the plan is devoted to the service functions of the house, the opposite wing to family bedrooms. The link between the two is devoted to living room and dining room. The genius behind the design is Henry's recognition of the opportunity for drama. By exploiting the subtle changes in the site's topography (the lot rises slightly from north to south and east to west) he created a series of elevation shifts in the roof line that give enormous interest to the exterior composition. This, along with Henry's careful adherence to the rules of proportion, imbues the house with an aura of repose and dignity more common to their larger designs. The deep overhang of the low eaves casts shadows over the terrace on the front elevation, and a row of rafter ends catches light. The supporting structure of the porch—broad beams and doubled posts on brick plinths—creates a visual screen in front of the entry. The compact interior follows the exterior's changes in elevation. The living room serves as entry area and access to the hall where family chambers occupy the north wing. Characteristically for Henry, a strict linearity is generally followed, even in the decorative ceiling trim and light-fixture plates. The exception is a subtle variation in the Chinese "lift" that softens

7

9 **Margaret B. S. Clapham Spinks house.**
Entry portico and covered terrace.

10 **Margaret B. S. Clapham Spinks house.**
East (rear) elevation.

9

10

the casement windows and doors. Under contractor August C. Brandt the careful finishing of the wood rivals that of the Greenes' finest commissions, indicating a cross-pollination of skill between Peter Hall's craftsmen and the Greenes' alternate builders. Glazed doors opposite the entry afford garden views beyond the courtyard, from which light floods into the north wing through a continuous wall of casement windows that open into the hallway serving the bedroom chambers. A soft, golden light filters through a stained-glass skylight over the hall. Adjacent to the living room and three steps above is an intimate dining alcove. The alcove is further separated from the living room by a low partition of bookcases flanking the three steps to the dining room. Over the steps a gateway-like structure stands like a Japanese *torii*, from which portieres were to hang to provide privacy to the dining dais. An open area between the bookcases and the ceiling maintains air circulation between the two rooms.

In 1910, Edward Savage Crocker retired from Crocker, Burbank & Company, his family's paper-manufacturing business in Fitchburg, Massachusetts. He and his wife, Adelaide, relocated to Pasadena, where they purchased Dr. Crow's house in January 1911.[15] It was Crocker who was responsible for doubling the size of the property by purchasing land to the west of the residence and enhancing it with extensive gardens and outbuildings. Because of his brother's absence in 1909, Henry Greene had been required to assert his design talents to a degree he had not previously enjoyed. One of the results was his being chosen by Crocker to continue as primary design architect for the house and gardens.

The gardens, now subdivided and developed with housing, originally reflected not only the linearity of the house itself (and of Henry's orderly character), but its subtlety as well. A fernery in the narrow rearcourt of the house gave way to a lawn and a rose garden. To the south, a cypress hedge screened the view of the garage, while behind the original property-line wall, with its rose-laden trellis, a regimented orchard of fruit trees was planted, recalling Henry Greene's orange grove designs for the H. M. Robinson house and the Spinks house. A path to the south, beyond a laurestinus hedge, led to a keeper's cottage. A walkway from the north end of the rose garden headed west, through a gate, past fruit trees, lilacs, and flower beds on

either side, to a junction of paths on a minor axis. The primary path ended at a small lily pool and fountain, with planters and seats forming a small outdoor room. The subsidiary path to the south terminated at a raised teahouse pergola. The subsidiary path to the north approached the property-line wall, then headed west under a wisteria trellis to the northwest corner of the lot. A turn to the south brought the path to stepping stones leading past a pair of taxus plants to a sundial in the vast rear lawn. Continuing along the property-line wall, with a climbing rose specified for its fence structure, one eventually came full circle to the teahouse. The Crow house and Crocker gardens are significant: they were Henry Greene's early independent triumph, accomplished entirely outside the sphere of his older brother's influence; but more importantly they gave him the confidence to sustain increasing independent design work in future years.

Also in 1909, Henry had the opportunity to design a large house in the firm's familiar wood idiom for Earle C. Anthony, on the southeast corner of Berendo Street and Wilshire Boulevard in Los Angeles. Anthony owned the Packard automobile franchise in California, as well as a radio station and prime real estate along Wilshire Boulevard. The design for his house had many of the characteristics of the Greenes' elaborate commissions of the previous three years, but without exotic materials, applied decoration, expensive cast hardware fittings, or custom furniture. The L-shaped plan, like the Thorsen house in Berkeley, was designed for an urban site. The Anthony plan was less rigid, however, with spaces that flowed into each other—a metaphor for the contrast between Southern California lifestyles and the more formal households, such as the Thorsens', to the north. While the exterior shares the same split-shake cladding, open porches, and terraces of the Blacker, Gamble, and Pratt houses, the interiors are plainer and more classically Craftsman, another reflection of Henry Greene's personal preference for sober, unadorned surfaces. The living-room fireplace treatment of a raised hearth of thick paving tiles resembles the treatment of the Irwin house living room of 1906. A small den, set off the living room, provides a secluded retreat. A series of french doors (since removed) provided outdoor access and garden views from the living room. A darkroom was also part of the original plan. In 1913, designs for leaded art glass, lanterns, carving over

11 **Dr. S. S. Crow house, Pasadena, 1909–10.**
East (front) facade.

12 **Dr. S. S. Crow house.**
Floor plan. Ink-on-linen presentation drawing.

13 **Dr. S. S. Crow house.**
Living room, view toward dining room, c. 1914.

14 Edward S. Crocker, second owner of Dr. S. S.
Crow house.

11

13   14

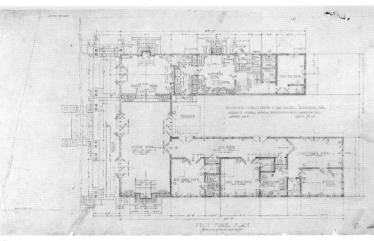

12

the living-room mantel, and additions to a sleeping porch and breakfast room were commissioned, though the lanterns and carving were never executed. In 1923, the house was moved to its present site in Beverly Hills by Mr. and Mrs. Norman Kerry, who commissioned Henry Greene to design the re-siting of the house on its new lot.

By all rights, the years following the successful creation of the Greenes' most refined residences in their popular wood idiom should have been doubly busy ones for the firm. They were not. In 1910, while several previous clients asked for additions and alterations, not a single new commission of a size similar to their 1907–09 work successfully progressed from design to construction. It has sometimes been suggested that the Greenes did not keep up with the public's fickle tastes, resulting in a decline in patronage. The facts controvert this view. Indeed, the Greenes presciently sidelined their elaborate wood residence designs at the precise moment that production of new Craftsman-style houses began to decline. In 1908, Pasadena's output of new Craftsman-style houses costing over $3,000 peaked at 97 percent of new construction at that cost level. It declined each subsequent year until the Colonial Revival and other period revivals virtually subsumed it by 1920.[16] The taste of the American house-buying public had begun to gradually shift away from the style with which the Greenes had become so closely associated, but there is nothing to suggest that they were not aware of this. When Charles returned from England, he attempted to guide the firm and its clients toward a new design vocabulary, but the cost of the work, and the slow pace, had made it increasingly uncompetitive.

Three relatively small projects for new clients were completed in 1910, as well as several additions and alterations for existing clients. More work was needed to complete the Thorsen house, too, notably the entry stairs, which was about the only thing keeping the Thorsen family from moving into their new home. Henry designed a modest two-story house for Ernest W. Smith, and a small bungalow for his friend, Sam L. Merrill, in northern Pasadena. Charmingly planned, with a library set off the living room, the Merrill house had features of the more expensive bungalows, including a variation on the Crow house treatment of partially separating the living

15

16

15 **Earle C. Anthony house, Los Angeles, 1909–10 (moved to Beverly Hills, 1923).**
Front facade, view from the southwest.

16 **Earle C. Anthony house.**
Living-room fireplace and raised hearth, similar in spirit to the treatment of the Theodore Irwin design.

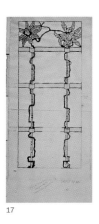

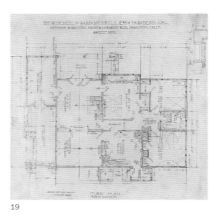

17   18   19

room and dining room with a gateway-like wall. A simple, two-story bunk house was designed, also by Henry, for Keith Spaulding's Sespe Ranch fifty miles away in rural Fillmore. Generally, however, the dearth of major new construction activity correlated with the high number of unrealized projects: clients wanted the Greenes' services until they discovered how dear they came. Their success rate in converting clients to home builders had fallen dramatically even though Henry worked hard to keep the work flowing and was amenable to working within the budget of potential clients. Indeed, he had a reputation for thriftiness. It seems that Charles, however, since his return from England, worked at an even slower, more inward-focused pace.

Emblematic of this phase of the firm's life was the project to design a large residence for John Lambert, a former Chicago resident and vice-president of the Crown City National Bank and president of the Pasadena Consolidated Water Company.[17] His house, as designed by the Greenes, was to have been built just east of a fashionable section of Orange Grove Avenue, at the southeast corner of Gordon Terrace and Waverly Drive. Had it been built, it would certainly have ranked among the largest and most impressive Greene and Greene commissions. The design was a dramatic departure from the wood vocabulary of their current fame, though it was in some ways a return to the Robinson house and Ford house aesthetic: a stucco exterior with exposed wood confined to the rafters, verge boards, major lintels, and beams. The roof pitch (3.5 in rise over a 12 in run) was consistent with the Greenes' classic wood houses, as was the overall horizontality that had characterized their large suburban designs in Southern California. Like the Robinson house, structural conventions of adobe building are present, too, including corner buttresses and tapered chimneys. These features, and stucco cladding, represented the new design order for the Greenes—materials that would replace split shakes, clinker bricks, and iron-strapped timbers. Lambert chose not to build, but the design exercise allowed the Greenes to develop and refine a hopeful vision of their future work.

Similarly, the firm's early-1911 design for Mr. A. M. Drake of Bend, Oregon, for a house in Oak Knoll recalled the Robinson house vocabulary of plaster and half-timbering. Remnants of the wood style remained, including

timber corbels bound with iron straps and wedges, and even the Chinese lift, which can be seen in the drawing of the lintel over the entry. The design was never built, though, with Mr. Drake having chosen another architect. Shortly after this defeat came another. A project to develop preliminary drawings for a landscape plan for the 1912 auto show at Fiesta Park in Los Angeles went nowhere. Charles's sketch for a waterfall, pool, and stream in the middle of the exposition grounds would have brought considerable charm to the commercial exposition, but it was not to be.

Later in 1911, there was a flurry of new work. Three large commissions came into the office in quick succession: the first, a country estate for Mortimer and Bella Fleishhacker of San Francisco; the second, a Santa Barbara home for Nathan Bentz, brother of the Greenes' former client, John Bentz; and the third, a large house for the three unmarried sisters of James Culbertson—Cordelia, Kate, and Margaret. The Fleishhackers wanted a country house built on their sizable estate in rural Woodside, on "the Peninsula" south of San Francisco. It was to be in the English style with formal gardens and provisions for a swimming pool to be added later. Mr. Bentz wanted a wood house, and the Culbertson sisters would get a residence with distinctly Chinese design overtones. The contract price of $152,809 was an immense sum—the Greenes' most valuable commission to date. Shortly after, Earle C. Anthony requested designs for his Packard automobile showroom in downtown Los Angeles, and along the way the city of Pasadena awarded the firm the commission to design the Henry W. Longfellow Elementary School. This wave of work was supplemented by several commissions for additions, alterations, smaller houses, and more work for the Pasadena Ice Company. In one year the firm had seemingly revived, from the ominously thinning schedule of 1910 to a full workload. It seemed as though the new design language, which relied on plaster, stucco, and stucco-like materials, might rekindle the firm's fortunes.

Green Gables, the Fleishhacker family's country estate south of San Francisco, stands intact today as the most extensive design ever conceived by Greene and Greene. Its seventy-five acres were developed during a twenty-year collaboration primarily between Charles Greene and his clients, Mortimer and Bella Fleishhacker. As president of the Anglo-California Trust

20 **John Lambert house, Pasadena, 1910** (project).
Artist's watercolor rendering of the Greenes' design,
which was never built.

21 **A. M. Drake house, Oak Knoll, Pasadena,
1910–11** (project).
Front elevation. Ink-on-linen presentation drawing.

20

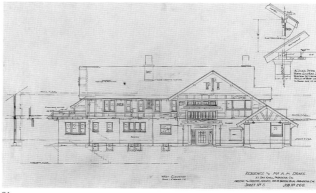

21

Company, Mortimer Fleishhacker was a successful businessman who had a sensitive and artistic side to his character as well. Mrs. Fleishhacker was a painter, and she and her husband shared an interest in supporting little-known artists of the day, including photographers Dorothea Lange and Edward Weston before they became established.[18] As Bella Fleishhacker recalled, "Henry Greene traveled to Woodside [only] a few times. He saw about the plumbing and such things."[19] The Fleishhackers apparently preferred Charles's pensive and gentle style, and even the Fleishhackers' young children sensed the distinction between the two, calling Henry "Pink Greene" and Charles "Green Greene," implying that Charles was the more authentic architect.[20] Ironically, the Fleishhackers did not particularly like the Greenes' Pasadena houses, which they thought "too Japanese."[21] It was Charles Greene, the man, whom they liked, no doubt because of his confident artistic sensibilities and exacting standards of work. For his part, Charles must have been very pleased. He had been hoping and preparing for work of this magnitude ever since he sent his "Sketch for a Dwelling Place for W. B. T." to the Louisiana Purchase Exposition in St. Louis in 1904.

The Fleishhackers specifically requested that the Greenes design for them an English-style house, with a "thatched roof, if possible," and they included the landscaping and gardens in the commission.[22] Charles was characteristically slow about submitting his design, and was remembered by the family as having sat for hours on what would become the swimming-pool hill, studying the topography and sight lines of the estate.[23] Charles finally decided to position the main house next to an established oak tree that emerged from the rear terrace, similar to the siting of the Gamble house near the prominent eucalyptus. He oriented the major views from the house toward the future garden to the south and parallel to the flanking mountains on the west.[24] This was inspired, since the drop-off at the end of the formal garden would give the impression of an endless estate. It still does. The Greenes also designed a barn and a dairy house shortly after the main house was under way, though only the barn was built at that time. The placement of roads, walkways, and exterior landscape elements, and the siting of the future swimming pool were also put in Charles Greene's hands, as was the design of the formal garden to the south of the house.

The main residence, designed primarily for summer use, was constructed around a dog-leg plan under a hipped roof, the main axis parallel to the front elevation and the rear terrace. The Fleishhackers did not care for the Greenes' legendary wood interiors, but requested instead a white-tinted plaster finish throughout, with any wood trim also to be painted white. Furniture was not part of the Greenes' initial commission, the family preferring to engage the decorating services of Elsie de Wolfe and Vickery, Atkins & Torrey. While the English design of the house seems alien to the Greenes' larger body of work, with the notable exception of the James Culbertson house, it follows some features of the unbuilt design project for the A. M. Drake house, and both reflect Charles's rekindled interest in Anglo-inspired forms following his return from England late in 1909. (Nor did the English theme cease with the Fleishhacker estate—the firm produced two major designs thoroughly influenced by English precedent within the next eighteen months.)

The material of choice for the Fleishhacker exterior was the new and innovative product (more correctly a process) called "Gunite," a fine cement that was applied with a patented pneumatic gun to a prepared surface (another indication that the Greenes were not set in their ways). Its easily manipulated spraying action allowed for complete coverage, and in the right hands could even allow for the spontaneous creation of uneven, sculptural surfaces. Because the system was new, its application at the Woodside estate was described and illustrated in *Architect and Engineer* in the April 1912 issue. Carnegie fire brick—more formal than clinkers—was used for exterior stairs, platforms, piers, and garden balustrades. Though the Fleishhackers had asked for a thatched roof, they got something more permanent and practical. A sawed-shingle roof was applied instead, built up in thick, undulating rows. Steam was used to shape the shingles to follow the curves of the eaves and surface. The rolling courses of shingles unified the various forms that made up the roof, including the hipped dormers, rolled and clipped gables, and eaves. The original plan called for a characteristically Greene and Greene shelter on the rear terrace, a wooden structure with overhead beams designed to fan out beyond the french doors from the entry hall. This idea was discarded, however, probably because it was "too

22 **Mortimer Fleishhacker, Sr., estate, "Green Gables," Woodside, 1911–12.**
Auto court elevation and entry portico, view from the north.

23 **Mortimer Fleishhacker, Sr., estate, "Green Gables."**
Early view of formal gardens at rear of residence, view from the south.

24 **Mortimer Fleishhacker, Sr., estate, "Green Gables."**
Early view of living room, before enclosure of west porch. The interior furnishings were designed by Elsie de Wolfe.

25 **Mortimer Fleishhacker, Sr., estate, "Green Gables."**
Steps leading from auto court to swimming pool, added in 1916.

22

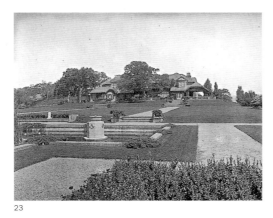

23

24

25

26 **Mortimer Fleishhacker, Sr., estate, "Green Gables."** Brick pedestals in rear garden support planters designed by Charles Greene.

27 **Mortimer Fleishhacker, Sr., estate, "Green Gables."** At the rear of the residence, an enormous oak tree shaded the house and terrace until the 1950s.

28 Overleaf:
Mortimer Fleishhacker, Sr., estate, "Green Gables." South (rear) facade of main residence, view across the pool at the end of the formal garden.

26

Japanese." A similar fate—and for the same reason—befell the structural supports of the original porch angled off the living room. Initially constructed of rounded and profiled timbers, the supporting posts and beams were changed at Mr. Fleishhacker's insistence to brick piers even before the house was completed.[25] If there were some elements that were not as English as they had hoped, the Fleishhackers would have appreciated the diamond-pane leaded windows (later replaced with plain glass), which put the finishing touch on their Anglo-California country house.

The genius of the Fleishhacker estate plan is in the harmony between the house and its gardens. On the south side of the house, a deep and broad terrace surrounded the immense oak tree (removed in the 1950s) against which the house was originally sited. Beyond a brick balustrade, steps lead past platforms with Greene-designed planters to a formal terraced lawn. Two long gravel paths, several feet below the level of the terrace, divide the main lawn into three sections and create separate axial views from the hall and the dining room. These views terminate at a reflecting pool, the extremity of the first phase of garden construction. This phase took more than two years to complete, involving numerous trips by Charles Greene from Pasadena to Woodside. Though the main residence had been accepted by the client on May 15, 1912,[26] a 1913 photo shows the muddy ground still unplanted behind the house.[27]

At the end of 1914, when Charles's involvement at Woodside was at a lull, Mr. Fleishhacker requested designs for extensive interior alterations to their Pacific Heights home in San Francisco (alterations worth about $18,000, according to the job book entry). This work, which included cut-glass designs for doors, a marble mantel, iron work, and decorative plaster ceiling designs, spanned most of 1915.[28] It was a festive year in San Francisco with the opening of the Panama Pacific International Exposition, a vast esplanade and series of pavilions built on landfill (later to become the Marina District). The Greenes attended the AIA convention there that year, and Charles took time to visit the fair, remarking publicly on the welcome use of color in building materials and finishes.[29] That year, the Fleishhackers also bought additional land adjacent to the southern property line of Green Gables, enabling later expansion of the gardens. (More than a decade would pass

27

29 **Henry W. Longfellow Elementary School, Pasadena, 1911 (altered).**
South (front) facade.

30 **Henry W. Longfellow Elementary School.**
North and east facades (rear of structure) with school children visible in the exercise yard.

31 **Cordelia Culbertson house, Pasadena, 1911–13.**
Courtyard garden, view from the south. Here the single-level portion of the house reaches the escarpment that allows the bedrooms in the north wing to be situated on an upper level.

29

30

before Charles Greene returned to design and execute, to spectacular effect, the next major phase of the garden plan.) In July 1911 the Greenes had also designed a swimming pool and two pool houses, which were finally constructed in 1916. Across the auto court from the entry to the main house, a broad brick stairway rises some twenty feet to a knoll, the top of which was excavated for the pool. The original *tsuba*-shaped basin design was later set aside in favor of a free-form configuration that was designed specifically to avoid disturbing the existing oak trees, the result being an unintentional harbinger of the kidney-shaped pools of today.[30]

While the Fleishhacker's main Woodside residence was under construction, Henry Greene was occupied with the design of the Longfellow Elementary School in Pasadena. Announced on May 16, 1911, in the *Pasadena Star*, it was to be "the first absolutely fireproof school in the city … [and] better ventilated and heated than any school building on the coast."[31] Henry designed the two-story, reinforced-concrete structure in a Classical idiom—with Ionic pilasters and faultless symmetry—that was nearly unrecognizable as a product of the Greene and Greene firm. Henry's pragmatism in producing a winning design would doubtless have been beyond his brother's high-art sensibilities at that time, especially if he had known that the school's budget, dictated by a city bond issue, was inflexible. It was characteristic of Henry's innate sense of economy that he persuaded the building committee to use shorter board lengths for flooring so he could specify more and bigger windows to bring added natural light to the interiors.[32] Substantially altered in the 1920s and 1930s, one of the few remaining original features to show Henry's careful specification of fixtures and materials is the nearly intact boys' lavatory facilities in the basement, with its monumental, gentlemen's-club-like urinals and stall dividers of beautifully figured marble.

Immediately following the submission of the Fleishhacker design, Greene and Greene embarked on the commission to design a residence for Nathan Bentz in Santa Barbara. Charles Greene claimed credit for the design, and its inventive plan and new (for Greene and Greene) use of materials exhibit his creative touch.[33] Charles also had much in common with Nathan Bentz, who, with his brothers, John and Philip, had become

successful curio dealers specializing in Chinese and Japanese art goods. Nathan Bentz, like Charles Greene, was thoroughly mystified by people who quibbled about the value of art. In one exchange, Bentz was reported to ask a friend "Would you like to see the most beautiful thing in the world?" He carefully removed from its box, so goes the story, an exquisite porcelain vase with a rare and beautiful cucumber crackle glaze. "This, to me, is the most beautiful thing in the world," said the dealer. "What is this porcelain worth?" his friend asked. "Nothing, if you do not love it," replied Bentz, "everything, if you do."[34] Apparently an appreciative client, Bentz lived in his Greene and Greene house for thirty years, until his death in 1942.

Outwardly, the Nathan Bentz house shares many of the characteristics of the firm's wood houses of the "classic" period from 1907 to 1909: a split-shake exterior, deep overhanging eaves, and the trademark exposed rafters. The angled plan, a dog-leg shape similar to that of the Fleishhacker house, allowed for stunning vistas toward the Channel Islands. A fully developed basement hidden behind a brick arcade of moorish pointed arches included a space dedicated to displaying a portion of Bentz's renowned collection of oriental art. The interiors were roomy, thanks to the use of steel I-beams that could span large spaces. In the living room, the beams were concealed (and simultaneously acknowledged) by deep plaster moldings, whose billowy, scalloped shapes softly reflected the light from the "eye-comfort" fixtures suspended from the ceiling. Vast picture windows gave views toward the ocean and provided ambient light for the display of art and artifacts against the painted plaster walls.[35] Charles's designs for interior spaces had become more self-effacing since his return from England, even to the point of being a vehicle for views, or a suitable backdrop for art, as much as a work of art itself.

While the Fleishhacker and Bentz projects were getting under way, the Greenes were also designing a residence for the three unmarried sisters of their former client, James Culbertson. The sisters had purchased a lot directly opposite the Blacker estate in Pasadena's Oak Knoll neighborhood and their house would be the last large Pasadena commission for Greene and Greene, encompassing residence, furniture, decorative arts, and landscaping. At sixty-one, Cordelia Culbertson was the eldest of the three

31

32 **Nathan Bentz house, Santa Barbara, 1911.**
Living room.

33 **Cordelia Culbertson house, Pasadena, 1911–13.**
Street facade, view from the northwest. The low-lying
profile belies the formidable structure in the rear.

34 **Cordelia Culbertson house.**
Entry hall.

35 **Cordelia Culbertson house.**
East pergola walkway, view toward the terrace over
the garage structure. A brilliant display of white
wisteria occurs in the spring.

32

33

34

sisters and acted as the official client. Her two younger sisters, Kate and Margaret, were fifty-eight and fifty-one, respectively, when the house was commissioned and they probably all expected it to be the home in which they would spend their remaining years. They also felt they could afford to spend a generous sum for its completion. No estimate was given, and no budget was set.[36]

From the street, the single-story elevation of the house appears deceptively unimposing. Most of its mass, and a spacious inner courtyard, is hidden from view. Equally obscured is the two-story height of the north wing, as well as the hillside where the extensive water gardens (now demolished) once existed. The unusual siting of the house was a creative solution to the clients' seemingly contradictory request that all of the rooms be on the same level and that the bedroom chambers be situated on an upper level. This was neatly solved by siting the back of the house directly over the escarpment to the north, thereby allowing for a sixteen- to twenty-foot drop from the bedrooms to the garden walkway below.[37]

Continuing to develop the theme of designing for nontimber materials, Greene and Greene specified Gunite for the exterior surface of the Culbertson residence, the same proprietary blown-on cement process used on the Fleishhacker's Woodside estate. In this case, Gunite was used not only as a cladding for the entire house but on the surrounding walls and fences as a transition material to the landscape. The concealing nature of the material meant that the expression of underlying structure was only sculpturally suggested, not explicitly articulated, as it had been by the massive timbers in the Greenes' earlier houses. This was a significant departure from the Arts and Crafts aesthetic, and again demonstrates that it was not a lack of willingness to change that shortened the Greenes' client list after 1909. Still, there were concessions to the traditional vocabulary of the firm, such as the timber purlins and ridge beams that project beyond the gable eaves, and rafter ends that are just visible under the low pitch of the roof. The roof's predominantly green field tiles, supplied by the Ludowici-Celadon Company, evoke a Chinese palace and recall similar roof treatments for the Tichenor house (1904–05) and the Oaklawn portals and shelter (1905–06). Dark-green tiles are intermixed with occasional red and

35

GREENE & GREENE

36 **Cordelia Culbertson house.**
The variegated coloring of roof tiles was a carefully planned aesthetic effect.

37 **Cordelia Culbertson house.**
Detail of loggia capitals showing two of Ernest Batchelder's series of four "minstrel" corbels, one of the earliest known uses of the tilemaker's wares.

38 **Cordelia Culbertson house.**
The lower-level loggia, a vast sheltered outdoor room (later enclosed) above which were situated the ladies' chambers.

39 **Cordelia Culbertson house.**
Interior view of dining room as originally furnished.

40 **Cordelia Culbertson house.**
Dining-room fireplace executed in Benou Jaune and Numidian marbles.

36

37

38

lighter-green pieces to give a lively variation in color to the large surface area.

Inside, wood paneling is nowhere to be seen, and yet the interiors are anything but self-effacing. Instead, sculptured plaster, velour fabric wall coverings, and exotic marble predominate. The high-ceilinged entry (reflected on the exterior by a separate, elevated section of roof) gives the impression of a reception hall rather than a transitional space. A Chinese-style carpet, woven in the same Bohemian workshops of J. Ginsky that had created the rugs for the Gambles' living room, was specified to cover the chevron-patterned oak flooring.[38] The enameled wood trim and columns of the entry are subtly and unevenly fluted, de-emphasizing the material and emphasizing the sculptural quality of the surface. The furniture, by contrast, remained unpainted. For the entry space, Charles Greene designed high-back armchairs and a large cloak-cabinet in dark crotch mahogany with inlays of koa, vermilion, and lilac root—all broodingly dark pieces. Dark mahogany was also used for the living-room chairs and case pieces. A dramatic shift had taken place. No longer did subtle variations in color between wood paneling and furniture predominate. Against the light paint and velour wall coverings, the very dark furniture established a contrast in color values far bolder than the Greenes' earlier interiors. There was an equally significant change in the sudden departure from the predominantly anti-historical designs of the pieces in the Blacker, Gamble, Thorsen, and Pratt houses, where soft curves and horizontal lines in the furniture echoed their architectural surroundings. By contrast, the Culbertson entry-hall and living-room furniture is linear, vertical, and more hard-edged than the Greenes' earlier pieces. A classicizing aesthetic was at work. Decorative inlays are tighter, more cramped, and less integral to the surfaces. Whereas the Thorsen dining-table inlay showed organic freedom in the low-relief design of the uprooted periwinkle, the rose-and-ribbon inlays of the Culbertson entry-hall pieces are tightly intertwined with the vertical edges of the panel borders. The inlay for the living-room chairs and table legs is delicate but rigid bundles of vertical lines with conventionalized flowers, golden in color to harmonize with the fixtures and velour wall covering. Glass panels in the case pieces are cut with a twining rose design similar to

39

40

41 **Cordelia Culbertson house, Pasadena, 1911–13.**
  Rear facade, view from the canyon behind the house.

42 **Cordelia Culbertson house.**
  Hillside water garden at the rear of the house
  (demolished), inspired by Italian precedent.

43 **Cordelia Culbertson house.**
  Engraved greeting card used by Mrs. Francis F.
  Prentiss, second owner of the house, showing a
  romanticized illustration of the water garden.

44 **Cordelia Culbertson house.**
  Living room with original furniture in place.

45 **Cordelia Culbertson house.**
  Garden room, view to the south toward the dining room.

41

42

43

44

45

the entry-hall inlays.[39] In the dining room, the walls were covered in silvery velour. The fireplace is of Benou Jaune marble with a center panel of Numidian marble. As in the living room, a plaster moulding shaped in a wave-like design meets the coved ceiling to produce a visually rich and soothing transition. The ceiling fixture medallion is a classicized egg-and-dart design encircling an acanthus-leaf canopy in the center. The dining-room furniture was a lighter and warmer mahogany than were the entry and living-room pieces, with a classicizing rope-and-sheaf inlay design. The tops of the sideboard and server are massive slabs of Numidian marble that relate the pieces to the fireplace. At the pivot-point of the plan is a garden room, with an ingenious pocket-wall with a glazed panel and separate screen that can be raised into a soffit overhead, opening a wide section of wall to views of the courtyard with its colorful fountain in custom-designed Pewabic tile.

In the fall of 1912, when the envelope of the house was largely completed, Charles Greene accompanied the Culbertson sisters on a shopping expedition to New York to select and purchase interior appointments for their home. Henry stayed behind to oversee the finishing of the floors and other final touches.[40] In earlier days Charles Greene had occasionally specified selected pieces of Craftsman furniture for the interiors of some houses of his design, but this was the only time that Charles was formally engaged to comprehensively appoint the interiors of one of his houses with furnishings not designed by him. He was no doubt aware that he was suddenly operating in the established sphere of interior designers such as Elsie de Wolfe, who was chosen by the Fleishhackers to decorate and furnish the white interiors of Green Gables. Charles certainly must have preferred having this responsibility himself compared with the alternative of the Culbertson ladies selecting another designer, or (worse) selecting their own furnishings unsupervised. In New York, Charles and the Culbertsons had an ambitious shopping agenda that included several visits to the interior decorator F. N. Dowling. There they selected bedroom rugs, bedspreads, and drapes, and the black-and-gold damask fabric used to make the living-room curtains and portieres. Charles would use the same strongly patterned fabric to upholster the furniture that he was still in the process of designing for the living room.[41] It was also at Dowling's that he purchased a suite of Louis XVI

46

47

bedroom furniture in grey enamel, an "English sofa" with down cushions in
red damask, and a suite of Queen Anne bedroom furniture. Elsie de Wolfe
would have approved. He also ordered seventy-eight interior and exterior
lighting fixtures from the Sterling Bronze Company catalog, fifteen pieces of
furniture from the Fifth Avenue antiques dealer A. J. Crawford, and a
chiffonier from Pottier & Stymus.[42] In less than two weeks, Charles Greene
had ordered nearly ten thousand dollars' worth of furnishings and fixtures
for his clients.

Directly below the Culbertsons' richly decorated bedroom chambers was
an open loggia (later enclosed) that overlooked the canyon. This outdoor
room with its octagonal columns, corbels, and beams, was also clad in Gunite,
allowing for softened edges reminiscent of the Greenes' timber years. The
capitals of the octagonal columns are decorated with Ernest Batchelder's
"minstrel" tiles, the first use of the tile-maker's products in the Greenes'
work.[43] Sadly, the most spectacular aspect of the Culbertson commission
does not survive, save for scattered remnants. The hillside water garden was
a master stroke of design that attracted praise and attention from the
architectural and popular press. A grand staircase on the steep hill
connected a portal near the northeast corner of the property with the garden
below. At the stairway's lower landing a division sent two sets of terraced
steps down in a half-ellipse curve to embrace the pool and sunken grassy
area below. In the upper staircase, a water channel—faced with Grueby
tile—was cut into the treads and risers to conduct overflow from the upper
courtyard fountain to the lower water garden. Italian cypresses flanked the
stairs, strengthening the Mediterranean imagery. The plasticity of Gunite
was ideal for creating the grotto-like drippings on the tiers of the lower
fountain structure, giving the instant appearance of antiquity at the focal
point of the water feature. A bench, trellis, and lath house were added in
1914 to complete the alfresco environment. The immediate inspiration for
the water garden may have been the Fountain of the Dragons at Villa d'Este,
Tivoli, or possibly the middle fountain at Villa Aldobrandini, Frascati, both of
which Charles and Alice Greene had toured on their honeymoon in 1901.[44]
Charles may have recalled seeing either of these fountains, but he probably
would have had to rely on published illustrations to supplement his memory.

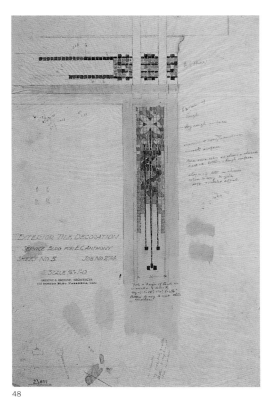

48

49

50

48 **Earle C. Anthony automobile showroom, Los Angeles, 1911 (demolished).**
Charles Greene's watercolor design for exterior decorative-tile scheme.

49 **Earle C. Anthony automobile showroom.**
West (front) facade in 1954.

50 **Earle C. Anthony automobile showroom.**
View of decorative plaster ceiling design.

Many popular books of the time had illustrations of Villa d'Este and Aldobrandini, and one in particular, entitled *European and Japanese Gardens* (1902) had a chapter dedicated to the principles of design in Italian gardens, and included several illustrations of both.[45] This book was in Charles Greene's personal collection.[46]

The Culbertson sisters, while enthusiastic about the Greenes' work, had spent nearly $200,000 on the house and grounds, and by 1917 they could no longer afford to keep, let alone keep up, the property. It was purchased by Mrs. Dudley P. (Elisabeth S.) Allen of Cleveland, Ohio, who shortly remarried and became Mrs. Francis Fleury Prentiss. Elisabeth Prentiss had the good judgment (and money) to maintain the Greenes' involvement in all of her future architectural and decorative requirements for 1188 Hillcrest Avenue. She named her new estate "Il Paradiso," no doubt in recognition of the Italian-inspired heavenly beauty of the water garden. In all, twenty-five separate job numbers were issued by the Greene and Greene firm to the second owner of the house between 1917 and 1937, representing a considerable flow of work for the brothers during otherwise lean times. Notable among these was a $3,000 commission in 1919 for Charles to paint five scenic panels for the entry hall.[47] In 1931, Henry Greene designed for her a charming lath house. Not all of the various projects for Mrs. Prentiss went well, especially one involving a project for Charles to design and carve nine decorative plaques for the dining-room walls. The first three plaques did not meet Mrs. Prentiss's expectations from an artistic standpoint, and she called the balance of the project to a halt. She had also asked Charles to design and produce a pair of travertine vases for the entry. These were duly installed, but the accompanying bill shocked her considerably. She wrote to Charles, saying, "It really never had occurred to me that they would reach such a sum."[48]

Immediately following the initial commission to design the Culbertson sisters' house, former client Earle C. Anthony commissioned an automobile showroom (now destroyed) near downtown Los Angeles. The project was to design exterior decoration, entry doors, and interior fittings for an existing commercial building designed by John Parkinson and Edwin Bergstrom. The contract for alterations and additions came with a budget of $33,000,

51 **S. C. Graham house**, **Los Angeles**, **1911** (project).
   Artist's watercolor rendering of the unbuilt house.

52 Charles S. Greene. Rosewood writing desk, 1912.

51

52

and Charles went to work. It was the firm's first success at winning a commercial project in several years. Grueby tiles were used to carry out the exterior's colorful decorative motif, which bore a resemblance to the rigid form of the Culbertson living-room furniture inlay. One of the most striking features of Charles's designs for the interior was the plaster relief on the ceiling, which depicted rays of sunshine emanating from behind overlapping stylized automobile grilles. The interior supporting columns were octagonal, like those of the Culbertson loggia, but were covered not in Gunite but tile, including custom-designed pieces of Pewabic. The hanging light fixtures, also octagonal, were reminiscent of the white-cedar basket lights in the Gamble house master bedroom. Decorative ironwork for the mezzanine balcony, stairway, and elevator doors was designed in a variation of the *tsuba* shape, with decorative rosettes as functional connectors. It was not long after this commission that Charles Greene purchased a Hudson automobile, which understandably put him out of favor with his Packard-dealer client, and Anthony awarded his future architectural commissions, both domestic and commercial, to Bernard Maybeck's office in San Francisco.

Returning to the English idiom that had been revived in the Fleishhacker house and A. M. Drake project drawings, Greene and Greene designed a residence for S. C. Graham that was announced in a *Los Angeles Times* newspaper article on December 10, 1911. A perspective drawing, based on the fully executed plans and elevations, illustrated the article.[49] The Graham house was designed to be a three-story, sixteen-room mansion for the Westchester Tract, a quasi-suburban setting just north of Pico Boulevard on South Arlington Street in Los Angeles. The L-shaped plan included a living room thirty-two feet by twenty-one feet, and a spacious stair-hall, library, and covered porch ranged along the street elevation of the ground floor. Service areas were to occupy the other leg of the plan, similar to the configuration of the Thorsen house. Like the Robinson and Drake houses, brick piers under a coat of stucco (or possibly Gunite) were to be supported by tapering buttresses. In the spirit of Greene and Greene's post-bungalow designs, exposed structural wood was present, but minimized. The interiors, however, were intended to be crisply defined sectional wood paneling rather than the broad, uninterrupted surfaces of the Blacker or Gamble house walls. Leaded

art-glass windows were specified for the oak-paneled library, ceilings were to be coved plaster throughout, and a brushed-and-carved redwood frieze was to embellish the dining room. Sadly, S. C. Graham was another client who chose not to pursue construction, and another carefully conceived design was relegated to the file cabinet.

No doubt disheartened, Charles undertook fewer and increasingly specialized projects during this period, primarily from former clients. He also concentrated on alterations to his own home and the design of a elaborately detailed rosewood writing desk. The form of the desk is similar to an earlier piece designed for the Gamble guest bedroom, and was also executed by John Hall though in the darker finish Charles had recently come to prefer. Inlaid with symbols of Charles's growing passion for celestial bodies and elemental symbolism, it is the most elaborate and mystical furniture design of his career. In it, an ivory moon floats among silver stars and the sun's rays shine among the carved outline of billowy clouds. It was a speculative piece, placed on consignment at Nathan Bentz's Santa Barbara shop, where it remained unsold for thirty years.

In late 1911, Henry designed three relatively modest houses for Charles P. Wilcox, C. G. Brown, and Mrs. Lena W. Huston, all in the six-hundred block of North Marengo Avenue in Pasadena (only the last of which stills stands). There was also more work coming in from the Pasadena Ice Company, and in early 1912 the firm designed two bungalows for Long Beach for Robert Blacker (another unbuilt project). In April a contract was signed for a two-story apartment block on Herkimer (now Union) Street in Pasadena. The symmetry, rationality, and overall simplicity of the building betrays Henry Greene's distinctive touch. Gunite cladding and a flat roof give Herkimer Arms a vaguely pueblo-like appearance, though decorative Chinese tiles on the parapet wall and the timber-trellis portals flanking the block connect with the firm's more familiar work. Despite this, however, the design is predominantly a product of the new Greene and Greene order with Henry in control. His ability to solve issues of space efficiency is shown in the trundle-type bed that rolls out from underneath a closet raised one step above the level of the living room. This was an improvement over the fold-out Murphy-style bed, since pictures could still be hung on the wall over the

53 **Annie Blacker house, Pasadena, 1912**.
East (front) facade. The four-square massing recalls
Henry Greene's earlier design for "A California House."

53

56

54 **Mary Marston Kew house, San Diego, 1912–13 (demolished).**
East (front) facade, facing Balboa Park.

55 **Mary Marston Kew house.**
View of rear facade from the tennis court.

56 **Mary Marston Kew house.**
Living room.

sleeping area. The chairs and tables that Henry designed for the apartments were equally dignified and economical, like their designer.

In his concept for a house for Robert Blacker's sister, Annie Blacker, Henry again drew from the "California House" concept he had developed in 1904–05, with some modifications. It is a simplified legacy of the wooden bungalow years, and represents a responsibility that Henry Greene felt to preserve the popular perception of the Greenes' classic work in wood for the discriminating few who still wanted it. The elongated plan is T-shaped, with a straightforward central hallway and stairs. The exterior, a simple facade under a spreading gable, comes to life because of its broad portico and large trellis structures that create a deep terrace on the ground level and a balcony (originally with a railing) above it.

In the late summer of 1912, before Charles left for New York to attend to the interior furnishings of the Culbertson sisters' house, he and his brother worked on the design of a large residence for Mrs. Mary M. Kew and her husband, Michael Kew, in San Diego. Simultaneously, Henry designed and oversaw alterations and additions for the home of Judge George A. Gibbs, designed alterations to two annexes of the Vista del Arroyo Hotel, and drew up plans for a teahouse, pergola, and garage with chauffeur's quarters for Dr. Robert P. McReynolds in Los Angeles. There were also projects on the boards for Mrs. Thomas Palmer in Highland Park, and Frank L. Palmer (possibly a relation) in North Pomona, much of which Henry would have handled while Charles was in New York. The most ambitious project pending at this time, however, was the house for Mary Marston Kew and her family. The design of the five-bedroom English-style residence, now demolished, combined aspects of the James Culbertson house (1902), the Fleishhacker house of 1911, and the recent S. C. Graham project. Mary Marston Kew was from an old-line San Diego family, and her husband, Michael Kew, was an attorney. The Kews, like the Fleishhackers, preferred the English style to the Greenes' more characteristic timber work, though remnants of the latter emerge in the rear pergola details. In massing and materials, the Kew house was particularly reminiscent of the James Culbertson house. Its disposition of pebble-dash on the ground level and half-timbering and shingle infill on the upper level was similar, as was its front elevation, where two gables projected from a transverse roof to flank the entry. This is not surprising, since Mr. Kew had hired the Greenes based on seeing an English house while driving around Pasadena one day. Kew asked who had designed it, and the Greenes were mentioned. It could only have been the James Culbertson house.[50] The Kew house in its final state was much more elaborately appointed, however, than the Culbertson house. Many labor-intensive features were specified, such as a rolled-eave roof with a subtly sculptured surface meant to resemble thatch. Like the Fleishhacker roof, the shingles were individually shaped to conform to the irregular surface treatment. The foundation was artistically handled, too: carefully placed stones at the base gradually gave way to a pebble-dash wall surface that continued to the second level. Small window panes were an added expense, as were the oak-paneled interiors carried out in a Tudor style, with linen-fold paneling and broad, dressed and carved stone fireplaces. Construction lasted over a year, from early 1913 and into 1914.[51] It is difficult to say which of the two Greenes had a greater hand in the design and execution of the Kew house. While the plan is characteristic of Henry, the richness and variety of surface textures and artistic masonry strongly suggest his older brother's involvement.[52]

From this time, Charles Greene's influence faded increasingly within the practice. For two decades Henry had played a supporting role to his brother's dominant one, and the realignment to primary design architect for the firm cannot have been an entirely easy one for a man whose nature it was to be accommodating. In short, he was far less likely to press innovative and creative ideas on a wavering client. He was stepping into a new role for which he had only sporadic previous experience. Perhaps sensing this, Henry planned a business trip to New York late in 1912 to meet with suppliers and fellow architects, writing to Charles that he believed such a trip might help him "in his line."[53]

The design for a house for Henry A. Ware followed the English tradition also, though on a significantly smaller budget than the Kew house had enjoyed.[54] Nonetheless, Henry produced a dignified and well-planned residence with several charming and distinctive elements, including a living room in brushed redwood. Below the beamed ceiling, sixty electric lights

57 **Henry A. Ware house, Pasadena, 1913.**
West (front) facade, perpendicular to the street. The
chimney at the back of the house was added in 1917.

58 **Henry A. Ware house.**
First floor plan. Ink-on-linen presentation drawing.

59 **William Mead Ladd house, Ojai, 1913.**
East (rear) terrace.

60 **William Mead Ladd house.**
Chimney stack on south facade.

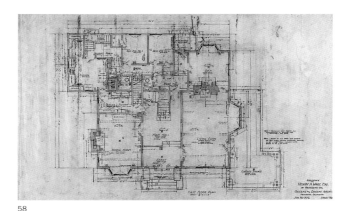

58

59

60

were concealed behind a redwood molding that curved subtly away from the
wall, acting as a continuous shield from incandescent glare around the room.
The result was a warm glow subtly circling the room at picture-rail height. A
shift in floor levels between the dining room and living room (by way of three
risers in the entry hall) recall Henry's subtle manipulation of levels in the
Crow house and the Herkimer Arms. Upstairs, a compact window seat on
one of the stair landings is a delightful appointment typical of Henry's keen
sense of spatial economy.

William Mead Ladd descended from one of the most prominent pioneer
families of Portland, Oregon. Ladd's father, William Sargent Ladd, had
arrived in Portland during the California Gold Rush and proceeded to build
the family's fortune, first in the liquor trade and later in land development
and real estate speculation. The younger William followed in his later
footsteps, successively becoming president of the Real Estate Title and Trust
Company, president of the banking house of Ladd & Tilton, and president of
Oregon Iron and Steel Co.[55] Though by 1913 building in stain-grade wood
was already on the wane, Ladd's timber-country instincts led him to Greene
and Greene to design a winter bungalow in the Ojai valley. The sobriety of
the plan and restraint of the decorative features is characteristic of its
designer, Henry Greene. The formal entry opened directly into the living
room from a porch on the west. By shifting this space off the primary axis of
the first floor plan, casement windows or french doors could be placed on all
four walls of the living room to give ample light, access to the terrace and
generous views of the spectacular mountains to the northeast. Designed for
casual living, a gallery-like hallway connects the living room to the dining
room at the far end, with two bedrooms between, placed opposite windows to
the rear terrace. A one-room upper level is reached by a staircase from the
hall, opposite which is another door to the terrace. Characteristically, even a
utilitarian corner of the house—the cellar door—is treated with style and
charm. The massive stone chimney of the living room shows a difference
between Charles Greene's approach to masonry work as opposed to his
brother's. Henry's chimney for Ladd has a predictable outline compared with
Charles's more broad-ranging choice of boulder sizes, for example, in the
chimneys of the Mary Cole house. The design of the Ladds' sandstone terrace

61 **William Mead Ladd house, Ojai, 1913.**
Decorative scuppers for drainage through the rear
terrace retaining wall.

62 **William Mead Ladd house.**
Plans and sections. Ink-on-linen presentation drawing.

61

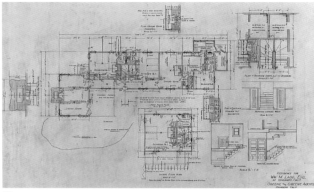

62

wall is more relaxed than that of the chimneys, though the line of the wall does not undulate as much as Charles's walls at the Irwin and Gamble houses. Stone scuppers and a view-lover's bench on the outside face of the wall are particularly charming appointments.

Later that year, Charles fell from grace with the firm's other Ojai client, Charles M. Pratt. The sting of rebuke is felt in a series of letters in which Charles defends himself against charges of insincerity, deception, and the high cost of his direct supervision of work. Pratt's accusatory letters do not survive, but their gist is clearly reflected in Charles's responses. First, his client was apparently critical of the firm's method of itemizing his bill for furniture and fixtures. Charles somewhat cryptically argues various angles, as if in an effort to convince himself as much as his client of his view of events.

"I could not understand your position. I have never been mistrusted before to my knowledge....In reply to your accusation of insincerity, I will say that as far as the office is concerned it is entirely unfounded. They are deadly sincere and perfectly convinced of their own portion. The charge must be laid directly to me. I understood just what your instructions were. I gave orders to have figures sent to you in items of complete cost for each piece. They [the office] say that I did not make it clear. I think that I did, but that need not concern you. I did not know how the bill had been made out....Before you telegraphed for items, we gave you a lump figure that included the complete cost to you of furniture and fixtures. All of this figuring was done by our accustomed rules and by the office. I did none of it. These figures prove themselves." Then, shifting ground, Charles admits of the error but blames his brother: "I know that the items of the list were incomplete contrary to your order as I understood it. My brother and I had some words about the way the list was to be made out. It was made according to our usual custom, not as I ordered it." Finally, acknowledging that his client had some basis for complaint, the frustrated Charles concluded, somewhat pathetically, "I still think that your sense of fairness must outweigh the contempt you might have for my business ability."[56]

In an undated letter, probably written shortly after his return from New York in the fall of 1912, Charles responded at length to Mr. Pratt's

complaint of the high bill for his personal supervision of landscape work. The defensive opening soon evolves into a passionate appeal for art patronage, revealing a deep commitment to art, and the root of his discontent with the profession. Mr Pratt's response, if any, does not survive.

Mr. C.M. Pratt
Cassa [*sic*] Barranca
Ojai

Dear Sir:
Your letter of the __th inst. was received and acknowledged by the office during my absence.

I have read [your letter] carefully and realize in full measure the discontent in it....I would have been glad had you been still more specific but am aware now (that it is too late) that I should have brought these business matters to your attention when you were in Pasadena. My excuse is that I had some landscape work in Los Angeles that was very trying as well as absorbing....Then, too, the papers were not ready to present to you at that time.

Of the trips I made to Nordhoff last summer, two were for the servants' room addition, one for some trouble about the roof and the other for color matching. The other seven trips were for the walls and grounds and were not for a day but for several days each. I did not think it advisable to make plans of the walls and terraces because it would be impossible to take advantage of the natural contours and trees, etc. So I had no levels taken but personally directed the work and carefully selected and placed the largest stones to harmonize with the surroundings. In some cases I made corrections in the work done when I was not on the ground. Of course this could have been done cheaper in the common way and by sending a man from the office instead of myself. But does not the result justify the expense? … This to my mind approaches the ideal of a transaction between artist and patron, and would be near indeed if you could but share my view.

Art reduced to a commodity of course cannot argue so, for investment seeks fixed financial return. But living art never can be so reduced. It must

63 **Charles M. Pratt house, Ojai, 1908–11.**
Stone portals and wall at roadside. The expense of
Charles Greene's personal supervision of this work
caused a rift with his client in 1913.

63

have become a curio in the hands of a dealer before it can be bartered
without any injury to the art. This is one good reason why living art
scarcely ever can compete with the old. Once exploited it ceases to be art.
You say that you have never before paid so high a price for this kind of
work; to which I reply that I believe you misjudge the character of mine. In
other words, is the comparison fair? Knowing what I do of the architectural
practice of today I cannot be very far wrong. Furthermore, there is no one to
my knowledge who has the temerity to limit the number of their
commissions to a person at supervision.

It is too much to expect that anyone may see the excellence of this
kind of thing in a few days. The work itself took months to execute and the
best years of my life went to develop this style. I realize that you are
concerned in affairs much more weighty than a little country house in the
Ojai, but trivial as it may seem to you my effort was for the best. My plea is
not so much for the fact as for the principle—not so much for the artist as
that art may find expression.

I do not claim for my management the strictest economy and I believe
that I understand how you must feel when for the greater part of your life
you have labored to bring to perfection the greatest of enterprises; how
those great undertakings could only be perfected by a systematic and rigid
restraint. How no saving could be too petty and order must be absolute.

My work is none of this. It is impossible that it should be so. Art and
commerce are divided and must ever be. Human natures in all classes are
far from perfect, in art natures perhaps less than others. But if I know so
well their weaknesses I also know their strengths....If one can afford to
have these things, does it not argue as well for you as for art that one
should have them? I do not speak on my own authority alone as to the
intrinsic art value of my work, though I could never have produced it
without knowing that. But do you know what a former president of the
American Institute [of Architects] says of it and also connoisseurs who
travel the world over in search of the rare and beautiful[?] I cannot find
reason for flattery in this, because for the most part they are unknown to
me, or of only slight acquaintance.[57] This sounds a bit egotistical but again I
recall that you are a very busy man and cannot be expected to hear of these

little things or read what is written of work that at a glance seems local.

Into your busy life I have sought to bring what lay in my power of the
best that I could do for Art and for you. How I wish I had the power to look
into your soul to more fully understand not what you *think* but what you
feel. I doubt not for a moment your power of appreciation, but I should know
better what to say without arguing.

I have known many people that love the beautiful but it is beyond
their reach. For you all these things are possible and, believe me, I have
given what I could personally because I thought you would like it and
because I felt sure that you would in the end appreciate.

C. Sumner Greene[58]

Over the next three years, Charles spent more time writing than
designing, although there were some notable exceptions. Fire screens,
andirons, and metal grill work designed for the Blacker and Thorsen houses
were manufactured during this period, and represent some of the Greenes'
finest decorative arts. Previous metalwork—both wrought and cast—had
been executed for the Greenes by Pacific Ornamental Iron Works of Los
Angeles. For these later, highly specialized pieces that required delicate
chasing of polished steel and subtle castings in bronze Charles shifted his
allegiance to George Burkhard and R. Lench of the Art Metal Company of
Los Angeles. The fire screens especially were exceptionally labor-intensive
projects that took the men months to complete, but the resulting work—
particularly the Thorsens' living-room fire screen in polished steel, described
in chapter five—stands out as one of his crowning artistic achievements.

At about this time, Charles wrote a novel entitled *Thais Thayer* that was
never published.[59] Its characters include a thinly veiled self-portrait in the
role of Roy Jones, an idealistic young architect recently graduated from MIT.
Jones is kidnapped and taken to a desert island by a wealthy merchant who
compels Jones to design a house for Thais Thayer, an operatic diva with
whom the mogul is in love. One quickly gets the impression that the novel is
merely a vehicle for the expression of the author's views on beauty and
spirituality, views that might conveniently be woven into a popular love
story. The architect falls in love with the diva, and his inspiration for the

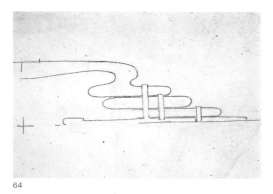

64

65

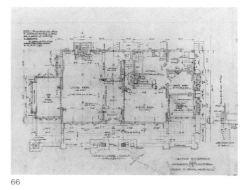

66

64 Charles S. Greene. Pencil sketch of firescreen detail for Robert R. Blacker house living room (1914).

65 **William E. Hamlin house, Pasadena, 1914–16 (project).**
Henry Greene produced scores of drawings like this one, but Hamlin died before anything was built.

66 **John T. Greene house, Sacramento, 1914–15.**
First floor plan. Pencil-on-tissue drawing.

design of her house comes from his romantic and zen-like contemplation of a Chinese bronze incenser. In one scene, he tells the singer, "There is a Japanese poem I have heard that expresses the simple thought of the soul … 'In the morning of Early Dew a maid went to a Spring to fetch Pure Water, when, lo! mysterious depths, two golden carp were there before.' 'I think I understand,' she said.…Life is a mysterious mingling. It is dual. Thought alone is pure.'"[60] Within the text Charles also manages praise for his own work, including a passage in which he apparently describes the Cordelia Culbertson garden (and presciently, the Fleishhacker water garden of 1927–28): 'She held in her hand an engraving … I saw an oblong pool closed on three sides by a mossy stone wall; a wide flagged terrace with a dwelling house surrounding it all. At the head of the pool a flight of steps led from the terrace to the rippled water. Clustered vines clung to the walls and entwined the porcelain balustrade.… I had never seen anything like it; so beautiful; I forgot to thank her.'[61] *Thais Thayer* was probably a necessary catharsis for Charles, and he was disappointed that it was never published. Nonetheless, it offers interesting insights into his state of mind in the years following the creation of his most revered work.

Henry proceeded with the design of most of the projects that were on the boards in 1914, and the firm's clients enjoyed a high level of personal attention from Henry precisely because business had fallen off so dramatically. Of the twenty-one jobs that were assigned numbers that year, all but two were minor alterations and additions, small decorative projects, or designs for houses that were never built. The exceptions included Henry's design for a $4,000 bungalow for Dr. Rosa Englemann. Though the design was not particularly innovative, it included an interesting built-in feature that was emblematic of Henry's talent for mechanical creativity. One of the living-room bookcase doors he fitted with a decoratively detailed strut attached to its facing panel. The strut was hinged on its top edge so that it could be swung out from the panel to support a table top, which was to be used for serving tea.

Among the unbuilt projects that year was a design for William E. Hamlin of Syracuse, who commissioned Greene and Greene to develop plans and elevations for a three-story mansion to be built on South Orange Grove

Avenue in Pasadena. One of Henry's schemes was an uncharacteristic Beaux-Arts design that controverted all of the ideals of function-driven form that the Greenes had followed for many years. Times were tough financially, however, and Henry accepted what work was available to him. In the end, however, Hamlin died before construction could begin, and his widow elected not to build.

The firm's more familiar legacy of wood architecture resurfaced in a design for the Sacramento real estate developer John Thomas Greene (no immediate relation to the architects). John Greene and his wife, Alvene, had purchased an interest in a farm on H Street Road opposite McKinley Park in east Sacramento, an area that had recently been incorporated into the city. The park-like setting encouraged John and Alvene to make several trips to the San Francisco area and Southern California to look at suburban houses that might suggest a suitable style for the development they planned for the farmland.[62] Like others before them, they were struck by the serene beauty of the Greenes' work in Pasadena, and especially by the Japanese qualities in the roof lines and overhanging eaves. The design that Henry created for them was a compact distillation of the classic wood vocabulary that the firm had effectively abandoned a few years earlier. The dimensions of the facade are based on the Golden Rectangle, the ancient law of proportion that controls the height as a function of the base length.[63] The plan shows Henry's preference for a central hall, though in this case the hall is also contiguous with the large living room and stair landing, creating a generous and hospitable reception area in a relatively modest-sized house. Especially notable is an intimate breakfast room adjacent to the dining area. Unstained, clear-heart redwood beams and paneling give the ten-foot-square space the intimate ambience of a Berkeley cottage in the style of Bernard Maybeck, but it was Henry Greene's refinement of the firm's legacy in wood.[64] Henry's floor plan—though not the articulated wood envelope of the structure—lived on even as public tastes shifted, and was subsequently used in another house in John Greene's development a few lots to the west. Meanwhile, in mid-1915, when Charles was involved with extensive decorative alterations to Mortimer Fleishhacker's house near San Francisco, Henry sketched a farmhouse for Mrs. Ruben H. Donnelly's property in Lake

67 John T. Greene house.
North (front) facade. Henry Greene's design is based on classical Golden Rectangle proportions.

68 John T. Greene house.
The deep reception hall and living area are flanked by contiguous smaller rooms that make for a generous flow on the first level.

67

68

70

69   71

Forest, Illinois. The house was never built, but the asymmetry, multi-leveled roofline, and glazed sun porch in Henry's sketches show a charm and compositional confidence that is reminiscent of his design for the Crow house of 1909.

The only new construction to proceed from a Greene and Greene design developed in 1915 was the two-story residence for Dr. Nathan H. Williams just north of Pasadena. Its aspect is unlike any other of the Greenes' houses. The organization of the windows and entry door is axially symmetrical on the street elevation, but the rear elevation shows the inventive composition of which Henry was also capable. The Gunite-clad front elevation seems overwhelmed by the visual weight of the portico and balcony structure, though this effect is softened in part by the perforated abstract designs in panels of wire mesh that span the structural steel of the portico, a technique originally used on the walls and fences for the Cordelia Culbertson house. Deep and low eaves cast shadows on the upper level while the lower-level windows have structurally integral hoods to shield the interiors from midday sunlight. Inside, the central hall plan is employed, with a staircase rising from it at a right angle. All surfaces are painted and the spaces are generous and welcoming. In the dining room the built-in sideboard is a faint echo of the grand statements made in the large houses of earlier years, but its crisp lines are a nod to modernity. The interiors are nearly devoid of decorative effects, save for the twisted-rope border and intricate flower medallions carved into the white marble of the living-room fireplace. Over the rear patio, an open structure with perforated Gunite panels at the corners originally sheltered an outdoor room (now enclosed). One detail in particular illustrates Henry Greene's courage in exploiting the fully concealing nature of the Gunite material: around the entire house the downspouts are permanently imbedded by the blown-on cement on the exterior walls. Henry Greene's garden plan for Dr. Williams was dominated by terraced expanses of lawn. It also included a small lily pond and secluded flower garden, however, as a quiet refuge at the rear of the property. By 1917, this unorthodox work of the Greene and Greene firm had been published in *American Country Houses of Today* by Aymar Embury II.[65]

At about this time, Charles took the revealing step of documenting his most cherished designs in a series of more than 150 photographs that he commissioned from Leroy Hulbert, a friend of Henry Greene's wife, Emeline, and a relative of Charles's former sweetheart, Bess Hulbert. Leroy Hulbert had come to Los Angeles from St. Louis, where Benjamin B. Hulbert was proprietor of the Gemelli Studios photographic business. Both Hulberts moved to California, and in 1903, Leroy Hulbert took a portrait of Henry Greene's son, Henry Dart Greene, at the family's Los Angeles home. Leroy advertised his business as the "Photographic Art Shop, Photography and Watercolors." Charles engaged Hulbert to document the firm's work in an artistic way, being specific as to how the views were composed, printed, and toned.[66]

Charles continued to pursue writing, most notably in a published article for *The Architect* in December 1915 that was printed again the following month in *Homes and Gardens*.[67] In it, Charles wore his professional discontent on his sleeve, much as he had in his novel, *Thais Thayer*. By inference, he painted himself as following a purist's credo while forced to operate among unenlightened clients: "To be true to the principle of all successful building, the bungalow architect must study carefully the practical conditions of the problem, and the personality of the owner forms one of the most difficult.... Many owners do not fully realize this duty of the architect and do not give him time enough to fully master these preliminaries. They demand pictures and drawings...." That he felt the need to complain is poignant given the exceptionally high quality of his work and the inspiration that it gave to so many. It also suggests how removed he had become from his fellow professionals, some of whom, such as Sylvanus B. Marston, had worked under him a decade before and had gone on to careers of relatively sustained financial success and regional acclaim. What Charles did not seem to fully appreciate was the profound and broad impact that the work of Greene and Greene had had on American architecture, and, ironically, the sheer impossibility of Charles's quality of work being replicated to his satisfaction by anyone else, even his brother. He might have contented himself with the knowledge that he had produced a remarkable body of progressive and artistic houses, but he was too close to the grind of daily business to see it that way.

The Elusive Client

73 **Dr. Nathan H. Williams house, Altadena, 1915–16.**
Entry hall and dining room.

74 **Dr. Nathan H. Williams house.**
Detail of entry hall stairs.

75 **Dr. Nathan H. Williams house.**
Detail of carved design in marble beneath living-
room mantel.

73

Early in 1916, Henry Greene produced designs for alterations to the
Louise Halsted house and the A. A. Libby house, and office alterations
(including a dumbwaiter) for the Pasadena Ice Company. On the latter he
took full credit for the design, for the first time even labeling one of his
drawings "Henry M. Greene, Architect." Charles had done this on occasion,
though usually only with regard to a speculative project such as the "Sketch
for Dwelling Place for W. B. T." (1903) or on drawings for his own house.
Officially, Henry's independent impulse was premature: the firm would keep
the name Greene and Greene until 1922. In practice, however, it
acknowledged the imminent planned departure of his brother for the
Northern California artists' hamlet of Carmel-by-the-Sea. Before Charles
left with his family, however, he designed a pair of stone portals, an iron
gate, wooden signs, and curb alterations for the two driveway ends of
Westmoreland Place, near the David B. Gamble and Mary Cole houses. The
homeowners on the private street reportedly had begun to complain of
sightseeing traffic in front of their homes, traffic generated by the numerous
postcards and illustrated periodicals promoting Pasadena. The
Westmoreland portals are formed by two piles of arroyo stones topped with
firebrick. Tall and slender compared with the squat piles of immense
boulders of the Oaklawn portals (1904–05), the Westmoreland portals and
gate take their form from their function: the gate had to be tall enough to
allow the automobiles of residents and guests to pass, but not so tall as to
allow the sightseeing buses to clear the top of the gate structure.
Recognizing their context, the stones and bricks were selected to harmonize
in size and color with the materials used in the porte cochere of the Cole
house. Charles also designed a wooden sign and another pile of boulders to
mark and identify the south end of the driveway. Within a few weeks, for
complex professional and personal reasons, Charles and his family had
packed their belongings and left town. For purposes practical and aesthetic,
the Greene and Greene partnership existed no more.

74

75

76 **Westmoreland Improvement Company, portals and gate, Pasadena, 1916.**
Remarkably intact, these portals still guard the north entrance to Westmoreland Place, a stone's throw from the David B. Gamble house.

76

7

Guarding a Legacy

1   Page 174:
    Walter L. Richardson ranch house, Porterville, 1929.
    Rear terrace, courtyard fireplace, and chimney (space
    now enclosed).

2   **Mortimer Fleishhacker townhouse, San Francisco,
    1916 (project).**
    Front elevation. Pencil-on-tissue.

3   Henry Mather Greene, c. 1935.

4   **Charles H. Stoddard house, Burlingame, 1916 (project).**
    Front elevation. Pencil-on-tissue.

5   **Charles H. Stoddard house.**
    Bird's-eye perspective from rear. Pencil-on-tissue sketch.

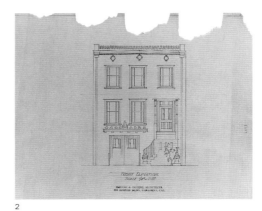

2

3

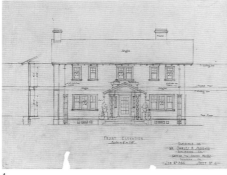

4

5

During the second half of 1916 the Greene and Greene office was in limbo. Following the departure of its senior partner and principle architect-designer, the future seemed uncertain. Although Charles Greene had moved his family to a rented cottage in Carmel, three hundred miles to the north, he had not formally declared an end to the twenty-two-year business partnership with his brother.[1] The remaining office staff, although diminished significantly in size from a decade earlier, must have wondered if Charles would return, and if so, when? Would Henry lead the firm? Increasingly, the answer seemed to be "yes," but the younger sibling, now forty-six, would have to do so without benefit of the clear authority and status that a definitive break between the two principals would have conferred on him.

Despite this, Henry proved willing to tackle the new role. After all, he had had experience with ambiguity. It was Henry who had kept the office work flowing during Charles's honeymoon in 1901, his residence in England in 1909, and his periodic absences to attend to the Mortimer Fleishhacker and Cordelia Culbertson jobs in 1911 and 1912. Henry had become accustomed to authoritative ambiguity in his own household, too, where the will of his mother-in-law was frequently felt under the shared roof of her house. Henry Greene's well-tempered demeanor, his work ethic and sense of duty, and his highly principled character helped him to navigate sea changes such as these. With little outward sign of difficulty Henry filled the vacuum left by his brother, though it could not have been an easy experience. Moreover, their father, Dr. T. S. Greene, who had been serving as the firm's bookkeeper for several years, expanded his role in an effort to facilitate a long-distance collaboration between Charles and Henry. Dr. Greene's frequent and detailed correspondence with Charles between 1916 and 1920 was designed in part to keep Charles interested in the work of the firm. At times, Charles seemed willing. At others, he would obliquely remind his father of his reasons for leaving Pasadena. Nothing could truly mitigate the physical and psychological break that had occurred with Charles's departure.

Henry became the de facto design principle and head of the office, but the economic stagnation of the war years, coupled with the sudden loss of the firm's strong creative direction, led to an inevitable decline in business.

The firm's fortunes never fully recovered, but Henry Greene persisted nonetheless, producing work of great quality, integrity, and dignity. Shortly after Charles's move, Henry designed alterations to the Los Angeles house of a former client, Dr. Robert P. McReynolds, who would give him occasional design jobs through 1926. Henry also oversaw new roof decking for the Blacker house, attended to Mrs. Tichenor's request for a garage addition to the east wing of her Long Beach house, and designed alterations for an apartment building in Pasadena. Other projects in the office at the time included a design for a house in St. Louis for William Bliss and a preliminary scheme for a speculative townhouse for Mortimer Fleishhacker in San Francisco.[2] Neither of these would be executed, however. The Fleishhacker townhouse design, which evokes the sobriety of Henry's work rather than the decorative flourishes more characteristic of Charles, represented the last job number assigned by the firm to Mr. Fleishhacker: all subsequent designs for him were produced in Charles's Carmel studio.

During this period, Henry also designed a residence for Charles H. Stoddard in the Northern California town of Burlingame, just south of San Francisco. Despite Charles's geographic proximity, Henry took charge of the job, which stalled before construction. On paper, the dignified and symmetrical colonial design showed Henry's willingness to work in traditional styles that suited the tastes of the day. The war in Europe was taking an economic toll in America even before the country's direct involvement, and as a result much of the design work performed in late 1916 never proceeded beyond preliminary sketches. By the beginning of 1917, Charles and his father were corresponding about their worries: the prospect of America committing battle troops abroad, the unusually cold winter, fuel shortages, the rationing of heating briquets, and the dismal performance of their business over the previous twelve months.[3] The only good news, it seemed, was that their client Charles S. Witbeck had authorized Henry to proceed to working drawings on his second scheme for an English-inspired house in Santa Monica.[4] In late-1916 the client had rejected an initial design as too expensive, but by January 1917 he had accepted the modified version, which had more modest detailing and less variation in the overall massing. A contract was signed for construction.

6

6 Charles S. Witbeck house, Santa Monica, 1916–17.
   North (front) facade.

7 Charles S. Witbeck house.
   Perspective sketch, first scheme.

7

The Witbeck house faces north along Santa Monica's Palisades Avenue, and a deep rear garden enjoys the sea breezes and sunny exposure on the south. By 1917, a $9,000 budget could not pay for an elaborate house, but the high-ceilinged stair-hall lighted by a large, north-facing window creates a dignified and dramatic entry. The exterior is distinguished by robust timbers in the portico and porches and characteristically close attention to detail in the hand-hewn joinery. The success of securing the design and construction of the Witbeck house emboldened Dr. Greene to express optimism in a letter to Charles on February 8, 1917: "I am in hopes we will get two or three large houses, but they come slowly."[5] One of the houses Dr. Greene referred to was probably for Dr. Martha J. Kuznick in Hollywood, for which Henry developed three different designs. Another was a projected $100,000 Pasadena residence for Major John H. Poole of Detroit, a project for which Charles would produce many conceptual sketches and mail them to the office for comment and formal drafting.

At about the same time, Henry was also at work designing a small house for Mrs. Howard F. Mundorff, the wife of a retired San Francisco baseball player who had settled in Fresno, in California's central valley. The Mundorff project successfully progressed to construction. In its design, Henry returned to the familiar concept of a single-story residence arranged around a courtyard, a plan similar in spirit to his house for Dr. S. S. Crow (1909). A smaller budget meant more modest materials, however, and the clapboard siding and interior plaster walls would be painted. Not only had budgets shrunk due to economic uncertainty caused by the war, but the quality of available wood had been steadily diminishing with the depletion of old-growth trees, making painted surfaces as much a necessity as a fashion. Decorative devices in the Mundorff house were limited to an inventive indirect-lighting design for the living-room wall sconces and a subtle organic design in the plaster moldings in the living room and hallway. A swimming pool and a detailed planting plan for the garden were also part of the commission. In the end, however, there was little reason for the optimism Dr. Greene had expressed in his letter to Charles. The Mundorff house was the last new residence from the Greene and Greene office to be constructed for another four years.

9 **Mrs. Howard F. Mundorff house.**
   Detail of living-room decorative plaster.

10 **Theodore A. Kramer garden, South Pasadena, 1918**
   Conceptual sketch for plan and elevation of
   garden bench.

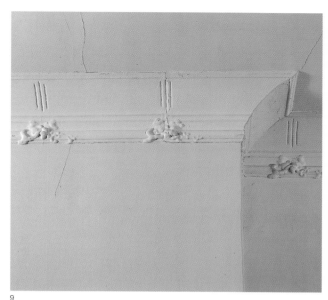

9

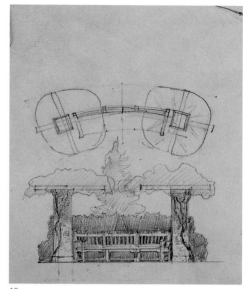

10

Another garden design project came that year from Theodore A. Kramer, a South Pasadena resident, who engaged Henry to produce a complete planting plan for the garden adjacent to his house, as well as alterations to the late-Victorian residence itself. Henry's drawing calls out over 150 different plant materials as well as furniture and other appointments, including a vine-shaded bench and a mirrored gazing-ball. The design included lawns and pathways of rigid geometry nearest to the house, but with the adjacent area to the north carried out in a naturalistic flow of winding paths, rock outcroppings, and water features, all under the shade of venerable oaks. The Kramer garden has since been subdivided and overgrown, but remnants of it persist as evidence of Henry Greene's skill in garden and landscape design.

Over the next several years, Henry Greene had little to do beyond the occasional alterations and additions for former clients. Among these was the new owner of the Culbertson sisters' house, Mrs. Dudley P. Allen, who remarried and was known as Mrs. Francis Fleury Prentiss not long after purchasing the Culbertson house in 1917. Henry's role included designing alterations to the house and garage, landscape and fence work, and, in 1921, a full planting plan for the additional land that Mrs. Prentiss purchased to extend her property to the northeast. Nor did the Culbertson sisters themselves desert the Greenes entirely after selling 1188 Hillcrest to Mrs. Allen. The sisters purchased the residence originally designed by the Greenes for Dr. William T. Bolton at 370 Elevado Drive (now Del Mar Avenue) that was occupied by Mrs. Belle Barlow Bush and her family. The Culbertson sisters retained Henry to design minor alterations to the house. Mr. and Mrs. Robinson also continued to be faithful clients, and for many years the Blackers and Pratts often had alterations or repairs for Henry to design and oversee.

A few new clients also emerged during the otherwise slow period between 1917 and 1921. Most of the projects, however, either never went past the conceptual stage or were abandoned prior to construction. One of these was Henry's design for a mansion in West Palm Beach, Florida. The design, for Hubert Francis Krantz, is mainly notable because it is the first of only two plans designed by Henry Greene to employ the oblique angles

favored by his brother. Charles Greene had pioneered angled plans for the firm in 1903 with the White sisters' house and the Samuel Sanborn house. He subsequently used angles often, either to promote a more relaxed interior circulation or to take advantage of particularly beautiful exterior views or topographical features. Henry had avoided designing plans with anything other than right angles, but for the Krantz design he angled the extremities of the T-shaped plan at forty-five degrees to embrace the rear garden, not only for better privacy and views but to acknowledge the triangular shape of the lot. Sadly, like others of the period, Henry's design for Krantz was never built. This was especially unfortunate, since Krantz was the developer of the entire Prospect Park subdivision in which it was to be built, and Krantz might have steered future work in the development toward Greene and Greene. Residential construction of any significant size eluded the firm. The clients of 1918–20, including Mrs. Carrie Whitworth of Altadena and Mrs. J. H. Jones of Pasadena, needed only minor alterations, additions, decorative fixtures, furniture, or garden plans. In 1920 Mrs. Datus C. Smith commissioned a garden (executed in 1924), which, similar to the Kramer plan, included a formal parterre near the house and a less structured orchard of fruit trees ranged among the existing oak and pepper trees.

Then, in 1921, Kate A. Kelly, Earl C. Anthony's sister-in-law, commissioned Henry to design a Mediterranean residence in stucco and mission tile, materials that had superseded the popularity of wooden bungalows following the unveiling of Bertram Goodhue's romantic and historically evocative buildings for the 1915 Panama-California Exposition in San Diego. Henry rose to the challenge of working in the relatively new idiom in the Kelly house, but also perpetuated specific details from the firm's earlier vocabulary, most notably the Chinese terra-cotta tiles that decorate the gable vents. The original L-shaped plan of the house (later expanded significantly) set the service wing away from the public spaces and created a sheltered entrance court. An adjacent fountain terrace originally gave dramatic views to the ocean toward the southwest. Essentially a one-story hillside residence, the house exhibits compositional variety and balance in its exterior elevations and roof line due to the

11 Scale drawings of furniture designs for Mrs. Carrie
    Whitworth house, Altadena, 1918. Ink on vellum.

12 Alterations for Mrs. Carrie Whitworth house. Sketch of
    wall sconce bracket. Pencil and crayon on tissue.

13 Mrs. J. H. Jones garden, Pasadena, 1920 (altered).
    Pencil and crayon on tissue.

14 Kate A. Kelly house, Los Angeles, 1921 (altered).
    Living-room section with detail of carved trusses.
    Pencil on tissue.

15 **Mrs. Datus C. Smith garden, 1920–24.**
    Site plan with pergola elevation. Ink on linen.

16 **Kate A. Kelly house.**
    Henry Greene's subtle sense of atmospheric color is
    evidenced in a pair of art-glass windows, representing
    dawn and dusk, for the master bedroom.

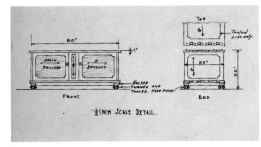

11

12

13

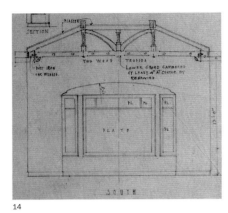

14

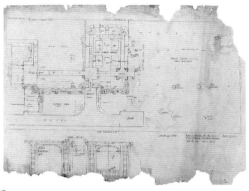

15

position of the high-ceilinged living room a few steps down from the main level. A dramatic and sweeping space, the exposed trusses were designed to be intricately carved with images of faces, the corbels bound together with the iron straps and wedges in the traditional Greene and Greene fashion. Henry's pencilled instructions on the drawings read "Carve free and bold. Vary expression in each [face] but keep [them] smiling." Mediterranean imagery extends also to the design of the chimney, whose shape recalls a medieval Italian campanile, and the heavy furniture designed for the house was similarly medievalized with elaborate carving and dark stains.[6] Henry's restrained, but by now highly evolved decorative sense was spectacularly demonstrated in a pair of subtly hued art-glass casement windows on the south wall of the master bedroom. Spare and evocative compositions, the left panel depicts a rosy-dawn sky, the other a lavender dusk, each with seagulls floating among billowy clouds.

Continuing economic uncertainty in the post-war years meant that contracts were scarce and generally of lower dollar value. Dr. and Mrs. Greene followed Charles's family to Carmel in 1921, leaving Henry to manage the Pasadena office entirely by himself, but the Greene and Greene name persisted as the official moniker of the firm until a formal reorganization was announced in April 1922.[7] After that, the business letterhead read "Henry M. Greene, Architect." Henry continued to rely on former clients for work. In 1921, Earle C. Anthony had asked Henry to design a model and topographical map to aid in the anticipated sale and relocation of his Berendo Street house in Los Angeles. Anthony planned to develop this property, which was at the busy intersection of Wilshire Boulevard, as a multistory luxury apartment building. Then, a fire damaged the garage of the house in 1922 and Henry was again called in to design and oversee the repairs. The future owners of the house, actor Norman Kerry and his wife, subsequently hired Henry to design a new site plan and landscaping for the house, whose relocation to Beverly Hills was finally announced in January 1923.[8] Beyond this, however, work was scarce. Joseph H. Huntoon, a friend of Henry's in the Central Valley town of Visalia, provided some work in 1922, though neither of two design projects he requested proceeded to construction. The more distinctive of the two was a

sketch for a duplex residence, with a half-story upper level that balanced the main mass of the lower level. An eyebrow dormer over one of the entry porticos and a gable over the other gave the scheme a pleasing asymmetry that was unusual for Henry.

One of the most intriguing design projects undertaken by Henry in the early 1920s was the design for a new cottage, a pair of gate portals, and alterations to existing cottages in the Wild Wood Park development owned by Walter D. Valentine in Altadena. Until recently, this village of cottages, hidden from public view at the end of a private driveway, has been virtually unknown as Henry Greene's work. Because the job to design the Valentine cottages came at a lean time for the office, Henry may have given the drawings more attention than they would have received at a busier time. And, since Charles's departure from the firm, Henry had been developing his rendering talents to provide his clients with more detailed drawings, something that his brother had usually resisted, claiming that it prejudiced clients and precluded making beneficial changes during construction.[9] Henry's drawings now frequently included shading to indicate texture, color-crayon garden plans, and even perspective views, complete with landscapes. The initial concept for the new Valentine cottage, an English Arts and Crafts design, was not adopted even though its woodsy aspect would have been highly complementary to the sylvan canyon of the Wild Wood Park parcel. Valentine instead chose an Americanized Craftsman aesthetic to reflect the existing board-and-batten structures for which Henry had also designed extensive additions. One of these additions was a dramatic new entry, living room, and terrace, all positioned a few steps down the hillside from the existing structure. Wrought-iron and mica lanterns hang from exposed trusses and the dark board-and-batten panels recall the prevailing aesthetic of a decade earlier. An arroyo-stone and clinker-brick chimney show Henry's ability and willingness to faithfully perpetuate the firm's classic legacy in the face of shifting trends.

Though mostly out of fashion by 1923, Henry Greene's design for an inexpensive wooden bungalow for Lloyd and Rachel Morrison is in a style similar to that used for modest builders' houses that were meant to emulate the Greene and Greene style at a lower cost. Amid neighborhoods of new

GREENE & GREENE

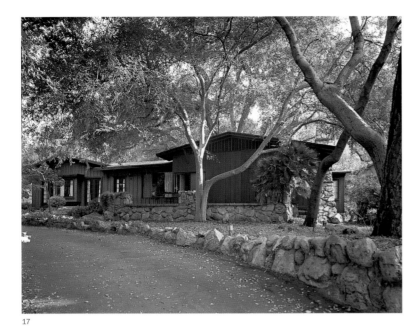

17

18

Spanish-Colonial Revival and other period-revival styles, the Morrisons' house must have seemed anachronistic, and they did not own the house for long. By 1926 it was sold to J. F. Rhodes, the owner of the adjacent residence to the east, a modest two-bedroom, stucco bungalow.[10] Built in 1925, the neighboring house seems also to have been designed by Henry Greene, though no documentary evidence exists. Evidence includes only the physical characteristics of the house and the recollection of Isabelle Greene McElwain that her father, in addition to designing two schemes for the Morrisons' house next door, had designed a second house for Mr. Morrison strictly as a speculative project. Interestingly, the undocumented stucco structure one house to the east is stylistically much more consistent with Henry Greene's residential work of the 1920s than the documented wood house. In addition to being solidly built, the stucco house also includes some of Henry's characteristic decorative devices, such as scored cement walks, a Batchelder fireplace flanked by built-in cabinets, and built-in cabinet doors in the dining room with a linear leaded-glass motif. Other more subtle signs can be seen, too, adding to speculation that Henry Greene may have been the designer.

Later in 1923, Henry designed a student pavilion for the campus of the California Institute of Technology. Plans were announced in 1921 to build a student clubhouse to be named "The Dugout" after a popular refreshment stand that had been discontinued in 1921. Cal Tech benefactors Mr. and Mrs. Robert R. Blacker offered to pay for the one-story, single-room building (now demolished), and the Blackers' influence no doubt steered the commission toward Henry Greene. Henry's design drew on proportions, materials, and detailing that were characteristic of earlier Greene and Greene structures: the interior space featured exposed timber trusses over a maple floor, with built-in benches along the east and west lengths of the forty-by-fifty-foot room. On three sides of the exterior was an eight-foot-wide, scored-cement walkway fully covered on the south and west sides by a post-and-beam shed roof with joinery details reminiscent of the Greenes' work of a decade or more before. In jobs such as this, Henry was faithfully carrying the legacy of the firm toward an uncertain era of Modernism, as fewer and fewer clients cared to be associated with a rustic, timber-based aesthetic. The students raised

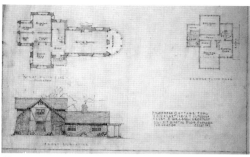
19

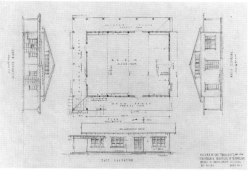
20

21

19 **Walter D. Valentine cottages.**
Conceptual sketch for unexecuted cottage.
Pencil on tissue.

20 **California Institute of Technology, student clubhouse, "The Dugout," Pasadena, 1923–24.**
Plan and elevations of student pavilion.

21 **Walter D. Valentine cottage b.**
Detail of living-room addition. Doors on either side of
the chimney open to a terrace equipped with an
outdoor fireplace.

funds to add a fireplace and chimney, a billiard table was added, and Henry Robinson donated a piano. The new building was dedicated with the enthusiastic approval of the students in February 1924.[11]

Another notable exception to Modernism emerged from Henry's design boards in the mid-1920s. Months at a time had passed without a new commission, until 1924, when Henry designed a two-story brick retail block for the Pasadena Drapery Company (owned by Ernest E. Wennerberg); a residence with English half-timbering detail for Dr. Edna T. Hatcher and her sisters in Pasadena's Allendale neighborhood; and a small, stucco duplex for Arthur Savage, a wood finisher who had previously done work for the Greenes. But the project that most closely related to the firm's popular identity was the house that Henry designed for Mr. and Mrs. Thomas Gould, Jr., in Ventura. Henry had first sketched a large wood house for Tom and Mabel Gould in 1920. Originally conceived as a two-story house on a J-shaped plan, the design generally reflected the large-bungalow aesthetic of years past. By the time the Goulds had purchased their hillside lot, however, economics had dictated a significantly more modest scheme. The second design, a more straightforward rectangular plan, was finally built in 1924–25. In Henry Greene's characteristic way, he managed to coax utility, dignity, inventiveness, and efficiency out of a limited space. As built, a large living room, sunroom, dining room, and "breakfast nook," make up the public spaces in the southwest corner of the house. The kitchen, service areas, hallway, and three of the five bedrooms comprise the balance of the lower level. A den alcove in the master bedroom gives semi-private reading space, and the two other ground-level bedrooms share a second sunroom. The half-story upper level, with two additional bedrooms, a bath, and storage space, is centered over the downstairs, but was not completed until 1932. Henry's manipulation of roof lines and pitches between upper and lower levels is calculated to impart visual life to the elevations. A shallow margin of shed roof over the entry strikes a strong horizontal line to visually anchor the base of the house, and to shelter the recessed entry portico and terrace. As a foil for the obscured entry, a dormer-like gable rises over a timber-braced planter box to squarely mark the front door.

22

The interior detailing of the Gould house includes some of Henry Greene's finest decorative work, and further hints at the unrealized promise of a creativity that had been too-little exercised during its prime. Particularly beautiful are the built-in drawers, whose facing boards and concave pulls are carved in billowy cloud forms. In the dining room, a brightly colored leaded art-glass design of birds and blossoms enlivens the china cabinet doors (later changed to casement window panels that open to the rear garden). Henry's design for delicate carving on the sideboard was expertly executed and picked out with stains of blue and red. Similar carving and staining treatments can be found in other places. Henry Greene gave the Goulds exceptional value, utility, and beauty in their home, and fulfilled their wish to live in an environment that evoked, if not recreated, the classic Greene and Greene interior work of fifteen years earlier. This knowledge, as much as the work itself, must have satisfied Henry. But, tellingly, he was disturbed that the job's costs came in slightly over budget. He chose to reduce his own commission to bring his clients' outlay closer to the original estimate.[12]

Former clients, and new owners of former clients' houses, continued to provide business, though not in large quantity. In 1923, Roy Wheeler had commissioned a significant addition to the 1904 Edgar Camp house. In 1924, John Bentz requested a design to finish the second story of the commercial block that the Greenes had designed for him in 1901. Mrs. Frances Swan returned, too, to ask for a new design with an estimated contract value of $70,100. This did not materialize, unfortunately, and she later decided to relocate her existing house, designed by the Greenes in 1899, to Altadena. Henry designed the alterations for the move in 1925. In 1924, Dr. V. Ray Townsend, the new owner of the Mary Darling house in Claremont (1903), commissioned a garage and alterations to the house, and R. Henry C. Green requested drawings for alterations to his 1904 house in Vancouver. While his own house was still in construction, Thomas Gould, Jr., called on Henry to engineer strengthening columns for the Ventura Union High School. Existing clients were often a source of new-client referrals, too. Mrs. Gould's sister, Mrs. C. P. Daly, came to Henry for a house design, also in Ventura.

Assigned a job number in 1925 but designed in 1926, the Daly project was Henry Greene's most elaborate creation (at least on paper) in the Spanish-Colonial Revival style that had by then become pervasive in Southern California.[13] Though the Daly design is nominally reminiscent of the Kate A. Kelly house of 1921, the drawings show that it was meant to be much larger and more articulated in its plan. The lifestyle that the drawings reflect is nonetheless servant-less and casual. The two-bedroom, one-and-a-half-story house was conceived to face the Pacific Ocean to the southwest with each functional space being treated nearly as a distinct pavilion projecting from the central mass of the house, allowing maximum flexibility in the placement of windows and doors. The main axis of the living room was to terminate in a large, multi-paned and arched window with narrow sidelights to give a dramatic view toward the water. Henry carefully sketched the placement of furnishings in all rooms. The intimate dining room was designed to project from the west side of the house at ninety degrees to the living room, also giving it a view to the south along one of its walls. A decorative covered balcony overlooked a sheltered patio in the rear, and an elevated terrace in the front provided added outdoor living space. The clear definition of the interior spaces on the exterior elevations gives an agreeable randomness to the design. The Daly design would have been one of Henry's most memorable houses had it progressed to construction.

Henry Greene's only significant new commission of 1925 was the design and construction of the William Thum house. Thum was a chemist who with his brothers had made a small fortune with the invention of a popular adhesive fly-paper called "Tanglefoot." He was also a former mayor of Pasadena (1911–13) and a close friend of Henry Greene and his family.[14] Indeed, Thum's son, John, and Henry's son, Henry Dart, were best friends. As mayor, William Thum had appointed Henry Greene—along with Frederick Roehrig, Myron Hunt, and Elmer Grey—to develop Pasadena's first "code of building procedure." Mayor Thum was especially concerned with directing public works projects and assuring the smooth operation of the municipal utilities. As a result, he was probably more interested in the

23 **Thomas Gould, Jr., house.**
Entry and staircase with hanging mirror. A built-in storage box has drawer pulls carved in the shape of clouds.

24 **Thomas Gould, Jr., house.**
Detail of leaded-glass cabinet door (converted to a window) over the dining sideboard.

25 **Thomas Gould, Jr., house.**
Drawer pulls on dining sideboard with faintly colored decorative carving.

23   24   25

engineering concerns of his residence than in their aesthetic demands.[15] He wanted a house that performed exceptionally well as a sheltering structure for his family and his extensive library, to keep them safe from fire and other dangers. Accordingly, the design of the house suggests a vault within a fireproof fortress. Nonetheless, Henry, in his subtly creative way, also injected decorative devices to add surface texture and visual interest. The materials and methods used on the portico of the Nathan Williams house (1915) were repeated here in constructing a side porch of steel poles, wire screen, and Gunite, sprayed on in a pattern of perforations that resemble the *tsuba* shape and other decorative forms from the Greene and Greene vocabulary.

In 1926, no new residential construction was undertaken save a small house for Henry Greene's neighbor, Mrs. James E. Saunders.[16] This project was never assigned a job number, though, and it was probably designed as a favor for a friend. The Saunders house had characteristics of the English Arts and Crafts movement, especially in the steep roof, timber portico, and iron strap-hinges on the planks of the front door. Alterations and repairs made up the balance of work in 1926. Mrs. Prentiss helped to keep Henry's bills paid that year with additions and repairs that amounted to nearly $15,000, and Henry M. Robinson proposed a promising job to redesign his Pacific Southwest Trust and Savings Bank office. Henry Greene's design for Mr. Robinson was traditional in its approach to the office itself—straightforward paneling, built-in bookcases, coffered ceiling. The furnishings he sketched, however, were Chinese in style, but somewhat blocky and heavy. The office was not constructed. The following year, 1927, Dr. V. Ray Townsend called on Henry Greene once again, this time regarding the 1904 Jennie Reeve house in Long Beach. Dr. Townsend wanted to relocate the house (its second move) to a more suburban setting, and asked Henry to provide a detailed garden plan, with plant materials specified, as well as designs for curtains and additional furniture to supplement the original Greene and Greene pieces that had remained with the house. This he did, and the job provided financial support during an otherwise lean spell. Smaller jobs for Mr. Blacker, Mrs. Prentiss, Mrs. Whitworth, and Kate A. Kelly was the only other work he had in 1927.

The following year was even more desperate. Two separate projects to design new residences, one for Mrs. Charles H. Kegley, the other for a client identified in the job book simply as "F. W.," did not progress beyond conceptual drawings. The new owner of the Nathan Williams house, J. B. Manning, requested alterations to the garage, and Henry also worked with Charles by corresponding regularly with him in Carmel to design and install a birdbath, with a basin in the shape of a lotus leaf, for Mr. and Mrs. Robert Blacker. Henry had proposed that the birdbath be made locally (where he could oversee its construction and on-time installation), but Charles proved that it would be cheaper to produce it in San Francisco through his contacts and then ship it south.[17] There was not enough work to support the rent, and Henry began to consider giving up the office space in the Boston Building. Then, in early 1929, Henry received two solid commissions for new residences, a development that brightened the financial picture considerably. The first was the design of a house for Estelle Strasburg in Covina, in the San Gabriel Valley east of Pasadena. The second was a ranch house in Porterville, California, near the foothills of the Sierra Nevada mountains. The Porterville house would be Henry's greatest late-career achievement and a worthy tribute to the Greene and Greene legacy.

Estelle Strasburg was an indecisive client. While Henry Greene patiently listened, Mrs. Strasburg rejected plan after plan, apparently based on the location of her own bedroom and the proposed circulation of foot traffic within the house. At last, they agreed on a design from which to build. The house would be sited in the wooded development of Adams Park, whose stately portals and winding streets aspired to set a quiet suburban tone.[18] The steep pitch of the roof immediately distinguishes the house from the majority of the Greenes' designs, though it is nominally aligned with their English-style residences. By 1929, times and tastes had changed, and suitable high-quality wood for exterior half-timbering and interior finishing had become increasingly scarce and unaffordable. Further, craftsmen who had learned woodworking and other trades in the "old country" had become scarcer, too, and the challenge of getting good work done—never easy in the best of circumstances—became progressively daunting as the Machine Age matured. The Strasburg house silently reflects these realities, though Henry

26 **William Thum house, Pasadena, 1925.**
South (front) facade.

27 **Estelle Strasburg house, Covina, 1929.**
East (front) facade.

28 **Walter L. Richardson ranch house, "Tenalu,"
Porterville, 1929.**
Northeast (front) facade showing rock foundation, steps,
and terrace. The client had wanted a facade oriented
due north, but the architect prevailed, angling the front
toward the Sierra Nevada mountain range.

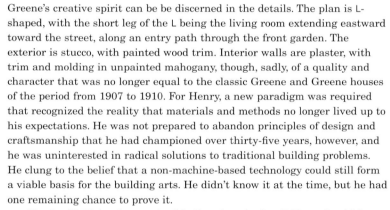

27

28

Greene's creative spirit can be be discerned in the details. The plan is L-shaped, with the short leg of the L being the living room extending eastward toward the street, along an entry path through the front garden. The exterior is stucco, with painted wood trim. Interior walls are plaster, with trim and molding in unpainted mahogany, though, sadly, of a quality and character that was no longer equal to the classic Greene and Greene houses of the period from 1907 to 1910. For Henry, a new paradigm was required that recognized the reality that materials and methods no longer lived up to his expectations. He was not prepared to abandon principles of design and craftsmanship that he had championed over thirty-five years, however, and he was uninterested in radical solutions to traditional building problems. He clung to the belief that a non-machine-based technology could still form a viable basis for the building arts. He didn't know it at the time, but he had one remaining chance to prove it.

Charles H. Richardson arrived in Pasadena in the 1880s and quickly grasped the rich potential of land ownership in the San Gabriel Valley. Richardson was a plant breeder and a builder who purchased thirty-five acres of land on South Molino Avenue (now El Molino, so named for the nearby mill that served the San Gabriel Mission). As a result of this and other land development deals (including construction of a Pasadena office building), Charles Richardson and his family benefited from the rise in land values during the "boom" years. Richardson was also a hearty outdoorsman who embraced a rugged lifestyle. He shot the last grizzly bear in California and tramped through the Sierra foothills with John Muir.[19] He was a friend of Don Juan Bandini, whose famous hospitality he enjoyed at the Bandini ranch.[20] Charles's son, Walter Linwood Richardson, followed his father's interests, not only going into land development but emulating the robust outdoor life. His family lived a *Craftsman*-magazine lifestyle in a well-built bungalow not far from some of the signature houses of Greene and Greene just after the turn of the century. Inevitably, the younger Richardson became aware of the Greenes' architecture.[21] Walter Richardson left Pasadena in 1917, and after spending a few years in the Imperial Valley finally settled with his family in Porterville. They moved into a small house where they remained for several years, and in early 1929, Richardson engaged Henry Greene to design a ranch house for his family. With such rich family history in Pasadena, Richardson's choice of architect was fueled in part by memories of the unique aesthetic environment of his childhood, an environment that had been shaped largely by the Greenes' work or influence.

The Richardson ranch house is called "Tenalu," after the Koyete Yokuts village that was originally located there.[22] The spectacular site overlooks Porterville's citrus fields from a hill the Indians called Pala Natsa, and the majestic, snow-capped Sierra Nevada range rises in the distance to the east. The most striking aspect of Tenalu is also its most natural. The rust-red walls of the house are adobe brick made from the earth of the hillside. Similarly, the foundation and chimney are of metamorphic rock extracted from the hill, and the terrace paving of sandstone flags was quarried from the site. Near the house, where the bedrock emerges above the soil, ancient "grinding rocks" show where the early native population processed food for the camp. By materials and history the structure is linked to the site. It could exist only in this place.

The modified U-shaped plan of the house was suggested by Walter Richardson, who probably realized that the Greenes had used the courtyard idea successfully in the past. Each leg of the U was shifted beyond the ends of the central block, however, to give greater width to the courtyard and added shade to the windows on the east and west gabled elevations. Unpainted wood shutters were placed at each window to allow maximum control of light and heat. The character of the elevations was dictated by the materials just as the materials were dictated by the natural resources. The challenge for Henry Greene was to create an aesthetically pleasing design, engineered with adobe and wood and supplemented with sills and headers of cast concrete, that would remain relatively cool in the summer and retain warmth in the winter. He did this by adapting to Porterville some of the devices that the firm had used successfully in Pasadena, including deep overhanging eaves and carefully positioned windows that would admit natural light without promoting dramatic swings in temperature due to direct sun. Structural timbers are lengths of Douglas fir that had been cut for the construction of oil derricks for the rich petroleum fields southwest of

29

30

31

Porterville. Indirectly benefitting from modern technology, Richardson bought the pre-cut timbers as salvage when it became clear that future derricks would be constructed of steel. This adaptive use of recycled material no doubt appealed simultaneously to Henry Greene's sense of thriftiness and anti-Modernism.[23] The roof is finished in sugar pine shakes from nearby forests.

The full-height foundation wall, made of the hillside's rock with its lichen left on, creates an above-ground basement level on the north and west legs of the plan. A sweeping staircase leads to the covered entry terrace. The front door opens directly into the living room, a large space dominated by a massive stone chimney.[24] Steel-sash casement windows open to views of the valley and mountains to the north and west. Overhead fourteen-by-fourteen-inch Douglas fir beams support a ceiling of two-by-fourteen-inch redwood tongue-and-groove panels, brushed and finished with a wax coat over a silver-grey stain (the formula of which Henry Greene kept secret from his clients). The interior walls were originally a yellow-ochre color, to complement the adobe and the multi-colored lichen on the building rock. The foundation and chimney work were supervised by a Pasadena stonemason. A local blacksmith named Crowfoot remained on the site for years to forge Henry's hardware designs for the house, including light fixtures and door and window hardware.

The dining room, an intimate space immediately to the east of the living room, was furnished with a brushed-redwood china cabinet and walnut dining table, both designed by Henry Greene in the spirit of simplicity that characterized some of his best mid-career work. The dining table in particular exhibits his love of "low-tech" mechanical solutions to design problems. As in similar tables, the dining surface can be lengthened by unfolding hinged leaves at each end. When not in use, Henry designed the underside efficiently so that the leaves could be secured to the underside by a notch at the end of a rail that catches the ends of the leaves. When they are folded out for use, it is the same rail that extends and locks in place to support the leaves.[25]

The overall organization of interior space is similar to Henry Greene's design for the Dr. S. S. Crow house of 1909, but with a different compass orientation. The Richardson kitchen and service areas occupy the wing to the

32

33

34

left of the entry and bedrooms are ranged along the opposite leg of the plan. A covered veranda provides exterior circulation on all three sides of the garden courtyard, similar to the Bandini plan of 1904. Facing the garden on the rear terrace is a massive exterior fireplace on the back side of the living-room chimney, a compelling focal point for outdoor life on cool evenings. Creating the Richardson ranch house was not the act of progressive architecture characteristic of the work of Greene and Greene in previous decades. But in composing a design of great utility and charm using local labor and natural resources close at hand, Henry Greene brought his career to a gracious close. The design and building of the Richardson ranch in many ways reflects the spirit of the best in collaborative Arts and Crafts building projects: Ernest Gimson's community of builders at Rodmarton Manor in the Cotswolds of England, or the varied sources of artistic input that built the Swedenborgian Church of San Francisco under the watchful eye of its minister, Joseph Worcester. Henry Greene's inspired design and quiet supervision, often from afar, resulted in a serene monument to the purity of his motives as an architect: to produce something that is useful as well as beautiful. There is nonetheless a tinge of wistfulness in the Richardson ranch project. Its design and construction pay tribute to a fast-disappearing level of artistic quality in building. More than that, it eulogized the Arts and Crafts movement, which by 1929 had become an inconvenient irrelevance in the face of Modernism. Henry Greene's last building summed up his feeling toward the past, the present, and the future, and he could not have ended his career on a finer note.

Later that year, the crash of the stock market and the ensuing economic depression made the fine art of architecture a lower priority. For Henry, the same few clients who had supported him modestly over the previous decade continued to support him during the 1930s, but the volume of work was too small to keep his practice active. In May 1930, Henry wrote to his brother in Carmel: "You wrote about finishing the working drawings for the Gothic room for Mr. Fleishhacker while he was away in Europe. I am not doing anything myself and I wonder if I could help you finish them if I came up? Could you afford a couple of weeks of expense drafting?"[26] In a letter to his brother the following year, Henry's tone had become more discouraged: "I

am doing nothing now and worrying about it, too. Can we not scrap these machines some way so the human animal will have a show again?"[27] Then, later still, "I hope, Charles, you have some work to do. All I have had is small alteration[s] which take so much time and do not pay enough."[28] Then, in June 1933, Henry wrote that he would be closing his office in the building where the firm had occupied a suite since 1907. "Hereafter address me at my house number."[29]

In 1935, Henry's beloved wife, Emeline, died of a heart attack a few days after surgery for an ovarian tumor. It was a terrible blow to Henry and the whole family, who had been very devoted to her. She was survived by her mother, Charlotte Whitridge, under whose roof Henry continued to live until shortly after her death in 1940. All of Henry and Emeline's children had long since moved away by then, and Henry rented the house and moved in with his son and daughter-in-law in Altadena, where he passed the last fourteen years of his life.

In 1951, at the age of eighty-one, Henry conferred on the design and construction of a house for his daughter and son-in-law, Isabelle and Alan McElwain, and their children. The budget was not large, and the family planned to build the house themselves. The chosen material had to be both inexpensive and easy to work with. Henry, who had always had sympathy for finding an inexpensive solution to a design problem, supported the choice of concrete block as the primary building material. The block was cheap, and constituted a modular unit that effectively dictated the dimensions of windows and doors, making it ideal for use by nonprofessional builders. Henry Greene's granddaughter, Isabelle Greene, who was twelve years old at the time, recalls that the house was built entirely as a "hands-on" family project, a fitting end to a long and distinguished career whose foundation had been a love of craftsmanship in the service of homebuilding.[30]

8

Seaside Bohemia

1 Page 190:
   Henry Greene (left) visiting his brother, Charles, at his
   studio in Carmel-by-the-Sea, December 1947.

2 Charles Greene's wife, Alice, with three of their
   children, on a camping trip in the summer of 1915.

3 Charles S. Greene, watercolor of Mission San Antonio
   de Padua, Monterey County, 1915.

4 Charles S. Greene, Southern Pine Association
   exhibition pavilion, New Orleans, 1916 (project).

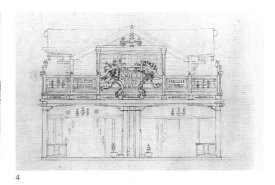

2   3   4

While working on Mortimer Fleishhacker's Woodside estate, Charles Greene became familiar with the life and climate of Northern California, and in the summer of 1915 he embarked with his family on an automobile touring and camping expedition with the ultimate goal of reaching the Panama Pacific International Exposition on the shores of San Francisco Bay. With their five children in tow, Charles and Alice Greene stopped at various points of interest along the way, including the Mission San Antonio de Padua at the foot of the Santa Lucia Mountains near the town of Jolon. Charles painted a picture of the mission while the children played and Alice cooked meals on the stone fireplace that Charles had constructed.[1] Responding to a request from a client, Charles disappeared for several days while Alice and the children remained, living like pioneers in the wilderness. When Charles reappeared, they resumed their journey to San Francisco, having had a chance to savor the clear air of central California and test their appetite for a less pampered life than they had known in Pasadena. In San Francisco, the PPIE was a dazzling sight, with its spectacularly lighted Tower of Jewels, the monumental Court of Ages, and the romantic Palace of Fine Arts. In an article he wrote for *The Architect* in December of that year, Charles remarked particularly on the appropriate use of color in the exposition's buildings, a notable contrast to the "White City" of the Chicago exposition he had seen twenty-two years earlier.[2] On the return journey, the family stopped in the sleepy village of Carmel-by-the-Sea. For some time Charles had been weary of what he perceived to be the materialism of Pasadena, and this quiet oceanside town of artists and writers suggested the perfect antidote to his increasingly unfulfilling career. Indeed, according to a family friend, he believed that lately he had been "prostituting his art."[3] During the family's visit to Carmel he made arrangements to rent a house there the following year.[4] Years later Charles described the decision to move: "I pondered, talked it over with my wife—'let's go to Carmel in the pine woods to find ourselves' ... She agreed and we have no regrets."[5] In the summer of 1916 the family rented a trailer, organized their personal belongings, and headed north. At the end of August their household furnishings were shipped, and by September the Carmel newspaper had announced the Greenes' rental of a cottage from Colonel Robert D. Fry, Jr., on the northeast corner of 13th Avenue and Carmelo Street. The spacious living room of the Craftsman-style cottage was paneled in raw redwood, and the broad windows of the dining room offered generous views to the west. But for the ocean, it must have seemed like many Pasadena houses of the period.[6] He continued to make himself available to his brother for consultation on various projects in the firm, but privately he was in search of his literary muse. In his own mind he had made a definitive break with his past life to concentrate on writing.[7] There was also some discussion of moving to Berkeley eventually, and Mortimer Fleishhacker offered Charles steady work designing tract homes if he would move to San Francisco. For Charles, this rang too much of commercialism, however, and they ultimately elected to remain in the quiet seaside enclave of artists and writers. Famous literary and artistic Carmelites at various times had included, among others, Robinson Jeffers, Mary Austin, George Sterling, Sinclair Lewis, Jack London, Lincoln Steffens (whom Charles later called "a great man with a high purpose"), Carl Sandburg, Pedro de Lemos, Charles Rollo Peters, Frank McComas, and Chris Jorgensen.[8]

During the first few years of the family's residence in Carmel, Charles responded to weekly letters from his father regarding the various jobs pending in the firm. His main occupation, however, was to seek inspiration from the beauty of the countryside and in the genial ambience and hospitality of Carmel's other creative citizens.[9] Charles wanted to write for a living, and he had been hoping for an assignment to write a book for the Southern Pine Association in New Orleans. He had also submitted the design of a permanent exhibition pavilion to the association, but nothing came of either project.[10] Meanwhile, he enjoyed attending occasional "philosophical evenings," and wrote to his father, "One never knows what kind of people one may stumble on here."[11]

In a letter slightly tinged with guilt from the as yet unrealized expectations of published work that he had raised among his family since leaving Pasadena, he wrote: "I am beginning to get my [next] article together for *The Architect*, but so far I have done no other writing. I have been reading lately some books on Art [and] am beginning to feel as if I

5 **Laurabelle A. Robinson house, Pasadena, 1905–06.**
Detail of carved paneling in sun-room addition, 1918.
Charles Greene had become enamored of celestial
bodies as decorative subject matter.

6 Charles S. Greene, conceptual sketch of the D. L.
James house, "Seaward," Carmel Highlands, 1918.
Watercolor on board. A bridge conceived as access to
the rocky island south of the house was never built.

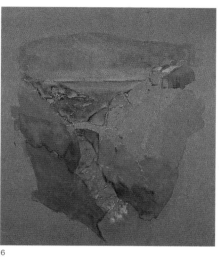

5

6

must start soon at my serious work. The everlasting tinkering seems to be drawing to an end, or rather such as remains can be left till it suits my convenience." This last remark was important, since it reveals Charles's pleasure in his new-found independence from the responsibilities of the firm.[12] By March, 1917, he had finished writing a major article entitled "Architecture as a Fine Art." In it, he justified his retreat from the profession, saying, "[architects] are pitted against a fast-prevailing economic contingent—the concentration of capital that seeks to control the entire field of building operation, combining real estate, building and investment." This was clearly anathema to Charles, who believed that the "art process" could exist only when economic considerations were minimized. His article gives little hope to the idealist, but concludes by saying: "The contemplative sensitive mind, altruistic and benevolent, cannot develop amongst the disordered hurry of commercial drive, nor can it be forced in the luxurious hothouse of a money-protected ego seclusion. It must be natural, or rather, spontaneous and free. Until there are enough of this kind of people to make themselves felt in the national will, there can be no national art product or architecture. No architect can by any power of his own put into form more of a national aim than he receives through his fellow countrymen."[13] This marked a politicization of Charles Greene that was not strictly confined to the architectural profession. He even became interested in anarchism, and wrote to his father, "Scientifically explained, [anarchism] has many good points if one could only find a way to bring it about."[14] He made a further study of Henry George's single tax (one of the topics of conversation with C. R. Ashbee in 1909), and told his father that he believed that the single tax would be a "grand thing for California."[15] Throughout this, Charles did not progress with his writing as he had led others to think, and his personality was equally ill-suited to political activism. Indeed, he kept his hand in architecture out of self-preservation and instinct, and he would soon be back into building on a scale he had never anticipated.

Early in 1917 Charles worked from afar on various schemes for a house for John Poole to be built in the Linda Vista neighborhood of Pasadena, and by the spring and early summer he was designing interior furnishings for Mrs. Dudley Allen, the new owner of the Cordelia Culbertson house. Charles

had met with Mrs. Allen for the first time at the Pebble Beach Lodge in April, at which time she asked him to prepare sketches for two mirrors and a screen for the dining room, a marble jardiniere for the hall, a lamp for the living room, and a piano case for the garden room. Typically, Charles explained that the furniture would have to have his personal supervision.[16] Mrs. Laurabelle Arms Robinson also reactivated herself as a client for the Greenes during this period and commissioned a sunroom to enclose the porch off the south end of her living room. For it, Charles designed a series of carved mahogany panels that demonstrated his growing interest in symbolism, and especially in the depiction of heavenly bodies. Charles chose tile and marble for the floors and baseboards, and Peter Hall performed the installation. The resulting paneled room, with the sun, moon, and stars amid the clouds is one of Charles's few Carmel-based carvings in Pasadena.[17]

In 1918, Charles was offered a commission that he could not refuse, despite a private promise he had made to cease practicing architecture.[18] Fortuitously, Theodore Criley, a local resident and amateur artist, introduced Charles to a visiting friend, a businessman and amateur writer named D. L. James. Mr. James, who was baptized with first and middle initials only, ran his family's successful Kansas City retail business in china, silver, and crystal. He fancied he had a creative streak, too, and counted numerous writers and artists among his friends. He and his wife had first come to Carmel in 1914 and ultimately purchased a spectacular parcel of land on a bluff south of Point Lobos directly over the water. After being introduced, and sensing a special opportunity, the Jameses showed Charles Greene the breathtaking cliff-top property. In two days he produced a watercolor sketch of a stone fortress emerging like an ancient ruin from the rocky bluff above the swells of the Pacific surf. His potential clients liked the rendering, and persuaded Charles to accept the commission. "It was the result of an afternoon tea and a little talk" wrote Charles of the vacation house he would design.[19] It was also the opportunity of a lifetime to design and build a house on his own terms. Theoretically, he was free to act as artist, architect, and contractor on behalf of sympathetic, seemingly unhurried, and wealthy clients. The Jameses would continue to live in Kansas City while the house was being built, allowing Charles the latitude to work unsupervised and at

7   D. L. James house, "Seaward," Carmel Highlands, 1918–22.
View through ceremonial arch to forecourt.

8   D. L. James house, "Seaward."
Forecourt and entry (center).

9   D. L. James house, "Seaward."
Service wing colonnade in Lombardy-Romanesque style.

10 D. L. James house, "Seaward."
Aerial view to the southeast from the sea.

7

8

9

his own pace.[20] Although Charles unexpectedly found himself practicing architecture again, the stars seemed well aligned to permit him to produce a crowning achievement for his career.

The James house, made of stone, may be an anomaly within Charles Greene's oeuvre, but the swift inspiration he had in creating the initial conceptual sketch could only have come spontaneously and sincerely from a lifetime of rich experience. More a work of sculpture than architecture, and more a monument to art than to domestic shelter, the James house is an appropriately enigmatic summation of Charles Greene. Given the fame of his earlier wooden designs, it seems surprising to imagine his professional epilogue written in granite. But far from being a dwelling for the warm flatlands or soft rolling hills of suburban Pasadena, it was conceived rather as a citadel over the craggy edge of the turbulent and chilly Pacific Ocean. This evoked memories of Tintagel, Clovelly, Lynton, and Porlock—the seaside towns Charles and Alice had visited years before—but the James house would also become everything that Charles had gleaned in his long search "to make pleasurable those things" that are necessary to life's journey.

For the foundations and walls, Charles ordered golden granite brought by horse cart from a quarry near Yankee Point, on the steep banks above Mal Paso creek. Local sandstone was used for steps, decorative pavers, and the top courses of the perimeter walls. Gladding McBean's "Medium Cordova" Latin Tiles were chosen for the roof in a range of soft terra-cotta colors. The exposed ends of each tile were chipped by hand to give a timeworn appearance. The ridges and surfaces of the roof were deliberately constructed to avoid precise alignment and evenness. The result was the look of an ancient, well-settled manse reminiscent of the Tintagel Old Post Office, which Charles had photographed in 1909.[21] Stonework, including corbels, impost blocks, and occasional decorative pieces, were carved out of Carmel Valley stone. Doors and windows are "Siam" teak supplied by White Brothers Hardwood of San Francisco, and window and door sills are white Vermont marble, drilled with weep holes as a safeguard against the accumulation of interior moisture.[22] The exterior walls of the house are carefully built-up courses of granite, each stratum a different thickness. Some are knife-blade thin, others inches deep, depending on the natural thickness of the slab-lines

11 **D. L. James house, "Seaward," Carmel Highlands, 1918–22.**
Southwest corner on the ocean side of the house.

12 **D. L. James house, "Seaward."**
The "Tintagel Arch" inspired by Charles's 1909 journey to Cornwall, England.

13 Charles S. Greene. Painting of the ruins of Tintagel, Cornwall, England, 1909. Watercolor on board.

14 **D. L. James house, "Seaward."**
Southwest point of foundation and stepped retaining wall.

12

13

11

14

along which they exfoliated from the mountainside. Since he could not supervise the laying of every rock, Charles Greene hired his longtime associate from Pasadena, Fred E. Coleman, as construction foreman. It was a daunting job. Any misplaced stone, or other deviation from Charles's vision, was subject to being unceremoniously ripped out and rebuilt. All mortar joints were to be struck well back of the surface to create emphatic strata and to allow appealing shadows to be cast. Straight lines are nonexistent; walls and chimneys rise at angles and bulge and weave according to the subtle changes in the bluff's topography.

Approaching the house from the highway, the noise of the sea rises gradually as a reminder of the wildness of the place. The pathway meanders according to the shape of the bedrock cliff, giving occasional glimpses of the ocean beyond. Passing through a ceremonial arch into the courtyard, there is only the house to confront, the noise of the sea being suddenly muffled. The inward-facing V-shaped courtyard plan, and its dramatic position near the edge of the cliff, was an inspiration suggested by the shape of the buildable portion of the site and the drama of its proximity to the water. Arches, appropriate to stone construction but relatively unfamiliar to Charles Greene's building vocabulary, provide a thematic rhythm for the house just as posts and beams had done in the Greenes' earlier timber buildings. One arch in particular frames a view from the perimeter wall on the south side, a near-literal translation of a ruined portion of the Norman-era castle at Tintagel that Charles had painted in watercolors a decade earlier.[23] He positioned the arch in a similar manner, too, hovering at the edge of the precipice directly over the roiling swells of the ocean. In addition to the imagery of the Cornish coast, a Mediterranean theme emerges in the James house. In January 1919, as the foundation was being constructed, Charles ordered from William Downing, a bookseller in Birmingham, England, a two-volume set of books entitled *Lombardic Architecture*.[24] Exterior details of the James house recall some of those of early Lombardic Romanesque structures, especially in the service-wing colonnade, which suggests a Romanesque cloister, and the arched recesses of the chimneys. The mixed regional imagery of England and Italy is entirely appropriate to Carmel, too, where the climate vacillates between surprisingly warm

15 **D. L. James house, "Seaward."**
Plans, elevations, and sections. Ink-on-vellum
presentation drawings.

16 **D. L. James house, "Seaward."**
View from entry hall through arched partition wall
toward the library.

17 **D. L. James house, "Seaward."**
Great room, view toward the entry-hall and library.

16

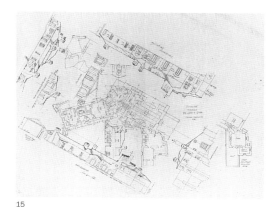

15

17

periods of sunshine and cool summer fogs. Though the house was not immune to leaks, the driving winter rains were picturesquely accommodated in the architecture, particularly in the roof gutters of upended tiles that terminate in elaborately carved downspouts of limestone. These conduct water into granite tubs that serve as fern planters, which, in turn, drip into a system of partially covered storm-drain ditches under the pavement of the courtyard, terraces, and pathways.

Beyond the seeming casual ramble of exterior walls, the interior floor plan is remarkably orderly. Charles may have completed his initial presentation sketch quickly, but the presentation drawing clearly took longer. Employing his prodigious ability to simultaneously conceptualize a design spatially and graphically, Charles presented to his clients a depiction of all elevations, plans, and sections oriented logically on a single sheet of paper. That they would fit on one sheet is less remarkable than the fact that any element of the plan could be visually related to its corresponding representation on any of the several elevations. For a courtyard house with few right angles this made for a complex drawing. But it shows how Charles approached his work: as a multi-dimensional totality rather than a conventional series of front, rear, and side elevations separate from the plans. This early drawing reveals that the house was initially conceived as a two-level structure featuring a small upper-level study. The Jameses ultimately rejected this part of the scheme, electing to keep the living areas on one level. The drawing also shows that the name of the house was initially "Pinecliffe," with the more romantic "Seaward" being adopted soon after.[25]

The entry is subtly distinguished from other doors on the exterior by its size and its position in relation to the entry path and courtyard. Gaining access to the entry hall, the visitor is rewarded with the first direct view of the ocean. Though partly screened by an interior colonnade that overlooks the library, the immediate presentation of a view to the exterior recalls many of the Greenes' best houses, where direct lines of sight from the front door to the rear garden were typical. A semicircular wall on the south end of the entry hall suggests a terminus, but two doors lead from it to the bedchamber wing. The first door opens to a hall leading to the bedrooms

18 **D. L. James house, "Seaward," Carmel Highlands, 1918–22.**
Main bathroom.

19 **D. L. James house, "Seaward."**
Main bathroom fireplace showing rhythmic diminution of blind arches.

19

20 **D. L. James house, "Seaward," Carmel Highlands, 1918–22.**
Detail of rain gutter and downspout, interior court.

21 **D. L. James house, "Seaward."**
Detail of great-room fireplace, showing sea birds in carved marble.

22 **D. L. James house, "Seaward."**
Detail of great-room fireplace, showing seaweed and other ocean life.

20

21

22

themselves. The master bedroom is first, with a fine view to the south and an intricately carved white marble mantel depicting a basket of flowers. The further of the two chambers, designed for the James's son, Daniel, is entered only by way of the master bedroom and a hall-like dressing area, or from the courtyard. Behind the second door from the entry hall a circular bathroom forms the pivotal joint of the V-shaped portion of the plan. An immense marble bathtub is set into the south wall at an oblique angle from a fireplace. Together with separate views to the land and the sea, these features represent the essential natural elements of earth, air, water, and fire.[26] Half-bowls of stone attached to the wall serve as reflective sconces casting light to the domed ceiling. Wispy carving on the gently bowed fireplace depicts seagulls in relief, flying low over the surf. Seaweed shapes are also carved into the capitals of the flanking marble posts. Down a short flight of stairs from the entry hall is the living room—more accurately a great room—that doubles as a refectory. Thirty-two feet long and more than twenty feet wide, the vastness of the space is mitigated by the warmth of the brushed redwood ceiling panels and beams, whose undersides are carved with images of local sea life. Plaster walls, originally pigmented an ivory tone, contrast softly with the white marble fireplace and its carvings of seaweed, pine cones, shells, and snails. Every surface is soft and sculptural with evidence of hand finishing virtually everywhere. French doors lead to a terrace on the point of the bluff, a spectacular lookout to the ocean, where whales can be seen migrating south to Mexico in the winter and north again in the spring. The intimate library off the great room, previously glimpsed through arches from the entry hall, is a separate retreat, where Mr. James could appreciate his collection of fine-press art books. The carved-marble mantel depicts ocean plant life floating on the sea, and a broad high window affords a vertiginous look at the churning water below. Tall cabinet doors of stained teak are accented with delicate and sinuous strap-hinges of wrought iron, forged in San Francisco by A. Laszolffy of Art Metal Works. The window seat of "rose antique" marble was carved, as was nearly all the marble in the house, by Jacob Schoenfeld of the Schoenfeld Marble Company, also in San Francisco.[27] The contrast of the sharp, rugged granite of the exterior and Schoenfeld's luxuriously smooth marble surfaces inside

gives the interiors the character of a cocoon-like sanctuary, despite the slightly menacing elements of nature depicted throughout the house.[28]

Begun when he was fifty, Charles's design for the James house carries the slightly melancholy aura of a finished career. In it, Charles combined his personal interpretation of the building arts with a nostalgic romanticism, all in a quest for perfection. It was probably the house he would have built for himself had circumstances permitted. Akin to Ernest Gimson's Stonywell Cottage near Leicester, England, it is a superb work of picturesque craft and art in harmony with its natural setting, but it lacks any inclination toward progressive architecture. For Charles, to design and build the James house was more an act of spiritual regeneration than of architectural practice, and it signaled the beginning of an intensified period of self-observation and the continued search for spiritual meaning in his life.[29]

In 1919, the Greenes were displaced from the Fry house, following which they moved to another rental property, a house owned by the Clamphet family. Here, Charles's daughter Bettie, a horse enthusiast, was able to keep her first mount. By 1920, though, it became clear that the Greenes were settling permanently in Carmel and more room was needed. Charles purchased land in the southerly section of town between 13th and Santa Lucia avenues and Lincoln and Monte Verde streets. He designed and built a single-story, board-and-batten house on a U-shaped plan, not dissimilar to the concept of the Bandini residence of 1903 but differing significantly in scale and detailing. A brick chimney faced the courtyard, and an uncovered brick path ran from one door to the next. The interior of its single-wall construction remained unfinished during the family's long occupancy, save for a marble fireplace probably made of material left over from the James house. It was the sole touch of elegance in the otherwise spartan shelter. (This detail was perhaps not lost on Charles's children as they watched their father erect a relatively elaborate studio next door two years later.) Nevertheless, the family was happy and busy, and Alice Greene, who had been brought up in a proper English household, did not complain about her reduced lifestyle as compared with the family's fashionable existence in Pasadena.[30] The children were involved in local theatrical performances staged by Carmel's Arts and Crafts Club and the Forest Theatre, and there

23 **Charles S. Greene house, Carmel-by-the-Sea, 1920.**
View into courtyard, with the Greenes' daughter, Alice,
standing in foreground, c. 1930.

24 **War Memorial, Carmel-by-the-Sea, 1921–22.**
West facade.

23

24

was usually a swarm of adolescent activity in the modest house. One frequent visitor in the 1920s remembers the house as always being "a bit of a shambles, but a comfortable, warm shambles."[31] Alice often had bread baking in the oven to serve visitors, invited or not, and it was a relaxed existence in a quasi-camp-like atmosphere.[32] The family socialized with like-minded neighbors, including architects Louis Christian Mullgart and John Galen Howard, who had weekend and summer retreats in town.[33] In 1921, on the southwest corner of his property, Charles also built a modest cottage for his parents, who had moved from Pasadena to spend their remaining years close to their eldest son.

In the fall of 1921, Charles donated his design services for the erection of a stone memorial to the fifty-six men of Carmel who had lost their lives in World War I. The plan was announced on Armistice Day, November 11, 1921, with a ceremonial laying of the first stone at the intersection of Ocean Avenue and San Carlos Street. Charles contributed his services for the supervision of its construction, too, but criticism was shrill from the local newspaper when it took a year to complete.[34] Its form suggests a mission bell tower, with dressed stones laid in an asymmetrical composition. The narrow opening of the arch is flanked by wide piers, and a hand-carved timber suspends a bronze bell within the arch. At the base was a drinking fountain (now missing), a white stone bowl designed and donated by Charles Greene, on which he had carved a design of breaking waves.[35]

In the spring of 1922, with Charles firmly settled in Carmel, the Pasadena partnership of Greene and Greene was officially dissolved. "Reorganized" was the official term used, but from that point forward, Charles's brother would practice independently as Henry M. Greene, Architect.[36] Charles, meanwhile, had been increasingly active in Carmel's civic affairs. In addition to the war memorial, he designed a new clubhouse for the Carmel Country Club (the project was later abandoned);[37] he submitted a design (not adopted) for a new Carmel City Hall;[38] and he designed alterations for the Carmel Club of Arts and Crafts, both for their Cassanova Street clubhouse and the Forest Theatre.[39] Because he was revered as a designer and was generous with his time and services he was sworn in as a member of Carmel's newly created Planning Commision on February 7, 1922.[40]

25 **City Hall, Carmel-by-the-Sea, 1921** (project).
Conceptual sketch. Pencil on tissue.

26 **Rudolph Schevill addition and alteration,
Berkeley, 1922–23.**
Interior elevations. Pencil on tissue.

27 **Rudolph Schevill addition and alteration.**
Charles Greene added the wing at the right of the house,
shown here in a period photo.

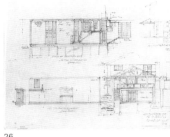

25   26   27

Immediately following the dedication of the war memorial in November 1922, Charles began work on the design of an addition to the Berkeley home of Rudolph and Margaret Schevill. The Schevills had met Charles on one of their visits to Carmel, and since Charles was occasionally invited to speak at the University of California by John Galen Howard, to have a project in Berkeley must have seemed manageable. Rudolph Schevill had come to Berkeley in 1912 to create a Department of Romantic Languages for the University, and at their Tamalpais Road home his personal study was located in the basement.[41] Wanting to move his books and files up to the existing living room, he and his wife, Margaret Erwin Schevill, engaged Charles to enclose their south porch and build an addition on that end of the house as a replacement for the former living-room space. Though Charles's drawings show "R. Schevill" as client, the project evolved as Mrs. Schevill's room—a place for her to entertain the many artistic friends with whom she kept company. The most striking features of the room are the dramatic proportions and the extreme treatment of the fenestration. Tall windows allow huge amounts of light to enter. Originally, sweeping vistas of San Francisco Bay could be had when there were fewer houses and trees to block the view. The fifteen-foot ceiling height gives the forty-by-twenty-foot volume a spacious and airy character. Stairs lead to a loft on the north end, a kind of minstrel's gallery supported by a massive pine beam and guarded by a redwood balustrade. The balustrade is the only feature in the room that is reminiscent of the Greenes' earlier devotion to building in wood. Charles made an excursion to San Francisco's Chinatown with Margaret Schevill to choose the lighting fixtures and a cabinet for the room.[42] He offered broken chips of marble, apparently left over from the James house project, to add decorative accents to the paving of the adjoining hallway. Several months after the addition was begun, fire struck the Berkeley hills. The house and addition were saved thanks to the swift action of the family and nearby university students. Once its reputation for excellent acoustics became known, composers and musicians asked to play or practice in the spacious, well-lighted chamber. Pablo Casals played his cello there and Dylan Thomas was fêted within its walls following a poetry reading.[43] The power of the space was such that the Schevill's son, James, wrote a poem about it, titled *The Big Room*:[44]

(1)
Believing in a radiant, visionary time
When imagination rides on spectacular wings
Beyond the confined pride of small-scale art,
My stubborn mother conceived and built an
Extraordinary living room she called the Big Room.

"When the community dances, everything comes
Alive," she smiled, "but it takes a Big Room.
In a small room, you can hide, my son,
But in a Big Room you must observe
How the community connects. In the end
You will find that the minimal glows in
Time's mirror only as a lovely, minor image."

Spying on the parties in the Big Room as a boy
Through a peephole in a gold Chinese Buddha
Fixed tranquilly on the balcony wall,
I peered down, fascinated, at the dancing guests.

All those people dancing around in impossible joy!

Transformed in the foot-tapping
Thrust of that rhythmical music,
I heard my mother whisper exultantly:
"Anyone who is afraid of wonder
Dares not enter the Big Room! This Room
Attacks the common, restricted possibilities!"

(2)
Older, I remember the Big Room aspiring
To a jubilant sense of communion, the pressure
Of light through majestic, high-laddered windows
Revealing the moon in a star-fused sky.

28

29

Eager dancers flowing below in joyous bursts
Like an enchanted white-rapids river.

Still, the Big Room questions me:
"Can you sing? Are you a natural phenomenon?
Can you perform magically in my presence,
Present yourself as a paragon of movement?
Can you see yourself as a strong shadow
Following masterly motion without being mastered?
In the Big Room, can you dance with others into
The impossible rhythm of happiness?"

Early in 1923, while work progressed on the Schevill addition, Charles began designing a live-in music studio for his friend and neighbor, Robert Tolmie, a pianist who owned several lots on Lincoln Street in Carmel, across from Charles's property.[45] Charles had taken Robert Tolmie, with his sister, Blanche, to see the James house before it was completed. Blanche was impressed, and later recalled the texture of the marble fireplaces and how Charles had designed them with uneven surfaces to "relieve the coldness."[46] The Tolmies planned to build a music studio, and they asked for Charles's help. Their lot was in Piedmont, in what was then a neighborhood of artists and writers in the hills above Oakland overlooking San Francisco Bay. Being only a short drive from the Schevill project in Berkeley, Charles could perform work for both clients during his visits from Carmel. He began in January 1923.[47] Blanche remembered Charles spending a total of six weeks on the project, during which time he lived across the street from the building site, in a studio that had once been used by the novelist Jack London.[48] Not surprisingly, the Tolmies' hillside studio-house has the modest scale of a Carmel cottage. Shingles lie in conspicuous irregularity, both in size and placement, and have a character similar to cottages by Carmel builder M. J. Murphy. Long wooden scuppers project exaggeratedly from the top of a bay on the north side of the house, giving a quaint and slightly whimsical appearance to the exterior. Inside, the main space resembles the Schevills' room in its dramatic ceiling height and tall

windows. Charles labored to achieve perfect acoustics, telling a later owner that he had adjusted the level of the ceiling several times to achieve the right effect.[49] Redwood panels, carved with figures of young musicians, decorate the balustrade of the loft area, and the plaster walls are decorated with impressions made from wood blocks carved by Charles into *tsuba* shapes and other abstractions. Charles seemed to have found a new outlet for his creativity, designing modest commissions for creative individuals whom he counted as personal friends. It was architecture with a smaller "a," and lacked the pressure he felt came from dealing with wealthy clients.[50]

After the Tolmie project, Charles soon began work on a studio for himself on the Lincoln Street side of his property. It was an economical project. At five dollars per thousand he purchased bricks salvaged from the demolished Pacific Grove Hotel. With his son, Patrickson, he cleaned the bricks of the old mortar, leaving just enough of the whitish grout so it would create a dappled effect of alternating red and white in the Flemish bond pattern of the exterior walls. Lumber was provided at no charge by White Brothers Hardwood in San Francisco, no doubt out of gratitude for supplying the rare and exotic woods for the James house. Remainder marble from the James job was used in the mantel and to pave a small vestibule and bath.

The interior spaces consist of a simple rectangle with smaller, subsidiary chambers appended on the east and south sides. A large skylight on the north of the pitched roof illuminates the main space, and french doors open to a terrace and garden off the south end.[51] Like the Tolmie studio the interior is plaster, with decorative images of leaves, rosettes, and other motifs from nature. These were personally added by Charles, who carved the small wood blocks used to press the images into the still-wet surfaces of the walls. Indeed, the studio's design is rich with Charles's personal symbolism. Two massive redwood beams span the twenty-foot width of the room and sit on roughly dressed limestone blocks (the load is actually borne by the buttressed exterior walls). Like the beams in the great room of the James house, these are carved with depictions of local sea life and other creatures: crabs, fish, birds, and shells. In his essay on the spirituality of Charles Greene, Travis Culwell notes that these carved forms carry specific symbolic relevance.[52] The bird, carved in three places, appears to be a falcon, the

31

34

32

33

30 **Charles S. Greene studio, Carmel-by-the-Sea, 1923–24.**
West (rear) facade.

31 **Charles S. Greene studio.** East (front) facade.

32 **Charles S. Greene studio.**
Front door, made of carved teakwood.

33 **Charles S. Greene studio.**
Decorative tiles accent the spandrel of an arch in the
garden wall.

34 (Left to right): Charles Greene, Lelia Mather Greene,
Alice Gordon Greene, and Alice Sumner Greene in the
garden of Charles's studio, c. 1930.

Japanese symbol of courage, power, and heroism. A pair of fish represents the spiritual freedom achieved in the state of Buddhahood. The crab is a symbol of reincarnation. Used here, the image of the crab also strengthens the link that Culwell has established between Charles Greene and Claude Fayette Bragdon, a contemporary architect and prolific writer on design and Theosophy. Greene actively read Bragdon at about this time and possibly earlier. His interest in Bragdon's writing was such that he laboriously transcribed lengthy passages, including detailed illustrations, from his book *The Beautiful Necessity: Seven Essays on Theosophy and Architecture* (1910). Among Bragdon's published theories that are brought to symbolic life in Charles's studio are the "Law of Radiation," illustrated by the crab; the "Law of Rhythmic Diminution," represented by carvings of wave forms and the spiral form of a shell;[53] and the theory of "Lower Space Systems in Our World," represented by the tomato vine carved into the entry door of the studio facing the street.[54] According to Bragdon, the tomato vine exemplifies a "lower-space" system of lines, planes, and solids in its stems, leaves, and fruit. Such systems lead to Bragdon's "higher-space conciousness," an intriguing Theosophical theory and an appropriate device at the entry to the studio of the increasingly spiritual Charles Greene. Nonorganic symbols are also suggested in various other carvings in the main studio space, including a disc with four opposing groups of radiating arms that recalls a common Native American depiction of the sun. Elsewhere, the symbol of a circle within a triangle relates to Bragdon's discussion of "lower spaces" contained in "higher spaces"; that is, geometries implying a larger number of dimensions.[55] The numerous carvings throughout the studio represent Greene's intensely personal symbolism: he declined to answer even his own family's queries about their exact meaning.[56]

Perhaps most cryptic of all is the carving that depicts Susanna and the Elders on a door panel inside the tiny bathroom. Taken from one of the apocryphal books of the Old Testament (detatched from the book of Daniel), the story tells of the unwanted advances of two old men rebuffed by the bathing Susanna. In retaliation for their rejection, the elders falsely accuse her of unchastity. Their plot is exposed by Daniel, who extracts contradictory accounts of the episode from Susanna's two accusers and

35 Mission San Miguel de Arcángel, San Luis Obispo County,
   whose arcade inspired a similar feature at Charles
   Greene's Carmel studio.

36 **Charles S. Greene studio, Carmel-by-the-Sea, 1923–24.**
   Interior of main studio space as it was furnished in 1954,
   three years before Greene's death.

37 **Charles S. Greene studio.**
   Studio interior today.

35 36 37

sentences them to death. While it is possible that the story held only superficial relevance for Charles, given the profound symbolism he indulged in elsewhere, not to say the sheer time and creative energy required to execute such a panel, there is probably more than passing significance for him in this cautionary tale. He may have intended the carving as a metaphor for his, and his brother's, career. In such a reading, Charles and Henry present to the world divergent theories on how to approach (and therefore represent) Beauty. They advance on their goal, but are ultimately rebuffed. While obvious differences exist from the original myth, this way of reading the carving aligns with Charles's view that perfection in representing beauty had ultimately eluded the partnership. Seen in this way, the Susanna carving also suggests a meaning for the carving on the door of Charles's adjacent workshop: a galleon at sea representing his never-ending journey toward the goal of perfection. Symbolism on various levels had appeared in Charles's work from as early as 1905, but in the 1920s it became a consuming interest. He ultimately wrote an essay on the subject, entitled "Symbolism" (c. 1930), which among other things proposes that symbols and symbolism are unexplainable in literal terms, and that the true essence of symbols must be experienced to be understood.[57]

While still working on his studio, Charles was engaged by Mortimer Fleishhacker to design a "sunroom" for the covered porch that extended at an angle off the living room of their Woodside residence. It was the second alteration of this particular space, the first being the rebuilding of the timber post-and-beam structure in brick while initial construction of the house was still in progress. This time, the space would be fully enclosed. The card room, as it was later known, represents a late revival of the classic Greene and Greene wood idiom with the added artistic touch of Charles Greene on every carved cabinet and panel. The use of polychrome-stained plaster on the walls and ceiling give lightness to the room that would otherwise be lacking had it been entirely of wood. Unlike the decorative panels that were installed in the Greenes' Pasadena houses, here Charles was personally responsible for the decorative carving. For subject matter, Charles's conceptual sketch shows simple depictions of trees, but the images he ultimately carved represent the continents of Asia, Africa, Europe, and

the Americas. The designs were approved in 1923 and the room completed in 1924.[58] Hand-carved furniture was planned for the room (the only furniture Charles would execute for the Woodside house), and in the fall of 1925 the Fleishhackers took delivery of Charles's exquisite card table with tooled-leather top, four side chairs, and an armchair, each with an intricately tooled and pigmented leather seat.

Woodcarving was a near-religious experience for Charles Greene. He studied books on Japanese carving methods and even made his own tools to get exactly the effects he wanted.[59] In an undated poem, Charles struggled to articulate his feeling toward this aspect of his creative life:

The Carver (Life)[60]

Over my bench in the twilight
Lieth the latent wood
Sealeth the struggle before me
Before my wavering sight.
Impelling me, Life lent me
All it could,
So tend me yet I must
To Life anon & trust
Life's way around me
To bear some of my good
My way to right
God in mine own sight!

In the ensuing years, Charles devoted increasingly more time to study of alternative religions, especially Buddhism and Theosophy, and a study group of about fifteen men and women began to meet at his home in the 1920s. Included in the group was one of Charles's fellow city planning commissioners, Susan Creighton Porter; an Arts and Crafts–period bookbinder from St. Louis named Mary E. Bulkley; and Dora Hagemeyer Comstock, who appears to have been the principal organizer of the group. Members of the group read the works of the Russian occultists George

38

39

Ivanovitch Gurdjieff and Peter Damien Ouspensky, and they followed the lectures of the internationally known theosophist A. R. Orage, who interpreted Gurdjieff's seemingly impenetrable theories. Orage spoke to the group in Charles's studio in November 1928, giving a lecture entitled "Neo-Behaviorism." Lincoln Steffens was on the periphery of the group and also played host to an Orage lecture that month.[61] Charles wrote: "The Orage method claims to increase being, so ultimately to reach understanding. Through self observation one may begin to find objective conscience. Through self awareness comes the distinction between the I and the It, and the relation of them to others must be increasingly realized; that is understanding. This requires energy, to overcome the inertia of subjectivity."[62]

Even while Charles attempted to overcome the inertia of subjectivity, he was still called upon occasionally to take up his former profession. Early in 1925, Charles designed an L-shaped concrete house for Carmel postmaster Jessie H. Payne. Probably for cost reasons, Payne purchased the drawings from Charles Greene and elected not to use his services to oversee construction of the house. He hired the popular Carmel contractor M. J. Murphy, who later took credit for the design as well.[63] Later that year, Jennie Crocker Whitman had Charles design a large house for her three-and-a-half-acre property on Cypress Drive in Pebble Beach. If not for the less spectacular site, the dwelling would have rivalled the James house as one of Charles's most romantic works had it been built. The plan for a spacious courtyard with pool and formal walkways held the promise of stately elegance similar to the upper garden of the Cordelia Culbertson house (1911). But the building material was to be a rustic "old brick," an informal material that would produce an effect more similar to that of his own Carmel studio. Also similar to a prominent feature of the studio, Charles included a long brick arcade, in this instance as a focal point for the rear of the Whitman garden. A prominent arcade was also a feature of Charles's project for the "Dwelling for W. B. T.," which Charles had exhibited at the St. Louis exposition in 1904. The long arcade related directly to the Franciscan missions that Charles loved, but in the abstract idea of the arcade there was also an opportunity to exercise another of Claude Bragdon's theories, the Law of Diversity in Monotony. This law was described in *The Beautiful Necessity*, and was illustrated by the arcade of the cathedral in Pisa, Italy, whose individual arches are deliberately different, varying to a small degree in their width and height from one to the next. Bragdon argued that such barely perceptible differences in dimension gave character and beauty to architecture, and consciously or not, Charles had used this "law" before to good effect in the James house. There, individual panes of glass that appear to be the same size as their immediate neighbor actually have slightly different height dimensions, giving a visual sensation, according to Bragdon, of "piquant variation."[64] Like the James house and his own studio, Charles intended the Whitman house to have the air of an ancient structure. To ensure this, he engaged the James house mason and construction supervisor, Fred Coleman, to work on the Whitman project, estimated to cost $88,000. In January 1926, however, the job was canceled, even though more than one hundred thousand bricks had been delivered to the site and White Brothers Lumber company in San Francisco was holding teak beams for the interior.[65]

If the big commissions were not bearing fruit for Charles, some smaller ones were. He designed and built a living-room addition to the cottage of Violet Campbell, a family friend, and a two-stall stable structure for Mrs. Willis Walker of Pebble Beach. He also designed and carved for Mrs. Walker a nine-foot-long cedar triptych panel—a carving of Christopher Columbus's West Indies landing in his ships the *Niña*, the *Pinta*, and the *Santa Maria*—for which he confidently brought together several of his favorite scenic elements, including mountains, trees, ships on the ocean, and sea birds. In 1927 and 1928, Charles collaborated with Henry on several decorative arts projects for Elisabeth Prentiss, owner of the Cordelia Culbertson house. These included a painted table, a folding screen for her bedroom, light boxes for the entry-hall paintings, a series of carved panels for the dining room, and the aforementioned pair of travertine jars for the entry portico. Charles's method of working very independently, without consulting his clients as to schedule and cost, had become a problem, however. Henry found himself in the position of having to make excuses for his brother's lack of attention. With regard to the series of carved panels Charles was to make for Mrs. Prentiss's dining room, Henry observed to Charles in a letter, "She

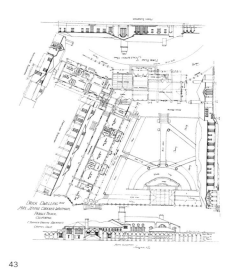

41

42

43

rather criticizes you for not letting her know costs and doing something so she would understand a little better what was to be done before doing it. I do not know what is wrong, unless it is your method of doing things."[66] Mrs. Prentiss was more to the point: "It would be a much happier condition if both you and your clients could know definitely what something will cost rather than to be utterly astounded. Surely in planning your time and the character of the work you can do this."[67]

In the spring of 1927 Mr. and Mrs. Mortimer Fleishhacker began discussions with Charles Greene to revive the former plan to build a dairy house that had been proposed in 1911 but never built. Charles presented new sketches for the structure, which was meant to be a teahouse retreat for Mrs. Fleishhacker. They showed a rustic stone folly nestled under an oak tree overlooking a stream running through the property. The Fleishhackers approved the design and made plans to proceed. At about the same time, Charles was given a far greater challenge. In 1915, the Fleishhackers had purchased an additional eleven and a half acres to the southwest of their estate, a parcel immediately beyond the existing lawn and pool at the rear of the house. This purchase would protect their unobstructed vista, and at the same time it afforded a new design opportunity for their landscape. At the end of the existing garden, an elevation drop of about sixty-five feet presented a challenging transition to the new parcel. First, Charles designed a balustrade at the top of the escarpment, using the same materials that he had for the hardscape of the main residence and garden.[68] A broad gap in the center of the balustrade would serve as the entry to a new lower garden, for which Charles had produced preliminary sketches by the spring of 1927. The vision was completed by the following year, when he produced designs for a dramatic arcade as a focal point at the end of the pool.

The dramatic stone steps, semicircular retaining wall, and long, shimmering reflection pool, together with the elliptical arcade at its terminus, constitute the most stunning and evocative landscape design of Charles Greene's career. Like the Cordelia Culbertson water garden, the concept was largely inspired by Italian precedent. The Canopus at Villa Adriana, Tivoli, is the historical basis for the long, rectangular shape of the

reflecting pool, while the rear wall and balustrade of the "Fountain of the Tivoli," or of the Tiburtine Sibyl, at Villa d'Este, suggest the specific imagery for the arched niches of the semicircular retaining wall at the north end of the pool. The arcade on the south end was evidently inspired by an ancient Roman aquaduct. Charles was familiar with these historical precedents, mainly because of his thirty-three-day visit to Italy in 1901. And, as previously noted, his personal library included at least one book profusely illustrated with Italian gardens, including Villa d'Este, Tivoli.

The view from the highest level of the Fleishhacker garden stairway is breathtaking, not only for the beauty of the constructed portions but for the seemingly endless vista of hills and forests to the southwest. Indeed, the genius of Charles Greene's design lay in his instinct to streamline, so as not to inhibit a full appreciation of the natural landscape. He wrote of his two schemes for the arcade: "I am inclined to think the larger number of arches is the better solution as it is lighter and more graceful, the other more monumental...."[69] The air of an ancient ruin is intentional, too, and is achieved in part by the overall design but also by the choice of materials. Like the James house, there are no even surfaces or hard lines. Irregularly shaped slabs of Napa sandstone were used for paving, and thousands of jagged bits of jasper constitute the wall and terracing.[70] The descent to the pool is by way of the terraced upper stairs, which split to embrace a series of planting beds, thus enabling oblique views of the pool and arcade from above. A broad landing above the pool's retaining wall allows a last view along the center axis before one is sidelined again to descend to the pool's north end. At the level of the pool, turning back to face the retaining wall, one is rewarded with a rich view of diverse forms: arches, niches, roundels, and eerily face-like weep holes built into the recesses of the main arches. Like the James house foundation, the design and materials are so thoroughly compatible with the site and its surrounding landscape that it seems as though the garden had always existed. In 1931, Garden City Pottery of San Jose delivered two hundred urns made to Charles Greene's design. These were installed as the finishing touch to the gardens and the completion of twenty years of work on the Fleishhackers' Woodside estate. Bella Fleishhacker asked Charles to design a small garden addition for her

44

45

44 **Mortimer Fleishhacker, Sr., estate, "Green Gables,"
Woodside, 1911–12.**
Reflecting pool designed in 1927–28, with elliptical
arcade inspired by Italian precedents.

45 Villa Adriana, Tivoli. View of Canopus, the historical
inspiration for arcaded reflecting pools.

46 **Mortimer Fleishhacker, Sr., estate, "Green Gables."**
Dairy house addition, 1927. North elevation. Ink-on-
linen presentation drawing.

47 **Mortimer Fleishhacker, Sr., estate, "Green Gables."**
Dairy house addition, 1927. South elevation. Ink-on-
linen presentation drawing.

48 **Mortimer Fleishhacker, Sr., estate, "Green Gables."**
View through arcade north toward reflecting pool,
retaining wall, and terraced stairway.

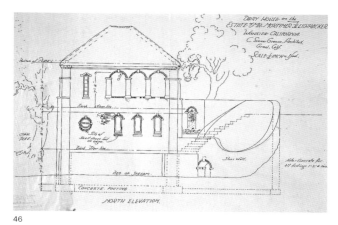

46

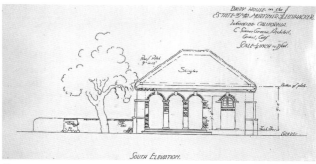

47

48

in 1935, but this was not constructed. Remarkably, the Fleishhacker estate has remained substantially as the Greenes designed it.

During the period immediately following the Fleishhacker water garden project, Charles engaged in only a few small architectural commissions. He gave art lessons, studied Theosophy and Buddhism, and generally led the life of a Carmel bohemian.[71] He cultivated the appearance of an artist, too, wearing his wavy hair in a Dutch boy cut and sporting a velour artist's smock. In 1929, he designed a pergola for the garden of Ralph C. Lee in Hillsborough, south of San Francisco. Like the Fleishhacker garden, it was to have been paved in Napa sandstone, and was meant to feature a double arcade terminating in a patio leading to a tennis court—an elegant landscape, if only the client had decided to go ahead with construction. Charles also designed a small shingle house in Monterey for John Langley Howard, the artist son of his friend and colleague, John Galen Howard, founder and head of the architecture department at the University of California at Berkeley.[72] The Howards had a summer home in Carmel and John Langley ("Lang") Howard had become friends with Charles's son, Nathaniel Patrickson ("Pat") Greene. The younger Howard had hired a builder and begun work on a house, but he was unhappy with the way it was progressing. Oddly, he asked his father's friend, Charles, rather than his father, to advise him. Charles suggested he demolish what was done and begin again with a different builder. He would provide the plans.[73] The simple cottage that resulted is noteworthy mainly for its quirky placement of shingles, a treatment similar to the Tolmie studio in Piedmont. With Charles's approval, his client personally carved the profiled ends of the rafters, leaving a whittled appearance that gives the house a hand-hewn rusticity.

In about 1929, Charles received a design commission that inaugurated another long-standing client-artist relationship. Martin Flavin was a highly successful playwright who, in 1929, had three of his works produced on Broadway simultaneously (*Children of the Moon*, *The Criminal Code*, and *Broken Dishes*). At about this time, Martin Flavin asked Charles Greene to help him design and build a small summer cabin along Cachagua Creek above the village of Carmel Valley.[74] It was following this modest project that Flavin commissioned additions and alterations to his English-style

house (designed by Charles Gottshalk, 1922) on the windswept bluff of Yankee Point in the Carmel Highlands. "Spindrift," as it was called, was a year-round retreat for the Flavin family, whose primary residence was in the Bel Air neighborhood of Los Angeles.

The first phase of Charles's work on Spindrift, most likely begun in late 1929 or early 1930, included the design of a perimeter wall and contiguous gatehouse at the roadway entrance to the property.[75] Flavin's growing fame and the highly exposed site that his house occupied on the point were likely causes for concern about security. The gatehouse, when occupied, would have afforded the greatest degree of protection, but it was never completed. Constructed of the same golden granite quarried for the James house, the perimeter wall presents a formidable barrier to entry. A pair of iron gates span the driveway gap and a solid-wood side gate (now unattached) stood to the left of the driveway, embellished with the name of the house in iron letters. In plan, the perimeter wall splits three ways at a Y-shaped junction to the right of the entrance gates, the tail of the Y curling back toward the road in an ever-tightening spiral. The spiral portion of the wall gradually diminishes in height until it fades into the earth at its end. This unusual geometric construction refers directly to Claude Bragdon's Law of Rhythmic Diminution, as described in *The Beautiful Necessity*. Indeed, according to Bragdon, the spiral vortex takes on exceptional significance as a form. "More and more, science is coming to recognize what theosophy affirms, that the spiral vortex, which so beautifully illustrates this law, both in its time and its space aspects, is the universal archetype, the pattern of all that is, has been, or will be, since it is the form assumed by the ultimate physical atom, and the ultimate physical atom is the physical cosmos in miniature."[76] Charles's use of the spiral was concurrent with his most serious explorations into Theosophy, further indicating his interest in linking his art with his spiritual search.[77] Also in 1930, Charles designed a breakfast-room porch addition to the ocean side of the house, dining-room candle sconces, draperies, and an elegant iron stairway and balcony for the living room.[78] Most significantly, however, he began to develop plans for a library adjacent to the Flavins' living room.

49 **Gate lodge for Martin Flavin house, "Spindrift,"**
Carmel Highlands, 1929–30 (project).
North (roadside) elevation and interior elevation. Ink-
on-linen presentation drawing.

50 **Martin Flavin house, "Spindrift."**
South wall of living room, with wrought-iron and
wood stairway and balcony railing and carved
redwood doors.

51 **Martin Flavin house, "Spindrift."**
Interior of library. Carved redwood doors are flanked
by bookcases equipped with portable torchlights.

52 **Martin Flavin house, "Spindrift."**
Library ceiling.

51

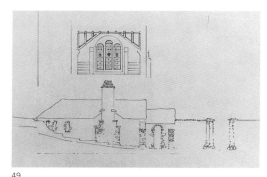

49

50

52

Martin Flavin's library addition at Spindrift was the most virtuoso artistic work of the post-James-house phase of Charles Greene's career. The intimate room, completed in 1931, was to be a quiet sanctuary in which the writer could work uninterrupted, without even the sound or view of the sea to distract him (a window to the west was opened in later years). Paneled entirely in vertical-grain redwood, the room was designed to contain bookshelves, a stained-glass triptych window, and a paneled ceiling set in a highly complex composition of opposing diagonals. The redwood wall and ceiling panels allowed Charles to take up his carving tools again, this time to depict various stylizations of plants. Just inside the library's double doors, two wall sconces with repoussé copper shades hang from the wall. Unhooked from their brackets, they can serve as hand-held electric torches to search for books in the otherwise subdued light of the room. Two additional wall-mounted copper lights were designed to rotate on their hinged brackets for easy positioning over a table or chair. Wrought-iron heat registers, executed by H. C. Steinmetz of Pacific Grove, echo the organic undulations of plant forms carved into the wall and ceiling panels. A leaded art-glass triptych window, manufactured by Cobbledick-Kibbe Glass Company of Oakland, was accidentally shattered in transit, and a replacement window, a compromise in conventional bottle glass, was substituted. Charles used a broken remnant of the original elegant window, however, as a lens insert above the living-room balcony door, a small light that gives a modest idea of the golden-red glow that would have suffused the redwood interior of the library had the original window survived. Following the delivery and installation of the library panels, Charles also designed a carved panel for the overmantel in the living room. After rejecting other possible designs, he and his client chose an image of the California oak tree, long one of Charles's favorite regional icons. The deeply carved redwood panel was his last bold design statement for Martin Flavin, although he undertook other alterations through 1941, including additional garden walls and minor interior work.

The remaining years of Charles Greene's design activity were notable mainly for the frustrations that resulted, even though they were of his own making. While Charles worked on Spindrift, he had also been involved with a commission from Martin Flavin's mother, Mrs. Louise A. F. Kelley, who wanted Charles to design a conservatory and tile fountain for "Ar-Kel Villa," her home in San Jose, California. The design and cost estimates were presented to her in the summer of 1929, and tile makers Solon & Schemmel of San Jose were awarded the job for the tile floor and fountain. The tile makers indicated their readiness to start immediately, as soon as the architect gave detailed instructions.[79] That fall the glass walls of the conservatory were partially erected, but they leaked in the winter rains. By May 1930 Mrs. Kelley was still awaiting its completion.[80] She wrote to Charles that she was "wildly anxious" to get it done."[81] "We are at home and waiting" read a telegram to Charles dated July 5, 1930. Two weeks later another: "When will you be here?" The work was finally completed later that year, but not without hard feelings on both sides.[82] Now age sixty-two, Charles had become incapable of accurately characterizing for his clients how long his work would take and how much it would cost. He was vague in his promises and seemed to be increasingly out of touch with his clients' wishes.

Mary J. Moore, the wife of San Jose physician Thomas Verner Moore, had visited Charles's studio with a friend and had admired a simple oak stool she noticed there. Charles said he would make a similar one for her. She wanted something for her son to use in his study. In April 1930, she wrote to say how pleased she was that he had agreed to make it, and added that she hoped the stool might be ready to present to her son on Mother's Day that year. She made a critical mistake, however, by adding: "I was glad when you consented to have the stool made....I did wish my son to have something extra pretty and uncommon."[83] She no doubt meant this last remark as a deferential compliment in recognition of the work of the celebrated designer, but Charles Greene took it as license to venture more broadly with her commission than originally discussed. After three more letters politely asking when she could expect her footstool, Mrs. Moore wrote in a panic in December: "I was so sorry you had so much trouble, first making that lovely stool, and then bringing it here. When I saw you in Carmel I thought you were to make a very plain but strong stool. I thought it was to be of oak, which would suit the furniture in Tom's den … so that he could enjoy sitting in front of the fire for a smoke. As I said to you when I saw the beautiful work on it that it was far too elaborate

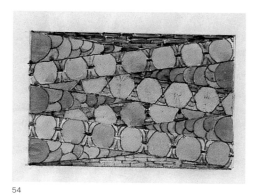

53

54

55

for the purpose it was to be used for. Then if the price you mentioned is correct—I was so astonished when you told me! That is prohibitive! I could not pay the amount you said. So I don't know that I could do anything else but send it back … I don't know when I was ever so sorry about a misunderstanding."[84] This missive did not go down well in Carmel, and Charles shot back a reply by return mail: "...when I received your letter [of April 11], I felt that you wanted something better...." In a postscript, he adds, "Since there is a sincere misunderstanding on each side I feel sure that we will be able to reach an understanding."[85] Mrs. Moore only restated her case more forcefully: "… [the] stool I saw at your house was not of ebony, neither was it carved, and certainly had no stones set in! You said you might have a man make the stool, the same shape as yours, and it was to be of oak, perfectly plain, which would match the chairs in the den.... You said at the time it would not be very expensive. I never for a moment thought it was necessary to ask you the exact price. I will ask my son to send the stool to you at once."[86] Inwardly driven to create something of exceptional beauty and uniqueness, Charles once again saw his client's role, consciously or not, as the financial vehicle to enable him to create a work of lasting artistic merit. The clash ended with Charles taking the piece back.

In the fall of 1929, following the successful completion of his water garden in Woodside, Mortimer Fleishhacker met with Charles Greene regarding the addition of a wing to his Pacific Heights residence in San Francisco. The timing of the meeting was especially interesting considering Mr. Fleishhacker's profession as a banker and the chaos that followed the market collapse on Wall Street in October of that year. Whether he was aware or not of the imminent onset of the Great Depression, Mr. Fleishhacker proceeded with plans to build a personal study that would serve as a showcase for antiques he had collected, including a pair of iron doors and a large tapestry, on his European travels. Charles had begun designing the addition by November 1929, and had alerted his favorite stone carver, Jacob Schoenfeld, of his intent to involve him in the project.[87]

Charles's idea was to design in the Gothic style, probably because of the provenance of the antiques to be housed in the addition. The first conceptual sketches show a street elevation that resembles the west end of a typical

English village church, but subsequent sketches show a more idiosyncratic interpretation of Gothic style, with an elaborately patterned brick exterior more reminiscent of the English Arts and Crafts church work of William Butterfield or George Edmund Street. The window muntins, however, were designed in a stone version of the familar Chinese "lift," the motif the Greenes had used so frequently in their classic designs in wood. The interior was to be a vaulted space, high enough to accommodate the hanging tapestry; a large fireplace was to be another focal point. The presentation drawings specify a combination of timbrel arches and vaulting of "Akoustolith" tile, to be provided and installed by the R. Guastavino Company, a New York– and Boston-based firm best known for its institutional projects, including portions of Pennsylvania Station, the Vanderbilt Hotel, and Tiffany & Co., which Charles had seen on his visit to New York in 1912.[88] The most intriguing decorative element of the design was the stone overmantel of the fireplace, meant to feature an elaborate carving of trees and plant life clinging to the flanks of a fuming volcano. This design, another symbolic expression from the spiritual mind of Charles Greene, was to be carved by Jacob Schoenfeld, who had executed the marble mantels of the James house a decade earlier.[89]

The Gothic Room was never built, both because of the slow pace of the design work and the contractor's prohibitive estimates. There is no mention of tight money or the deteriorating financial markets, however, in any of Fleishhacker's correspondence, indicating that the construction estimates were simply more than the client wanted to pay. Letters between Charles Greene and his consulting engineer, Victor Poss, indicate considerable time spent working out engineering issues throughout 1930. In December, Charles wrote to his brother, "Mr. Fleishhacker's plans are not done yet, but I think I am getting it worked out. It has been the hardest work I have ever done, but I hope to make a success of it if he has the patience to wait for me....I have been putting lots of time on it. I have nothing else."[90] In early 1931, Charles made contact with the Guastavino representative in San Francisco, who promised a significant discount if the Gothic Room work could be installed that spring, concurrent with the firm's work on the walls and main ceilings of Grace Cathedral in San Francisco (Louis P. Hobart, 1928–33). By that time,

56 **Mortimer Fleishhacker, Sr., Gothic Room addition,**
San Francisco, 1929–32 (project).
Proposed south (front) elevation and wall section.
Ink-on-linen presentation drawing.

57 **Mortimer Fleishhacker, Sr., Gothic Room addition.**
Proposed interior elevations (south and west).
Ink-on-linen presentation drawing.

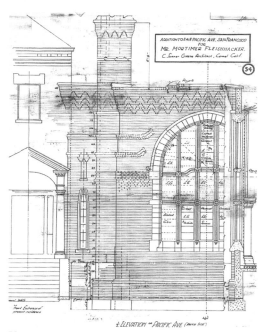

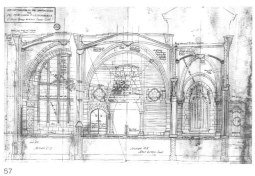

56

57

however, communications had broken down between Charles and his consulting engineer. On April 13, 1931, Mr. Fleishhacker's assistant, H. M. Simons, wrote to Charles: "Can you advise as to the status of the work...? Mr. Poss ... has been in several times complaining as to various things... I advised him I would write you...."[91] Charles replied immediately that he would contact Mr. Poss and be ready with figures by the end of the month. This was apparently unacceptable to Mr. Fleishhacker, who instructed Simons to reply: "In view of the fact that the matter has dragged on so long, Mr. Fleishhacker has decided to let it drop for the time being."[92] At the bottom of the letter, Charles scribbled in pencil, "Saw M. F. in person: 10 days grace from 25th."

The real reason for the delays, however, was due to more than Charles's usual slow pace of work. He was apparently somewhat out of his element in dealing within the exacting engineering tolerances required by a substantial masonry structure on an urban lot. The consulting engineer and the Guastavino Company were hampered by Charles's lack of experience in this area, and as late as June 1931, Poss and Guastavino both complained that there was insufficient structural support planned for the proposed vaulting. This could be fixed, but Charles incorrectly assumed that his client's reluctance to proceed had to do exclusively with money. He wrote to Mr. Fleishhacker: "The reason for the high stone figure is the hand work over the entire surface of the stone. Of course the real beauty of the job is the hand work. Stone is a cold impassive substance when finished by machine and stone dominates the room."[93] By then, Mr. Fleishhacker had lost his appetite for the project, which had grown to be far more time-consuming than he had imagined. In an effort to keep the project alive, however, Charles independently solicited bids for increasingly cheaper materials. Mr. Fleishhacker definitively dropped the Gothic Room plan in the spring of 1932, citing cost as the excuse, but the record indicates that it clearly had more to do with the pace of work.

After this disappointment, Charles did less and less design work. He spent most of his time studying Buddhist texts and Theosophical writings. Group-study meetings continued at his studio, and he occasionally took up his pen to write. Hugh Ferriss, the New York designer, architectural renderer, and futurist, wrote an article for *The Carmelite* in the fall of 1930 about Modernist architecture's search for a design soul. Charles Greene wrote a reply for the following week's issue, stating flatly, "there are no creative artist-builders of today."[94] Pursuing Theosophy, he painstakingly transcribed a vocabulary of terms required to unlock the considerable mysteries of G. I. Gurdjieff's writings; he also transcribed key phrases from Dwight Goddard's *Buddhist Bible*.[95] He had not entirely lost his will to create, however, and in 1934 designed and carved a three-panel teak and leather screen for his former client Mrs. Willis Walker. By all accounts she had been happy with both of his previous efforts, which had included the small stable and carved panel of Columbus's landing. But, like Mrs. Moore and her stool, Mrs. Walker rejected Charles's latest work as being different from what she had wanted. Slightly daunted, Charles tried to interest Mr. and Mrs. Fleishhacker in buying the teak screen, writing to them, "I would rather you would have it than anyone else in the world."[96] They declined, however, saying they did not have a use for it, and mentioned that they felt it would be an extravagance, "beautiful as it is."[97] Charles's artistic spirit was further tested when Walter Heil, director of the de Young Museum in San Francisco, declined to exhibit the screen that year.[98]

In 1934, Charles went along with an ill-advised attempt to use a land developer as an intermediary to attract wealthy clients in the San Francisco Bay area. The scheme was sponsored by Park Abbott, a well-meaning but naive man who was ineffective at selling Charles's ideas or reputation. The first attempt at selling a design met with outright rejection from a prospective client named Reinhart. The scheme was dropped for a few years, then revived in 1937. Abbott produced an attractive prospectus, printed by fine-pressman Wilder Bentley, but weakly confessed to Charles, "I'm mailing very few of the announcements, first because it would be very grievous to me if some architect should take exception to them and write to you, secondly because I still do not know many people who have taste. I will attempt to enlarge my acquaintanceship to remedy this, because I am confident there is a large amount of good taste and good spirit that will welcome my search."[99]

The last design commission of Charles's career was from D. L. James, who wanted an expanded library for Seaward. Mr. James and Charles

58

59

58 D. L. James house, "Seaward," Carmel Highlands, 1918–22.
Library alterations and additions, 1938–44. South wall of library (wood surround and mantel added).

59 D. L. James house, "Seaward."
Library alterations and additions, 1938–44. Detail of stone vent on north wall of library.

Greene corresponded about the possibilities beginning in 1938, the first idea being to convert the unusual round bathroom into a library. This was abandoned, however, and it was ultimately decided that Charles would design an alteration to the basement space under the service wing, facing the ocean. Several schemes were drawn up, including one for an addition of a shed-roof bay that would have extended beyond the granite face of the house. The design work was slow in coming. In September 1939, Jacob Schoenfeld provided an estimate for the bulk cost of materials to be used, but by July 1940 he wrote to Charles, now seventy-one, to ask for instructions, noting that he had "received an inquiry from Mr. James as to how we are getting along with the job, as he was in the impression that it should be about done."[100] Charles pressed his brother into service that fall to design the structural engineering aspects of the job, but by 1941, Schoenfeld had still been unable to finish cutting and carving the stone, for lack of drawings.[101] Charles complained to him vaguely of "interference," "complications," and a general inability "to get work done when promised."[102] In fact, so little progress was made on the ground that the client refused to pay Schoenfeld for the work he had done. The stone carver, in turn, threatened a lein on the property. James sent a truck to collect his marble, and it was not until the summer of 1943 that Charles engaged a replacement, a San Francisco marble sculptor named L. Cardini. The stonework was nearly completed when D. L. James died suddenly on March 10, 1944. His son, Daniel, and Mrs. James eventually resumed the work of the library addition and it was completed in the early 1950s with help and encouragement from *House Beautiful* editor Elizabeth Gordon, who had published several articles on the Greenes.

In the end, the library was small but elegant, with simple granite arches on the exterior that blended with the masonry of the house. Large, mullioned windows give views to the ocean, and bookcases and drawers (now removed) lined the east wall. High above the fireplace on the south wall is an elaborately carved decorative stone vent, with a complementary vent on the north wall. Each depicts a different interpretation of water flowing onto the earth, and in each the sun rises over banks of stylized clouds, symbolizing the elements of fire and air. Charles's fascination with the traditionally mystical and elemental imagery of Tintagel persisted here, in his last effort for the James house.[103] The image of water flowing through a stone circle came to Charles from St. Nectan's Kieve, a spectacular natural feature at Trethevy, near Tintagel, where the waters of the Trevillet river fall into a rocky basin and out through a circular stone opening.[104] Charles's designing days had concluded at last, but it was fitting that they should end with a project that was emblematic of his fifty-year career. The James library was slow to conceive, slow to execute, but impeccable in its craftsmanship, provocative in its symbolism, and enduring in its beauty. It was everything the architect had envisioned, and this one last time, he had mustered the courage and energy to obtain it.

1 Henry Mather Greene (seated) and Charles Sumner
Greene in a portrait by Cole Weston at the D. L.
James house, "Seaward," Carmel Highlands,
December 1947.

The impact of the Greenes' work on the architecture of early-twentieth-century America was strong, but fleeting in its day. Promoted in national and international publications, including *Ladies' Home Journal*, *The Craftsman*, *Country Life in America*, and *The International Studio*, the Greenes' designs had excellent recognition and exposure, in both text and photographs, from 1902 through 1919. Like Frank Lloyd Wright's prairie-style houses of the Midwest, the Greenes' Asian-influenced Craftsman idiom represented a fresh regional design language for Southern California when it needed it most, during a rapid growth in population following the beginning of the new century.

The Greenes' designs were adapted by other builders for less expensive construction as early as about 1904, but the decline of the brothers' output after 1911 had more to do with changing tastes and values than with a cheapening of the product through careless imitation by others. Neither Charles nor Henry elected to play into the hands of Modernism, and they remained stubbornly on the periphery of changing trends for the rest of their careers. Their professional peers and the press virtually ignored their work from 1930 until after World War II. It was as if they had never existed. Then, in 1947, the Southern California chapter of the American Institute of Architects discussed the "advisability of ... honoring in some way the work of architects Charles S. Greene and Henry M. Greene."[1] They did so the following year, based on the recommendation of Charles Greene's former neighbor, chapter president Myron Hunt, and his associate, Henry Eggers. In 1948, the Greenes' work was illustrated in James Marston Fitch's *American Building: The Forces That Shaped It*, and over the next several years various architecture and trade journals began to publish reassessments of the Greenes' work under the bylines of architect Lloyd Morgan Yost, editor Elizabeth Gordon of *House Beautiful*, architectural historian Clay Lancaster, and Jean Murray Bangs, wife of architect Harwell Hamilton Harris, who wrote, "Greene and Greene ... understood beauty in terms of simplicity, fitness and repose."[2] Bangs, in particular, sought to secure for the Greenes a position of appropriate prominence in the history of American architecture.

In 1952, the American Institute of Architects honored the Greenes with a Special Citation, which read: "Architects much honored in your homeland for great contributions to design, sensitive and knowing builders who reflected with grace and craftsmanship emerging values in modern living in the western states, formulators of a new and native architecture, The American Institute of Architects honors you Henry Mather Greene and Charles Sumner Greene for your contributions to the design of the American home. Your gifts have now multiplied and spread to all parts of the nation, and are recognized throughout the world, influencing and improving the design of small as well as great houses. You enrich the lives of the people. You have made the name of California synonymous with simpler, freer and more abundant living. You have helped shape our distinctively national architecture, and in giving tangible form to the ideals of our people, your names will be forever remembered among the great creative Americans."[3]

The Greenes lived long enough to sense the genuine revival in appreciation of their work. Henry Mather Greene died in Pasadena on October 2, 1954, at the age of eighty-four. He is remembered by most who knew him as a quiet man of erect bearing, always in a pressed suit and tie, always gracious and courteous. According to his family, he had a twinkle in his eye that showed a profound contentment with his place in the world. Charles Sumner Greene died at the age of eighty-eight, on June 11, 1957, in Carmel-by-the-Sea. He was fittingly remembered by one acquaintance as "a man of immense spirituality, almost to the point of abstraction ... as though he were only one-third with us in the real world."[4] The two men were never known to have spoken a harsh word to each other, and they corresponded until they could no longer, always maintaining a cordial relationship.

In the 1950s, historians Lewis Mumford, Henry-Russell Hitchcock, Vincent Scully, Jr., Talbot Hamlin, Frederick Gutheim, and Esther McCoy redressed the omission of the Greenes from the principal architectural history texts of the first half of the twentieth century, and in 1960, Randell Makinson, a young instructor at the University of Southern California, wrote a chapter in Esther McCoy's regional history, *Five California Architects*, about the Greene brothers. It is primarily his work since then that has guided our understanding of the Greenes.

Perhaps one of the greatest legacies of Charles and Henry Greene, along with their extraordinary houses, decorative arts, and other tangible output, is the uncompromising will of two men in a quiet corner of California who toiled for a level of perfection that each felt to be unobtainable, but worth striving for. In doing so, they created some of the most enduring masterpieces of the last century.

Notes

Key to abbreviations

Avery: Avery Architectural and Fine Arts Library, Columbia University, New York
CSG: Charles Sumner Greene
GGL: Greene and Greene Library, San Marino, California
HMG: Henry Mather Greene
LMG: Lelia Mather Greene
TSG: Thomas Sumner Greene
UCB: Environmental Design Archives (formerly Documents Collection), College of Environmental Design, University of California at Berkeley

Introduction

1   Frank Purcell, "City's Almost Forgotten Geniuses," *Pasadena Independent*, 6 March 1949.

Chapter One: Yankee Forebears, Midwest Boys (pp. 6–21)

1   "Williams' Cincinnati Directory" for 1868 and 1870 lists Thomas Greene's residence as "Ernst Station," which became known as Brighton Station by 1871. No street address is listed for the family residence until the 1873 directory, which names only "Walker Miller Road. Brighton Sta." as the Greenes' address. According to Cincinnati ward maps, Walker Miller Road was renamed State Street at about this time.

2   Elihu and Mathilda Greene are listed in the Cincinnati directory as living on State Street as early as 1871. They may have lived in the same house as their son and his family, though this is neither proved nor disproved by the directory listings.

3   The youngest child of a large family, Elihu Greene had left the Greene family home, the "Old Forge," along the banks of the Potowomut River in Warwick, Rhode Island, to seek his fortune in Ohio in the 1830s (Elihu Greene letters, Rhode Island Historical Society).

4   The different approaches to child rearing can be recognized in letters from the parents to their sons sent during the five years the boys attended MIT and apprenticed in Boston, from 1888 until 1893.

5   This well-worn book, along with other items from Charles Greene's childhood, are included in the Charles Sumner Greene Collection housed at UCB. I am grateful to Professor Stephen Tobriner, curator of the collection, and to its director, Waverly Lowell, for access to these important materials (a gift of Charles Greene's wife, Alice Storey White Greene, and son, Nathaniel Patrickson Greene, in 1959).

6   Calvert Vaux, in his essay "A New Scale of Values," recommended architecture as a profession, asking rhetorically, "Should not parents speculate for their sons in this line?" (*Villas and Cottages*, 1857).

7   Christopher P. Monkhouse, "Thomas Waldron Sumner," *East India Marine Hall: 1824–1974*, ed. Philip Chadwick Foster Smith (Salem, Mass.: Peabody Museum of Salem, Massachusetts, 1974), n.p.

8   Louise Brown Clark, *The Greenes of Rhode Island with Historical Records of English Ancestry, 1524–1902, Compiled from the Mss. of the Late Major-General George Sears Greene, U. S. V.* (New York: 1903).

9   He was discharged as a captain in Company A, 47th U. S. Col'd Infantry Volunteers.

10   "Civil War Memoirs of Thomas Sumner Greene: 1861–1866" are in typescript form prepared by T. S. Greene, 23 October 1917 (GGL, courtesy Jane McElroy, granddaughter of Charles Greene).

11   Miles Greenwood, "to whom it may concern," 11 June 1867 (collection of Virginia Dart Greene Hales, granddaughter of Henry Greene).

12   Lelia Mather Greene's descendents recalled hearing her tales of daring nocturnal rides through enemy lines. Isabelle Horton Greene McElwain, Henry Greene's daughter, recalled hearing it directly from her grandmother, and told her own version of this story to the author in a taped interview on 22 February 1998. Family members have recorded other similar versions.

13   Examples of Charles Greene's early artwork are at UCB. Examples of both of the Greenes' early sketches are at the GGL.

14   Hallie M. Greene to TSG, 3 August 1879 (collection of Virginia Dart Greene Hales).

15   I am grateful to Bruce Smith for generously sharing his Greene family genealogical file with me. I am also indebted to the local History Room staff of the Cabell County Public Library, Huntington, West Virginia, for their friendly and personal assistance.

16   Virginia Dart Greene Hales, interview with the author, 11 February 1998.

17   The family of Thomas Sumner Greene is shown as residing in Cabell County, West Virginia, in the federal census of 1880.

18   See "Pulte Medical College, Cincinnati. Annual Announcement, Session of 1881–82," Cincinnati Medical Heritage Center, University of Cincinnati Medical Center, Cincinnati, Ohio.

19   One of Dr. Greene's business cards from this period is at the GGL.

20   TSG to CSG and HMG, 3 March 1891: "Dr. Brandon … still wants to buy right to practice my treatment…." (GGL).

21   See Charles M. Dye, "Calvin Woodward and the Development of Polytechnic Education at Washington University," *Bulletin, Missouri Historical Society* 34, no. 1 (October 1977): 17–21.

22   Calvin Milton Woodward, *The Manual Training School* (Boston: D. C. Heath & Co., 1887), 2–4.

23   Charles Alpheus Bennett, *History of Manual and Industrial Education, 1870 to 1917* (Peoria, Ill.: The Manual Arts Press, 1937), 322. Woodward is quoted as saying, "To Russia belongs the honor of having solved the problem of tool instruction." I am grateful to Bruce Smith for providing a copy of this important published history.

24   The full motto was actually a brief poem by Woodward: "Hail to the skillful cunning hand! Hail to the cultured mind! Contending for the World's Command, Here let them be combined." See W. T. Bawden, "Some Leaders in Industrial Education: Calvin Milton Woodward," *Industrial Arts and Vocational Education Magazine* 36 (September 1947): 280.

25   *Manual Training School of Washington University*, prospectus dated 1884, Washington University Archives.

26   Ibid., 347 (from the school's establishing ordinance, 6 June 1879).

27   Woodward, *The Manual Training School*, 4.

28   A descriptive geometry assignment book from the class of 1886 is in the Washington University Archives, Manual Training School collection.

29   Washington University Archives. I am grateful to Carole Prietto for her kind assistance.

30   Calista Halsey, *Two of Us* (New York: G. W. Carlton & Co., 1879), 159–62. Betty Patchin Greene, daughter-in-law of Charles Greene and Halsey's granddaughter, brought this early feminist novel, about two young women seeking self-sufficiency in an artistic trade, to my attention. Calista Halsey went on to become the first female reporter for the *Washington Post*.

31   Charles Greene's grade report is housed at UCB (the registrar's office of Washington University was unresponsive to requests for additional grade information for the Greenes).

32   Henry Greene's tribute, dated 25 May 1910, was printed in "Alumni Echoes, a collection of testimonials of representative graduates from the St. Louis Manual Training School of Washington University, selected from several hundred received upon the occasion of the retirement from active service of its founder and director, Dr. Calvin M. Woodward, to whom these sentiments were presented, as inscribed upon original parchments, bound in a hand-tooled album, on June 10, 1910" (Washington University Archives).

33   CSG, miscellaneous writings, c. 1943 (UCB).

34   Charles C. Savage, *The Architecture of the Private Streets of St. Louis* (Columbia, Missouri: University of Missouri Press, 1987), 158–62. I am very grateful to Bruce Smith for leading me to this information.

35   See "Report of the Department of Architecture" submitted by William Ware in 1872, Massachussetts Institute of Technology Museum archives. See also Kimberly Alexander Shilland, "William R. Ware and the Origins of American Architectural Education," *Drawings at Work* (Boston: MIT Museum, 1992), the catalog of an eponymous exhibition at the MIT Museum, May–October 1992.

36   See Francis Ward Chandler file, MIT permanent Historical Exhibit, Faculty and Administrative Officers, MIT Museum archives. See also *Massachusetts Institute of Technology, Boston, Twenty-fourth Annual Catalogue of the Officers and Students with a Statement of the Courses of Instruction and a List of the Alumni, 1888–1889* (Cambridge, Mass.: University Press, 1888), 32–33.

37   See Francis Ward Chandler file, MIT Museum archives. I am grateful to Kimberly Alexander Shilland for sharing her insights on Chandler.

38   See Walter Muir Whitehill, *Boston: A Topographical History* (Cambridge, Mass.: Harvard University Press, 1959), and Anthony Mitchell Sammarco, *Boston's Back Bay* (Dover, New Hampshire: Arcadia Publishing, 1997), 7.

39   Margaret Henderson Floyd, *Architectural Education and Boston* (Boston: Boston Architectural Center, 1989), 12–19.

40   Margaret Henderson Floyd, *Henry Hobson Richardson: A Genius for Architecture* (New York: The Monacelli Press, 1997), 104.

41   TSG to CSG and HMG, 1 July 1890 (GGL): "I differ with you Charlie about the value of the Tech certificates. I think you will find that without them you will not be able to enter any of the Architectural Societies and in order to take proper work among first class architects you will have to join the associations."

42   Regarding being kept from the club, Charles Greene wrote "…one [student] black-balled me out of the architectural club because I criticized the old Rogers Building." He also mentioned how he had a "sinking feeling when walking up the dull red sandstone steps of the Rogers Building and numbly fumbled through a darkish hall." CSG, miscellaneous writings, c. 1943 (UCB).

43   I am grateful to the registrar's office at the Massachusetts Institute of Technology for providing photocopies of the original transcripts for Charles and Henry Greene.

44   In an interview with the author, 21 June 1990, Charles Greene's eldest son, Nathaniel Patrickson Greene, explained how his father had commanded the respect of his contractors and workmen by effectively demonstrating and explaining exactly how he wanted a job done.

45   Charles's MIT notebook giving details of Materials class notes is at UCB.

46   Unfinished examples of these drawings are at UCB.

47   See Edward S. Cooke, Jr., "Talking or Working: The Conundrum of Moral Aesthetics in Boston's Arts and Crafts Movement," in Marilee Boyd Meyer, *Inspiring Reform: Boston's Arts and Crafts Movement* (New York: Harry N. Abrams, 1997), 27.

48   CSG, miscellaneous writings, c. 1943 (UCB).

49   CSG, miscellaneous writings, c. 1943 (UCB).

50   Dumas Malone, ed., *Dictionary of American Biography*, vol. 19 (New York: Charles Scribner's Sons, 1936), 70–71.

51   TSG to CSG and HMG, 20 November 1890 (GGL): "Have you joined the Art class yet?"

52   CSG, miscellaneous writings, c. 1943 (UCB).

53   In the MIT class picture of 1891, Ernest Machado and Charles Greene are seated next to each other. In Charles Greene's MIT yearbook (UCB), Machado's name is checked off in pencil. Machado's interests and working history are outlined in an unpublished biographical sketch by Elizabeth Osborn, his grand-niece.

54 See Van Wyck Brooks, *Fenollosa and his Circle* (New York: E. P. Dutton, 1962).

55 CSG, miscellaneous writings, c. 1943 (UCB).

56 See *"A Pleasing Novelty": Bunkio Matsuki and the Japanese Craze in Victorian Salem* (Salem, Mass.: Peabody and Essex Museum, 1993).

57 Ibid., 62–64.

58 CSG to Miss Claire W. Ditchy, December 1951. Typescript in the collection of Robert Judson Clark (original at UCB).

59 TSG to CSG and HMG, 1 August 1892 (GGL): "Your letters Hal 16 and 22 July we found awaiting us here....We were awfully disappointed Charlie not to get a letter from you....Do write regularly." And, LMG to CSG and HMG, 22 January 1893 (GGL): "I suppose Charlie you do not intend to write again. It is a good thing for us that you have a brother who will let us hear from you."

60 TSG to CSG and HMG, 18 November 1891 (GGL).

61 LMG to CSG, 2 November 1890 (GGL).

62 Draft of a letter from CSG to Blanche Lawton dated 1891. From the context of the letter it is clear that it was written late in August, prior to classes beginning again in September (GGL).

63 Letter from Mary L. Jones to CSG, 17 May 1890. In it she says, "I enclose the business cards of two of my friends, Mr. Harker and Mr. Jaques, to whom I have spoken of you and your brother. They both will be glad to see and talk with you when you are ready to take places."

64 Mariana Griswold Van Rennselear, *The Architecture of Henry Hobson Richardson* (Boston, 1888), 27–32.

65 Floyd, *Henry Hobson Richardson*, 104. See also James F. O'Gorman, *Living Architecture: A Biography of H. H. Richardson* (New York: Simon & Schuster, 1997), 24, and "Class of '77, MIT, 1877–1910" (Boston: Puritan Press, 1910), 2–3.

66 Barbara Ann Francis, "The Boston Roots of Greene and Greene" (master's thesis, Tufts University, May 1987). In this detailed and insightful study, Ms. Francis establishes the Boston activities of the Greenes and analyzes many of the projects they encountered. I have relied on this thesis (on file at Tufts University, with a copy at the GGL), for much of my understanding of this phase of the Greenes' careers.

67 Construction began in 1890 and was still underway in 1891 after Charles had left the firm. I am indebted to Roger Reed of the Brookline Historical Commission for his generous assistance in taking me to visit Pine Manor College and for his help with additional information on the Cox commission.

68 While Barbara Ann Francis makes a strong case for the Greenes' exposure to the Paine house, it can only be conjectured. Certainly, if they had seen it, it would have been an epiphany for them, since so many of the details and materials that became dear to the Greenes later are represented in this remarkable house, one of Richardson's greatest.

69 TSG to CSG, 8 October 1890 (GGL): "I hope you will succeed in getting into Mr. Walker's office."

70 TSG to CSG, 5 November 1890 (GGL): "I am glad you have got into another office Charlie and hope you will find it more agreeable than the other." In a 1906 career summary that Charles provided to Charles Fletcher Lummis, then librarian for the Los Angeles Public Library, he lists his Boston office affiliations. He included R. Clipston Sturgis along with Andrews, Jaques and Rantoul, H. Langford Warren, and Winslow and Wetherell. Because of specific references in dated letters, the Sturgis appointment, by process of elimination, would have fallen into this time period, though no conclusive evidence survives.

71 TSG to HMG and CSG, 5 February 1891 (GGL): "I hope Charlie you will soon get into a place." Also TSG to CSG, 17 February 1891 (GGL): "So glad you have secured a place and do hope you will find it agreeable."

72 H. L. Warren to CSG (GGL).

73 Engraved notice is on file at UCB.

74 Floyd, *Henry Hobson Richardson*, 51.

75 (GGL).

76 *American Architect and Building News (AABN)*, 11 April 1891. The first mention of the commission, however, was made in an earlier item, *AABN,* 28 March 1891, xxiii.

77 Maureen Meister, "Patterson Smith's Winchester: Professor Langford Warren," *The Winchester* (Mass.) *Star*, 9 June 1994, p. 7A. I am grateful to Ms. Meister for her enthusiasm and kind assistance in Boston, and for her valuable insights into the life and work of H. Langford Warren.

78 *The Chronicle* (Brookline, Mass.), 1 July 1893.

79 Indeed, all of these elements can be found in Charles Greene's own house (1902–15) in Pasadena.

80 CSG to his parents, 24 November 1891 (GGL).

81 While Charles's own words on the subject are lost, his father's correspondence from the summer of 1893 indicates his son's contentment.

82 In October 1890, Dr. Greene wrote to CSG and HMG, "I think after the first of January the people you boys are with should pay you some money" (GGL). On 17 February 1891, he writes again, "I know you will both make yourselves so useful that you will soon be earning better remuneration." Sometime during this interval the Greenes began to draw a salary.

83 LMG to CSG and HMG, 11 November 1891 (GGL): "Hal, I think it so strange Mr. C. did not invite you to his wedding don't you? I don't like it because you work in his office."

84 Frederick Stickney file, Lowell Historic Board, Lowell, Massachusetts. See also Jeffrey A. Harris, "*Frederick W. Stickney*," in *A Biographical Dictionary of Architects in Maine* 7 (1995), published by Maine Citizens for Historic Preservation.

85 See Barbara Ann Francis, "The Boston Roots of Greene and Greene," an invaluable resource for an understanding of the Greenes' apprenticeships and influences on later work.

86 TSG to CSG and HMG, 6 May 1891 (GGL): "It is a good thing to get outside work as it is experience you will need. Will you have any such opportunities, Charlie?"

87 Benton's office records are in the archives of the Society for the Preservation of New England Antiquities, Boston (Gift of Christopher Monkhouse).

88 The present-day firm of Shepley, Bullfinch, Richardson & Abbott has kept the Shepley, Rutan and Coolidge archive in an excellent state of preservation in their Boston offices. I am obliged to Katherine Meyer and Robert Roche for their cooperation and interest in allowing me to review the relevant files and ledger books. See especially Drawing Book no. 5, dated 1884–94, pp. 84–85, 90–91, and 116–17.

89 Dated invoices for the Chinese tiles at Olana are in the Olana Archives, Hudson, New York.

90 Numerous references to his investments and dwindling practice are found in the letters to "the boys" between 1890 and 1893 (GGL).

91 TSG to CSG and HMG, 2 June 1892 (GGL), in which he discusses purchasing "round-trip tickets" to California. See also LMG to CSG and HMG, 19 June 1892 (GGL): "...we have not told anyone we are not coming back."

92 TSG to CSG and HMG, 4 October 1892 (GGL). The regional economy was only beginning to emerge from the bust cycle of a previous building boom.

93 LMG to CSG and HMG, 18 June 1893 (GGL): "I wish ... Charlie [you would] get more pay and a better position....I am beginning to think you will never work into an office as partner. I hope you will make a good thing out of Mr. Avery's house."

94 TSG to CSG and HMG, 7 July 1893 (GGL). While Dr. Greene does not specifically mention the World's Columbian Exposition, it is unlikely that he means for them to stop there for any other reason than to see it. The exposition was the greatest popular attraction in the United States, and in any case, the Chicago terminal was not far from the entrance to the exposition. See note 1, Chapter Two.

Chapter Two: "To Make Pleasurable Those Things" (pp. 22–39)

1 That the Greene brothers attended the exposition is strongly suggested in family correspondence, and confirmed in an interview between Henry Greene and Clay Lancaster in the early 1950s. According to Mr. Lancaster, Henry Greene mentioned that he and his brother had visited both the World's Columbian Exposition in 1893 and the San Francisco Mid-Winter Fair in 1894 (Clay Lancaster, interview with the author, 21 March 1998).

2 J. W. Buel, *The Magic City* (Philadelphia: The Historical Publishing Company, 1894), n.p.

3 LMG to CSG and HMG, 6 August 1893 (UCB).

4 *The Twilight Club of Pasadena*, a privately printed booklet marking the 75th anniversary of the club, pp. 5–6.

5 Francis Fenelon Rowland, M.D., "Cross-Country Riding," *The Californian* 1, no. 2 (January 1892): 1.

6 In mid-December of 1893, Charles and Henry Greene's MIT classmate Ernest Machado received a letter from Shepley, Rutan and Coolidge informing him that they were not sure they would have enough work to retain him and informing him to look elsewhere for employment. I am grateful to Elizabeth Machado Osborne for providing this information in her unpublished biographical sketch of Ernest Machado.

7 For the impact of the panic of 1893 on Pasadena, see Henry Markham Page, *Pasadena: Its Early Years* (Los Angeles: Lorin L. Morrison, 1964), 168–69.

8 The Massachusetts Institute of Technology was often referred to as the Boston School of Technology, or simply Boston Tech.

9 Hiram A. Reid, A.M., M.D., *History of Pasadena* (Pasadena, Calif.: Pasadena History Company, 1895), 226.

10 My thanks to Trevor Todd of the British Architectural Library for information on T. William Parkes.

11 My thanks to Kirk Meyers and the Pasadena Historical Museum for information on J. J. Blick.

12 Elaine D. Engst, *125 Years of Cornell's College of Architecture, Art, and Planning* (Ithaca, New York: Cornell University Library, 1996), 5. Ironically, Babcock was succeeded at Cornell by Alexander B. Trowbridge, a man Charles Greene's age who had worked with him at Winslow and Wetherell and who sought to transform Cornell's curriculum into a Beaux-Arts based program in the image of MIT.

13 Contract cost and project information is compiled from several sources, including gifts of Jean Murray Bangs and her estate to Avery, and the University of Texas at Austin, the GGL, and an unpublished, annotated bibliography of Greene and Greene compiled in 1993 by Margaret Meriwether (GGL).

14 The church was moved to South Pasadena in 1907 and is now called the Grace Brethren Church.

15 This important discovery is detailed by Barbara Ann Francis, "The Boston Roots of Greene and Greene."

16 Charles Greene's pencil sketches for these details are pasted into his scrapbook (GGL).

17 The unsuccessful bids included a residence for Dr. and Mrs. Adelbert Fenyes, who selected architects Dennis and Farwell to design a Moorish palace for them. The Greenes were also denied the contract to design alterations and additions to the Green Hotel.

18 *The Twilight Club of Pasadena*, 6.

19 Ibid., 23. Henry played the flute, Charles the violin. Henry was also a member of a vocal group, the Amphion Quartet.

20 An interim sketch in Charles Greene's hand traces the evolution toward the final design (Avery).

21 Notes in Charles Greene's handwriting entitled "Sunday March 6/98" (Avery). Travis L. Culwell points out that Charles had exhibited philosophical curiosity as early as 1893 in writing a poem that contained a Transcendentalist's view of Nature and man's place as a philosophical seeker within it. Culwell, "The Spirituality of Charles Sumner Greene" (master's thesis, University of California at Berkeley, 1995), 4–5.

22 Beverly Brandt, "The Essential Link: Boston Architects and the Society of Arts and Crafts," *Tiller* 2, no. 1 (September–October 1983): 10. See also Meyer, *Inspiring Reform: Boston's Arts and Crafts Movement*.

23 Edward S. Cooke, Jr.'s article "Talking or Working: The Conundrum of Moral Aesthetics in Boston's Arts and Crafts Movement" deftly surveys the important role of Charles Eliot Norton and his circle in the shaping of the American movement.

24 The *Pasadena Star* announced on 3 September 1897 that the Wotkyns house was "being erected." An image of the Wotkyns house was published in *American Architect and Building News* 64 (27 May 1899): 71, plate 1222.

25 The W. G. Low house was first published in 1939 by Henry-Russell Hitchcock, who included it in an exhibition catalogue published by the Rhode Island Museum Press. My thanks to Richard Guy Wilson for this information.

26   The Mills house would have been relatively easy for the Greenes to see, since it sits close to the street not far from where both brothers' employers had houses under construction during the Greenes' years in Boston.

27   See Richard Guy Wilson, "The Big Gable," *Architectural Review* 166, no. 1050 (August 1984): 52–57.

28   Originally located at 306 North Raymond Avenue, Pasadena, the Brockway house was later moved to 860 Arden Road, where it stands today.

29   See Virginia Dart Greene Hales, ed., *The Memoirs of Henry Dart Greene and Ruth Elizabeth Haight Greene* (La Jolla, Calif.: privately published, 1997).

30   The Whites lived at 989 East Colorado Street and the Greenes at 848 East Colorado Street, according to the city directory of 1893–94.

31   Jane Storey White, sister of Alice Gordon White, interview with Robert Judson Clark, 2 January 1960, Atascadero, California. Typescript of interview courtesy of Robert Judson Clark.

32   John Storey White and Daisy White, Violet's twin sister, died in childhood.

33   "Storeys of Old; Historical, Biographical and Genealogical Observations on the Storey and Story Families," *Cross Fleury's Journal* (March 1912): 8–9. The passenger list from the *S. S. Celtic* is courtesy of Bruce Smith. A memorial stone, placed by the White sisters in remembrance of their father, mother, and brother, still stands in the parish yard in front of Emmanuel Episcopal Church, Greenwood, Virginia, west of Charlottesville.

34   Thomas Gordon Greene, interview with the author, 21 January 1997.

35   Dr. Greene's obsession with money was demonstrated repeatedly in early correspondence with his sons in Boston, when letters regarding failed investments, straightened circumstances, and the need for Charles and Henry to work once they arrived in Pasadena, were routine. This tendency was perhaps held in higher regard by the Greenes when in later years Dr. Greene began to keep the books for his sons' architectural practice.

36   Jane Storey White interview 2 January 1960. I am greatly indebted to Robert Judson Clark for sharing his notes with me.

37   According to Probate Archives of the Los Angeles County Superior Court (case no. 1546), George Storey White left to his daughters more than $40,000, in addition to his house, when the probate was settled in 1897. By contrast, Charles and Henry each had inherited $250 from their paternal grandmother Mathilda Ray Sumner Greene, who stipulated an additional $1,000 to each of her sons and daughters after her death in 1898. An acrimonious probate battle between the surviving siblings ended in opposition to Dr. Greene's role as one of the two executors. (Probate Archives, Los Angeles County Superior Court, case no. 2602.) When the protracted case was finally closed, almost nothing remained to divide after court costs and attorneys fees.

38   Charles Greene's travel journal and memorabilia (UCB).

39   See Sara Holmes Boutelle, *Julia Morgan, Architect* (New York: Abbeville Press, 1988), 30.

40   See Linda Parry, ed., *William Morris* (London: Philip Wilson Publishers in association with The Victoria & Albert Museum, 1996), 140–41.

41   For an excellent analysis of Voysey's contribution to design, architecture, and craft at the turn of the twentieth century (and on Broadleys and Moorcrag), see Wendy Hitchmough, *C F A Voysey* (London: Phaidon Press, 1995).

42   Charles Greene's copy of the official catalog for the exhibition was signed by him and dated 3 July 1901. It is housed in the Rare Books Room of the Environmental Design Library, University of California at Berkeley.

43   Roger Billcliffe, *Mackintosh Furniture* (Newton Abbott, U.K.: Cameron & Hollis, Moffat in association with David and Charles Publishers, 1984), 76–77.

44   Perilla Kinchin and Juliet Kinchin, *Glasgow's Great Exhibitions: 1888, 1901, 1911, 1938, 1988* (Wendlebury, U.K.: White Cockade Publishing, 1995), 67–68. This book offers an excellent survey of the exhibition. I am indebted to Alan Crawford for bringing this book, and especially the Russian Village, to my attention.

45   While the former objective was accomplished, the latter notion was tragically shaken by the assassination of President McKinley in the exposition's Temple of Music in early September, a few weeks after the Greenes' visit.

46   Barry Sanders, *A Complex Fate* (New York: John Wiley & Sons, 1996), 28.

Chapter Three: A California House (pp. 40–71)

1   Virginia Dart Greene Hales, *The Memoirs of Henry Dart Greene and Ruth Elizabeth Haight Greene*, 13.

2   Lisa See, *On Gold Mountain: The One-Hundred-Year Odyssey of a Chinese-American Family* (New York: St. Martin's Press, 1995), 87.

3   The All Saints alteration drawings are at Avery.

4   H. Langford Warren, Charles Greene's former employer, was especially interested in reviving the American Colonial style as evidenced in the work done in his office during Greene's tenure there.

5   *Ladies Home Journal* 18, no. 2 (January 1901). The favor was returned. Cram was one of the Greenes' greatest admirers in later years. See Ralph Adams Cram (preface), *American Country Houses of Today* (New York: The Architectural Book Publishing Company, 1913).

6   "Hon. William C. Culbertson," in *Nelson's Biographical Dictionary and Historical Reference Book of Eire County*, 788–89. William Culbertson also owned timber land in North Carolina and Missouri, was a railroad director, and was elected to Congress in 1888.

7   The Culbertson son's death has sometimes been attributed to a brain tumor.

8   Invoices in the Greene and Greene Library show that Culbertson was a customer of John Bentz, the Pasadena dealer of Asian art goods and client of Greene and Greene.

9   *Official Catalogue of Exhibits, Department of Art, revised edition, Universal Exposition, St. Louis, 1904* (St. Louis, Missouri: Catalogue Company, 1904), 65. Charles Greene also submitted under his own name a proposed design for a "Dwelling for W. B. T. near Pasadena," probably referring to a new project for the firm's earlier client, William B. Tomkins.

10   Ibid.

11   The interior alterations involved bedroom fittings and furnishings, possibly for a servant's room, according to documentary evidence donated to the GGL by Mary and Howard Durham and Lois and John Cocanougher.

12   I am indebted to independent researcher John Ripley, whose meticulous database on bungalow building in Pasadena tracks this and other statistics using data from building permits and other documents.

13   The ink-on-linen presentation drawings show the bench well to the left of its later position as built.

14   Una Nixson Hopkins, "A Study for Home-Builders," *Good Housekeeping* 45 (March 1906): 259–64.

15   Edward S. Morse, *Japanese Homes and Their Surroundings* (New York: Harper & Brothers Franklin Square, 1895; orig. published 1886), 174, fig. 150. Charles's copy of this highly influential book is inscribed "Chas. Sumner Greene, Dec 1st/03" (GGL).

16   Invoice dated 1 December 1907 details Grassby's carving services (GGL, 1998 gift of Mary and Howard Durham in honor of James and Nora Culbertson).

17   Avery drawing.

18   Conceptual sketches with detailed instructions in Charles Greene's hand, dated 26 July 1910 (Avery).

19   Charles Greene's pencil drawings for the fixtures are dated 26 July 1910 (Avery, Greene and Greene drawings 00955 and 00956).

20   From a database compiled by independent researcher John Ripley on construction trends in Pasadena from 1903 to 1918.

21   "Among the Architects," *Builder and Contractor*, 5 February 1903, p. 1.

22   Charles Sumner Greene, "Bungalows," *Western Architect* 12 (July 1908): 3–5.

23   Identical pieces are illustrated in the April and May 1903 issues of *The Craftsman*. I am grateful to David Cathers for providing his expert opinion on this rare leaflet.

24   "American Domestic Architecture," *Academy Architecture and Architectural Review* 24, no. 2 (London: Academy Architecture, 1903): 51, 54, and 55.

25   Lucretia R. Garfield to CSG, 17 December 1903 (UCB).

26   Pasadena Historical Museum biographical files.

27   The oft-disputed setting for the fictional *Ramona* was based on the Rancho Camulos adobe, the former Del Valle family home, in Ventura County. See James A. Sandos, "Historic Preservation and Historical Facts: Helen Hunt Jackson, Rancho Camulos, and Ramona," *California History* 67 (1999), no. 3: 169–85.

28   Morse, *Japanese Homes and Their Surroundings*.

29   The first house for Josephine van Rossem, for example, had a contract value estimated at $3,800.

30   Orientations are as the house was originally located at 306 Cedar, Long Beach, California, before being moved first in 1917, and again in 1927 to its current site.

31   Morse, *Japanese Homes and their Surroundings*, fig. 275.

32   The Stickley pamphlet had appeared prior to the arrival of Harvey Ellis, who brought ornament to the firm's work by late May 1903.

33   Hanging lanterns had also been designed for the Darling house, but they were never executed.

34   Adelaide Tichenor to CSG (postmarked) 9 November 1904 (UCB).

35   The lot's size, more than subsequent budgetary concerns, most likely affected the Reeve project. The $6,500 contract value of the Sanborn house, with its more sprawling, angled plan, for example, was $900 less than the estimated value of the Reeve house contract. (Estimated contract values are recorded in the Jean Murray Bangs papers at Avery and at the University of Texas at Austin.)

36   See Daniel Gregory, "The Nature of Restraint: Wurster and His Circle," in *An Everyday Modernism: The Houses of William Wurster*, ed. Marc Treib (Berkeley, Calif.: University of California Press, 1995): 98–113.

37   Henry Greene's daughter, Isabelle Horton Greene McElwain, recalled that her father sometimes felt that it was not good, from a professional viewpoint, for the family not to be living in a house that he owned. (Isabelle Horton Greene McElwain, interview with the author, 22 January 1998 and 30 December 1998.) I am grateful to Maria Nichols Kelly and Ted Wells for arranging to videotape the January 1998 interview with Mr. and Mrs. McElwain.

38   Lucretia Garfield to CSG, 25 May 1903 (GGL).

39   CSG to Lucretia R. Garfield, 1 June 1903 (GGL).

40   CSG to Lucretia R. Garfield, 5 June 1903 (GGL).

41   CSG to Lucretia R. Garfield, 5 June 1903 (GGL).

42   Lucretia R. Garfield to CSG, 5 March 1904 (GGL).

43   Lucretia R. Garfield to CSG, 14 August 1903 (GGL).

44   Lucretia R. Garfield to CSG, 21 August 1903 (GGL).

45   CSG to Lucretia R. Garfield, 6 September 1903 (GGL).

46   As was frequently the case, it was the lady of the house whose name appeared on the drawings.

47   Randell L. Makinson, *Greene and Greene: Architecture as a Fine Art* (Salt Lake City, Utah: Peregrine Smith, 1977), 94.

48   "The Mother of Long Beach Left Legacy," *Long Beach Press-Telegram*, 28 March 1996, p. A4.

49   Correspondence between Mrs. Tichenor and Charles Greene indicates that he, not Henry, dealt primarily with the client in this case. The Tichenor/Greene letters are at UCB.

50   According to the sequence of the Greenes' own job numbers, the Tichenor commission followed the R. Henry C. Green job, for which the Greenes announced they were preparing plans in April 1904. The job that came after Mrs. Tichenor's was contracted out in June 1904, so the Tichenor commission came into the office sometime between April and June 1904.

51   The drawings are not dated, but his correspondence indicates none of the re-drawing that was needed for Mrs. Garfield's job.

52   Clay Lancaster, *The Japanese Influence in America* (New York: Walton Rawls, 1963; reprint, Abbeville Press, 1983), 141 (page citations are to the reprint edition).

53   Most of these clippings are from the *Cosmopolitain* 37 (Sept. 1904) (UCB).

54 Long Beach is situated on an atypical portion of the California coast that runs east-west, with the ocean to the south.
55 Randell L. Makinson, *Greene and Greene: The Passion and the Legacy* (Salt Lake City, Utah: Gibbs Smith Publishers, 1998), 70.
56 Lancaster, 109.
57 Randell Makinson, "Greene and Greene: The Adelaide Tichenor House," *The Tabby* 1, no. 3 (July-August 1997): 23–38.
58 (Avery).
59 Office addresses are confirmed by newspaper articles that detail the Greenes' move from office to office. See Meriwether, unpublished annotated bibliography of Greene and Greene (GGL).
60 Charles Sumner Greene, "Impressions of Some Bungalows and Gardens," *The Architect* 10, no. 6 (December 1915): 252. "The perfect bungalow should be designed to fit the needs of a particular owner. A house built to sell is like a slop-shop coat; it will cover most any man's back but a gentleman's, unless misfortune preclude a choice."
61 Copies of the specification of "A California House" are at Avery.

Chapter Four: Stones of the Arroyo (pp. 72–103)
1 *Pasadena Star*, 23 December 1904, p. 7.
2 Contractors and owners typically signed the ink-on-linen presentation drawings signaling an understanding of, and agreement to, the architects' plans.
3 *Pasadena Star*, 9 December 1904, p. 1.
4 The classicized portico and the Golden Rectangle proportions of the front elevation are more closely aligned with the known work of Henry Greene.
5 For background on the Hall brothers and their employees during the years they worked with the Greenes, see Edward S. Cooke, Jr., "Scandinavian Modern Furniture in the Arts and Crafts Period: The Collaboration of the Greenes and the Halls," in *American Furniture 1993,* ed. Luke Beckerdite (Hanover, N.H., and London: Chipstone Foundation, dist. by University Press of New England, 1993), 55–74.
6 I am grateful to descendents Gary Hall, Gregson Hall, and Robert Hall for their assistance.
7 In a long and impassioned letter (undated, c. fall 1913) to a later client, Charles Greene described his personal supervision of masonry work as essential to the artistic success of the job (Pratt client reference file, GGL).
8 Nathaniel Patrickson Greene, interview with the author, audiotape recording, Pasadena, Calif., 21 June 1990. Charles's son described his father as being highly revered by Peter Hall and his workers because he (Charles Greene) could do so many of the things he asked of them.
9 *Pasadena News*, 14 January 1905: 11. As it happened, the permit for the Oaklawn portals was taken out by A. C. Brandt, not Peter Hall. It may be, however, that both men worked on the project. Since Peter Hall had not yet been officially recognized as a contractor, he may have associated with Brandt in order to be qualified for the project, which had semi-official status with the city of South Pasadena.
10 *Los Angeles Builder and Contractor*, 9 March 1905.
11 *Pasadena News*, 7 March 1905, p. 7.
12 Though technically not in Park Place, the Edith Claypole house was located just a few doors south of the Halsted house until it was demolished in the 1960s for the construction of a freeway.
13 David M. Renton acted as general contractor.
14 Ralph Adams Cram, "A Country House of Moderate Cost," *Ladies Home Journal* 18, no. 2 (January 1902): 15. Charles Greene had clipped and placed the article in his scrapbook. In it, Cram wrote, "The living room, as should always be the case, is the largest room in the house...."
15 The Willett house, at $3,500, was small, but not considered cheap, since more than 85 percent of houses built in Pasadena in 1905 cost less than $3,000 according to John Ripley's database, entitled *Pasadena Houses of the Craftsman Era: 1904–1918* (unpublished, January 1995).
16 "The Easy-Housekeeping Bungalow," *Ladies Home Journal* 25 (November 1907): 50.
17 Rockwell Hereford, *A Whole Man and a Half Century* (Pacific Grove, Calif.: The Boxwood Press, 1985): 18–19.
18 Ibid, 42–43.
19 Ibid, 45. Wives' names were also frequently listed as sole owners of real property to expedite probate proceedings in the event that a husband died before his wife did.
20 New fireplace drawings, dated 11 February 1906, eliminated the original concept for what would have been the Greenes' first use of Grueby tiles, replacing it with pale yellow firebrick.
21 Dated furniture drawings for the Robinson house are at Avery.
22 Henry Mather Greene, "The Use of Orange Trees in Formal Gardens," *California Southland* 4 (April 1919): 8.
23 *Out West* 23, no. 1 (July 1905): 86.
24 Vroman addressed the Twilight Club with a lecture entitled "The Enchanted Mesa," a widely used description of Acoma, on 18 September 1897. Since Vroman was noted for his photographs, he probably illustrated his talk with lantern slides of Acoma's early Native American buildings (c. 1300) and seventeenth-century Spanish mission.
25 Charles Greene was interested enough in Indian baskets at about this time to correspond with the Fred Harvey Company in Albuquerque, New Mexico, to confirm the identity of a Shoshonian cooking basket (UCB).
26 The Robinson dining room has been meticulously re-created, with original furnishings, at the Greene and Greene Exhibition in the Virginia Steele Scott Gallery of the Huntington Library, Art Collections and Botanical Garden, San Marino, California.
27 See Cooke, "Scandinavian Modern Furniture in the Arts and Crafts Period: The Collaboration of the Greenes and the Halls," 60.
28 The written estimate for the glass in the chandelier is consistent with, and in the same handwriting as, Lange's estimates for other Greene and Greene work.
29 Makinson, *Greene and Greene: Architecture as a Fine Art*, 142.
30 Makinson, *Greene and Greene: The Passion and the Legacy*, 85.
31 The original bay was replaced in the 1920s by a larger, rounded, leaded-glass bay designed by Garett van Pelt.
32 Charles Greene had first expressed interest in artistic wood inlays at the St. Louis Exposition of 1904, where he had taken the business card of Armand Tuerk, manager of Charles Spindler Works of Arts, located in the Olbrich Pavilion. The card read "Inlaid Wood, Natural Colors—Not Painted." Greene wrote a letter of inquiry to Tuerk, and received a solicitous reply on 14 December 1904.
33 Charles Greene's travel diaries (UCB).
34 *Pasadena Star*, 29 March 1906, p. 14.
35 Makinson, *Greene and Greene: Architecture as a Fine Art*, 113.
36 A. V. Saph, "Cement and Concrete: A Discussion of a Reinforced Concrete Arch," *Architect and Engineer* 6 (August 1906): 51–55.
37 Makinson, *Greene and Greene: The Passion and the Legacy*, 82.
38 Mrs. Robert W. de Forest, *A Walloon Family in America: Lockwood de Forest and his Forebears 1500–1848* (Boston and New York: Houghton Mifflin Company, 1914), 309.
39 *New York Town and Country*, 17 December 1910. I am grateful to Michael John Burlingham for his assistance in providing genealogical information on the de Forests.
40 In 1906 alone there were eleven magazine articles illustrating the Greenes' work in national or international publications, including *House Beautiful, International Studio, Good Housekeeping,* and *Architectural Record*. While their Pasadena business flourished, there was apparently little call for their work outside the region.
41 Jennie A. Reeve to Charles S. Greene, 5 June 1906 (Courtesy Robert Judson Clark).
42 The Pasadena city directory for 1906–07 shows Mr. and Mrs. Robert Pitcairn, Jr., and Robert Pitcairn, Sr., living at 998 San Pasqual Street. By then, Robert Pitcairn, Sr. (1836–1909) had retired as vice-president of the Pennsylvania Railroad, but remained as director and stockholder of eleven Pittsburgh corporations (The John Pitcairn Archives, Bryn Athyn, Pennsylvania).
43 Though the building permit names the client as contractor, the characteristically precise milling of the doors and the distinctive detailing of the timbers and other fittings is too similar to Peter Hall's work in the Robinson, Gamble, Blacker, Thorsen, and Pratt houses to be coincidental. Hall apparently worked as a subcontractor in this particular case.
44 For an excellent overview of the differences and similarities between European and Japanese joinery, see Klaus Zwerger, *Wood and Wood Joints: Building Traditions of Europe and Japan* (Basel, Switzerland: Birkhauser, 1997).
45 The Irwin family history is described in an unpublished account written by Nanine Hilliard Greene (Nanine Hilliard Greene Collection, Department of Rare Books and Special Collections, Ekstrom Library, University of Louisville, Kentucky; book 17).
46 No documentary evidence has been found to suggest that the Greenes were involved in the design of the 1903 alterations, or in any other work on the property preceeding the major 1906 alterations and additions commissioned by Theodore Irwin.
47 Nanine Hilliard Greene Collection, book 17, pp. 99 and 205.
48 Earl C. Anthony (Los Angeles Packard dealer) to Theodore Irwin, Jr., 22 January 1928: "Do you remember you bought the first Packard we sold? It was 1906...." (Nanine Hilliard Greene Collection, book 17, p. 180).
49 *The Craftsman* published exterior images of the Irwin house as early as July 1907, in an article by Henrietta Keith, "The Trail of Japanese Influence in Our Modern Domestic Architecture" (vol. 12, pp. 446–51). Irwin's granddaughter, Nanine Hilliard Greene, speculates in her unpublished family history on how carefully her grandfather would have had to compose his interior photographs (Nanine Hilliard Greene Collection, book 17, p. 129). Happily, the Irwin house is furnished by today's owners much as it was in the Irwins' day.
50 The Greenes' 1906 drawings, showing the stair landing in place, were later marked with the word "out" in pencil to indicate its deletion.
51 They had specified, but not used, Grueby tiles for living-room fireplaces in earlier designs for the Robinson and Pitcairn houses, and Charles Greene had ordered two Grueby pots for Adelaide Tichenor in 1904.
52 Notes taken by Charles Greene dated 2 July 1907 (Avery, Greene and Greene Collection, document no. 00785).
53 See examples of these in Alph H. Secakuku, *Following the Sun and Moon: Hopi Kachina Tradition* (The Heard Museum, Phoenix, Arizona: Northland Publishing Company, 1995).
54 These windows are now on loan to the Greene and Greene Exhibition in the Virginia Steele Scott Gallery of The Huntington Library, San Marino, California.
55 Botanical analysis of inlays for the Thorsen house (1908–10), for example, indicates that Charles Greene's design is not based on a pattern book but rather on a species of periwinkle peculiar to Southern California.
56 Samuel B. Morris to Charles and Henry Greene, 30 March 1948. Charles Greene's drafted response included this confession: "The houses you mention kept me very busy, so busy that I did not have time to give to all the fellows [but] a few curtailed admonitions and a bit of encouragement with my blessings" (UCB).
57 Samuel B. Morris to Charles and Henry Greene, 30 March 1948 (UCB). Marston's son, Keith Palmer Marston, recalled in an informal interview with the author in 1993 how his father had worked for the Greenes, probably during the summer of 1906 while home from Cornell's architecture program. J. Cyril Bennett's son, Robert Bennett, also told the author in a 1993 interview that Marston had worked for Greene and Greene, and that his father had also worked for the Greenes before joining Marston's own firm in 1909. Except for Deland W. Harris and Leonard W. Collins, whose long employment with Greene and Greene is documented by Randell L. Makinson, most of the remaining names are specifically mentioned as office staff in the Morris letter cited above. Harris became a San Diego architect and was listed in *Who's Who in the Pacific Southwest* (1913). Others are listed in Pasadena directories.

58 It is also worth noting that David M. Renton, who was a contractor for a few of the Greenes' houses (Halstead, de Forest, Serrurier), had learned enough from the experience that he became a designer/builder capable of fine work that emulated their style.
59 Mary L. Ranney owned the house she designed at 440 Arroyo Terrace until 1913, though it was advertised as early as October, 1907 as rented furnished. See "Bachelor Maid House is Now Completed," *Pasadena News*, 12 October 1907.

Chapter Five: The Tree of Life (pp. 104–137)
1 Miscellaneous writings by CSG (UCB).
2 "City Loses Modest Unselfish Friend in Robert Blacker," *Pasadena Star News*, 18 September 1931. See also "Robert R. Blacker, An Unostentatious Man," *Pasadena Star News*, 12 December 1916.
3 Ann Scheid, "The Oak Knoll Neighborhood," in *Oak Knoll 1910* (Pasadena, Calif.: The Gamble House, published privately, 1995).
4 Herbert Croly, "Some Houses by Myron Hunt and Elmer Grey," *Architectural Record* 20 (October 1906): 281–95.
5 Makinson notes an oral tradition that Mr. Blacker was dissatisfied with Hunt and Grey's response to questions about the earthquake readiness of their design, following the disastrous April 1906 earthquake and fire in San Francisco.
6 The lotus motif in the Blacker house is often mistaken for a waterlily.
7 I am grateful to Mrs. Stephen Mengos, granddaughter of Blacker construction supervisor William Issac Ott, for allowing me to examine her grandfather's weekly time book for the Blacker project (copy on file at the GGL).
8 The Robinson and Bolton pieces were in production well before the Blacker pieces, as evidenced by the dated furniture drawings issued by the Greenes' office. Even so, there was a delay in building the Blacker furniture, which seems to have been made simultaneously with, or even following, the Gamble furniture. In a letter from Peter Hall, dated 9 August 1909 and addressed to Charles Greene at a rented townhouse in London, Hall writes: "The Gamble House is ready to be accepted and the furniture about completed. It will be all ready for Mr. Gamble when he arrives. The Blacker furniture is well under way and is working out beautifully. It will all be ready when he [Mr. Blacker] arrives except for the inlaying and finishing which cannot be done until the inlaying is done."
9 A birdbath was designed in 1928 by Charles Greene and added to the garden just outside the Blackers' entry hall. It was made in San Francisco by marble carver Jacob Schoenfeld and shipped by rail to Pasadena, where installation was overseen by Henry Greene.
10 The *New York Times* writer Joseph Giovannini suggested this intriguing idea in an article in the 1 October 1998 issue of the *Times*, published to coincide with the opening of the newly restored house for a temporary public tour.
11 Morse, *Japanese Homes and Their Surroundings*, 137, fig. 118.
12 The final drawings, originally dated 21 September 1906, were marked "revised" and redated 26 June 1907 (Avery).
13 Subsequent owners have significantly altered the house, removing the upper level of the original entry hall and den, clipping the rafters, and replacing the malthoid roof with Mission tiles.
14 The photographs in question are from the September 1904 issue of *Cosmopolitain*, p. 548 (UCB).
15 I am especially grateful to John Selmer and Barbara Goldeen for their assistance in providing me with background on Native American design traditions. The Greenes may have seen a copy of George Wharton James, *The Indians of the Painted Desert Region* (Boston: Little, Brown and Company, 1905), which depicts Hopi ceremonial headresses.
16 A note in Charles Greene's handwriting describes a $335 estimate for gold leaf to be applied in the Ford living room and dining room (UCB).
17 "Ford House to be Finished," *Pasadena News*, 14 March 1908, p. 1.
18 "Architects Are on Plans for Mr. Gamble," *Pasadena Star*, 14 June 1907, p. 2.
19 A separate commission for additional living-room furniture (a desk, a chair, and a lamp) came to the Greenes as late as 1914.
20 See D. B. Gamble client-reference file, UCB.
21 Charles Greene did have ample opportunity to see Mackintosh's work in published journals, however.
22 D. B. Gamble client-reference file, UCB.
23 Leuders was a Pasadena coppersmith about whom little is known. For an illustration of a similar piece, see Kenneth R. Trapp, ed., *The Arts and Crafts Movement in California: Living the Good Life* (New York: Abbeville Press, 1993), 37–38.
24 According to Mrs. Gamble's wish, these rugs were to be "more green than brown." The original watercolors were faithful to her request, showing intense greens throughout. The actual rugs themselves have doubtless faded over time, but may never have shown the intensity of the watercolors. Correspondence at UCB shows that the rugs were custom-manufactured in Maffersdorf, Bohemia (now Vratislavice, Czech Republic) by Ignatz Ginzkey of Haas & Ginzkey. For more on Haas and Ginzkey, see Sarah B. Sherrill, *Carpets and Rugs of Europe and America* (New York: Abbeville Press, 1993), 232.
25 The *ramma* tradition was clearly illustrated in Charles Greene's copy of Edward S. Morse's *Japanese Homes and Their Surroundings*. The Gamble panels may have been executed by Ernest Grassby, a sculptor and woodcarver who subcontracted to Peter Hall for some of the Greenes' work, including the James Culbertson additions in 1907.
26 Charles Greene's handwritten notations on lighting for the Gamble living room are at UCB.
27 The town of Nordhoff, now called Ojai, was originally named for Charles Nordhoff (1830–1901), who authored the widely read book of regional boosterism, *California for Health, Pleasure, and Residence* (1872).
28 Ron Chernow, *Titan: The Life of John D. Rockefeller, Sr.* (New York: Random House, 1998), 162–64.
29 Joseph F. Grady, *The Adirondacks' Fulton Chain-Big Moose Region: The Story of a Wilderness* (Old Forge, New York: North Country Books, 1933), 158–59. I am especially grateful to David S. Brown and Edward Comstock, Jr., of the Adirondack League Club for their assistance.
30 Edward Comstock, Jr., ed., *The Adirondack League Club: 1890–1990* (Old Forge, New York: The Adirondack League Club, 1990), 261.
31 *Bulletin of Vassar College, Alumnae Biographical Register Issue* (Poughkeepsie, New York: Vassar College, 1939), 44.
32 It will be recalled that the Blacker floor plan was designed not by Greene and Greene but by Myron Hunt and Elmer Grey, and the Gamble house design had been constrained by a Westmoreland Place covenant (GGL) that required all homes in the private enclave to face the street squarely.
33 Both early design schemes are at UCB.
34 I am grateful to Robert Judson Clark for allowing me to draw from the typed notes of his personal interview in 1960 with Thaddeus S. Timms, caretaker of Casa Barranca from 1920 to 1947.
35 *The Ojai* 20, no. 2 (4 February 1911): 2.
36 Tracings for the Pratt living-room furniture are dated 7 May 1912 (UCB).
37 The Greenes may have seen Mackintosh's ladderback chair for Windyhill in one of Hermann Muthesius's essays on the subject in *Dekorative Kunst* 9 (1902) (p. 203) and *Das Englische Haus*, vol. 3 (Berlin: 1904–05), pl. 254.
38 The original Pratt conceptual sketches remained among Charles's personal posessions throughout his life, suggesting that it had been his hand guiding the design of the house. Henry Greene told the Pratts' caretaker, Thaddeus S. Timms, that his brother "was the artist" and "actual designer" of the house, and the furniture's conceptual sketches are in Charles's hand. Construction of the house began immediately upon Charles's departure for England in the spring of 1909, and Thaddeus S. Timms further recalled that Henry Greene came to the house every four or five years for six weeks to oversee a meticulous maintenence program (Timms interview, courtesy Robert Judson Clark).
39 According to the Manistee Historical Society, Thorsen had a handsome Victorian residence in town that had been designed by the Chicago architect and engineer William Le Baron Jenney.
40 Frances Phillips, "The Story of a Bungalow," *Country Life in America* 4 (October 1903): 411–13. I am grateful to Robert Judson Clark for bringing this article to my attention, and to Tim and Karen Robertson, current owners of Thorwald, for additional information regarding their house.
41 Original plan documents have not been found, though a revised map from the late 1860s confirms Olmsted's involvement in the design (archives of Berkeley Architectural Heritage Association).
42 Edward R. Bosley, Robert Judson Clark, and Randell L. Makinson, eds., *Last of the Ultimate Bungalows: The William R. Thorsen House of Greene and Greene* (Pasadena, Calif.: The Gamble House, privately published, 1996), 30–31. Notes made prior to the design phase of the project are in Charles Greene's handwriting, as are preliminary conceptual sketches (UCB). The earliest extant dimensioned plan, entitled "Second scheme, Revised," dated 16 November 1908, appears to be in Henry Greene's hand (Collection of Robert Judson Clark).
43 The Thorsens lived in this house while their own was being built; from it they could literally oversee construction.
44 Mrs. J. W. Beswick-Purchas to Mr. and Mrs. William R. Thorsen, 17 December 1909, unpublished typescript courtesy of Robert Judson Clark, originally from the collection of Mr. and Mrs. Eric Thorsen.
45 Lange's pricing lists for the Thorsen project, as well as Charles Greene's preliminary watercolor schemes, are at UCB.
46 "Eye-comfort" was used in the Greenes' notes to describe a fixture that directed light upward so as not to bother the eyes. By itself, it would have shed far less light than the final design for multiple fixtures.
47 Since 1943, the Thorsen house has been home to the Alpha of California chapter of the Sigma Phi Society, a college fraternity. Through their efforts, the house has been maintained well in its near-original state. The furniture, however, was removed at the time of sale, and is now in the collection of The Gamble House, USC, and is on exhibit at the Huntington Library's Virginia Steele Scott Gallery, San Marino, California.

Chapter Six: The Elusive Client (pp. 138–173)
1 Ashbee Papers, Modern Archive Centre, King's College Library, Cambridge University (doc. no. 108a).
2 For more on Ashbee, see Alan Crawford, *C. R. Ashbee: Architect, Designer, Social Reformer* (New York: Yale University Press, 1985).
3 Ashbee Papers, p. 6.
4 Charles J. Morse to CSG, 13 January 1909 (UCB). Kevin Nute, in his excellent text on the Japanese influence on Frank Lloyd Wright, suggests that Charles Morse may have been related to Edward S. Morse of Salem, Mass., the author of *Japanese Homes and Their Surroundings*.
5 "Pasadena, Jan." journal entry, Ashbee Papers (doc. nos. 72–74). Permission to quote from Ashbee's journal, given by his daughter, Felicity Ashbee, is gratefully acknowledged. Ashbee's mention of Charles Greene was first published by Dr. Robert W. Winter in "American Sheaves from C. R. A. and Janet Ashbee," *Journal of the Society of Architectural Historians* 30 (December 1971): 317–22. Winter used Ashbee's "memoirs" (typescript edited from the manuscript journal) at the Victoria & Albert Museum in London. The careful reader will note that the manuscript journal entries vary slightly, but in significant ways, from the typescript memoirs. For example, "fetched us *again*..." (emphasis mine) suggests at least one other excursion Ashbee made in Charles Greene's car, an incident heretofore unremarked upon due to the omission of the word "again" from the typescript.
6 Assuming Ashbee was right about the materials he saw, these were the only walnut and lignum vitae pieces designed by the Greenes during this period. A letter from Peter Hall to CSG, dated 9 August 1909, states that the Gamble furniture was "about completed." The approximately fifty pieces of furniture for the Gambles could easily have been underway since before January of that year.
7 It has been conjectured that Charles Greene had, or was close to having, a physical breakdown that precipitated his sudden departure for England. There is, however, scant evidence to support this. The decampment of a family of seven for six months or more, though admittedly with a nanny, is not likely to have been the result of hasty planning. Nor does lengthy train travel, followed by a week's crossing of the Atlantic with one's young children, seem a particularly soothing plan of recovery from

physical collapse. While it seems plausible that Charles was mentally and physically weary from the volume of work, as he claimed in later writings, there is nothing to suggest something more acute.

8 The original lease document is at the GGL.

9 *Builder* 96 (Jan.–June 1909): 698. I am grateful to Alan Crawford for helping me to know more about current events in the world of art and architecture in London during Charles Greene's visits.

10 Alice Greene to Jane White, July 1909 (GGL).

11 Peter Hall to CSG, 9 August 1909 (UCB).

12 Charles Greene's travel diary for 1909 (UCB).

13 According to a database compiled by John Ripley of houses built in Pasadena between 1903 and 1918, Will A. Taylor had built only six houses in Pasadena prior to the Spinks house, all for other designers, and all were of a lesser value than the work he did for the Greenes.

14 Peter Hall to CSG, 9 August 1909 (UCB).

15 I am grateful to Ruth Ann Penka of the Fitchburg Historical Society for background information on the Crockers. Sale of the Crow house to E. S. Crocker was announced in the *Pasadena Star* on 12 January 1911, p. 1.

16 I am again grateful to John Ripley for access to his detailed and carefully compiled database of Pasadena building from 1903 to 1918.

17 *Pasadena Star,* 27 May 1909, p. 1.

18 Anne Bloomfield, "The Evolution of a Landscape: Charles Sumner Greene's Design for Green Gables," *Journal of the Society of Architectural Historians* 47, no. 3 (September 1988): 233. This excellent study carefully traces the complete Fleishhacker commission from 1911 to 1931.

19 Mrs. Mortimer Fleishhacker, Sr., interview with Robert Judson Clark, San Francisco, 1960. I am grateful to Professor Clark for making available to me typed notes from his interviews with the Fleishhacker family.

20 Mortimer Fleishhacker, Jr., interview with Robert Judson Clark at Green Gables, 13 March 1960.

21 Ibid.

22 Mrs. Mortimer Fleishhacker, Sr., interview 1960.

23 Ibid.

24 Ibid.

25 Ibid.

26 Bloomfield, "The Evolution of a Landscape," p. 237.

27 H. T. Lindeberg, "Some Observations on Domestic Architecture," *Architect and Engineer* 33 (June 1913): 59.

28 Mortimer Fleishhacker, Sr., to Charles Greene, 27 December 1914 (UCB): "We are contemplating making some alterations to our home here on Pacific Avenue and want you to advise us how to do the work, and prepare plans as soon as possible … the work to begin in the early spring."

29 Charles Sumner Greene, "Impressions of Some Bungalows and Gardens," *The Architect* 10, no. 6 (December 1915): 278.

30 Mr. and Mrs. Mortimer Fleishhacker, Jr., interview with Robert Judson Clark.

31 "Coming School to Be Most Modern," *Pasadena Star,* 16 May 1911, p. 1.

32 Isabelle Greene McElwain (daughter of Henry Greene), Paso Robles, Calif., to the author, 17 November 1998.

33 CSG to Bella Fleishhacker, Jolon, Calif., 22 August [1915] (UCB): "…the house I designed … for Mr. Nathan Bentz.…" The year of the letter is known because in it CSG responds directly to Mrs. Fleishhacker's letter of 1 August 1915 (UCB).

34 "World Lost Great Oriental Art Dealer in Nathan Bentz," *Santa Barbara News Press,* 15 February 1942.

35 Awnings had to be added to shield the interiors from the intense southern light flooding through large windows.

36 This is according to Charles Greene, who admitted to the subsequent owner, "Speaking of estimates, it seems to me that you do not know, or you have forgotten that your house and all in it were completed without an estimate and exceeded all expectations." CSG to Elisabeth Prentiss, 15 February 1928 (UCB).

37 "Culbertson Residence, Pasadena, Cal.," *The Pacific Coast Architect* 7, no. 1 (March 1914): 10.

38 Documents confirming the source of the Culbertson rugs are at the GGL.

39 "Culbertson Residence, Pasadena, Cal.," p. 10.

40 HMG to CSG in New York, 18 October 1912 (UCB): "The Culbertson work is progressing slowly. By the time you return the floors will be laid and have first coats on.…Did you feel you accomplished a good deal east with the Culbertsons?"

41 On the back of F. N. Dowling's order confirmation letter dated 28 October 1912 is Charles Greene's conceptual sketch in pencil for the Culbertson sisters' upholstered living-room armchair (UCB).

42 Invoices dated 6 and 7 November 1912 (UCB).

43 Ernest Batchelder's biographer, Dr. Robert W. Winter, estimates that the tile-maker's manufacturing began in Pasadena at about the time the Culbertson house was being built.

44 Documentation of the Greenes' visit to southern Italy in 1901 is in his diary notebooks at UCB. A photo of Aldobrandini, with Charles Greene's handwritten caption, is at the GGL.

45 Glenn Brown, ed., *European and Japanese Gardens* (Philadelphia: Henry T. Coats & Co., 1902).

46 This volume was given with Charles's personal effects to the University of California at Berkeley in 1959, and was subsequently placed in circulation in the university's Environmental Design Library.

47 Payments for the panels are recorded in CSG's cash account book on 14 April 1919 (on account) and 14 February 1920 (final payment).

48 Elisabeth S. Prentiss to CSG, 9 February 1928 (UCB).

49 I am grateful to Alfred Willis for bringing this newspaper article to my attention.

50 William S. W. Kew to Robert Judson Clark, 1 April 1961 (GGL).

51 William S. W. Kew to Robert Judson Clark, 19 April 1961 (GGL).

52 Charles's participation is confirmed in a letter from HMG to CSG in New York, dated 18 October 1912 (UCB). "Mr. Kew told me that he had a friend who wanted to build and he would have you see

her when you go down [to San Diego] again." Charles had no other business in San Diego but the Kew house at that time.

53 HMG to CSG, 18 October 1912 (UCB). Notes taken by Henry on his New York trip are in the Henry Mather Greene reference box, GGL.

54 The $15,000 approximate cost of the Ware house was not a small sum, but fell well short of the Kew house budget of $40,000.

55 MacColl, *The Shaping of a City* (Portland, Ore.: The Georgian Press Co., 1976), 358–64.

56 CSG to Charles M. Pratt, letter dated October 1913, C. M. Pratt client-reference file (GGL). The letters to Mr. Pratt, in Charles Greene's handwriting, are either drafts or, more likely, the holographic copies of his letters that he characteristically kept for his personal files.

57 One of the connoisseurs to whom he refers is C. R. Ashbee, who preferred the Greenes' work over that of Frank Lloyd Wright. See Robert W. Winter, "American Sheaves from C. R. A. and Janet Ashbee," *Journal of the Society of Architectural Historians* 30 (December 1971): 317–22. In his preface to the 1911 Wasmuth portfolio of Wright's work, Ashbee wrote: "I have been in houses along the Arroyo that appeal to me more than Frank Lloyd Wright.…"

58 CSG to Charles M. Pratt, undated copy of letter written late 1912 or early 1913 (GGL).

59 Nathaniel Patrickson Greene, interview with Robert Judson Clark, April 1959. Patrickson Greene recalled that his father wrote the manuscript in his Pasadena home in about 1914 (I am grateful for the use of the typescript notes of this interview in the collection of Robert Judson Clark).

60 Charles Greene, *Thais Thayer*, from an unpublished manuscript copy at the GGL, p. 48.

61 *Thais Thayer*, 46–47.

62 Preston Greene to Robert Judson Clark, 16 April 1960.

63 I am grateful to Ted Wells, restoration consultant for the John T. Greene house, for sharing this observation with me.

64 The current owners have lovingly restored this house in recent years, and Henry Greene's interest in landscaping would be particularly gratified by the Japanese-inspired garden recently created behind the house.

65 Aymar Embury II, *American Country Houses of Today* (New York: Architectural Book Publishing Company, 1917), 50–51.

66 CSG to TSG, Carmel, Calif., 7 March 1917 (UCB).

67 Charles Sumner Greene, "Impressions of Some Bungalows and Gardens," *The Architect* 10 (December 1916): 251–52, 278; and *Homes and Gardens I*, San Francisco, January 1916.

Chapter Seven: Guarding a Legacy (pp. 174–189)

1 "Pine Needles," *Carmel Pine Cone*, 20 September 1916. "Green [sic] family occupying Frye cottage at Carmelo and Thirteenth Avenues.…"

2 No drawings or other documentation exist for the Bliss project apart from the job book entry.

3 TSG to CSG, Pasadena, 3 January 1917 (UCB): "We are having a fuel famine here such as we had in 1907 while we were living in Los Angeles.…We have only enough briquets to last ten days. I grieve we will have to burn the barn. Everybody is tired of the cold weather which began in September." Also see TSG to CSG, Pasadena, 6 January 1917 (UCB): "…herewith a memorandum of business done by Greene and Greene last year (1916) showing expenses etc. and a small profit of about 20% on the amount done.…You will see from this that you each have to your credit $1688.58." Also, CSG to TSG, Carmel, 10 January 1917 (UCB): "I certainly hope that 1917 will make a better showing. It wouldn't take much to beat [1916]."

4 TSG to CSG, Pasadena, 6 January 1917 (UCB).

5 (UCB).

6 Drawings for the Kelly house and furniture are held at Avery.

7 "With the Architects," *Architect and Engineer* 64 (April 1922): 112. "Mr. Henry M. Greene … has assumed entire charge of the business which will be continued at the same address under his name alone."

8 *Southwest Builder and Contractor* (19 January 1923): 35.

9 Charles Sumner Greene, "Impressions of Some Bungalows and Gardens," *The Architect* 10 (December 1915): 251–52, 278. See also Makinson, *Greene and Greene: The Passion and the Legacy*, 178.

10 Permit records for the Morrison and Rhodes houses, showing Rhodes as owner of both properties by 1926, are in the permit archive, South Pasadena, Calif., City Hall.

11 "The Dugout," *Big "T" 1924* (Pasadena, Calif.: Associated Student Body of the California Institute of Technology, 1924), 77–78.

12 A letter from Henry Greene to Mr. Gould (Pasadena, Calif., 24 February 1925) sheds lights on why Henry Greene seemed often to be in financial straits. He writes: "I am very glad to know you and Mrs. Gould are pleased with the house.…I have made out my bill and enclose it in this letter. As long as it has over run in cost I have made my bill about on the basis of the proposed cost and not the actual cost and I hope you will both be entirely satisfied with it. I have waived the clause in our contract of additional fee on account of separate contract, although this increases my work." (This letter is in the personal collection of Virginia K. Gould, daughter-in-law of the original clients. I am indebted to Mrs. Gould for furnishing me with a copy of this document.)

13 I am again grateful to Virginia K. Gould for furnishing me with copies of the Daly house sketches.

14 Virginia Dart Greene Hales, ed., *The Memoirs of Henry Dart Greene and Ruth Elizabeth Haight Greene*, 23–24.

15 Ibid., 24.

16 Drawings at the GGL.

17 Correspondence at UCB.

18 In some previous publications this house has been incorrectly listed as demolished. It stands today in its original location at 225 North Cedar Drive (formerly Adams Park Drive) in Covina, California.

19 William Richardson (son of the original client), interview with the author, 13 November 1997, p. 22 of author's typescript. Richardson's grizzly was shot in Tujunga Canyon and is documented by the

University of California Museum of Zoology as the last of its species in the state. The skin and skull were given to the university.

20   John Richardson, great-grandson of Charles H. Richardson, kindly provided this information from the family archives.

21   William Richardson, interview with the author, 13 November 1997, p. 2 of author's typescript. Many of the details of the construction history of the house were furnished in this interview, and by John Richardson, grandson of the client. I am grateful to the family for their generous cooperation.

22   Frank F. Latta, *Handbook of Yokuts Indians* (Santa Cruz, Calif.: Bear State Books, 1977, reprint of 1949 ed.), 196.

23   Ibid., 3–4. On the subject of thriftiness, Henry Greene's granddaughter, landscape architect Isabelle Greene, recalls how her grandfather would rub his fingers on his nose and face to collect the natural oils to lubricate small mechanical parts, thus avoiding the need to buy a commercial oil. On Henry Greene's anti-modernist sentiment during this period, see HMG to Alice Greene, Pasadena, 12 November 1930 (UCB): "Most people have succombed [*sic*] to the 'machine' and are trying hard to think they like it when, in truth, they do not like it. But it surely dominates everything just now, willy-nilly."

24   Originally, the door was positioned a few feet to the right of its present location, and other alterations have been undertaken, but always with sensitivity to the original design.

25   Alan Marks, "Greene and Greene: A Study in Functional Design," *Fine Woodworking*, September 1978, 43–44.

26   HMG to CSG, Pasadena, 11 May 1930 (UCB).

27   HMG to CSG, Pasadena, 13 February 1931 (UCB).

28   HMG to CSG, Pasadena, 3 November 1931 (UCB).

29   HMG to CSG, Pasadena, 12 June 1933 (UCB).

30   Isabelle Greene, telephone interview with the author, 8 June 1999.

Chapter Eight: Seaside Bohemia (pp. 190–215)

1   Thomas Gordon Greene (son of CSG), interview with the author, Carmel, Calif., 12 July 1999.

2   Charles Sumner Greene, "Impressions of Some Bungalows and Gardens," *The Architect* 10, no. 6 (December 1915): 278.

3   Janette Howard Wallace, interview with Robert Judson Clark, 13 June 1988 (notes courtesy of Robert Judson Clark).

4   Thomas Gordon Greene interview, 12 July 1999. This impression is supported by the action Charles took at about this time to engage photographer Leroy Hulbert to document the firm's work.

5   Charles Sumner Greene, miscellaneous writings, c. 1943 (UCB).

6   Thomas Gordon Greene, interview with the author, 21 January 1997.

7   Mary B. Sands to Mrs. Charles S. Greene, Pasadena, 4 July 1916 (UCB): "Carmel is quite conducive to inspire one to do what is especially in his line. Mr. Greene will soon become acquainted with the writers and they will be a help to him in his work."

8   Thomas Gordon Greene interview, 21 January 1997. CSG quote regarding Lincoln Steffens is from *Carmel Pine Cone*, 16 February 1934. Famous figures in Carmel are detailed in various books, oral history accounts, and other resources in the Henry Meade Williams Local History Room of the Harrison Memorial Library, Park Branch, Carmel, Calif. I am grateful to Arlene Hess for her friendly assistance. An excellent source of Carmel cultural history is Franklin Walker, *The Seacoast of Bohemia* (San Francisco: The Book Club of California, 1966; 2nd ed. Salt Lake City, Utah: Peregrine Smith, 1973).

9   CSG to TSG, Carmel, Calif., 10 January 1917 (UCB). Charles wrote enthusiastically of visiting the home and studio of the respected watercolorist William C. Watts (1869–1961), who had arrived in 1915. Regarding W. C. Watts, see "Pioneer Artist W. C. Watts Dies in His Carmel Home," *Monterey Herald*, 15 May 1961.

10   CSG to TSG, Carmel, 13 February 1917 (UCB).

11   CSG to TSG, Carmel, 5 February 1917 (UCB).

12   CSG to TSG, Carmel, 16 February 1917 (UCB).

13   "Architecture as a Fine Art," unedited typescript (UCB).

14   CSG to TSG, Carmel, 17 April 1917 (UCB).

15   Ibid.

16   CSG to TSG, Carmel, 27 April 1917 (UCB).

17   CSG to TSG, Carmel, 9 November 1917 (UCB).

18   Charles Sumner Greene, miscellaneous writings, c. 1943 (UCB): "I broke my vow just once, for one house to grow out of a rock cliff over-hanging the Pacific Ocean…"

19   Ibid.

20   Charles later claimed bitterly, and possibly somewhat unfairly, that he had been rushed to finish during the five years that it took to build the James house, suggesting that he had not been given a chance to complete the work. "I am everything, without office boys, draftsmen and secretary, etc. with a very unruly client. My efforts have strenuous exacting [*sic*]… against incompetency and disarrangements [*sic*]… and the owner's prodding me to speed me to a finish before we were stopped." (Charles Sumner Greene, miscellaneous writings, c. 1943 [UCB]).

21   Charles Greene photographed the charming medieval manor house, known as the Old Post Office, and he may have been aware of its rehabilitation in 1895 by the Arts and Crafts architects Detmar Blow and Herbert North on behalf of William Morris's Society for the Protection of Ancient Buildings. See Michael Drury, "The Wandering Architects," in Alan Crawford and Colin Cunningham, eds., *William Morris and Architecture* (London: The Society of Architectural Historians of Great Britain, 1997), 88.

22   Information on building materials and other facts regarding construction are at UCB.

23   Robert Judson Clark first made this all-important connection between the James house and Tintagel in the 1960s and I am profoundly grateful to him for sharing his many research notes from that period.

24   Downing's invoice and shipping confirmation are at UCB.

25   I am grateful to Sherry C. Birk, Director of Collections at The Octagon, the Museum of the American Architectural Foundation, Washington, D.C., for providing this drawing.

26   Culwell, "The Spirituality of Charles Sumner Greene," 55.

27   See marble-carving invoices for the James house (UCB).

28   For further study of the James house see Charles Miller, "The James House: Charles Greene's Masterpiece in Stone," *Fine Homebuilding* 24 (December 1984–January 1985).

29   For an excellent analysis of Charles Greene's spiritual quest, and symbolism in the James house, see Culwell, "The Spirituality of Charles Sumner Greene."

30   Thomas Gordon Greene interview, 21 January 1997.

31   John Langley Howard (former client of Charles Greene and a family friend), interview with the author, 9 July 1997.

32   Howard interview, 9 July 1997.

33   Thomas Gordon Greene interview, 21 January 1997.

34   Editorial, "The Soldier Memorial," *Carmel Pine Cone*, 20 April 1922, p. 4. "It's about time something was done to complete the Carmel soldier memorial begun with such a hurrah last Armistice Day five months ago. The work in its present state is a disgrace and is the subject of frivolous and uncomplimentary remarks by residents and visitors…."

35   One published report says the fountain bowl was removed in the 1960s out of fear of vandalism. The entire memorial was demolished by a runaway vehicle on 6 August 1977, but was subsequently restored and rededicated a few months later on the eleventh hour of Armistice Day, the eleventh day of the eleventh month, 1977.

36   "With the Architects," *Architect and Engineer* 64 (April 1922): 112.

37   "Country Club Plans Progressing," *Carmel Pine Cone*, 6 October 1921, p. 1; "Country Club," *Carmel Pine Cone*, 16 March 1922.

38   Pencil sketch at UCB.

39   "Club Members Discussing Building Alterations," *Carmel Pine Cone*, 22 December 1921; "Little Theatre Assured…," *Carmel Pine Cone*, 19 January 1922, p. 1.

40   "Early City Records #2," Henry Meade Williams Local History Room of the Harrison Memorial Library, Park Branch, Carmel, Calif.

41   James Schevill, *Years of Becoming*, Contemporary Authors Autobiography Series 12 (Detroit, Mich.: Gale Publishing Company, 1989), 254.

42   Margaret Schevill, notes solicited by questionnaire submitted to Mrs. Schevill by Robert Judson Clark, Tucson, Arizona, 8 April 1960. I am grateful to Robert Judson Clark for sharing this information with me.

43   James Schevill (son of Rudolph and Margaret Schevill), interview with the author, 9 July 1997. "My mother, particularly, wanted a new living room. My mother liked parties … one purpose of the living room [was] to have parties where she could have dances…."

44   From James Schevill, *The Complete American Fantasies* (Athens, Ohio: Swallow Press/Ohio University Press, 1996), 48–49. Reproduced with kind permission from the author.

45   Park Abbott, interview with Robert Judson Clark, May 1959. I am grateful once again to Robert Judson Clark for generously sharing his interview notes with me.

46   Miss Blanche Tolmie (sister of Robert Tolmie), interview with Robert Judson Clark, Carmel, 27 July 1960.

47   Charles Greene's records show subsequent trips in April, May, and June 1923, and payments coming in installments from Mr. Tolmie in 1923 and 1924.

48   Mrs. Alfred W. Crapsey (purchased the studio from Blanche Tolmie), interview with Robert Judson Clark, Piedmont, 7 December 1959.

49   Ibid.

50   According to Blanche Tolmie, Charles said that he "loved Carmel, where there was no pressure from people with money." Interview with Robert Judson Clark, Carmel, 27 July 1960.

51   In the 1960s the studio was sensitively altered to communicate with a residential addition on the west, not visible from Lincoln Street.

52   Culwell, "The Spirituality of Charles Sumner Greene," 69.

53   Claude Bragdon, *The Beautiful Necessity*, 4th ed. (New York: Alfred A. Knopf, 1939), 57–59.

54   Claude Bragdon, *A Primer of Higher Space*, 2nd rev. ed. (New York: Alfred A. Knopf, 1938), plate 17.

55   Bragdon, *Primer*, plate 9.

56   Thomas Gordon Greene, interview 12 July 1999.

57   Charles Sumner Greene, "Symbolism," n.d. (GGL).

58   Correspondence and invoices at UCB.

59   Charles's copy of *A Course of Instruction in Wood–Carving According to the Japanese Method* (London: The Studio, n.d.) is at the GGL. His son, Nathaniel Patrickson Greene, showed some of his father's self-made tools to the author in 1990.

60   Original manuscript at UCB.

61   "Calendar," *The Carmelite*, 24 October 1928. See also "Orage Goes beyond Behaviorism," *The Carmelite*, 7 November 1928, p. 13.

62   Undated notes, UCB.

63   Carmel Architectural and Historic Survey, Comprehensive Research Form, 10 March 1994. In an undated printed piece promoting Murphy's work, an illustration of the Payne house is captioned "plans drawn and built by M. J. Murphy, Inc." I am grateful to Robert Judson Clark for sharing this information with me.

64   Bragdon, *The Beautiful Necessity*, 50–53.

65   CSG to Mr. C. H. White (White Brothers Lumber), 23 January 1926 (UCB).

66   HMG to CSG, 27 January 1928 (UCB).

67   Elisabeth F. Prentiss to CSG, 9 February 1928 (UCB).

68   Charles Greene cash book entry, 13 September 1926, for Mortimer Fleishhacker: "balustrade, Woodside: $180" (UCB). This amount would have been Charles Greene's design fee.

69 CSG to Mortimer Fleishhacker, 30 October 1928 (UCB).

70 Arthur Payne to Robert Judson Clark, 6 April 1960. Payne, a contractor who had worked for Charles Greene on the Fleishhacker project, specifically recalled the "collecting of jasper nodules at Coyote Point, San Mateo, to be used on the stairs and balustrade." See also CSG to Simons, 12 March 1928, regarding Napa stone (UCB).

71 In 1928, Charles gave private art lessons at five dollars per session. Mrs. J. A. Mackenzie invoice from Charles Greene, 17 June 1928 (UCB).

72 Though John Galen Howard was four years older than Charles Greene, the two architects had much in common, both having been students at MIT and apprentices in Boston. See Loren W. Partridge, *John Galen Howard and the Berkeley Campus: Beaux-Arts Architecture in the "Athens of the West,"* (Berkeley, Calif.: Berkeley Architectural Heritage Association, 1978).

73 John Langley Howard, interview with the author, San Francisco, 9 July 1997. I am grateful to the artist and his daughter, the late Ann Bernstein, for their willingness to be interviewed. I am also grateful to Alan Temko for introducing us.

74 Sean Flavin, interview with the author, Monterey, Calif., 23 January 1997. He recalled in particular that his father had talked of Charles Greene helping to construct the fireplace and chimney from stones gathered from the adjacent riverbed. The exact date of construction cannot be verified since no Monterey County building permits exist for this period.

75 While no permit records exist, correspondence with contractors and Charles's own copy of his invoice to Martin Flavin for the entrance gates and subsequent work (dated 27 July 1931) indicate that the first phase began in 1930, or possibly as early as 1929. Charles Greene would often postpone billing his clients for many months, or even years. See Martin Flavin client reference file, UCB.

76 Bragdon, *The Beautiful Necessity*, 54–55.

77 Travis Culwell's important discovery of the link between Charles Greene and Claude Bragdon's writings has contributed significantly to a better understanding of Charles Greene's Carmel years, and I am grateful to him for sharing his insights with me.

78 Bids for breakfast room dated April 1930; Martin Flavin to CSG, 21 July 1930, regarding dining-room fixtures and carving of balcony door; invoice from H. C. Steinmetz, Pacific Grove, 24 July 1930, for forging balcony railings, etc. (UCB).

79 Solon & Schemmel to CSG, 22 August 1929 (UCB).

80 Louise A. F. Kelley to CSG, 1 February 1930 (UCB).

81 Mrs. Frank J. Kelley "by Kenneth Adcock" to CSG, 9 May 1930 (UCB).

82 Charles pursuaded Mortimer Fleishhacker to order a duplicate of the Kelley fountain for their Woodside estate, possibly to reduce the cost of the initial casting to Mrs. Kelley.

83 Mary J. Moore to CSG, 11 April 1930 (UCB).

84 Mary J. Moore to CSG, 29 December 1930 (UCB).

85 CSG to Mary J. Moore, 2 January 1931 (UCB).

86 Mary J. Moore to CSG, n.d. (UCB).

87 Johns-Manville Co. to CSG, 14 November 1929 (UCB). "We are informed by Mr. Schoenfeld … that you are designing a new addition for Mr. Fleishhacker's residence.…"

88 The famous Oyster Bar Restaurant in Grand Central Terminal was not completed until 1913, the year after Charles's visit. For more on the R. Guastavino Company, see Janet Parks and Alan G. Neumann, *The Old World Builds the New* (New York: Avery Architectural and Fine Arts Library and the Miriam and Ira D. Wallach Art Gallery, Columbia University, 1996).

89 Culwell, "The Spirituality of Charles Sumner Greene," 84–99. Culwell presents an intriguing case for a deeper spiritual meaning behind Greene's design for Fleishhacker's Gothic Room.

90 CSG to HMG, Carmel, 1 December 1930 (UCB). In fact, Charles was readying the panels for the Flavin library at the same time.

91 H. M. Simons (Anglo-California Trust Company) to CSG, San Francisco, 13 April 1931 (UCB).

92 H. M. Simons to CSG, 17 April 1931 (UCB).

93 CSG to Mortimer Fleishhacker, 14 June 1931 (UCB).

94 Charles Sumner Greene, "Architecture and the Machine Age: A Response to Hugh Ferriss," *The Carmelite* 3, no. 37 (30 October 1930): 3.

95 Charles Greene had correspondence with Dwight Goddard from 1931 to 1935, according to evidence in CSG's papers (UCB).

96 CSG to Mr. and Mrs. Fleishhacker (CSG copy), 21 July 1934 (UCB).

97 Bella Fleishhacker to CSG, n.d. (UCB).

98 Walter Heil to CSG, 12 September 1934 (UCB).

99 Park Abbott reference file, UCB.

100 Jacob Schoenfeld to CSG, 3 July 1940 (UCB).

101 HMG to CSG, 13 September 1940 (UCB).

102 CSG to Jacob Schoenfeld, 14 June and 8 July 1941 (UCB).

103 For more on the importance of the natural elements to the Tintagel legends, see Paul Broadhurst, *Tintagel and the Arthurian Mythos* (Launceston, U.K.: Pendragon Press, 1995).

104 St. Nectan's Kieve is described and illustrated in Charles's 1909 guidebook for the North Cornwall and Devon region. Charles Greene papers, gift of N. Patrickson Greene, 1990 (GGL).

Conclusion (p. 216)

1 *Minute Book 1947–1951* (Los Angeles: Southern California Chapter of the American Institute of Architects) 8 December 1947, 2.

2 Jean Murray Bangs, "America Has Always Been a Great Place for the Prophet without Honor," *House Beautiful* 92 (May 1950): 138–39, 178–79.

3 "A Special Citation to Henry Mather Greene and Charles Sumner Greene," *Journal of the American Institute of Architects* 18, no. 1 (July 1952): 4–5.

4 Anne Bernstein (daughter of John Langley Howard), interview with the author, San Francisco, 9 July 1997.

Selected Bibliography

Andersen, Timothy J., Eudorah M. Moore, and Robert W. Winter. *California Design 1910*. Los Angeles: California Design Publications, 1974.

Bennett, Charles Alpheus. *History of Manual and Industrial Education, 1870 to 1917*. Peoria, Ill: The Manual Arts Press, 1937.

Bowman, Leslie Greene. *American Arts and Crafts: Virtue in Design*. Boston: Little, Brown and Company, 1990.

Current, William R, and Karen Current. *Greene & Greene: Architects in the Residential Style*. Fort Worth, Texas: Amon Carter Museum of Western Art, 1974.

Clark, Robert Judson, ed. *The Arts and Crafts Movement in America: 1876–1916*. Princeton, New Jersey: Princeton University Press, 1972.

Cooke, Edward S., Jr. "Scandinavian Modern Furniture in the Arts and Crafts Period: The Collaboration of the Greenes and the Halls." In *American Furniture* 1993, edited by Luke Beckerdite. Hanover, N.H., and London: Chipstone Foundation, dist. by University Press of New England, 1993.

Davey, Peter. *Arts and Crafts Architecture*. London: Phaidon Press Ltd., 1995.

Duschscherer, Paul, and Douglas Keister. *Inside the Bungalow: America's Arts and Crafts Interior*. New York: Penguin Studio, 1997.

Germany, Lisa. *Harwell Hamilton Harris*. Austin: University of Texas Press, 1991.

Hales, Virginia Dart Greene, ed. *The Memoirs of Henry Dart Greene and Ruth Elizabeth Haight Greene*. La Jolla, Calif.: Privately published by Virginia Dart Greene Hales, 1996.

Hitchmough, Wendy. *Arts and Crafts Gardens*. London: Pavilion Books Ltd., 1997.

Kaplan, Wendy. *"The Art that Is Life": The Arts and Crafts Movement in America, 1875–1920*. Boston: Little, Brown and Company, 1987.

Lancaster, Clay. *The Japanese Influence in America*. New York: Abbeville Press, 1983.

———. "Metaphysical Beliefs and Architectural Principles: A Study in Contrasts between Those of the West and Far East." *Journal of Aesthetics and Art Criticism* 14, no. 3 (March 1956).

Makinson, Randell L. *Greene and Greene: The Passion and the Legacy*. Salt Lake City, Utah: Gibbs Smith Publisher, 1998.

_____. *Greene and Greene: Furniture and Related Designs*. Salt Lake City, Utah, and Santa Barbara, Calif.: Peregrine Smith, Inc., 1979.

_____. *Greene and Greene: Architecture as a Fine Art*. Salt Lake City, Utah, and Santa Barbara, Calif.: Peregrine Smith, Inc., 1977.

_____. *A Guide to the Work of Greene and Greene*. Salt Lake City, Utah, and Santa Barbara, Calif.: Peregrine Smith, Inc., 1974.

Miller, Charles. "The James House: Charles Greene's Masterpiece in Stone." In *Craftsman-Style Houses*. Newton, Conn.: The Taunton Press, 1991: 52–58.

Morgan, Bret. *Shingle Styles: Innovation and Tradition in American Architecture, 1874 to 1982*. New York: Harry N. Abrams, Inc., 1999.

Nute, Kevin. *Frank Lloyd Wright and Japan: The Role of Traditional Japanese Art and Architecture in the Work of Frank Lloyd Wright*. New York: Van Nostrand Reinhold, 1993.

Smith, Bruce, and Yoshiko Yamamoto. *The Beautiful Necessity: Decorating with Arts and Crafts*. Salt Lake City, Utah: Gibbs Smith Publisher, 1996.

Smith, Bruce. *Greene & Greene Masterworks*. San Francisco: Chronicle Books, 1998.

Streatfield, David C. *California Gardens: Creating a New Eden*. New York: Abbeville Press, 1995.

Trapp, Kenneth R., ed. *The Arts and Crafts Movement in California: Living the Good Life*. New York: Abbeville Press, 1993.

Winter, Robert, ed. *Toward a Simpler Way of Life: The Arts and Crafts Architects of California*. Berkeley, Calif.: University of California Press, 1997.

Winter, Robert. *American Bungalow Style*. New York: Simon & Schuster, 1996.

12 October 1868

Charles Greene born, Cincinnati, Ohio.

23 January 1870

Henry Mather Greene born, Cincinnati, Ohio.

1874

Greene family moves from Cincinnati to St. Louis, Missouri.

1884

Charles Greene enrolls in Manual Training School of Washington University, St. Louis.

1885

Henry Greene enrolls in Manual Training School.

1887

Charles has one-year apprenticeship with architect Alfred F. Rosenheim in St. Louis.

1888

Charles and Henry Greene enroll in the "Partial Course" in Architecture, Massachusetts Institute of Technology, Boston.

28 March 1891

Charles and Henry attend baccalaureate service at Trinity Church, Boston, recognizing completion of Partial Course.

1890–93

Charles and Henry apprentice with several prominent Boston architects.

August 1893

Charles and Henry move to Pasadena, California, by way of Chicago, to join their parents, who had relocated from St. Louis the year before.

January 1894

The Greenes open their first architectural office in the Eldridge Block, Room 8, 62 East Colorado Street, corner of Raymond Avenue, Pasadena, California.

January 1897

Office relocates to the Greene-designed Kinney-Kendall Building, 63–65 East Colorado Street, corner of Raymond Avenue, Pasadena.

22 August 1899

Henry Mather Greene marries Emeline Augusta Dart in Rock Island, Illinois.

11 February 1901

Charles Sumner Greene marries Alice Gordon White in Pasadena. The newlyweds spend four months touring England, Scotland, and the European continent.

October 1901

Second Greene and Greene office opens in the Henne Building, Room 207, 122 West Third Street, Los Angeles. Henry relocates his family from Pasadena to Los Angeles that year.

January 1902

Los Angeles office relocated to the Potomac Building, Room 110, 217 South Broadway.

February 1903

Pasadena office closed. Charles Greene works out of his home in Pasadena.

Los Angeles office moved again, to the Grant Building, Room 722, 355 South Main Street.

July 1904

Charles Greene visits Louisiana Purchase Exposition in St. Louis, Missouri, on behalf of his client, Adelaide Tichenor.

March 1906

Los Angeles office moved to the Pacific Electric (Huntington) Building, Rooms 396–398, 608 South Main Street.

February 1907

Los Angeles office closes; firm consolidates in Pasadena in the Boston Building, Room 215, 35 North Raymond Avenue.

January 1909

Charles Robert Ashbee visits Charles Greene in Pasadena.

March 1909

Charles Greene and his family leave for six-month residence in London. Henry assumes design responsibility for the firm in his brother's absence.

1910–1916

Apart from the notable exceptions of the Fleishhacker, Cordelia Culbertson, and Kew commissions, the Greenes had little success persuading new clients to have the firm design and supervise construction of elaborate houses. Henry assumes design responsibility for most of the other built commissions of this period, and his father, Dr. Thomas Sumner Greene, performs bookkeeping duties for the firm. Charles focuses on completing existing furniture commissions and explores writing as a second career.

September 1916

Charles Greene and his family relocate from Pasadena to Carmel-by-the-Sea, California, three hundred miles to the north. The firm continues under the name Architects Greene and Greene, though Henry Greene unofficially assumes day-to-day office responsibilities.

1918–1922

Charles creates his great, late-career masterpiece, the D. L. James house, in the Carmel Highlands.

April 1922

The firm of Architects Greene and Greene ceases to exist legally. Charles continues to practice out of his studio in Carmel, while Henry maintains the Pasadena office as Henry M. Greene, Architect, in the Boston Building, Room 215, 35 North Raymond Avenue.

1929

Henry Greene designs his eloquent homage to building with nature in the W. L. Richardson adobe ranch house in Porterville, California.

June 1933

Severely hit by the depression, Henry closes his Pasadena office, thereafter working out of his home at 146 Bellefontaine Street, Pasadena.

1935

Henry's wife, Emeline Augusta Dart Greene, dies in Pasadena, aged 59.

1940

Following the death of his mother-in-law, Henry moves from her Bellefontaine Street house into his son's home at 1405 La Solana Drive, Altadena.

1944

Charles Greene ceases work on his last architectural commission, a library addition for D. L. James in the Carmel Highlands, following the death of his client. Construction of the library had begun in 1938 and is completed by Mrs. James in the 1950s.

9 March 1948

Southern California Chapter of the American Institute of Architects presents a Certificate of Merit to Charles and Henry Greene.

1951

Henry Greene designs his last house, a concrete block structure for his daughter's family in Granada Hills, California. Built entirely by the family, the house is completed in 1953.

26 June 1952

At the national convention of the American Institute of Architects held at the Waldorf-Astoria hotel, New York, the Greenes are awarded a special citation that describes them as "formulators of a new and native architecture," responsible for important contributions to the design of the American home.

2 October 1954

Henry Greene dies in a Pasadena rest home, aged 84.

11 June 1957

Charles Greene dies at his home in Carmel, aged 88.

Key to Abbreviations

AAF	Prints and Drawings Collection, The Octagon, Museum of the American Architectural Foundation, Washington, D.C.
Avery	Avery Architectural and Fine Arts Library, Columbia University, New York
BSG	Bettie Storey Greene
CPC	*Carmel Pine Cone*
dem.	Demolished
DPB	*Daily Pacific Builder*
GGL	Greene and Greene Library, San Marino, California
IHGM	Isabelle Horton Greene McElwain
JB	Job Book, typescript by Jean Murray Bangs, Harwell Hamilton Harris Collection, Blake Alexander Archives, University of Texas, Austin
JLH	John Langley Howard
LABC	*Los Angeles Builder and Contractor*
LAJ	*Los Angeles Journal*
n.r.	Not recorded
PN	*Pasadena News*
PPA	Pasadena Permit Archive, Hale Building, City of Pasadena
PS	*Pasadena Star*
RJC	Robert Judson Clark research files
RLM	Randell L. Makinson's *A Guide to the Work of Greene and Greene*, 1974
SF	Sean Flavin
SWBC	*Southwest Builder and Contractor*
SWCM	*Southwest Contractor and Manufacturer*
TGG	Thomas Gordon Greene
UCB	Environmental Design Archives (formerly Documents Collection), College of Environmental Design, University of California at Berkeley

Job List Methodology

Jobs, projects, and competitions undertaken by the Greenes are listed in order of job number or other reliable chronological evidence, usually newspaper accounts as noted. Gaps in the numbering sequence indicate that no information for that job number is extant. The large gap in the numbering sequence between jobs 63 and 90 (1902) is unexplained, but likely due to renumbering within the firm. Client names are as shown on drawings or other reliable sources. One spouse's name is often used, sometimes but not always indicating primary involvement with the architects. Addresses in parentheses indicate the originally anticipated location of an unbuilt project. Addresses of built projects are provided for research purposes only, as all of the houses except The Gamble House are private residences and are not accessible to the public. The most important sources for original job numbers include the drawing files at Avery Library, the Greene and Greene Library, and the Environmental Design Archives at the University of California at Berkeley. These were supplemented by significant additional data found in a partial typescript of the Greenes' original job book discovered by the author in the Harwell Hamilton Harris collection at the University of Texas, Austin, as well as a file-card record transcribed from the job book by Jean Murray Bangs at Avery Library. The dollar figures also come from these two sources. The late Megs Meriwether's 1993 detailed bibliography of the Greenes' work was also a valuable source for identifying jobs and projects, as was Randell Makinson's published job list of 1974 and its later addendum. Sources cited are not exclusive but in the author's judgment represent reliable sources that verify a job's date of inception or other important information. Any errors are attributed to the author.

Job Number
Client Names
Original Address of Job/Client
Estimated Value of Contract ($)
Selected Source Information

1894

1 Flynn, Mrs. Martha
96 North El Molino Avenue, Pasadena (demolished)
$2,460
21 September 1894: "work commenced on house" (PS).

2 Breiner, John
826 East Colorado Street, Pasadena (moved)
$1,307
21 September 1894: "preparing plans for house" (PS); house moved to 740 N. Mar Vista Avenue, Pasadena.

3 Pasadena Security Investment Co.
80 South Madison Avenue, Pasadena (dem.)
$2,350
30 October 1894: "contract for house" (LAJ); sold to Charlotte Gartzman same month (PS).

4 Pasadena Security Investment Co.
100 South El Molino, Pasadena (dem.)
$1,756
28 November 1894: "contract for house" (LABC); sold to Charles E. Getchell, Feb. 1895 (PS).

n.r. King, Mary P.
(North Raymond Avenue, Pasadena)
n.r.
Competition: 14 November 1894, "preparing plans for eight-room residence" (LABC); project not awarded to Greene and Greene.

1895

5 Covelle, Conrad A.
250 North Los Robles, Pasadena (moved)
$1,510
29 January 1895: "preparing plans" (PS); relocated to 920 Seco Street, Pasadena (1982).

n.r. Unidentified
(unspecified)
$25,000
Project: 13 March 1895, "preparing plans for large unidentified project" (LABC).

6 Eason, Willis M.
442 North Summit Avenue, Pasadena
$1,705
20 May 1895: plans completed for six-room cottage (PS).

n.r. Eason, Robert
448 North Summit Avenue, Pasadena
n.r.
Attributed to Greene and Greene.

7 Eldred, Mrs. Charles
881 North Raymond Avenue, Pasadena (dem.)
$2,539
8 July 1895: preparing plans for residence (PS).

9 Riggs, Dr. Thomas J.
49 South Madison, Pasadena (dem.)
$2,900
26 August 1895: preparing plans for residence (PS).

n.r. First Presbyterian Church
Colorado Street at Worcester (re-named Garfield) Avenue, Pasadena (moved/altered).
n.r.
3 August 1895: New Sunday School Rooms... (PS); moved to 920 Fremont Avenue, South Pasadena (1907).

10 Crump, Edward S.
716 Hull (re-named Union) Street, Pasadena (dem.)
$1,108
6 September 1895: preparing plans for cottage (PS).

1896

11 Unidentified
(Altadena, California)
n.r.
Project: 8 January 1896: preparing plans for twelve-room house (LABC).

n.r. Helmke, Jacob
(930 East Colorado Street, Pasadena)
n.r.
Competition (not awarded): 8 January 1896, preparing plans for two-story house and barn (LABC); moved to 1250 E. Washington St., Pasadena.

15 Allen, Robert S.
325 South Euclid Avenue, Pasadena (dem.)
$2,475
24 June 1896: work commenced on cottage (PS).

n.r. Kinney, Joseph N.
63-65 East Colorado Street (renamed Boulevard), Pasadena (altered)
$17,365
11 June 1896: Pasadena's Latest Building (PS).

16 Miller, Rollin H.
292 Bellefontaine Street, Pasadena (dem.)
$1,255
3 July 1896: plans prepared for house (PS).

17 Gartzman, Charlotte
54 North Madison Avenue, Pasadena (dem.)
$2,722
18 August 1896: plans prepared for two-story house (PS).

1897

18 Neumeister, Col. John G.
415 South Lake Avenue, Pasadena (dem.)
$2,692
5 February 1897: preparing plans for house (PS).

n.r. Fenyes, Dr. and Mrs. Adelbert
(251 South Orange Grove Avenue, Pasadena)
n.r.
Competition (not awarded): 10 February 1897, preparing plans for house (PS).

19 Hosmer, Edward B.
(229 South Orange Grove Avenue, Pasadena)
n.r.
Project: 7 April 1897: preparing plans for house (LABC).

20 Gordon, Theodore, P.
820 North Los Robles Avenue, Pasadena (dem.)
$3,992
7 April 1897: plans prepared for house (PS).

n.r. Green Hotel
(82 South Raymond Avenue at Green Street, Pasadena)
n.r.
Competition (not awarded): 27 April 1897, preparing plans for Hotel Green Annex addition (LABC).

21 Hull, Dr. George, S.
46 North Los Robles Avenue, Pasadena (dem.)
$2,374
11 May 1897; house announced (PS).

23 Longley, Howard and Etta
1005 Buena Vista Street, South Pasadena
$3,876
6 August 1897: preparing plans for house (LAJ).

n.r. Kendall, Bela O.
South Los Robles Avenue, Pasadena (dem.)
n.r.
6 September 1897: alteraltions to house (PS).

n.r. McLean, Elizabeth A.
450 North Raymond Avenue, Pasadena
$1,938
6 September 1897: work commenced for
two-story house (PN).

24 Hull, Dr. George S.
36 North Los Robles Avenue, Pasadena (dem.)
$1,045
2 November 1897: preparing plans for office
building (PS).

1898
n.r. Hull, Dr. George, S.
46 North Los Robles Avenue, Pasadena (dem.)
$1,200
Alterations to house to add porte cochere and
sunroom (Avery).

n.r. Roberts, Dr. W. Hume
29 North Euclid Avenue, Pasadena (dem.)
$968
16 February 1898: plans completed for office
building (PN).

27 Bennett, Mary A.
104 North Los Robles Avenue, Pasadena (dem.)
$2,695
22 March 1898: preparing plans for house (LAJ).

n.r. Pasadena School District
(SE Corner East Walnut Street and North
Marengo Avenue, Pasadena)
n.r.
Competition (not awarded): 28 May 1898,
Greene and Greene and others present plans for
additions [to Wilson Elementary School] (PN).

28 Fay, Winthrop B.
71 South Euclid Avenue, Pasadena (dem.)
$9,852
1 June 1898: plans prepared for house (LABC).

29 Tomkins, Wm. B.
400 South San Rafael Avenue, Pasadena (dem.)
$5,628
30 September 1898: contract for house (LAJ), to
include barn, wash house and keepers' cottage.

30 Swan, James
515 East Colorado Street, Pasadena
(moved/altered)
n.r.
1 December 1898: contract for mansion (PN);
first scheme, unbuilt.

31 Swan, James
515 East Colorado Street, Pasadena
(moved/altered)
$18,556
23 May 1899: contract signed for Torrington
Place; relocated (1925) to 2162 North Holliston
Avenue, Altadena.

32 Swan, James
515 East Colorado Street, Pasadena (dem.)
$2,912
Design for stable (Avery).

33 Hollister, Charles W.
310 Bellefontaine Street, Pasadena
$6,800
19 October 1898: plans prepared (LABC).

1899
n.r. Brockway, A. F
306 North Raymond Avenue, Pasadena (moved)
n.r.
21 June 1899: [Greene and Greene] consulting
architects (LABC); house moved to 860 Arden
Road, Pasadena.

34 Sanborn, Samuel P.
(695 East Colorado Street, Pasadena)
$6,800
Project: 27 July 1899, plans prepared for
two-story house (PS).

n.r. Coffin, George H.
(315 Bellefontaine Street, Pasadena)
n.r.
Project: 20 November 1899, preparing plans
for house (PS).

n.r. Pasadena Public Library
(SE corner Raymond Avenue and Walnut Street,
Pasadena)
n.r.
Project: 10 November 1899, plans submitted for
addition (PS).

1900
36 Smith, Mary M.
370 West Colorado Street, Pasadena (dem.)
$7,500
14 March 1900: contract for house (PS); also
addressed as 125 Terrace Drive.

38 Bolton, Dr. W. T.
101 North Los Robles Avenue, Pasadena (dem.)
$4,000
18 April 1900: contract for house (LABC).

39 Milnor, Mary R.
385 South Euclid Avenue, Pasadena (dem.)
$5,500
13 June 1900: contract for house (PN).

40 Ford, Tod
(Ocean Park, California)
$1,000
Project: 28 February 1901, preparing plans
for two bungalows (LABC).

41 Sickler, Mrs. Carrie C.
221 North Euclid Avenue, Pasadena (dem.)
$5,000
12 July 1900: contract for house (LABC).

n.r. Orth, Grant
(326 West Walnut Street, Pasadena)
n.r.
Project: 13 September 1900, plans prepared
for brick warehouse (LABC).

1901
n.r. Radebaugh, Dr. John M.
(33 North Euclid Avenue, Pasadena)
n.r.
Project: design for alterations to house (UCB).

45 Ker, James F.
165 North El Molino Avenue, Pasadena (dem.)
$6,500
7 March 1901: contract for house (PS).

46 Pasadena Ice Company
899 South Broadway Avenue (now Arroyo
Parkway), Pasadena (dem.)
n.r.
July 1901: contract for office, ice house, and
stable (Avery).

47 Bentz, John C.
49-55 South Raymond Avenue, Pasadena (dem.)
n.r.
9 July 1901: plans prepared for Bentz block (PS).

48 Brown, Mrs. Benjamin C.
120 North El Molino Avenue, Pasadena (dem.)
$4,500
9 July 1901: plans prepared for house (PS).

49 Swett, Miss H. Sybil
343 Waverly Drive, Pasadena (dem.)
$4,500
24 July 1901: contract for house (PS).

n.r. All Saints Episcopal Church
126 North Euclid Avenue, Pasadena (dem.)
n.r.
31 July 1901: plans for alteration to church
donated by H. M. Greene (PS).

n.r. Hansen, Anna J. (Mrs. L. P.)
1000 San Pasqual Street, Pasadena (dem.)
n.r.
10 October 1901: contract for house (LABC).

1902
51 Dowling, Frank M.
570 North Raymond Avenue, Pasadena
$2,906
31 January 1902: contract for house (PS).

n.r. Pasadena Ice Company
899 South Broadway Avenue (renamed Arroyo
Parkway), Pasadena
$9,400
13 March 1902: contract for business structure
(LABC).

n.r. Greene, Charles S.
368 Arroyo View Drive (renamed Arroyo
Terrace), Pasadena
$2,310
21 March 1902: construction begun on house
(PS).

52 Phillips, Mrs. Metilde
151 South Fair Oaks Avenue, Pasadena (dem.)
$4,462
27 March 1902: work commenced on house (PS).

n.r. First Presbyterian Church
NW corner East Colorado and Worcester
(renamed Garfield) Avenue, Pasadena (moved).
n.r.
2 April 1902: work commenced on renovation
(PS); church moved to 920 Fremont Street,
South Pasadena (May 1907).

n.r. Byington, C. S.
950 San Pasqual Street, Pasadena (dem.)
n.r.
3 April 1902: contract for stable and carriage
house (PS).

n.r. Pasadena Ice Company
786 Keller Street, Los Angeles, California (dem.)
n.r.
9 April 1902: contract for business structure
(LAJ).

55 Barker, George H.
505 South Grand Avenue, Pasadena (altered)
$23,108
22 April 1902: contract for mansion (PN).

n.r. Hunt, G. S.
(North Los Robles Avenue, Altadena, California)
n.r.
Project: 15 May 1902: preparing plans for house
(LABC).

n.r. Auten, P. L.
North El Molino Avenue, Pasadena (dem.)
n.r.
21 May 1902: plans prepared for house (PS).

56 Rasey, Mrs. Rose J.
158 North Euclid Avenue, Pasadena (dem.)
$9,860
7 July 1902: plans prepared for boardinghouse
(PN).

60 All Saints Episcopal Church
126 and 132 North Euclid Avenue,
Pasadena (dem.)
$4,586
24 July 1902: preparing plans for alteration [to
church] (LABC); design and construction of
rectory.

n.r. Talcott, William G.
150 South Orange Grove Avenue, Pasadena
(dem.)
n.r.
24 July 1902: contract for alterations to house
(PS).

n.r. Hollister, Charles W.
(Los Angeles, California)
n.r.
Project: 14 August 1902, plans prepared for
house (LABC).

n.r. Kendall, Bela O.
(213 South Los Robles Avenue, Pasadena)
$1,800
Project: 14 August 1902, preparing plans for
alterations (PS).

61 Bolton, Dr. W. T.
284 South Madison Avenue, Pasadena (dem.)
$3,600
30 October 1902: contract for house (LABC).

62 Poor, W. F.
(Pasadena Avenue, Highland Park, California)
$2,000
Project: 4 September 1902, plans prepared for a
house (LABC).

n.r. Bean, Jacob
(Alhambra, California)
n.r.
Painting specifications for addition to house;
unsigned contract dated 1902 (GGL).

63 Averell, A. J.
(unspecified)
$1,800
Date of contract: 25 July 1902 (Avery).

n.r. Springer, Issac
154 North Hudson Street, Pasadena (dem.)
$900
30 October 1902: preparing plans for alterations
(LABC).

90 Culbertson, James A.
234 North Grand Avenue, Pasadena (altered)
$8,265
Date of contract: 25 July 1902 (Avery).

91 Guyer, George G.
Mariposa at SE corner Santa Rosa Ave.,
Altadena, California
n.r.
11 December 1902: preparing plans for
alterations (LAJ).

n.r. Lutz, Harrison M.
(155 South Orange Grove Avenue, Pasadena)
n.r.
Project: 18 December 1902, preparing plans for
addition to house (LABC).

n.r. King, Mary P.
(unspecified)
n.r.
Project: design of house (Avery).

1903
92 Martin, F. J.
225 North Madison Avenue, Pasadena (dem.)
$10,000
13 February 1903: contract for apartment
building (PN).

93 Black, Emma M.
(210 South Madison Avenue, Pasadena)
n.r.
Project: first scheme for design of house (Avery).
See also job #102.

94 White, Mss. Martha, Violet, Jane
370 Arroyo View Drive (renamed Arroyo
Terrace), Pasadena
$4,500
13 February 1903: contract for house (PN).

96 Darling, Mrs. Mary Reeve
807 North College Avenue, Claremont,
California
$3,500
27 March 1903: plans prepared for house (PN).

97 Lund, Dr. George J.
1227 Maryland Avenue, Los Angeles, California
(dem.)
$4,200
22 June 1903: contract for house (LAJ).

99 Auten, P. L.
117 North Madison Avenue, Pasadena (dem.)
$13,000
7 March 1903: contract for house (PS).
and
99 Auten, P.L.
119 North Madison Avenue, Pasadena (dem.)
$2,000
10 October 1903: contract for auto stable (PS).

100 Van Rossem, Mrs. Josephine
400 Arroyo View Drive (renamed Arroyo
Terrace), Pasadena
$3,800
29 May 1903: contract for house (LABC).

102 Black, Emma M.
210 South Madison Avenue, Pasadena (moved)
$2,250
May 1903: second scheme (Avery); house moved
to 1070 North Marengo Avenue (1999).

103 All Saints Episcopal Church
126 North Euclid Avenue, Pasadena (dem.)
$1,995
21 March 1903: plans for remodeling (PS);
13 November 1903: alterations to chancel (PS).

107 Sanborn, Samuel P.
999 East Colorado Street, Pasadena
(moved/dem.)
$1,000
Stable (Avery).

108 Garfield, Lucretia R.
1001 Buena Vista, South Pasadena
$5,500
7 August 1903: plans prepared for house (PS).
First scheme; construction dealyed—
see job #129 (Avery).

109 Bandini, Arturo
1149 San Pasqual Street, Pasadena (dem.)
$2,800
19 November 1903: contract for house
['El Hogar'] (PN).

110 Sanborn, Samuel P.
999 East Colorado Street, Pasadena (moved)
$6,500
14 October 1903: contract for house (PS);
relocated to 65 N. Catalina Avenue, Pasadena
(1930).

111 Rowland, Dr. Francis Fenelon
55 South Marengo Avenue, Pasadena (moved)
$6,000
29 September 1903: newspaper description of Dr.
Rowland's New House (PS); alterations and
relocation in 1912 to 225 West State Street,
Pasadena.

112 Sanborn, Samuel P.
(unspecified)
$1,000
Project: Beach cottage (Avery).

113 Claypole, Edith, J.
50 North Grand Avenue, Pasadena (dem.)
$3,195
6 August 1903: contract for house (PS).

114 Reeve, Mrs. Jennie A.
306 Cedar Avenue, Long Beach, California
(moved)
$7,436
25 February 1904: contract for house (LABC);
relocated to 1004 Pine Avenue, Long Beach
(1917), and to present location at 4260 Country
Club Drive (originally Magnolia Avenue), Long
Beach (1927).

115 Darling, Mrs. Mary Reeve
807 North College Avenue, Claremont,
California
$500
Design for stable (Avery).

116 W.B.T. Esqr.
(Pasadena)
$7,500
Drawing exhibited at St. Louis Exposition
(1904) as sketch #2406: Projected Dwelling for
Mr. W. B. T., near Pasadena.

121 Kinney, Joseph N.
63–65 East Colorado Street, Pasadena (altered)
n.r.
Alterations to 3rd and 4th floors (Avery).

125 Culbertson, James A.
235 North Grand Avenue, Pasadena (altered)
$300
Contract to build wall; permit issued 30
December 1903 (PPA).

1904
126 Camp, Edgar W.
497 West Grandview Avenue (re-addressed 327
Sierra Woods Drive), Sierra Madre, California
$3,700
2 August 1904: plans prepared for house (LAJ).

127 Whitridge, Mrs. C. A.
146 Bellefontaine Street, Pasadena (dem.)
$6,500
11 February 1904: contract for house (PS).

129 Garfield, Lucretia R.
1001 Buena Vista Street, South Pasadena,
Calfironia
n.r.
14 April 1904: contract for house (LABC).

130 Reeve, Mrs. Jennie A.
1265 Loma Vista, Long Beach, Calfornia
$2,772
Speculative cottage (Avery).

n.r. Barker, George H.
505 South Grand Avenue, Pasadena (dem.)
$600
Pergola added to residence (1902); permit dated
2 Aug 1904 (PPA).

131 Hollister, Mrs. Cora C.
163 North Cahuenga, Hollywood, California
(dem.)
$5,200
24 November 1904: contract for house (LABC).

132 Green, R. Henry C.
1919 Robson Street, Vancouver, British
Columbia (dem.)
$8,500
21 April 1904: preparing plans for house (PS).

133 Tichenor, Mrs. Adelaide
First Place at Ocean Boulevard (re-addressed
852 Ocean Boulevard), Long Beach, California
(altered)
n.r.
9 March 1905: contract for house (LABC).

134 Van Rossem, Mrs. Josephine
210 North Grand Avenue, Pasadena
$5,100
16 June 1904: contract for house (PS).

n.r. A California House
(unspecified)
n.r.
Drawings and specifications, circa 1904 (Avery).

136 Abbott, Dr. George E.
161 North Los Robles Avenue, Pasadena (dem.)
$5,195
7 July 1904: contract for house (PS).

138 Palmer, Jane E. (Mrs. Thomas)
5036 Echo Street, Highland Park, Los Angeles,
California (dem.)
n.r.
25 August 1904: contract for addition to house
(LABC).

n.r. Heap, Josephine B.
356 West California Street, Pasadena
$2,500
3 August 1904: contract for alterations to house
(PS).

n.r. Bolton, Dr. W. T.
284 South Madison Avenue, Pasadena (dem.)
n.r.
September 1904: contract for alterations to
1902 house (Avery).

141 Merwin, Rev. A. Moss
267 West State Street, Pasadena
$7,195
9 December 1904: contract for house (PS);
drawings dated 23 July 1904 and 18 April
1905 (Avery).

143 White, Mrs. Kate A.
1036 Brent Avenue, South Pasadena
$3,727
1 August 1904: contract for house (LABC).

144 Willett, C. J.
(424 Arroyo View Drive [renamed Arroyo
Terrace], Pasadena)
n.r.
Project: design of residence (Avery).

148 Bowen, William A.
(443 East Calaveras Street, Altadena,
California)
n.r.
First scheme (Avery). See also job #150.

n.r. Sanborn, Samuel P.
999 East Colorado Street, Pasadena (moved)
n.r.
December 1904: drawings for alteration to
front door; porch (Avery); house moved to 65
N. Catalina, Pasadena.

1905
150 Bowen, William A.
443 East Calaveras Street, Altadena, California
n.r.
30 January 1905: contract for house (LAJ),
storehouse, chicken house, and corral.

151 Halsted, Mrs. Louise T.
90 North Grand Avenue, Pasadena
n.r.
4 February 1905: contract for house (LAJ).

152 South Pasadena Realty and Improvement Co.
Oaklawn Residential Park, South Pasadena,
California
n.r.
23 December 1904: contract for entrance gates
and fence (PS).

153 Ford, Mrs. E. A.
(San Pasqual Street near Lake Avenue,
Pasadena)
n.r.
Project: 4 February 1905, plans prepared for
house and auto barn (PN).

154 Libby, Dr. Arthur A.
665 South Orange Grove Avenue, Pasadena
(dem. 1968)
n.r.
8 June 1905: contract for house (LABC).

159 Willett, C. J.
424 Arroyo View Drive (renamed Arroyo
Terrace), Pasadena (altered)
n.r.
20 April 1905: contract for house (LABC).

161 Wheeler, Miss Lucy E.
2175 Cambridge Street, Los Angeles
n.r.
27 April 1905: contract for house (LABC).

160 Van Rossem, Mrs. Josephine
223 North Orange Grove, Pasadena (dem.)
$7,688
27 March 1906: contract for house (PN).

163 Serrurier, Iwan
805 East California Street, Pasadena (dem.)
n.r.
11 May 1905: contract for house (LABC).

n.r. Parker, J. F.
(572 East Colorado Street, Pasadena)
n.r.
Project: 8 June 1905, plans prepared for
alterations to house (LABC).

164 Brandt, A. C./I. Serrurier
1086 Mariposa Street, Altadena
n.r.
August 1905: design for speculative
residence (RLM).

n.r. Ford Sr., Tod
257 South Grand Avenue, Pasadena (dem.)
$2,000
Additions to house; permit dated 15 August
1905 (PPA).

169 Robinson, Mrs. L. A.
195 South Grand Avenue, Pasadena
n.r.
Design for residence and grounds; permit dated
25 August 1905 (PPA).

171 Bentz, Mrs. Louise
657 Prospect Square (re-named Boulevard),
Pasadena
$6,376
28 July 1906: contract for house (PN).

174 Serrurier, Iwan
(Pasadena)
n.r.
Project: design for residence (Avery).

n.r. White, T. Stewart
(Santa Barbara, California)
n.r.
Project: August 1905, design for residence
(Avery).

176 Porter, Mrs. L. G. and Miss Marion A.
1957 South Hobart Boulevard,
Los Angeles (dem.)
$7,314
28 September 1905: contract for house (LABC).

1906

178 Robinson, Mrs. L. A.
195 South Grand Avenue, Pasadena
$1,915
Design for auto barn (Avery).

180 Bolton, Dr. William T.
370 Elevado (now Del Mar Ave.), Pasadena (altered)
$17,868
19 July 1906: contract for house (LABC).

181 Merrill, Samuel, Jr.
(unspecified)
$4,723
Project: conceptual sketches for residence (Avery).

182 Culbertson, James A.
235 North Grand Avenue, Pasadena (altered)
$670
Addition to 1902 residence (Avery).

n.r. South Pasadena Realty and Improvement Co.
Oaklawn Residential Park, South Pasadena
$20,434
8 March 1906: contract for bridge [and waiting station] (LABC).

n.r. Pasadena Ice Company
980 South Broadway Avenue, Pasadena (dem.)
$3,410
1 March 1906: plans prepared for [office] building (PN).

183 de Forest, Miss Caroline S.
530 West California Street, Pasadena
$7,873
20 April 1906: contract for house (PS).

n.r. Hyde, Louis K.
(North Plainfield, New Jersey)
n.r.
Project: drawings dated 16 April 1906 (Avery).

185 Reeve, Mrs. Jennie A.
187 North Mountain Trail, Sierra Madre, California
$1,359
Design of cottage (Avery; UCB).

188 Phillips, John Bakewell
459 Bellefontaine Street, Pasadena
$10,694
2 June 1906: contract for house (PS).

190 Pitcairn, Robert Jr.
289 West State Street, Pasadena
$18,915
2 July 1906: contract for house (PN).

191 Bank competition
(unspecified)
n.r.
Project: conceptual sketches only (Avery).

192 Ford, Freeman A.
215 South Grand Avenue, Pasadena
$43,200
Initial design for residence dated 21 September 1906 and revised 26 June 1907. Second scheme (project on same job number) dated May 1907. Permit dated 7 July 1907 for construction of revised initial scheme (Avery; GGL).

n.r. Neil, Mrs. James W.
400 Arroyo Terrace, Pasadena
n.r.
Alterations to 1903 Josephine van Rossem house (Avery).

n.r. Hawks, F. W.
(408 Arroyo Terrace, Pasadena)
n.r.
Project: drawings dated 12 July 1906 (Avery).

193 Irwin, Jr., Theodore
240 North Grand Avenue, Pasadena
$28,181
August 1906: major alterations to Katherine Duncan house, completed January 1907 (Avery).

195 Cole, Mrs. Mary E.
(2 Westmoreland Place, Pasadena)
$26,480
15 September 1906: To build in Westmoreland (PN). First (unbuilt) scheme drawings dated 28 August 1906 (see also job #213; Avery).

197 Hawks, F. W.
408 Arroyo Terrace, Pasadena
$10,668
6 August 1906: contract for house (LABC).

n.r. Greene, Charles S.
368 Arroyo Terrace, Pasadena
n.r.
27 September 1906: addition to house (LABC).

198 Irwin, Jr., Theodore
240 North Grand Avenue, Pasadena
$2,604
Design for two-car garage (Avery).

199 Culbertson, James A.
235 North Grand Avenue, Pasadena
$1,603
Garage: drawings dated November and December 1906 (Avery).

1907

n.r. Stahlhuth, Fred
380 South Pasadena Avenue, Pasadena (moved)
$2,000
Attributed to Greene and Greene, designed for the Greenes' stonemason; permit dated 9 February 1907; (moved to 131 East Washington Boulevard, Pasadena).

203 Ranney, Miss Mary L.
440 Arroyo Terrace, Pasadena
$7,736
14 February 1907: contract for house (LABC).

204 Pasadena Hospital Association
(Fairmount Street, Pasadena)
n.r.
Project: design for proposed nurses' home (Avery).

205 Culbertson, James A.
235 North Grand Avenue, Pasadena (altered)
$6,778
Addition of service wing (removed); drawings dated 26 February 1907. Other alterations on same job number designed in May and December 1907 (Avery).

206 Leffingwell, Charles W.
Santa Gertrudes Avenue, Whittier, California (dem.)
$7,563
21 August 1907: Ranch house flag raising (PN); drawings (April 1907) by Mary L. Ranney in office of Greene & Greene, Architects (Avery).

207 Blacker, Robert Roe
1177 Hillcrest Avenue, Pasadena
$5,771
17 April 1907: work commenced on [keeper's cottage and garage] (PS).

209 Blacker, Robert Roe
1177 Hillcrest Avenue, Pasadena
$70,925
4 May 1907: plans completed for R. R. Blacker house (PN).

212 Spinks, Mrs. Margaret B. S. C.
1344 Hillcrest Avenue, Pasadena
$11,000
Discussions begun re. design of residence in 1907; drawings dated 31 March 1909; permit issued 23 April 1909 (Avery).

213 Cole, Mrs. Mary E.
2 Westmoreland Place, Pasadena
$26,480
11 May 1907: contract for house (PN); second scheme drawings dated 11 April 1907 (Avery).

215 Gamble, David Berry
4 Westmoreland Place, Pasadena
$81,105
14 June 1907: architects on plans for Mr. Gamble (PS); presentation drawings dated 19 February 1908 (Avery).

218 Bolton, Dr. William T.
370 Elevado Drive (renamed Del Mar Avenue), Pasadena
$3,710
Furniture (drawings dated March 1907) and alterations for Mrs. Belle Barlow Bush for W. T. Bolton house (Avery).

219 Ford, Freeman A.
215 South Grand Avenue, Pasadena
$2,144
Design for garage (Avery).

220 Irwin, Jr., Theodore
240 North Grand Avenue, Pasadena
$1,388
Addition of bath and closet (Avery).

222 Stimson, G. Lawrence
227 Oaklawn Avenue, South Pasadena
$2,823
30 April 1908 (PN): description of Greene and Greene interiors in house to be sold by G. L. Stimson to a Mr. Pryor (Avery).

n.r. Chapin, Lon F.
140 West California Street, Pasadena (dem.)
n.r.
June 1907: alterations and additions, bookcases, dining room (Avery).

n.r. Shelter for View Lovers
Monk Hill, Pasadena (dem.)
$300
19 November 1907: Charles Greene donates plans for casino at Monk Hill (PS).

n.r. Wadsworth, John
685 East Colorado Street, Pasadena
n.r.
Alterations to house (PPA).

1908

223 Ford, Jr., Tod
257 South Grand Avenue, Pasadena (dem.)
$11,209
13 December 1907: contract for alterations (PN); drawings dated January 1908 (Avery).

225 Culbertson, James A.
235 North Grand Avenue, Pasadena (altered)
$245
Alterations (Avery).

227 Gamble, David Berry
4 Westmoreland Place, Pasadena
$4,173
Design for garage (GGL).

228 Halsted, Mrs. Louise T.
90 North Grand Avenue, Pasadena
$834
Alterations (Avery).

230 Pratt, Charles Millard
1330 Fairview (renamed North Foothill) Road, Nordhoff (Ojai), California
$31,293
Presentation drawings dated 18 March 1909 (GGL).

231 Lawless, William J.
585 Central (renamed Sierra Madre Blvd.), Sierra Madre, California (altered)
$6,062
28 May 1908: plans prepared for house (LABC).

233 Thorsen, William Randolph
2307 Piedmont Avenue, Berkeley, California
$83,600
Design begun summer 1908; 13 April 1909: contract for house (DPB).

234 Scofield, Miss Belle D.
(1070 South Orange Grove Avenue, Pasadena)
n.r.
Project: alterations to house (Avery).

236 Irwin, Jr., Theodore
240 North Grand Avenue, Pasadena
$1,467
Addition of steps, door, and portico to front of house, drawings dated 25 July 1908 (Avery).

n.r. Armenian Pilgrims Church
(Fresno, California)
n.r.
Project (UCB).

n.r. Lawless, William J. and George H. Letteau
585 and 609 Central (renamed Sierra Madre Blvd.) Sierra Madre, California (dem.)
n.r.
Pergola to connect houses; drawing dated 18 November 1908 (Avery).

1909

n.r. Silent, Judge Charles K.
(NW corner of Palm Drive at Grand, Glendora, California)
n.r.
Project: 16 April 1908, ...contemplates building a house (LABC).

238 Anthony, Earl C.
666 South Berendo Street, Los Angeles (moved)
$26,412
7 April 1910: contract for house (LABC); drawings dated 24 December 1909 (Avery). Moved to 910 North Bedford Drive, Beverly Hills, 1923.

241 Spinks, Mrs. Margaret B. S. C.
1344 Hillcrest Avenue, Pasadena
$1,065
Design for garage; drawings dated 2 April 1909 (Avery).

242 Lambert, John
(SE corner of Gordon Terrace at Waverly Drive, Pasadena)
n.r.
Project: drawings dated 11 March 1910 (Avery).

243 Culbertson, James A.
235 North Grand Avenue, Pasadena (altered)
$7,818
Alterations: drawings dated 31 March 1910 (Avery).

245 Crow, Dr. S. S.
979 South El Molino Avenue, Pasadena
$12,216
September 1909: design for residence (Avery).

246 Crow, Dr. S. S.
979 South El Molino Avenue, Pasadena
$1,029
Design for garage (Avery).

247 Culbertson, James A.
235 North Grand Avenue, Pasadena (garage moved)
$572
Design for second garage, later moved to different site on same property (Avery).

1910

249 Blacker, Robert Roe
1177 Hillcrest Avenue, Pasadena (pergola dem.)
$1,321
Design for pergola (Avery).

250 Blacker, Robert Roe
1177 Hillcrest Avenue, Pasadena
$3,650
Design for billiard room (Avery).

n.r. Neumeister, Col. John G.
(Redondo Beach, California)
n.r.
Project: design for bungalow, sketch dated
1 March 1910 (Avery).

251 Smith, Ernest W.
272 South Los Robles Avenue, Pasadena
$9,822
Drawings dated 22 March 1910 (Avery).

252 Merrill, Samuel Jr.
1285 Summit Avenue, Pasadena
n.r.
26 March 1910: plans prepared for house (PS).

253 Lambert, John
(SE corner Gordon Terrace at Waverly Drive,
Pasadena)
n.r.
Project: drawings for garage and keeper's house
dated March 1910 (Avery).

254 Bradley, Henry K.
(Pasadena)
n.r.
Project: design for residence; five schemes dating
from 13 January through 18 June 1909 (Avery).

256 Sanborn, Samuel P.
999 East Colorado Street, Pasadena (moved)
$230
Alterations to residence later moved to 65 N.
Catalina, Pasadena (Avery).

257 Blacker, Robert Roe
(Long Beach, California)
$1,529
Project: design for beach cottage (Avery).

258 Pratt, Charles M.
1330 Fairview (renamed North Foothill) Road,
Nordhoff (Ojai), California
$940
Addition to residence (Avery).

259 Spaulding, Keith
2896 West Telegraph Road, Fillmore, California
$6,123
27 October 1910: taking bids for building at
Sespe Ranch (LABC).

260 Drake, Mr. A. M.
(1274 Hillcrest Avenue, Pasadena)
$418
Project: design for fence and gardener's cottage
(Avery).

n.r. Bolt, Frank C.
1005 Buena Vista Street, South Pasadena
n.r.
3 September 1910: alterations to [Howard
Longley] house (PN; Avery).

262 Bentz, Mrs. Louise
657 Prospect Square (renamed Blvd.), Pasadena
n.r.
Design for garage (Avery).

263 Halsted, Mrs. Louise T.
90 North Grand Avenue, Pasadena
$490
Alteration (Avery).

265 Robinson, Mrs. L. A.
195 South Grand Avenue, Pasadena
$1,110
Alterations and furniture (Avery).

1911
266 Drake, Mr. A. M.
(1274 Hillcrest Avenue, Pasadena)
$16,100
Project: design for residence, drawings dated
25 March 1911 (Avery).

267 Licensed Motor Car Dealers Assoc. of
Los Angeles
(Fiesta Park, Los Angeles)
n.r.
Project: design for proposed landscape, including
waterfall, pool, and stream (Avery).

268 Fleishhacker, Mortimer
329 Albion Avenue, Woodside, California
$70,465
Residence and grounds for country estate;
completed plans and contract announced
20 April 1911 (LABC).

269 Fleishhacker, Mortimer
329 Albion Avenue, Woodside, California
n.r.
Remodel of cottage (Avery).

270 Crocker, Edward Savage
979 South El Molino Avenue, Pasadena
$7,706
Rugs and furniture for residence purchased
from Dr. S. S. Crow January 1911 (Avery).

271 Crocker, Edward Savage
979 South El Molino Avenue, Pasadena
$1,760
Drawings for walls, gates, fences, and addition
to garage, dated 13 May 1911 (Avery).

n.r. Pasadena School District
1065 East Washington Street, Pasadena
(altered)
$40,637
Proposed plans announced for the building of
Longfellow Elementary School 16 May 1911
(PS); additions in 1928 and later remodeling
by others.

272 Bentz, Nathan
1708 Olive Avenue (re-addressed as 1741
Prospect Avenue), Santa Barbara, California
n.r.
Design for residence (Avery).

273 Culbertson, Miss Cordelia A.
1188 Hillcrest Avenue, Pasadena
$152,809
27 July 1911: A Pasadena Residence (LABC);
permit dated 31 July 1911.

274 Anthony, Earl C.
1000 South Hope Street, Los Angeles (dem.)
$33,435
9 May 1912: contract for showroom (LABC);
design of interior and facade of Packard
dealership; John Parkinson and Edwin
Bergstrom, architects of existing block (Avery).

276 West, Mrs. William F.
1344 Hillcrest Avenue, Pasadena
$222
Alterations to house (1909) purchased from
Judge and Mrs. William Ward Spinks (Avery).

277 Anthony, Earl C.
1000 South Hope Street, Los Angeles (dem.)
n.r.
Continuation of Job #274 (Avery).

278 Fleishhacker, Mortimer
329 Albion Avenue, Woodside, California
$4,925
Barn, pumphouse, gate, and fence (Avery).

279 Fleishhacker, Mortimer
329 Albion Avenue, Woodside, California
n.r.
6 July 1911: preparing plans for stable, garage,
dairy house, swimming pool (LABC).

280 Fleishhacker, Mortimer
329 Albion Avenue, Woodside, California
$3,500
Design for pool and room addition (Avery).

281 Graham, S. C.
(South Arlington Street, Los Angeles)
n.r.
Project: 15 December 1911, preparing plans
for sixteen-room house (PN).

282 Wilcox, Charles P.
675 North Marengo Avenue, Pasadena (dem.)
n.r.
31 August 1911: plans prepared for house
(LABC).

283 Brown, Charles G.
665 North Marengo, Pasadena (dem.)
$5,800
Design for residence (illustrated in PS,
1 January 1913).

285 Pasadena Ice Company
899 South Broadway Avenue, Pasadena (dem.)
$12,641
Design for new ice house; office alterations
(Avery).

286 Huston, Mrs. Lena W.
605 North Marengo Avenue, Pasadena
$4,288
21 October 1911: contract for house (PN).

288 Pasadena Ice Company
899 South Broadway Avenue, Pasadena (dem.)
$1,400
28 December 1911: plans completed and
contract let for brick addition to Ice and Cold
Storage building (LABC).

1912
289 Blacker, Robert Roe
(Long Beach, California)
$3,200
Project: design for two bungalows (JB).

291 Blacker, Robert Roe
1177 Hillcrest Avenue, Pasadena
$544
Design for additional furniture (JB).

292 Graham, S. C.
(South Arlington Street, Los Angeles)
n.r.
Project: design for garage (Avery).

293 Earl, Mary Maud (Mrs. J. Parker)
527 Herkimer Street (renamed Union Street),
Pasadena
$17,451
25 April 1912: [contract] for apartment house
(PS).

294 Pratt, Charles Millard
1330 Fairview (renamed North Foothill) Road,
Nordhoff (Ojai), California
$4,823
Living-room furniture, alterations to residence;
drawings dated 7 May 1912 (Avery).

295 Blacker, Miss Annie
675 South Madison Avenue, Pasadena
$14,075
18 April 1912: contract for house (LABC).

296 Blacker, Miss Annie
675 South Madison Avenue, Pasadena
$1,005
Design for garage (Avery/JB).

298 Crocker, Edward Savage
980 South Madison Avenue, Pasadena (dem.)
n.r.
Drawings dated 29 June 1912: maid's cottage
and yard, lily pool, brick at rear of 979 South
El Molino Avenue (Avery).

299 Halsted, Mrs. Louise T.
90 North Grand Avenue, Pasadena
$764
Addition to residence (Avery).

300 Kew, Mrs. Mary M.
3224 Sixth Avenue, San Diego (dem.)
$42,185
19 September 1912: preparing plans for house,
garage and landscaping (LABC); blue prints
made 7 January 1913 (Avery).

301 Gibbs, Judge George A.
305 East California Street, Pasadena (dem.)
$3,494
8 August 1912: contract for alterations and
additions to house (LABC).

302 Vista del Arroyo Hotel
100 South Grand Avenue, Pasadena (dem.)
$13,409
12 October 1912: plans completed for additions
and improvements to hotel annex (PN).

303 Vista del Arroyo Hotel
505 Del Rosa Drive, Pasadena (dem.)
$5,049
24 October 1912: alterations to houses (LABC).

304 McReynolds, Dr. Robert P.
20 Berkeley Square, Los Angeles (dem.)
$3,323
Plans (1912) and contract (9 January 1913;
LABC) for teahouse, pergola, garage, chauffeur's
quarters (Avery).

305 Palmer, Frank L.
(Foothill Blvd. at North Garey Avenue, North
Pomona, California)
n.r.
Project: 28 November 1912, preparing plans
for house (LABC).

n.r. Silverberg, J. S.
(San Mateo, California)
n.r.
Project: alterations to house (UCB).

1913
306 Ware, Henry A.
460 Bellefontaine Street, Pasadena
$15,399
19 April 1913: preparing plans for house (PN).

307 Anthony, Earle C.
666 South Berendo Avenue, Los Angeles (moved)
$3,677
Drawings for leaded art-glass, lanterns, mantel
carving, and additions to sleeping porch and
breakfast room (Avery).

308 Angle, Dr. Edward H.
(South El Molino Avenue, Pasadena)
n.r.
Project (Avery).

309 Ladd, William M.
818 Fairview (renamed North Foothill) Road,
Nordhoff (Ojai), California
$10,456
Design for winter residence (Avery).

310 Blacker, Robert Roe
1177 Hillcrest Avenue, Pasadena
n.r.
Design for toolhouse (JB).

311 Ballentine, Mrs. J. Herbert
600 East Alameda Street (re-addressed 2259
North Santa Rosa Avenue), Altadena (altered)
$2,380
Alterations and additions to house (JB).

312 Gamble, Sidney David
(Escondido, California)
n.r.
Project: first scheme for bungalow (Avery).

313 Thorsen, William Randolph
2307 Piedmont Avenue, Berkeley, California
$543
Designs for fire screens, irons, garage trellis,
gates, fence (Avery).

314 Neil, James W.
400 Arroyo Terrace, Pasadena
n.r.
Addition and alteration to house to add
maid's room (JB).

n.r. Forsman, S. W.
408 Arroyo Terrace, Pasadena
n.r.
Alterations to house (RLM).

1914
315 Blacker, Robert Roe
1177 Hillcrest Avenue, Pasadena
$1,019
Enclosure of southwest balcony, design of
metal register grills and fire screens (Avery).

316 Gamble, Sidney David
(Escondido, California)
n.r.
Project: second scheme for stucco bungalow (JB).

317 Culbertson, James A.
235 North Grand Avenue, Pasadena (altered)
$4,878
Design for pergola, bay windows and yard
(Avery/JB).

318 Halsted, Mrs. Louise T.
90 North Grand Avenue, Pasadena
$1,800
Design for garage alterations, scheme #4
(Avery).

319 Bradford, L. T.
(unknown)
n.r.
Project: design for residence (JB).

320 Englemann, Dr. Rosa
1235 San Pasqual Street, Pasadena (dem.)
$4,000
14 February 1914: contract for house and
garage (SWCM).

321 Hadley, Mrs. A. T.
(unknown)
$103
Design for tea table (JB).

322 Pasadena Ice Company
899 South Broadway Avenue (renamed Arroyo
Parkway), Pasadena (dem.)
n.r.
28 March 1914: permit for brick freezing room
(SWCM).

323 Hamlin, William E.
(150 South Orange Grove Avenue, Pasadena)
n.r.
Project: design for residence, scheme #1 (JB).

324 Pratt, Charles Millard
1330 Fairview (renamed North Foothill) Road,
Nordhoff (Ojai), California
n.r.
Alterations in windows (JB).

325 Costello, Frank T.
(unknown)
n.r.
Project: design for residence (JB).

326 Pasadena Ice Company
899 South Broadway Avenue (renamed Arroyo
Parkway), Pasadena (dem.)
n.r.
Alterations to ice-house condenser tower A;
including wind stress diagram and detail of
Howe-type truss (Avery).

327 Fleishhacker, Mortimer
(San Francisco)
n.r.
Advising only (JB).

328 Culbertson, Miss Cordelia A.
1188 Hillcrest Avenue, Pasadena
$1,706
Upper and lower pergolas, lath house, trellis and
balcony (Avery).

329 Pomona Valley Ice Compnay
1163 East Second Street, Pomona, California
(dem.)
n.r.
Freezing tank for Pomona facility (Avery).

330 Greene, John T.
3200 H Street Road (renamed H Street),
Sacramento, California
$8,000
Design for residence (Avery).

331 Gibbs, George A.
(unknown)
n.r.
Project: brick public garage (JB).

332 McReynolds, Dr. Robert P.
20 Berkeley Square, Los Angeles (dem.)
n.r.
Trellis, sash for sun porch, driveway gates, table
for sun porch (Avery).

333 Gamble, David Berry
4 Westmoreland Place, Pasadena
$1,531
Design for desk, chairs, lamp (JB).

334 Hamlin, William E.
(unknown)
n.r.
Project: design for a log cabin (JB).

n.r. Vista Del Arroyo
(124 South Grand Avenue, Pasadena)
n.r.
Project: design for hotel building (Avery).

1915
335 Culbertson, James A.
235 North Grand Avenue, Pasadena (altered)
$256
Alteration to living room (JB).

336 Fleishhacker, Mortimer
2418 Pacific Avenue, San Francisco
$18,642
Alterations to house, including decorative
plaster ceilings, marble mantel, front-door
molding (UCB).

337 Valentine, Walter D.
(unspecified)
n.r.
Advice, service (JB).

338 Hamlin, William E.
(150 South Orange Grove, Pasadena)
n.r.
Project: scheme #2.

339 Culbertson, Miss Cordelia A.
1188 Hillcrest Avenue, Pasadena
$1,688
Designs for vase, fountain, bird dish, lamp
(Avery).

340 Blacker, Robert Roe
1177 Hillcrest Avenue, Pasadena
$643
Replacing wood deck following dry rot; add
floor in billiard room (JB).

341 Pratt, Charles M.
1330 Fairview (renamed North Foothill) Road,
Nordhoff (Ojai), California
$1018
Addition to bathroom (JB).

342 Donnelly, Mrs. Ruben H.
(Lake Forest, Illinois)
n.r.
Project: design for residence (JB).

343 Williams, Dr. Nathan H.
1145 Albany Street (renamed Sonoma Drive),
Altadena, California
$11,428
24 September 1915: contract for house (PN).

344 Hamlin, William E.
(150 South Orange Grove Avenue, Pasadena)
n.r.
Project: designs for garage and outbuildings
(JB).

345 Thorsen, William R.
(2307 Piedmont Avenue, Berkeley, California)
n.r.
Project: design for light fixtures in
living room (JB).

346 Halsted, Mrs. Louise T.
90 North Grand Avenue, Pasadena
$4,145
Alterations to west bedrooms, dining room,
addition of trellis (JB).

1916
347 Williams, Dr. Nathan H.
1145 Albany Street (renamed Sonoma Drive),
Altadena
$1,275
Design of garage (JB).

348 Libby, Dr. Arthur A.
665 South Orange Grove Avenue, Pasadena
(dem.)
$4,183
Addition to residence (JB).

349 Fleishhacker, Herbert
Corner of El Camino Real and Fair Oaks Lane,
Atherton, California (dem.)
$10,070
Addition of maid and guest rooms (RJC/JB).

350 Pasadena Ice Company
899 South Broadway Avenue, Pasadena (dem.)
$9,354
Design for dumbwaiter in office; other
alterations and additions (Avery).

351 Pasadena Ice Company
899 South Broadway Avenue, Pasadena (dem.)
$10,105
Addition of ice storage room (Avery).

352 Hamlin, William E.
(150 South Orange Grove Avenue, Pasadena)
n.r.
Project: garage details (JB).

353 Hamlin, William E.
(150 South Orange Grove Avenue, Pasadena)
n.r.
Project: entrance gates (JB).

354 Garfield, Lucretia R.
1001 Buena Vista Street, South Pasadena
$2,264
Alterations to accommodate elevator (JB).

355 Murray, Mrs. Lucy Wheeler
(2175 Cambridge Street, Los Angeles)
n.r.
Project: design for elevator (JB).

356 Procter, Thomas Hardy
(Cocoa Nut Beach, Florida)
n.r.
Project: design for residence and grounds (JB).

357 Westmoreland Improvement Co.
Westmoreland Place, Pasadena
$550
Design of north gateposts and iron gates (JB).

358 Blacker, Robert Roe
1177 Hillcrest Avenue, Pasadena
$270
New deck roofs (JB).

359 Bliss, William H.
(St. Louis, Missouri)
n.r.
Project: design for residence (JB).

360 Hall, J. Herbert
(105 Ford Place, Pasadena)
$83
Project: alterations and additions to apartment
house (JB).

361 McReynolds, Dr. Robert P.
20 Berkeley Square, Los Angeles
$3,901
Alteration and addition to residence: second-
story sitting room, laundry house (Avery).

362 Tichenor, Mrs. Adelaide
First Place at Ocean Boulevard (re-addressed
852 Ocean Boulevard), Long Beach, California
(altered)
n.r.
Design of garage addition (JB).

363 Fleishhacker, Mortimer
(San Francisco)
n.r.
Project: design for townhouse (JB).

364 Stoddard, Mr. Charles H.
(Burlingame, California)
$3,500
Project: design for residence; drawings dated
October 1916 (JB).

365 Irwin, Jr., Theodore
240 North Grand Avenue, Pasadena
$52
Chinese trays for boxes (JB).

366 Leeds, Charles T.
370 Elevado Drive (renamed Del Mar Blvd.),
Pasadena
$500
Addition of bathroom (JB).

367 Witbeck, Charles S.
226 Palisades Avenue, Santa Monica, California
$9,183
Design for residence; drawings begun 1916,
house constructed 1917 (JB).

1917
368 Kuznick, Dr. Martha J.
(Hollywood, California)
n.r.
Project: three schemes for residence, drawings
date from 2 January 1917 (JB).

369 Poole, Maj. John H.
(Mira Vista Development [Linda Vista],
Pasadena)
$100,000
Project: first scheme for residence (JB).

370 Ware, Henry A.
460 Bellefontaine Street, Pasadena
$250
Addition of chimney to residence (JB).

371 Irwin, Jr., Theodore
240 North Grand Avenue, Pasadena
$69
Wood base and monogram for bronze Buddha
(JB).

372 Mundorff, Mrs. Howard F.
3753 Balch Street, Fresno, California
$14,511
Residence, pool, and planting plan (JB).

373 Witbeck, Charles S.
226 Palisades Avenue, Santa Monica, California
$452
Garage (Avery).

374 Anthony, Earl C.
666 South Berendo Street, Los Angeles (moved)
$2,831
Addition of bath and addition to garage (JB).

375 Mundorff, Mrs. Howard F.
3753 Balch Street, Fresno, California
$1,584
Design for garage (JB).

376 French, Steuart F.
(Linda Vista, Pasadena)
n.r.
Project: design for residence (JB).

377 Allen, Mrs. Dudley P.
1188 Hillcrest Avenue, Pasadena
$1,899
Design for wardrobe; alterations to grounds (JB).

378 Ballentine, J. Herbert
Santa Rosa Avenue at Alameda Street
(re-addressed 2259 Santa Rosa Avenue),
Altadena (altered)
$342
Alterations to dining room (JB).

379 Bernhard Brothers
(71 Palmetto Drive, Pasadena)
n.r.
Project: design for shops (JB).

1918
380 Kramer, Theodore A.
1725 Milan Avenue, South Pasadena
(property divided)
$16,722
Additions to residence, garden plans, planting
plan, pergola, arbor, and bench (Avery).

381 Robinson, Mrs. L. A.
195 South Grand Avenue, Pasadena
$6,868
Addition of sunroom, bathroom, sleeping porch,
and alts. to maids room (Avery/JB).

382 Culbertson, Miss Cordelia A.
370 Elevado Drive (renamed Del Mar Avenue),
Pasadena (altered)
n.r.
27 April 1918: drawings for sleeping porch,
mould for finishing over wall-fabric in living
room, telephone case for second floor (Avery).

383 Whitworth, Mrs. Carrie
2612 North Lincoln Avenue, Altadena
$9,125
Additions to existing residence (Louis B. Easton,
architect): grounds, new pergola and trellis,
case pieces (Avery).

384 McReynolds, Dr. Robert P.
20 Berkeley Square, Los Angeles (dem.)
$60
Addition to laundry (JB).

385 Coulter Dry Goods Company Store
(Seventh and Olive Streets, Los Angeles)
n.r.
Project: alterations to existing building (Avery).

387 Prentiss, Mrs. Francis F.
1188 Hillcrest Avenue, Pasadena
$7,961
Design for incinerator, wall, fences on east lot,
and gate details (Avery/JB).

1919
390 Poole, Maj. John H.
(Mira Vista [Linda Vista], Pasadena)
$12,373
Project: scheme #2 for residence; begun, then
suddenly stopped (JB).

392 Krantz, Hubert F.
(Prospect Park, Palm Beach, Florida)
n.r.
Project: design for residence (Avery).

394 Prentiss, Mrs. Francis F.
1188 Hillcrest Avenue, Pasadena
$2,565
Alterations to residence (JB).

396 Khazoyan, Haigag H.
487 South Los Robles Avenue, Pasadena (dem.)
$1,160
Bay window, garage, and cement drive for
residence (JB).

1920
397 Gould, Thomas Jr.
3441 Gale Way (re-addressed 402 Lynn Drive),
Ventura, California
$18,427
Design begun March 1920; plans revised and
house built in 1924–25 (JB).

399 Angle, Dr. Edward H.
(unknown)
n.r.
Alterations to house designed by D. St. C.
Donnelly (Avery).

401 Whitworth, Mrs. Carrie
(2612 North Lincoln Avenue, Altadena)
$3,500
Project: sketches for cottages (JB).

402 Riggin, Dr. L. Lore
(2085 West Avenue, Pasadena)
$13,000
Project: design for residence and garage (JB).

404 Jones, Mrs. J. H.
960 North Los Robles Avenue, Pasadena
(altered)
$737
Garden, garage, and birdhouse; drawings dated
14 June 1920 (Avery).

405 Curtis, Carl C.
2444 North Lincoln Avenue, Altadena (dem.)
$1,804
Alterations to residence (JB).

406 Smith, Mrs. Datus C.
487 West California Street, Pasadena
$1,232
Addition to residence and garden design,
executed 1924 (Avery).

n.r. Stewart, Percy M.
(unspecified)
n.r.
Drawings of the P-M System of Fireproof
Construction—witnessed by HMG—dated
May-September 1920 and November 1921
(Avery).

407 Martin, Edson J.
3237 North Lake Avenue, Altadena (dem.)
$299
Alterations to residence and garage (JB).

408 Prentiss, Mrs. Francis F.
1188 Hillcrest Avenue, Pasadena
$558
Alterations to garage (JB).

1921
409 Kelly, Kate A.
(2550 Aberdeen Avenue, Los Angeles)
n.r.
Project: design for residence; see also job #416
(JB).

410 Mundorff, Mrs. Howard F.
(3753 Balch Street, Fresno, California)
n.r.
Project (JB).

411 Anthony, Earl C.
666 South Berendo, Los Angeles (moved)
$433
Model and topographical map for move of house;
see also job #443 (JB).

412 McReynolds, Dr. Robert P.
20 Berkeley Square, Los Angeles (dem.)
$10,000
Addition to residence, executed 1924 (Avery).

414 Prentiss, Mrs. Francis F.
1188 Hillcrest Avenue, Pasadena
$100
Design to pipe part of property (JB).

415 Culbertson, Mrs. James A.
235 North Grand Avenue, Pasadena
n.r.
New roof on garage (JB).

416 Kelly, Kate A.
2550 Aberdeen Avenue, Los Angeles (altered)
$33,146
Design for residence and furniture (JB/Avery).

419 Khazoyan, Haigag H.
38 South Raymond Avenue, Pasadena (altered)
$100
Alterations to store building (JB).

420 Prentiss, Mrs. Francis F.
1188 Hillcrest Avenue, Pasadena
$7,570
Garden planting plan, lath house, cane-seat
chair in bedroom.

421 Day, Clarence P.
492 Eldora Road, Pasadena
$300
Alterations to cottage (JB).

422 Day, Clarence P.
492 Eldora Road, Pasadena
n.r.
Project: alterations (JB).

423 T. & W. Store
(corner Colorado and Lake, Pasadena)
$1,200
Project (JB).

n.r. Denison, F. G.
(341 South Mariposa Avenue, Beverly Hills,
California)
n.r.
Project: Landscape plan (Avery).

1922
424 Wilson, Mrs. O. G.
2734 South Normandie Avenue, Los Angeles
$1,000
Alterations to residence (JB).

425 Hibbard, Rev. Charles H.
156 Bellefontaine Street, Pasadena (dem.)
$144
Addition of front porch, executed
1924 (Avery).

428 Rice, Paran F.
(237 [now 225] Highland Place, Monrovia,
California)
$333
Project: addition of lattice entry to residence
of Jean D. Gunder (JB).

429 Anthony, Earl C.
666 South Berendo, Los Angeles (moved)
$4,064
Repair garage after fire (JB).

430 Hoyt, H. W.
965 New York Drive, Altadena
$600
Addition to residence (JB).

431 Day, Clarence P.
(492 Eldora Road, Pasadena)
$1,700
Project (JB).

432 Huntoon, Joseph H.
(Visalia, California)
$5,000
Project: two schemes for duplex residence
(Avery/JB).

433 Crocker, Edward Savage
979 South El Molino Avenue, Pasadena
$750
Repair to residence and outbuildings (JB).

434 McReynolds, Dr. Robert P.
20 Berkeley Square, Los Angeles (dem.)
$1,350
Alteration of sunporch into library; addition
of second-floor gallery and studio (Avery).

435 Khazoyan, Haigag H.
38 South Raymond Avenue, Pasadena
$365
Design for lighting store display window (JB).

436 Blumenthal, A. C.
(NW corner of Lucern St. and Wilshire Blvd.,
Los Angeles)
n.r.
Project: residence and grounds (JB).

437 Blacker, Robert Roe
1177 Hillcrest Avenue, Pasadena
$978
Addition to garage (JB).

438 Valentine, Walter D.
1425 (re-addressed 1419 and 1421) Palm Street,
Altadena
n.r.
Designs for new cottages and alterations to
existing structures designed (possibly by HMG)
c. 1915; Wild Wood Park portals (Avery/JB).

439 Gehrig, A. C.
(54 South Oak Avenue, Pasadena)
n.r.
Project: design for bungalow and garage (JB).

440 Wheatere, S.
(unknown)
n.r.
Project: design for residence (JB).

441 Rice, Paran F.
368 Arroyo Terrace, Pasadena
$933
Alterations to former Charles S. Greene
residence (JB).

442 Prentiss, Mrs. Francis F.
1188 Hillcrest Avenue, Pasadena
$1,090
Repairs to garage (JB).

443 Kerry, Mrs. Norman
910 Bedford Drive, Beverly Hills, California
(altered)
$2,000
Design of grounds and relocation of Earl C.
Anthony house from 666 South Berendo, Los
Angeles (Avery/JB).

444 Huntoon, Joseph H.
(Visalia, California)
$3,000
Project: residence and garage (JB).

1923
445 Cox, J. D.
(unknown)
n.r.
Advise (JB).

446 Morrison, Lloyd E. and Rachel
(1414 Alhambra Road, South Pasadena)
$4,122
Project: design of residence, see also job #450
(JB).

448 Wheeler, Roy B.
497 West Grandview Avenue (re-addressed 327 Sierra Woods Drive), Sierra Madre, California
$24,804
Alterations to 1904 Edgar Camp house (JB).

449 Prentiss, Mrs. Francis F.
1188 Hillcrest Avenue, Pasadena
$60
Base for lamp (JB).

450 Morrison, Lloyd E. and Rachel
1414 Alhambra Road, South Pasadena
$4,122
Residence and garage. Permit issued 9 June 1923. L. C. Johnson, contractor (JB/City of South Pasadena).

451 Blacker, Mrs. Robert Roe
1177 Hillcrest Avenue, Pasadena
$670
Upholstery and painting (JB).

452 Prentiss, Mrs. Francis F.
1188 Hillcrest Avenue, Pasadena
$1,489
Chairs, sink, lantern, chaise, front hall alteration (Avery).

453 California Institute of Technology
1201 East California Street, Pasadena (dem.)
$1,700
Student union, "The Dugout," donated by R. R. Blacker, August 1923 (Avery/JB).

1924

454 Wennerberg, Ernest E.
236 South Raymond Avenue, Pasadena (dem.)
$5,085
Two-story brick shop-building for Pasadena Drapery Company (Avery/JB).

455 Hatcher, Dr. Edna L.
63 Club Road, Pasadena
$16,851
Design of two-story residence, constructed 1925 (SWBC).

456 Savage, Arthur
1299–1301 North Marengo Avenue, Pasadena
$7,291
Duplex residence designed for wood finisher who had done work for the Greenes (JB).

457 Whitworth Corporation
1504 Monterey Road, South Pasadena (dem.)
$1,425
Interior alterations (JB).

458 Bentz, John C.
(55 and 64 South Raymond Avenue, Pasadena)
n.r.
Project: design for finishing second story of store (JB).

459 Swan, Mrs. Frances B.
(155 Colorado Street, Pasadena)
$70,100
Project: two-story residence and garage (JB).

460 Townsend, Dr. V. Ray
807 North College Avenue, Claremont, California
$2,940
Garage, repairs and alterations to residence (JB).

461 Coats, Ray
(unknown)
n.r.
Project (JB).

462 Ventura Union High School
(2155 East Main Street, Ventura, California)
$6,000
Project: design for strengthening walls, requested by Thomas Gould (JB).

463 Murphy, Elmer R.
400 Arroyo Terrace, Pasadena
$200
Addition of east gates to 1903–6 van Rossem–Neill house (JB).

464 Mardian, Samuel Z.
1517–1525 East Washington Street, Pasadena (altered)
$5,000
Store and apartment building, drawings dated 2 December 1924 (Avery).

1925

465 Swan, Mrs. Frances B.
2162 North Holliston Avenue, Altadena (altered)
n.r.
Relocation of James Swan house (1899) from 515 East Colorado, Pasadena (Avery).

466 Wolfskill
(San Francisco)
n.r.
Project: design for residence (JB).

467 Daly, Mrs. C. P.
(Ventura, California)
n.r.
Project: design for residence; drawings dated 29 May 1926 (JB).

469 Curtis, Carl C.
2444 North Lincoln Avenue, Altadena (dem.)
$112
Cover sink and drainboards with monel metal (JB).

470 Green, R. Henry C.
1919 Robson Street, Vancouver, British Columbia (dem.)
$5,770
Alterations to 1904 residence; drawings dated 7 April 1925 (JB).

471 Thum, William
1507 East Mountain Avenue, Pasadena
$29,295
Design of residence and garage (JB).

472 Brandt, August C.
(San Pasqual, Pasadena)
$9,000
Project: design for alterations to Dr. Walker residence (JB).

473 Walker, Dr. Myron W.
(2265 San Pasqual, Pasadena)
$8,000
Project: additions to residence (JB).

474 Prentiss, Mrs. Francis F.
1188 Hillcrest Avenue, Pasadena
$3,472
Addition to veranda, north hall and repairs (JB).

475 Ventura Union High School
2155 East Main Street, Ventura, California (dem. 1956)
$9,000
Strengthen buildings by adding columns (JB).

1926

476 Pacific Southwest Trust and Savings Bank
(234 East Colorado Boulevard, Pasadena)
$1,000
Project: alterations to office and design of furniture for Henry M. Robinson (Avery/JB).

477 Culbertson, Miss Kate
370 Elevado Drive (renamed Del Mar Avenue), Pasadena (altered)
$1,609
Alterations of east porch (JB).

478 Prentiss, Mrs. Francis F.
1188 Hillcrest Avenue, Pasadena
$11,487
Repairs to residence (JB).

479 McReynolds, Dr. Robert P.
20 Berkeley Square, Los Angeles (dem.)
n.r.
Alteration of reception room into library (JB).

480 Smith, Thomas P., Jr.
240 North Grand Avenue, Pasadena
$6,626
Alterations to garage of 1906 Irwin house (JB).

n.r. Saunders, Mrs. James E.
130 Bellefontaine Street, Pasadena (dem.)
n.r.
Design of residence (RLM).

1927

481 Townsend, Dr. V. Ray
4260 Magnolia Avenue (later renamed Country Club Drive), Long Beach, California
$22,744
Moving of Jennie Reeve house from 1004 Pine Avenue, Long Beach, including shrubs and plant list, planting plan, curtain designs, etc. (Avery).

482 Blacker, Robert Roe
1177 HIllcrest Avenue, Pasadena
$630
Repairs (JB).

483 Whitworth, Mrs. Carrie
2612 North Lincoln Avenue, Altadena
$2,272
Additions and repairs to residence (JB).

484 Prentiss, Mrs. Francis F.
1188 Hillcrest Avenue, Pasadena
$3,164
Steppingstones in garden, repairs, hall pictures, light (JB).

485 Kelly, Kate A.
2550 Aberdeen Avenue, Los Angeles (altered)
$5,400
Alterations and additions to residence (Avery).

1928

486 W., F.
(unspecified)
$38,800
Project (JB).

488 Birch, William A.
(unknown)
$180
Addition to gates and entrance (JB).

489 Prentiss, Mrs. Francis F.
1188 Hillcrest Avenue, Pasadena
$201
New grills in maid's room, and lantern (JB).

490 Blacker, Robert Roe
1177 Hillcrest Avenue, Pasadena
$1,248
Bird fountain [near] patio, design begun 1927 (JB/UCB).

491 Crocker, Edward Savage
(979 South El Molino, Pasadena)
n.r.
Project: sketches of proposed second-story addition to residence (Avery/JB).

492 Doherty, Mary R.
304 Fillmore Street, Pasadena
$2,945
Move residence and put [in] foundations, cellar and repairs (JB).

493 Culbertson, Miss Kate
370 Del Mar Avenue, Pasadena
$100
Cabinet in living room (JB).

494 Prentiss, Mrs. Francis F.
1188 Hillcrest Avenue, Pasadena
$1,551
Wardrobe and repairs (JB).

495 Gibbs, George A.
305 East California, Pasadena (dem.)
$663
Repair foundation (JB).

496 Isham, Howard F.
460 Bellefontaine Street, Pasadena
$1,200
Alterations to 1913 Henry Ware residence (JB).

497 Manning, J. B.
1145 Albany Street (renamed Sonoma Drive), Altadena
$3,150
Alterations to garage of 1915 Williams house (JB).

498 Robinson, Mrs. L. A.
195 South Grand Avenue, Pasadena
$400
Alterations to garage (JB).

499 Birch, Mrs. A.
(unknown)
$4,390
Addition to east wall (JB).

500 Kegley, Mrs. Charles H.
2175 Cambridge Street, Los Angeles
$17,136
Design of alterations to 1905 Lucy Wheeler house (Avery).

1929

501 Strasburg, Estelle
225 Adams Park Drive (renamed North Cedar), Covina, California
n.r.
2 August 1929: contract (SWBC).

502 Richardson, Walter Linwood
27349 Avenue 138, Porterville, California
$18,000
Ranch house and outbuilding (JB/GGL).

503 Robinson, Mrs. L. A.
195 South Grand Avenue, Pasadena
$7,732
Alterations to enlarge library, add dressing room and bath (JB).

504 Prentiss, Mrs. Francis F.
1188 Hillcrest Avenue, Pasadena
$1,038
Repairs to residence (JB).

505 Blacker, Robert Roe
1177 Hillcrest Avenue, Pasadena
$2,247
Pantry alteration, oiling woodwork and furniture (JB).

506 Whitworth Corporation
1504 Monterey Road, South Pasadena (dem.)
$626
Repairs to residence (JB).

1930

507 Love, Thomas G.
701 South Oakland Avenue, Pasadena
n.r.
Alterations to residence (JB).

508 Prentiss, Mrs. Francis F.
1188 Hillcrest Avenue, Pasadena
$3,058
Repairs to residence (JB).

509 Blacker, Robert Roe
1177 Hillcrest Avenue, Pasadena
$1,750
Changing heating systems to gas (JB).

510 Whitworth, Mrs. Carrie
2612 North Lincoln Avenue, Altadena
$383
Additions to sleeping porch (JB).

511 Robinson, Mrs. L. A.
195 South Grand Avenue, Pasadena
$1,340
Pergola and retreat (JB).

n.r. Brininstool, Frank M.
(unknown)
n.r.
Alterations to house (RLM).

n.r. Horne, Mrs. Fred W.
1166 Hillcrest Avenue, Pasadena
n.r.
Alterations to house (RLM).

1931
512 Prentiss, Mrs. Francis F.
1188 Hillcrest Avenue, Pasadena
$3,285
Repairs (JB).

513 Black, Emma M.
210 South Madison Avenue, Pasadena (moved)
$513
Alterations and additions to residence (add windows); moved to 1070 North Marengo, Pasadena in 1999 (Avery/JB).

514 Prentiss, Mrs. Francis F.
1188 Hillcrest Avenue, Pasadena
$6,639
Potting shed, concrete wall, steps, paving (Avery).

515 Pratt, Mrs. Charles M.
(1330 Fairview [renamed North Foothill Road, Nordhoff [Ojai], California)
n.r.
Advised on work done by Hall (JB).

516 Gain, George W.
(312 Grant Street [renamed Cordova Street], Pasadena)
n.r.
Project for alterations to shop (JB).

1932
517 Blacker, Robert Roe
1177 Hillcrest Avenue, Pasadena
$649
Re-roof decks (JB).

518 Kendall, B. O.
Merced, California
n.r.
Project: design of barn for client's sister (JB).

519 Prentiss, Mrs. Francis F.
1188 Hillcrest Avenue, Pasadena
$139
Termite work and repairs (JB).

520 Blacker, Robert Roe
1177 Hillcrest Avenue, Pasadena
$2,265
Alterations and addition of bookcases (UCB/JB).

521 Gould, Thomas, Jr.
3441 Gale Way (re-addressed 402 Lynn Drive), Ventura, California
$1,500
Finished second story and bath (JB).

522 Kendall, B. O.
Merced, California
$300
Select barn lumber for client's sister in Merced (JB).

1933
523 Prentiss, Mrs. Francis F.
1188 Hillcrest Avenue, Pasadena
$1,882
Repairs (JB).

524 Kernaghan, George F.
(1144 Lura Street, Pasadena)
n.r.
Project: design for cottage (JB).

525 Curtis, Carl C.
(South Fair Oaks Avenue, Pasadena)
n.r.
Project: design for store and apartment building (JB).

526 Rapp, William H.
(982 Emerson Street, Pasadena)
n.r.
Project (Avery).

527 Howard, James
900 Cypress Street, Pasadena (dem.)
$7,600
Design for cottage (JB).

1934
528 Prentiss, Mrs. Francis F.
1188 Hillcrest Avenue, Pasadena
$1,369
Termites, repairs, and pergola (JB).

529 Beeson, William M.
(unknown)
$250
Project: design of brick store and show window (JB).

1935
530 Buck, Howard K.
(Grace Hill, Pasadena)
$8,000
Project: design of two-story residence (JB).

531 Prentiss, Mrs. Francis F.
1188 Hillcrest Avenue, Pasadena
$2,634
Two lanterns, repairs (JB).

532 Johnson, Lucas C.
1066 Concha Street, Altadena
$600
Design for garage (JB).

533 Schiffman, Rudolph
505 South Grand Avenue, Pasadena (altered)
n.r.
Alterations to 1902 George H. Barker house (JB).

534 Sloan, William A.
(823 Brent Avenue, South Pasadena)
n.r.
Project: alterations to garage (JB)

535 Ritson, J. H.
2062 El Sereno Avenue, Pasadena
$150
Alterations to residence designed by J. Springer (JB).

1936
536 Prentiss, Mrs. Francis F.
1188 Hillcrest Avenue, Pasadena
$6113
Repairs (JB).

1937
537 Pratt, Mrs. Charles M.
1330 North Foothill Road, Ojai, California
$5,697
Addition to maid's bedroom; roof over cellar door (JB).

538 Prentiss, Mrs. Francis F.
1188 Hillcrest Avenue, Pasadena
$1,729
Repairs (JB).

539 Pratt, Mrs. Charles M.
1330 North Foothill Road, Ojai, California
n.r.
Protective stonework in barbecue; advice only (JB).

540 Prentiss, Mrs. Francis F.
1188 Hillcrest Avenue, Pasadena
n.r.
Repairs (JB).

541 Gould, Mrs. Thomas, Jr.
3441 Gale Way (readdressed 402 Lynn Drive), Ventura, California
$193
Magazine shelves in den; desk in den (JB).

1939
542 Greene, Henry M.
(146 Bellefontaine Street, Pasadena)
n.r.
Gravestone for Mrs. H. M. Greene (d. 1935) (JB).

1940
543 McElwain, Alan and Isabelle
772 North Catalina Avenue, Pasadena
n.r.
Addition of chimney and fireplace (JB).

544 Greene, Henry M. and family
146 Bellefontaine Street, Pasadena (dem.)
$1,300
Alterations (JB).

545 Saunders, James E.
(130 Bellefontaine Street, Pasadena)
n.r.
Project: alterations and additions to residence (JB).

1941
546 Pratt, Mrs. Charles M.
1330 North Foothill Road, Ojai, California
$656
Renewed floors and woodwork; new cabinet sink (JB).

547 Thum, Mrs. Louise
570 East Sierra Madre Avenue, Glendora, California
$1,300
Additions to residence, bedroom, bath, and porch (JB).

1944
n.r. Greene, William Sumner
(SW corner Central and Elm Streets, Pittsburgh, California)
n.r.
Project: design for residence for HMG's son (GGL).

1951
n.r. McElwain, Alan and Isabelle
18000 Bull Canyon Road, Granada Hills, California
n.r.
Design of concrete block residence for family of HMG's daughter (IHGM).

List of Independent Work of C. Sumner Greene: 1916–1944

1916
Southern Pine Association
(New Orleans, Louisiana)
Project: design for permanent commercial exhibition building (UCB).

1918
James, D. L.
State Highway One, Carmel Highlands, California
Design of summer residence. Survey completed August 1918, owners occupied in 1922 (UCB).

1920
Greene, C. Sumner
Lincoln Street near Thirteenth Avenue, Carmel-by-the-Sea (dem.)
Design for own house (UCB).

1921
Greene, Dr. Thomas Sumner
Monte Verde Street near Thirteenth Avenue, Carmel-by-the-Sea (dem.)
Design for parents' cottage (TGG).

Carmel Country Club
(Junipero Avenue at Ocean Avenue, Carmel-by-the-Sea)
Project: 6 October 1921, plans for clubhouse (CPC).

City of Carmel War Memorial
Ocean Avenue at San Carlos Street, Carmel-by-the-Sea
10 November 1921: description and sketch of Soldier's Memorial Fountain (CPC).

City of Carmel
(Carmel-by-the-Sea)
Project: design for City Hall (UCB).

Carmel Club of Arts and Crafts
Monte Verde Street at Ninth Avenue, Carmel-by-the-Sea (burned and rebuilt)
22 December 1921: plans presented for alteration of clubhouse (CPC).

1922
Forest Theatre
Mountain View and Santa Rita, Carmel-by-the-Sea
19 January 1922: plans for Little Theatre alteration presented by Charles Greene (CPC).

Schevill, Rudolph
77 Tamalpais Road, Berkeley, California
Addition of living room and entry hall (UCB).

1923
Tolmie, Robert
250 Scenic Avenue, Piedmont, California
Music studio and residence (UCB).

Montezuma Mountain School
(Los Gatos, California)
Project: design for portals on school property (UCB).

Fleishhacker, Mortimer
329 Albion Avenue, Woodside, California
Design for game room, presented 20 May 1923, completed 1924 (UCB).

Greene, C. Sumner
Lincoln Street near Thirteenth Avenue, Carmel-by-the-Sea
Design and construction of own studio, permit dated September 1923 (UCB).

1924
Greene, Bettie
Junipero Avenue near Fifth Avenue, Carmel-by-the-Sea (dem.)
Design for daughter's commercial stables (BSG).

1925
Payne, Mr. Jessie H.
SW corner of Seventh Avenue and Carmelo Street, Carmel-by-the-Sea
Design of residence; permit issued March 1925 to contractor, M. J. Murphy (not built under CSG supervision) (UCB).

Whitman, Jennie Crocker
(Cypress Drive, Pebble Beach, California)
Project: design for brick residence; land survey dated 9 December 1925 (UCB/RJC).

1926

Greene, Alice Sumner
Lakeport, California (dem.)
Deisgn of residence for daughter (RLM).

Chamberlin, Edith
(Woodside, California)
Project: design for garden, 17 September 1926
(UCB).

Walker, Mrs. Willis
Pebble Beach, California (dem.?)
Design of two-stall stable (UCB).

Campbell, Violet
Thirteenth Avenue near Lincoln Street, Carmel-
by-the-Sea
Addition to cottage; permit dated December
1926 (UCB).

1927

Prentiss, Mrs. Francis F.
1188 Hillcrest Avenue, Pasadena
Design for tea table (UCB).

Fleishhacker, Mortimer
329 Albion Avenue, Woodside, California
Design for lower-garden, stairs, and reflecting
pool (UCB).

Fleishhacker, Mortimer
329 Albion Avenue, Woodside, California
Design for dairy house; materials calculations
dated 24 July 1927 (UCB).

Blacker, Robert Roe
1177 Hillcrest Avenue, Pasadena
Design for birdbath, see also job #490 (UCB).

1928

Fleishhacker, Mortimer
329 Albion Avenue, Woodside, California
Design for arcade and seats at end of reflecting
pool; sketches dated October 1928 (UCB).

1929

Flavin, Martin A.
18100 Cachagua Road, Carmel Valley,
California
Design and construction of summer cabin (SF).

Lee, Ralph C.
(224 West Santa Inez, Hillsborough, California)
Project: garden pergola (UCB).

Howard, John Langley
86 Ave Maria Road, Monterey, California
Design of house; construction executed by client
(UCB/client).

Flavin, Martin A.
Spindrift Road, Carmel Highlands, California
Design of entrance gates and wall (UCB).

Kelley, Mrs. Louise A. F.
Keyes Street at Senter Road, San Jose,
California
Addition to Ar-Kel Villa, including solarium and
servant's wing (UCB).

Fleishhacker, Mortimer
(2418 Pacific Avenue, San Francisco)
Project: Gothic Room addition (UCB).

1930

Moore, Mary J.
(625 South Sixteenth Street, San Jose,
California)
Design for stool with leather seat (UCB).

Flavin, Martin A.
Spindrift Road, Carmel Highlands, California
Additions and alterations to house: living-room
balcony, redwood door, breakfast porch, curtain
design, etc. (UCB).

1931

Fleishhacker, Mortimer
329 Albion Avenue, Woodside, California
Ceramic fountain and pots for garden (UCB).

Flavin, Martin A.
Spindrift Road, Carmel Highlands, California
Redwood library; carved panel over living-room
fireplace (UCB).

Greene, C. Sumner
(Monterey Cemetery, Monterey, California)
Design of grave marker for Thomas Sumner
Greene (UCB).

Kelley, Mrs. Louise A. F.
Keyes Street at Senter Road, San Jose,
California
Additions to residence (UCB).

1932

Flavin, Martin A.
Spindrift Road, Carmel Highlands, California
Skylight, waterproofing, repairs to house (UCB).

1933

Flavin, Martin A.
Spindrift Road, Carmel Highlands, California
Design and supervision of garden wall (UCB).

1934

Reinhart
(Oakland, California)
Project: designs for houses (UCB).

1935

Fleishhacker, Mortimer
(329 Albion Avenue, Woodside, California)
Project: design for small garden beside lower-
garden stairs (UCB).

1937

Abbott, Park
(Oakland, California)
Projects: designs for houses and office (UCB).

1938

Flavin, Martin A.
Spindrift Road, Carmel Highlands, California
Grading, rock work, stone arch, son's bedroom
(UCB).

1939

James, D. L.
State Highway One, Carmel Highlands,
California
Design for library addition (UCB, AAF).

Flavin, Martin A.
Spindrift Road, Carmel Highlands, California
Enclosure of kitchen steps (UCB).

1941

Flavin, Martin A.
Spindrift Road, Carmel Highlands, California
Minor alterations (UCB).

Picture Acknowledgments:

Mark Fiennes was specially commissioned for the principal color photography in this book.

Drawings and Archives Departments, Avery Architectural and Fine Arts Library: p27 figs9,10; p29 fig14; p30 figs15, 16,17,19; p31 figs20,21,24; p32 fig27; p33 figs28,29; p37 figs37,38; p43 fig5; p49 fig19; p51 fig22; p53 figs25,26; p54 fig29; p58 figs38,39; p59 fig42; p60 fig45; p61 figs46,47,48; p63 figs54,55; p64 fig57; p65 fig59; p67 fig65; p70 figs71,72; p71 fig73; p75 fig6,8,9; p78 fig14; p79 figs17,18; p84 figs26,27; p88 fig36; p89 fig39; p94 fig53; p96 figs 57,58; p101 figs67,68; p102 figs69,70; p112 figs21,22; p130 figs57,58,59; p131 fig62; p142 fig6; p146 figs12,13; p148 figs17,19; p149 fig21; p150 fig23; p157 figs38,39; p158 figs42,44,45; p165 fig58; p166 fig62; p168 figs65,66; p170 fig71; p176 figs2,3,4,5; p177 fig7; p179 fig10; p180 figs11,12,13,14,15; p183 figs19,20; p192 fig4. **Drawings and Archives Departments, Avery Architectural and Fine Arts Library/Leroy Hulbert Photograph**: p69 fig70; p107 fig3; p107 fig5; p159 figs46,47; p161 fig52. **Drawings and Archives Departments, Avery Architectural and Fine Arts Library/Maynard Parker Photograph**: p156 fig32. **Environmental Design Archives, University of California, Berkeley**: p11 figs 8,9; p13 fig12; p14 figs 13,14; p18 fig22; p44 fig6; p47 fig13; p48 figs14,15; p53 fig27; p59 fig41; p60 fig44; p62 figs49,50,51,52; p64 fig58; p66 fig62; p68 fig67; p69 fig69; p76 figs10,11; p77 fig12; p79 fig16; p80 fig19; p81 figs22,23; p88 figs33,34,35; p89 fig37,38; p103 fig72; p134 fig68; p140 fig2; p141 fig5; p150 fig24; p158 fig43; p160 fig48; p167 fig63; p168 fig 64; p170 fig70; p172 fig73; p202 figs25,26; p211 figs46,47; p213 figs54,55. **Environmental Design Archives, University of California, Berkeley/Leroy Hulbert Photograph**: p67 fig64; p81 fig24. **John Bethell/The Garden Picture Library**: p210 fig45. **Courtesy Edward R. Bosley**: p17 fig20; p21 fig28; p26 fig8; p74 fig3; p141 fig42; p215 fig59. **Collection of Boston Athenaeum/***American Architect and Building News***(24 Oct. 1891)**: p18 fig 23; **Collection of Boston Athenaeum/***American Architect and Building News***(25 Mar. 1891)**: p28 fig11. **The Brookline, Massachusetts Preservation Commission**: p17 fig21. **Chicago Historical Society**: p22. **Courtesy Cincinnati Historical Society Library**: p8 fig2. **Courtesy Robert Judson Clark**: p50 fig21; p89 figs40,41; p101 fig66; p107 fig4; p114 figs24,25; p128 fig51; p132 figs65,66; p148 fig18; p154 figs29,30; p192 fig3; p203 figs28,29; p205 fig34; p209 fig43; p214 figs56,57. **Courtesy Connecticut Valley Historical Museum, Springfield, Massachusetts**: p19 fig 25. **Courtesy Alan Crawford, with permission from Felicity Ashbee**: p140 fig3. **Courtesy Howard and Mary Durham**: p49 figs17,18; p50 fig20; p52 fig24. **© Mark Fiennes**: Frontispiece; p2 fig2; p44 fig7; p55 fig31; p56 fig32; p57 figs36,37; p72 fig1; p85 fig28; p91 figs44,45; p92 figs47,48; p93 figs49,50; p95 figs54,55; p97 fig59; p98 fig60; p99 figs61,62,63; p100 figs64,65; p102 fig71; p103 fig74; p104 fig1; p105 fig2; p108 figs7,8,9,10; p109 figs12,13; p110 figs14,15,16; p111 figs17,18; p115 fig27; p117 figs29,30; p118/119 fig31; p120 figs32,33; p121 figs34,35; p122 figs36,37,38,39,40; p123 figs41,42,43; p124/5 fig44; p125 fig45; p126 figs46,47,48; p127 figs49,50; p128 fig52; p129 fig54; p130 figs55,56,60; p131 figs61,63; p137 fig78; p138 fig1; p143 fig7; p144 fig8; p145 fig9,10; p146 fig11; p147 figs15,16; p150 figs22,25; p151 figs26,27; p152/3 fig29; p155 fig31; p156 figs33,34,35; p157 figs36,37,40; p164 fig57; p165 figs59,60; p166 fig61; p170 fig69; p173 fig76; p174 fig1; p178 fig8; p179 fig9; p184 fig22; p185 figs23,24,25; p187 fig28; p188 figs29,30,31; p193 fig6; p194 figs7,8,9; p195 fig10; p196 figs11,12,13,14; p197 fig16,17; p199/200 fig18; p200 fig19; p200 figs20,21,22; p201 fig24; p205 fig30; p205 figs32,33; p206 fig37; p207 figs38,39; p208 fig40; p209 figs41,42; p210 fig44; p211 fig48; p212 figs50,51,52; p213 fig53. **Fitchburg Historical Society**: p146 fig14. **Thomas Gordon Greene**: p201 fig 23. **Greene and Greene Library**: p8 fig3; p9 fig5; p10 fig 7; *American Architect and Building News* p19 fig24; figs2,3,4; p25 fig25; p37 fig39; p38 fig40; p39 fig41; p52 fig23; p54 fig30; p63 fig53; p64 fig56; p74 fig2; p75 figs4,5,7; p91 fig46; p128 fig53; p163 figs54,55,56; p189 fig34; p190 fig1; p192 fig2; p206 fig35. **Greene and Greene Library/***The Architect***/Academy Architecture/1903**: p57 figs34,35; **Greene and Greene Library/Gift of Nathaniel Patrickson Greene**: p56 fig 3; **Greene and Greene Library, Gift of the Richardson Family**: p189 figs32,33; **Greene and Greene Library/© Winstead's Photography, Long Beach**: p68 figs66,68. **Courtesy, Virginia Dart Greene Hales**: p15 fig15; p35 fig34; p65 figs60,61; p86 fig29. **Photo by Lamson, courtesy William Richardson**: p189 fig33. **Clay Lancaster**: p160 figs49,50; p206 fig36. **Courtesy, Tom Leffingwell**: p103 fig73. **Richard Rice Long, AIA**: p31 fig23. **University of Louisville, KY/Nanine Hilliard Greene Collection**: p96 fig56. **Maine Historic Preservation Commission**: p21 fig27. **© Erika Marrin**: p4 fig2; p5 fig3; p40; p44 fig8; p45 fig9; p46 fig10; p82/3 fig25; p87 fig30; p88 figs31,32; p93 fig51; p109 fig11; p112 fig20; p113 fig23; p162 fig53; p169 figs67,68; p171 fig72; p172 figs74,75; p177 fig6; p181 fig16; p182 figs17,18; p183 fig21; p186 fig26; p187 fig27; p193 fig5; p205 fig31; p215 fig58. **Massachusetts Institute of Technology Museum Archives**: p6 fig1; p16 fig18. **Kirk Meyers Collection**: p67 fig63. **Mrs. Stephen Mengos**: p107 fig6; p132 fig64. **Courtesy Jack Moore**: p111 fig19. **Prints and Drawings Collection, The Octagon, Museum of the American Architectural Foundation, Washington, DC**: p197 fig16. **The National Trust**: p90 fig42. *The Pacific Coast Architect*/**March 1914**: p158 fig41. **Pasadena Historical Museum**: p28 fig12; p29 fig13; p30 fig18; p31 fig22; p32 figs25,26; p34 fig30; p35 fig33; p36 figs35,36; p42 fig2; p43 figs3,4; p47 figs11,12; p48 fig16; p58 fig40; p71 fig74; p78 fig14; p79 fig15; p80 fig20; p81 fig21; p90 fig43; p94 fig52. **Pasadena Illustrated Souvenir Book, Board of Trade Publication 1903. Courtesy of André Chaves**: p26 fig7; p34 figs31,32; p48 fig16; **Courtesy Peabody Essex Museum, Salem MA**: p16 fig 19. **Courtesy, Anthony Mitchell Sammarco**: p15 fig16. **Courtesy James Schevill**: p202 fig27. **Courtesy Shepley, Bulfinch, Richardson + Abbott, Boston MA**: p21 fig29. **Society for the Preservation of New England Antiquities (SPNEA)**: p20 fig 26. **Society for the Preservation of New England Antiquities, Gift of Earle G. Shettleworth, Jr.**: p9 fig 4; p20 fig 26. **© Michael Stebbins**: p149 fig20; p161 fig51. **© Tim Street-Porter**: p115 fig26; p133 fig67; p134 fig69; p135 figs70,71,72; p136 figs73,74; p137 figs 75,76,77,79. **Washington University Archives, St. Louis, Missouri**: p12 figs10,11.*The Western Architect*/**July 1908**: p53 fig28. **© Cole Weston**: p217 fig1.

Acknowledgments

To scan the list of individuals who helped create this book is to appreciate the compelling nature of the subject matter. The mere mention of a pending book on the Greenes opened many doors, not just to their houses but also to the stories of the people whose lives had been touched by their work. To the many friends who looked out for my non-book life during the writing and research, I owe a special debt. I am particularly grateful to my wonderful family, who sacrificed tremendously. During my various absences the excellent staff at The Gamble House managed very well (annoyingly so at times), and I appreciate their support and patience. The members of the Docent Council of The Gamble House, particularly those who staff the Greene and Greene Library, also deserve special thanks for their understanding and support. I am also very grateful indeed to Robert H. Timme, FAIA, Dean of the USC School of Architecture, who offered encouragement along the way.

It is impossible to overstate the value of past scholarship to the present work. Randell L. Makinson's original writings on the Greenes continue to inform and inspire us all. Other important touchstones include the writings of L. Morgan Yost, Jean Murray Bangs, Clay Lancaster, Janann Strand, and Karen Sinsheimer Current with the late William Current. More recent texts have shed important new light on the Greenes, too, including those by Randell Makinson and Bruce Smith, and master's theses by Dr. Barbara Ann Francis and Travis Culwell. I owe a great debt to Robert Judson Clark for so generously sharing the rich results of his groundbreaking research undertaken from the late 1950s to the early 1960s. Margaret Meriwether's exhaustive bibliography of Greene and Greene, completed in 1993, has been tremendously valuable, as has John Ripley's survey of Craftsman bungalows in Pasadena from 1903 to 1918. I thank them for sharing their data with me so freely. My gratitude also goes to Barbara Ealy, Alan Crawford, James Elliott Benjamin, Mary Helen Wayne, Bruce Smith, and my mother, Phyllis Bosley, each of whom spent many hours generously assisting my research in the field. My sister, Kathy Bennett, and her husband, David, provided lodging during my research visits to the University of California at Berkeley; Mary Helen and Bob Wayne opened their doors to me whenever I was in Carmel; and Kelly and Steve McLeod generously provided peace and quiet in the Sierra foothills. Sarah Davis hosted me frequently in New York, and my father-in-law, Christopher Davis, made available his Adirondack farmhouse many times during the winter and spring of 1999. Without this silent sanctuary, especially, I could not have completed the text.

Foremost among the many archivists and librarians who provided assistance are Janet Parks, Curator of Drawings and Archives, and her assistant, Anne-Sophie Roure, at Avery Architectural and Fine Arts Library of Columbia University in New York. The vast quantity of the Greene and Greene firm's drawings (placed there by Jean Murray Bangs in 1960) meant numerous visits over several years and repeated requests for information and photographs, all of which were cheerfully accommodated. I also thank Angela Giral, head of Avery Library, for her willingness to allow so many of these important drawings to be published here. Equally accommodating were Waverly Lowell, Kelcy Shepherd, and Jody Stock at the Environmental Design Archives of the University of California at Berkeley (to which Charles Greene's personal papers were donated by members of his family in 1959, a gift facilitated by Robert Judson Clark). Needless to say, the descendents of Charles and Henry Greene have provided especially valuable information that has led me to a better understanding of their lives and careers. In particular I would like to acknowledge Thomas Gordon Greene and Betty Patchin Greene, the late Bettie Storey Greene and the late Nathaniel Patrickson Greene, Isabelle Horton Greene McElwain, and Alan McElwain, Isabelle Greene, FASLA, Virginia Dart Greene Hales, Ruth Greene, Jane McElroy, Alice Cory, and Thomas Casey Greene.

I am tremendously grateful to Mark Fiennes for the eloquent new photography he has provided to accompany the text, and to Caroline Fiennes for her help and company during the photography. Erika Marrin and Tim Street-Porter have also provided several beautiful images, and Cole Weston kindly printed for me the portrait of the Greenes from a negative he had made at the James house late in 1947.

I cannot say enough to express my deep appreciation for the cooperation and interest of the following homeowners, archives and libraries, and other individuals:

Greene and Greene Homeowners

David and Catherine Alexander, Harry Anderson, John and June Armstrong, Barbara Babcock, Bill and Rosemary Barbus, John and Shannon Bowman, Jill Brown, David and Judy Brown, Marilyn and George Brumder, Stephanie Buffington, Ann and Andre Chaves, Andrew Chute, Mr. and Mrs. Thomas Cotter, Leslie Dixon and Tom Ropelowski, Wayne DuCharme, the Fleishhacker family, Eunice and Dan Goodan, Mrs. Virginia Gould, Did and Betty Greene, Charlotte Hayden, the late Lilith James, Maria and Robert Kelly, Rob and Peggy Kincaid, Harvey and Ellen Knell, Mark and Ann LaSalle, Mark and Phaedra Ledbetter, Joseph and Judy Lord, George and Judith Lowe, Dr. and Mrs. C. Burke Maino, Amy and Michael McGrade, Bill and Jennifer Moses, the Neighborhood Church, Ruth and Robert Peck, Ed and Margene Remund, John and Beverly Richardson, William B. Richardson, Joseph Ritchie, Susan Schevill and James Schevill, The Sigma Phi Society Alpha of California Chapter, Peter and Jackie Slabaugh, Denise and Zachary Snyder, Carol and Brad Sturtevant, Kathleen Thorne-Thomson, Mr. and Mrs. Fred Ulan, Judy Webb, Martin Eli Weil, Westridge School, Gwen and Robert Whitson, Doug and Norvene Vest, and Susanna Yoakum.

Libraries, Archives, and Historical Societies

Avery Architectural and Fine Arts Library, Columbia University, New York: Angela Giral, Head; Janet Parks, Curator of Drawings and Archives; Anne-Sophie Roure, Assistant to the Curator; Ted Goodman, Avery Index

Greene and Greene Library, San Marino, California: Louise Mills, Chairman; Ann Scheid, Archivist

The Huntington Library, San Marino, California: Edward Nygren, Director of Art Collections; Amy Meyers, Curator of American Art; Jacqueline Dugas, Registrar of Art Collections

Environmental Design Archives (formerly Documents Collection), College of Environmental Design, University of California at Berkeley: Waverly Lowell, Director; Kelcy Sheperd, Archivist; Jody Stock, Reference Specialist

Environmental Design Library, University of California at Berkeley: Elizabeth Douthitt Byrne, Head

Pasadena Historical Museum Library: Tania Rizzo, Archivist

Blake Alexander Archives, University of Texas, Austin: Beth Todd and Nancy Sparrow

Prints and Drawings Collection, The Octagon, Museum of the American Architectural Foundation, Washington, D.C.: Sherry C. Birk, Director of Collections

Architectural Collections, the MIT Museum, Cambridge, Massachusetts: Kimberly Alexander Shilland, Curator

Shepley Bulfinch Richardson and Abbott, Boston: Katherine Meyer and Robert J. Roche

Society for the Preservation of New England Antiquities: Lorna Condon, Curator of Library and Archives

Permit Center Archives, City of Pasadena: Mary Jo Winder, Senior Planner, Design and Historic Preservation

Fitchburg (Massachusetts) Historical Society: Ruth Ann Penka, Executive Director

Brookline (Massachusetts) Preservation Commission: Roger Reed, Preservation Planner

Cincinnati Historical Society Library: Peter Bahra, Collections Manager

Connecticut Valley Historical Museum, Springfield, Massachusetts: Cynthia Murphy

Maine Historic Preservation Commission: Earle G. Shettleworth, Jr., Director

Rhode Island Historical Society: Rick Stattler, Manuscripts Curator

Missouri Historical Society: Dennis Northcott, Reference Librarian

Washington University, St. Louis, Missouri: Carol Prieto, University Archivist

Harrison Memorial Library, Carmel-by-the-Sea, California: Arlene Hess, Local History Librarian

Houghton Library, Harvard University: Anne Anninger, Curator of Printing & Graphic Arts

Peabody Essex Museum, Salem, Massachusetts: Robert E. Saarnio and Dean Lahikainen, Curators

Ekstrom Library, University of Louisville, Kentucky: Delinda Buie, Director; Susan Knoer, Archivist

University of Cincinnati Medical Heritage Center: Billie Broaddus, Director

California Institute of Technology Archives: Bonnie Ludt, Administrator; Charlotte Erwin, Associate Archivist

Modern Archive Centre, King's College, Cambridge, U.K.: Jacqueline Cox, Archivist

Los Angeles County Hall of Records: Donald Cameron, Archivist

The John Pitcairn Archives, Bryn Athyn, Pennsylvania: Walter C. Childs II, Archivist

Vassar College, Poughkeepsie, New York: Nancy MacKechnie, Curator of Rare Books

Royal Institute of British Architects: Trevor Todd

The Victoria & Albert Museum, London: Dr. Clive Wainwright

Cabell County Public Library, Huntington, West Virginia: Nina Johnson, Local History Room

California Views, Monterey, California: Pat Hathaway

The following individuals also helped in very significant ways: Felicity Ashbee, Bill Benson, the late David Shipman Brown, Michael John Burlingham, Douglas and Dordo Byles, David Cathers, Susan and Kirk diCicco, Mr. and Mrs. John Cocanougher, Edward Comstock, Jr., Edward S. Cooke, Jr., Joseph Cotter, Julie Dercle, Mary and Howard Durham, Astrid Ellerseick, Flags Pasadena Photo Center, Sean Flavin, Lauren Gabor and Scott Goldstein, Leslie Clark Gray, Nanine Hilliard Greene, Gary Hall, Gregson Hall, Tim Hansen, David Heller and Lori King, Wendy Hitchmough, John Langley Howard and the late Ann Bernstein, Dan Kany, John and Nina Kirby, Tom Leffingwell, Richard Rice Long, Los Angeles County Museum of Art, Jim Marrin, Delaney and Bob Marron, Ann and Scott McCready, Dorothy McMillian, Maureen Meister, Mrs. Stephen Mengos, Kirk Meyers, Jack Moore and Joan Frederick, Eliot Morgan, Jean and Roger Moss, James O'Gorman, Tavo Olmos, Ellen Palevsky, Mary Jane Penzo, Greg Porter, Eleanor M. Richardson, Enid Sales, Anthony Mitchell Sammarco, John Selmer and Barbara Goldeen, Jeff and Amelia Silverman, Michael Stebbins and Andrea Kraus, Jack and Mary Alice Stumpf, Margaret Gamble Swift, Christine Thompson, the late Elisabeth Kendall Thompson, Jim Tranquada, Kathleen Tuttle, Verticare Helicopters of Salinas, Jim and Marlene Webster, Ted Wells, Alfred Willis, Ellen and Richard Guy Wilson, and Philip Wright.

Finally, I would like to thank the many good people at Phaidon Press who showed an interest in this book, especially David Jenkins, Anita Moryadas, Sophia Gibb, Iona Baird, Julia Joern, Jeri Poll, Karen Stein, and Megan McFarland. Inevitably I have neglected to name someone who should have been mentioned here. Please forgive the omission and know that your help was appreciated, too.

Dedication

To Kirby, Will, and Julia, who wanted to keep me.

Phaidon Press Limited
Regent's Wharf
All Saints Street
London N1 9PA

Phaidon Press Inc.
180 Varick Street
New York, NY 10014

www.phaidon.com

First published 2000
Reprinted in paperback 2003
© 2000 Phaidon Press Limited

ISBN 0 7148 4357 1

A CIP catalogue record of this book is available from the British Library.

Designed by Karl Shanahan, Robbie Mahoney
Printed in Hong Kong

Jacket illustrations:
Charles Greene, c. 1906 (front jacket)
Henry Greene, c. 1906 (back jacket)
Plans and elevations for the Gamble House, Pasadena, California, 1907–09

Endpapers:
Detail of living-room frieze for The Gamble House

Index